UNDERSTANDING THE COMMON AGRICULTURAL POLICY

The majority of recent publications on the Common Agricultural Policy (CAP) of the European Union address current issues and specific applications. There is little available which attempts to increase understanding of the nature of existing policies, their development, intentions, problems and successes.

The aim of this book is to improve knowledge and understanding of the 'policy process' and its application to the CAP, focussing on the principles of policy analysis. For while the details of agricultural and environmental policies evolve, the principles upon which they are based endure. The author uses economics as a basis for his exploration, as fairly simple economics holds the key to understanding many of the fundamental pressures to which agriculture and rural areas are subject. He explains the importance of the political and administrative context in which the process occurs, acknowledging the influence of environmental and sociological concerns.

Such knowledge of the conceptual framework of the 'policy process' and its application to the CAP is essential for all concerned with agriculture and rural livelihoods, both within the European Union and in those countries trading with the EU. This includes both students and professionals. The book provides an understanding of these principles in terms of how and why policy changes, thus increasing the efficiency and efficacy of the process.

Berkeley Hill is Emeritus Professor of Policy Analysis at Imperial College London, and was President of the Agricultural Economics Association for 2008/9. He is well-known internationally for consultancy, research and publication on the analysis of agricultural and rural policy.

UNDERSTANDING THE COMMON AGRICULTURAL POLICY

Berkeley Hill

publishing for a sustainable future
London and New York

First published 2012
by Earthscan
2 Park Square, Milton Park, Abingdon, Oxon OX14 4RN

Simultaneously published in the USA and Canada
by Earthscan
711 Third Avenue, New York, NY 10017

Earthscan is an imprint of the Taylor & Francis Group, an informa business

British Library Cataloguing in Publication Data
A catalogue record for this book is available from the British Library

Library of Congress Cataloging in Publication Data
Hill, Berkeley.
   Understanding the common agricultural policy / Berkeley Hill
      p. cm.
   "Simultaneously published in the USA and Canada" – T.p. verso.
   Includes bibliographical references and index.
   1. Agriculture and state – European Union countries.
   2. Agriculture – Economic aspects –European Union countries.
   3. European Union countries – Politics and government.
   4. European Union countries – Economic policy. I. Title.
   HD1918.H53 2012
   338.1′84–dc23   2011023875

ISBN: 978–1–84407–777–9 (hbk)
ISBN: 978–1–84407–778–6 (pbk)
ISBN: 978–0–84977–561–8 (ebk)

Typeset in Baskerville
by HWA Text and Data Management, London

Printed and bound in Great Britain by
TJ International Ltd, Padstow, Cornwall

CONTENTS

FIGURES

TABLES

BOXES

PREFACE

There is no shortage of written material on the Common Agricultural Policy (CAP) and the other policies which impinge on rural areas in the European Union. In addition, over the last decade there has been an explosion of information on the internet, both from official and non-official sources, that has transformed the approach to gaining awareness of the CAP. Internet search engines will rapidly throw up vast amounts of material. Why, then, should there be one more book aimed at students and others concerned with agriculture, the countryside, rural areas and related subjects?

The justification lies in the fact that most of the literature, including what is available on the internet, is about the details of the day – for example, of the latest proposals from the European Commission for reform of the CAP, or the views of interested parties on the way that CAP rules should or should not apply, or what has happened to the support prices for agricultural commodities and the conditions for intervention buying, or the most recent proposals from opposing camps in international trade negotiations. Though essential for people who operate in the commercial world and government, such material is only of fleeting relevance. Surprisingly little is available which attempts to *increase understanding* of why the policies are as they are, how they attempt to tackle the underlying problems faced in the European Union and the degree of success they achieve, and the prospects for change. In short, there are few attempts to place the CAP within the conceptual framework of the 'policy process'. Yet this is precisely the sort of material which students require. Knowledge of this process and how it can be applied is important to gaining a good understanding of the CAP. During their working lifetime the details of agricultural and rural policies will change many times, and the number of Member States may increase further; any book that deals only with them is bound to be out of date soon. Yet the principles of policy analysis as applied here to the CAP will endure and should be of lasting use as details evolve. These principles are the focus of this book.

Economics provides the main toolkit, as this discipline holds the key to understanding many of the fundamental pressures to which agriculture and rural areas are subject. This book has in mind a reader who is already familiar with basic economics, including elementary demand and supply theory, though the material should be comprehensible to someone without this background. However, much of the explanation has to take into account factors that lie outside the narrow toolbox of conventional economics. For example, while all economists are concerned with the allocation of scarce resources between alternative uses, those working in agricultural economics have often overlooked the importance of the political and administrative environment in which CAP decisions are made. Thus, political economy, especially theory of public choice and the behaviour of bureaucratic organisations, is also drawn upon. In understanding such vital areas, non-economist readers will not be at a disadvantage.

The book is not arranged to be read straight through, though this is one option. After the first chapter, the others can be taken in whichever order the reader finds most relevant. Because there are so many linkages involved, it is impossible to package the material linearly. While each chapter is more or less self-contained, the implications for aspects of policy covered elsewhere should be constantly kept in mind. A feature of the book's structure is that the emphasis is on the CAP as it is now, with each chapter containing only enough material on how we got here to make it intelligible. A final chapter gives a more detailed account of the historical development of the CAP, and this is accompanied by a chronology that takes the reader up to events of 2011.

The way of presenting things chosen for this book came from my experience of teaching generations of students at Wye College (University of London) and latterly Imperial College London (Wye campus). This left me with an impression of what is important to the understanding of this very complex area. This includes both what to present and the order of doing so.

In a sense, the ready availability of information on the internet about the CAP has been liberating. It has enabled the avoidance of what seems to me to be excessive and passing detail in favour of the bigger picture and, in my view, the more important explanatory factors to understanding the CAP and how it is changing. Inevitably this incurs a degree of subjectivity, since interpretation often involves stepping beyond what is fully researched and documented. Of course, not everyone will agree with this approach!

The intention was to write in collaboration with former colleagues at Wye/Imperial. As things turned out, this proved impractical, so I am responsible for all the chapters. This book is, therefore, a personal approach to what seems to be necessary to understand the CAP.

I am particularly grateful to Professor Robert Ackrill, of the Nottingham Business School (Nottingham Trent University) for his detailed comments on a draft of this book. Of course, I alone am responsible for all errors, omissions and poor judgements.

Useful websites

The following organisations have websites from which detailed information can be obtained.

European Union (Europa), a portal website for the institutions of the EU.

European Commission

European Parliament

Council

Court of Auditors

OECD

Economic Research Service (US Department of Agriculture)

Defra (UK Department for Environment, Food and Rural Affairs)

1

UNDERSTANDING
THE POLICY PROCESS –
WHAT IS POLICY?

Key topics

- The policy cycle: problem formulation, policy formulation, objectives, implementation by instruments, impact, evaluation.
- Hierarchy of objectives.
- Intermediate and final objectives.
- Interaction between agricultural and non-agricultural policies.
- The rationales for policy intervention.
- The notion of an 'efficient' policy.

1.1 Introduction

It may seem odd to start a book on understanding the Common Agricultural Policy (CAP) and the other policies of the European Union (EU) which are targeted at rural areas with a chapter which does not attempt to deal in detail with the specifics of these policies. However, as was pointed out in the Preface, this book is primarily directed at providing an *explanation* rather than with a *description* of current activities. Over time the details will alter; before the ink is dry on this page some changes will have been made to the CAP which would make a catalogue of income support mechanisms, quota arrangements, import tariffs and so on out-of-date. This enormous body of rapidly changing detailed material is well covered in the flow of official publications from the EU institutions and by information disseminated by commercial news networks and by organisations supporting farmers and other groups that are directly affected by the CAP. Much of this is now freely available in electronic form. In contrast, an understanding of the general principles and the forces at work is likely to be more enduring, providing the means to explain why policies are as they are, and an ability to assess and analyse future developments as they occur. The aim of this book is to assist the reader to reach such an understanding. The starting point must be an examination of the what we mean by 'policy' – *any* policy.

Various approaches can be used to explain and to understand the CAP. Here we mainly use economics because the toolbox this discipline provides is, in practice, immensely helpful. Economics can be described as 'the study of how individuals and society allocate scarce resources between alternative uses in pursuit of given objectives'. As such, we can look at the objectives of policy and the way that decisions are taken to allocate resources to reach those objectives. We can recognise that some of the policy objectives are primarily political or environmental rather than to do with production or incomes, and that the outcomes of policy decisions are heavily influenced by the way in which those decisions are made. But the central thread is the scarcity of resources, which means that decisions have to be made on their allocation. This is a problem that belongs to economics.

Nevertheless, economics does provide a complete explanation the behaviour of individuals and society. Indeed, at its margins the discipline merges into political science, sociology, biology and other ways of looking at society. We will find that, in explaining the CAP and rural policy, there is a need to go some way in all these directions.

1.2 The policy process

In the present context the term 'policy' implies that there is some attempt by public authorities (often simplified to the 'government' or the 'state') to affect the way things are or how they turn out. Thus there may be an attempt to maintain the number of people working in the agricultural industry above the level that would otherwise occur, or to increase the area of land used for low-intensity farming beyond what would happen in the absence of government intervention. A decision *not* to intervene, while clearly forming a policy option, is not usually labelled as a policy, although in the UK there have been long periods in our history when such a *laissez faire* attitude was the norm as far as agriculture was concerned.

Policy is not just a list of state interventions (such as income support payments to farmers, grants for investment or retraining, legislation to prevent degradation of the appearance of the countryside etc.). These are merely the instruments by which policy is put into practice. Rather, policy can be seen as a *process of related steps or stages* in which each step leads to the next in a logical progression – a 'rational' model – in an attempt to tackle problems faced by society. This approach seems particularly appropriate for EU policies directed at agriculture and rural development where the aims are set out in legislation.

We must start with an outline of the *policy process*, as this forms the framework of all that follows. Later parts of this book tackle various parts of the process in greater detail. The policy process has four basic stages, shown in Figure 1.1, namely *Problem formulation, Policy formulation, Policy implementation* and *Policy impact*. Other writers have identified a greater number of stages by subdividing these four, but the basic framework of the approach is broadly agreed. These stages relate to four fundamental questions:

1 What is the problem that makes the policy necessary?
2 What is the policy trying to achieve in order to solve (or partly solve) the problem?
3 What mechanism (instrument) is used to achieve the objective?
4 How successful is the chosen mechanism in relation to the policy problem that started the process off?

From the purpose of analysing existing policies, including the CAP, such a set of logical stages is very helpful. It is the approach traditionally taken in introductory books on public policy, and the hope is that readers will find it a convincing and useful way of looking at the CAP. However, it must be conceded that in the real world the ways in which decisions are reached can at times be far removed from the 'rational' model. Some analysts of public policy on defence or healthcare or immigration question whether governments have much of an idea about what they are trying to achieve, suggesting that they are primarily concerned with 'muddling through' and that public resources are often used irrationally. Even where the *policy process* model is more obviously applicable, as in agriculture and rural development, people responsible for making decisions in national government departments or EU institutions

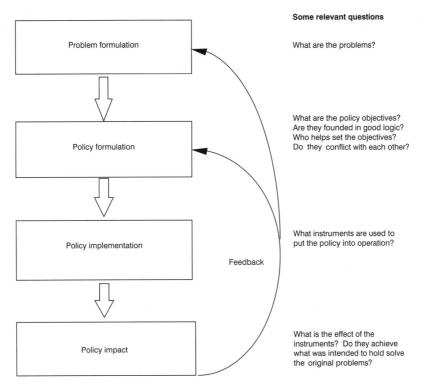

Figure 1.1   The policy process

often face confused situations in which crises arrive unpredicted and demand quick fixes which are often less than perfect solutions to the problem in hand and which can carry implications that are often unforeseen. Even when time is not so short, pressure comes from bodies representing people affected by the policy to take decisions that favour their members. Information on which to base decisions, including the nature of the problem and what can be done about it, may be incomplete or biased, The institutions of government themselves often have their own motives for favouring certain decisions (such as departments wanting to extend their powers and budgets) and individual politicians and administrators may also see advancement of their careers being helped or hindered by the way that decisions go. Alternative views of the way in which the process actually works can be taken, touched on later.

Nevertheless, the view of the policy process as a set of stages linked systematically by an underlying rationale is a useful starting point for explaining policy, even helping to predict it. Though a simplification, it can usually be detected behind what goes on in the complex real world.

1.3 Problem formulation

The first stage is the recognition that there is a need for some public intervention. In some cases the need for action is blindingly obvious. For example, if people are in danger of starving because the nation's food supply is threatened by war or its aftermath (as happened in many countries of Western Europe in the 1940s), any reasonably competent government will realise that it faces a problem and will wish to do something about it. In many other cases, though, the recognition of a problem's existence will be less immediate. For example, the awareness in many European countries (including the UK) that farming has been encroaching on wildlife to the extent that society now wishes to protect the natural environment required the recognition that there was a danger in continuing in the old ways. Government was forced to come to terms with the fact that changes were taking place largely because individuals and then groups started to make a fuss which, eventually, politicians and senior civil servants in departments responsible for agricultural and environmental policy had to take seriously. Questions then were asked by government, such as: 'What is the real extent of the loss of hedgerows and birds?' and 'Does it matter?'

The specific problems that the EU's Common Agricultural Policy is attempting to address are considered in detail later (Chapter 2). Here it is convenient first to set out in a general way the basic sorts of problems that policy has to contend with. It will become clear that those tackled by the CAP fit into (or are 'nested' within) these general problems.

1.3.1 Inherent problems of a capitalist market economy – 'market failure' and the motives behind policy

Some problems arise because of the very nature of the type of economic system in which we live. It is worth reminding ourselves that, in the Member States of the EU, the market mechanism, with its associated prices for inputs and products, is the main way in which the fundamental decisions of what is produced, how it is produced and who gets what is produced are settled, though in agriculture there has been a history of state intervention in the system. The free interaction of supply and demand in the market has many admirable properties for this purpose.

- It operates as a way of reflecting willingness to purchase and to produce without the need for a mass of data collection and planning (as was the case in the formerly centrally planned countries of Eastern Europe). Those entrepreneurs who respond to meet consumer demands sell their output and prosper, serving the interests of both themselves and their customers. Industries where demand is growing will expand and those where demand is falling will contract.
- Competition between producers means that resources go to those who can use them in the most effective way. Efficient producers grow, while the inefficient are squeezed out and new technologies which make production more efficient get taken up.
- Comparative advantage leads to specialisation and exchange, resulting in trade both within countries and across national boundaries.
- Because the market mechanism involves equilibria, such as between supply and demand, the system is largely automatic and can for the most part be left to itself as tastes change, incomes rise which alter the pattern of demand, new technologies and new products are developed and so on.

However, a completely free market is not a perfect way of solving the basic economic problems. Flaws occur in various forms and governments will wish to intervene to modify the outcomes, 'correcting' for what they perceive to be problems caused by the failures of the system and aimed at achieving a better overall result in terms of the welfare of society as a whole – in other words correcting for 'market failure'. The main deficiencies can be classed broadly as follows:

- **Externalities.** The market mechanism is not good at taking externalities into account. These are the outputs from production and consumption that are disregarded by the producers or consumers in their decision-making. Some are positive, such as the benefit which a farmer who installs bees in his orchard to improve the fruit yield has on the yields of neighbouring farms and gardens, whose owners benefit without bearing any cost. And a landscape shaped by 'traditional' farming systems may be attractive to tourists and firms looking for places in which to set up, bringing economic benefits to the local economy. However, many of these externalities are negative, such as the pollution caused by a farmer who makes silage without care to the effect of effluent on local water supplies, or the use of sprays which, in addition to controlling harmful pests on crops, kills butterflies and other insects. By failing to take into account externalities the market system does not ensure the optimum use of resources from society's standpoint (see Chapter 8). Control of many negative externalities, especially water and air pollutions, often has to be tackled on a co-operative EU-wide basis as the causal chemicals are no respecters of national boundaries. Externalities are particularly relevant to public goods and merit goods, which form increasingly important concerns of agricultural and rural policy (see Box 1.1).

Box 1.1 Public and merit goods

Public goods, of which the best example is the country's defence system, are those it is impossible to exclude people from benefiting from (they are non-excludable), and when the more there is for one person, the more there is for everyone else (they are non-rival). Markets would not provide such goods at the socially optimal level because of the incentives for individuals to opt out of paying (the 'free-rider problem'). Consequently, defence has to be organised collectively by the state and financed from taxation. A visually attractive countryside and a diverse and rich natural environment both have aspects of non-excludability and non-rivalness and have claims to be public goods. Increasingly agricultural policy is concerned with such conservation and landscape issues.

Merit goods: somewhat controversially, externalities also form the basis of the rationale for the public finance or support of 'merit goods'. These are good and services whose consumption is believed to confer benefits on society as a whole that are greater than those reflected in consumers' own preferences (and thus in their willingness to pay) for them. Examples include subsidies provided to grand opera companies that allow ticket prices to be reduced, to the repair of large country houses, and to historic church buildings. It is not always easy to spot a plausible externality. For example, how does attending performances of Wagner operas subsequently enable the listeners to pass tangible benefits to other people or improve the productivity of society at large? On the other hand, evidence of the benefits to the community of providing a subsidised university education to those capable of tackling it is much firmer.

- **Imperfect knowledge.** The demand side of the market mechanism comes, directly or indirectly, from consumers expressing their wants through their purchasing patterns. However, consumers are not always in the best position to know what is in their personal interest, as in the cases of smoking and safety precautions. This may stem from imperfect information on the part of consumers (they are genuinely not aware of the implications of their actions) or a disregard of implications of their actions beyond the immediate future. Those of us with weight problems who nevertheless still go to restaurants to celebrate minor events with calorie-laden feasts are heavily discounting the longer-term results of our indulgence. Society may take the long view that the actions of this generation must not disregard the welfare of future generations. This is particularly pertinent in periods leading up to a war, when a government may need to safeguard the nation's ability to feed itself and the market mechanism cannot be relied on the make the necessary preparations (ensure that there are stocks of fertiliser, that land improvements are undertaken etc.). Even in peacetime there will be some people who claim that finite resources should not be depleted, and that the consumption of oil reserves by the motorcars of today is depriving energy supplies to the earth's inhabitants of the next century. The term 'sustainable' is often used to mean policies that safeguard the interests of future generations. A detailed consideration of such issues would be inappropriate here, but it is important to note that they bear heavily on policy decisions to avoid the use of growth stimulants in cattle (because of the fear of long-term consequences on human health), to protect natural resources, the natural and built environment, our cultural heritage and so on.
- **Monopolies and other forms of imperfect competition.** The market mechanism is also subject to the growth of market power by single or groups of buyers and sellers. In agriculture it is often felt that the individual farmer is at a disadvantage when bargaining with the small number of very large businesses that buy the bulk of many agricultural commodities (wholesale dairies, cereal merchants etc. who themselves may be subject to the influence of a few large supermarket chains). The EU has a strong policy on competition, backed up with legislation and large fines, which aims at maintaining a satisfactory degree of competition within the overall economy.
- **Friction in the market mechanism.** The real world is a dynamic place in which changes are constantly occurring (for example, changes in the technology of production etc.). The market will signal the adjustments needed to match new conditions (for changes in output by firms and the reallocation of the resources used in production). However, the adjustments usually do not take place immediately, easily and without cost to at least some individuals and firms. In particular, people may not move from types of occupation (and locations) where the demand for their services is falling to other types of jobs (and places) where opportunities are greater. In part this friction may result from lack of information, housing, suitable skills or stickiness in wages. As will be seen later, immobility of factors present a particular problem in agriculture, where new technology and higher productivity implies that less labour is needed but where the outflow from farming is often slow (the associated economic and social problems are discussed later). Rural areas also tend to suffer from remoteness and relatively poor communications.
- **Weak self-correcting forces.** We also know that, at aggregate level, the whole economy does not automatically operate simultaneously at high levels of employment,

low inflation and sustained moderate growth rates. In part this is a reflection of market friction but goes beyond it to involve how the various parts of the economy relate and interact with each other. While there are some self-correcting mechanisms at work, and economists vary in their view of how strong they are, in practice some steering of the economy seems to be necessary. Unfortunately, the workings of the macroeconomy are only imperfectly understood and governments are unlikely to apply the exactly required amount of stimulus or brake. Attempts to control inflation by damping down aggregate demand can be too zealous (even assuming that this action will be effective), with a serious impact on employment. Often a new round of intervention is needed to 'correct' the impact of an earlier round. And because economies are increasingly interlinked, particularly among the Member States of the EU, what one government does can have widespread implications for other countries. As yet, steps towards a collective action at tackling general economic problems in the EU have proved to be faltering.

- **Failure to reflect non-economic goals**. The market mechanism is 'amoral', in the sense that it does not apply a set of ethical values to the solutions it achieves. The market is sensitive to purchasing power, and those without this power will not have a direct impact on what gets produced and on who consumes it. Hence the market will reflect the present distribution of income (and wealth) in society, which may not be fair (equitable) judged from some moral or ethical standpoint. For example, in a completely free market system, where education had to be paid for by the person receiving it, there are grounds to think that those from poorer backgrounds would be disadvantaged in terms of their access to it, and thus would be excluded from the many advantages that a good education can bring (economic, social, cultural etc.) both to the individuals concerned and the community at large (see Box 1.1 on 'merit goods'). A market-determined solution to the provision of education may not reflect what society prefers. In democracies one way of indicating preferences is through the political system, including the way that people vote in elections. Politicians may propose that, in the national interest, all young people *should* have equal educational opportunities irrespective of where they live or their type of home background. If these proposals attract votes and form part of government programmes the market solution can be modified, for example by providing state education, university scholarships, student loans etc. Even so, modified outcomes can fall far short of what some critics would regard as an ethically fair and just way of organising the use of a country's resources for the benefit of its inhabitants, present and future. In reality the situation is complex; there will be a variety of opinion in society of what is fair and reasonable, and the political system is not flawless at reflecting the balance of the wishes of citizens.

Although the interventions to correct for market failure are well-meant, it is by no means certain that governments acting alone or collectively achieve in practice a better outcome than the admittedly fallible market system. Tinkering with what constitutes a complex set of inter-relationships, often only partly understood, is likely to introduce additional problems. Thus 'state failure' also exists, and a balance will have to be struck between 'market failure' and 'state failure'. For example, in farming the persistently falling prices of agricultural commodities means inevitable structural adjustment, with falls in the number of people operating farms and increasing average farm sizes. Because of friction in the reallocation of resources, in the short term some farmers will find themselves trapped on units too small to generate a satisfactory income. The traditional way that policy has attempted to ease their pain has been by intervening in the market mechanism and supporting commodity prices against the trend. However, this has resulted in widespread inefficiency (because incentives for efficiency-enhancing structural change are reduced) and high costs to consumers (because food prices have been kept up) and to taxpayers (because the 'need' for support they finance becomes embedded). This example will be returned to on numerous occasions in this text.

Given that these sources of problems exist, three basic rationales can be identified for public policy action that attempts to modify the situation. These are:

- **Efficiency**, in that the actions will improve the relationship between the national output of the economy and its use of resources. If only private goods and services are considered (which would include the value of commodities produced by farming), an improvement in efficiency will lead to an increase in national income, as conventionally measured. But a broader view can also be taken, so that output of public goods is also included (such as the non-market environmental services that agriculture and forestry can provide by enhancing biodiversity and landscape appearance). Greater efficiency would be achieved if the sum of both market and non-market output increased in relation to the resources available and used.
- **Equity**, in that the actions will improve the fairness of society. There is no easy measure of this, and views will differ as to what is fair or not. However, in practice some indicators may be useful (such as the numbers of people falling below a poverty line, though the level at which this is set is open to dispute).
- **Political economy**: sometimes it is necessary to facilitate the policy process by offering incentives to people or organisations who would otherwise be obstructive to attempts to tackle policy problems. For example, if operators of businesses have become used to a particular form of subsidy, they are likely to oppose changes that leave them worse off, even if these changes are beneficial to society as a whole. The offer of compensation may shift their attitudes and allow the policy change to go through the legal system, still leaving a net gain for society.

In reality, often the rationale for action is a mix of these three. The issue of motives will be encountered later (Chapter 12) when the reform of agricultural policy is described.

1.3.2 The background to problem formulation

In the policy process the step of problem formulation requires someone or some institution to realise that things are happening that require corrective action. Awareness of a possible problem is only a necessary first step; the next is to convince politicians that it is a serious problem for which solutions should be sought, thereby putting the issue on the policy agenda for consideration of what actions are appropriate.

Some important characteristics of problem formulation should be noted:

- **What is considered a problem will be a reflection of the set of social values prevalent at the time.** Examples of these values include the preference for a reasonably stable society, so that political, economic and social stability is thought of as 'good' and instability as 'bad'. Economic growth is 'good' because it enables people to enjoy a greater consumption of goods and services and, given the choice, people will usually prefer more to less. Equality of opportunity is thought desirable (though in agriculture the opportunity for entry to this occupation in many EU countries is less now than 50 years ago unless the entrant is a member of a farming family). A more efficient use of national resources is thought better than a less efficient use. Maintaining a low-pollution environment for future generations is thought 'good' and the consuming of non-renewable resources is 'bad' (though there is often an assumption that future generations will be constrained to the sorts of technology found today). Conditions which force young people to leave rural communities in order to find work or housing are also thought to be 'bad' because they threaten family support networks and can unbalance the age profile of communities .

- **Different groups in society are likely to have different sets of social values, and hence some may see problems where none are apparent to others.** As a generality, it seems that society's current concern with the problems of the environment and landscape originated from members of the non-agricultural community (people interested in wild birds, rare plants, fishing etc., many of whom live in urban areas), rather than from farmers. The issue of access to the countryside for recreation is of concern primarily to ramblers; indeed the use of land for this purpose can constitute a problem for those engaged in agricultural production. Perhaps the greatest clash of social values occurs over field sports (hunting with dogs, shooting game birds etc.). Often the views of people who own or control agricultural land differ from those who do not.

- **Priorities change.** In times of severe national food shortage, such as might occur during a war, environmental considerations would not count highly. But when food is plentiful and there is the opportunity to take into account the broader aims of society, a greater priority might be attached to conserving the quality of the environment; in such circumstances any loss of wildlife becomes a 'problem'. We now think that we should attach a larger value to preserving part of the national stock of old buildings than was the case twenty years or so ago. On the other hand, the idea that everyone should have a job has been given a lower priority in the attempt to achieve other policy aims, such as the control of inflation, especially if unemployment benefits are available. The point is that what is not a problem worth government intervention at one time and in one set of circumstances may be viewed as a real problem at other times, and vice versa.

- **Different societies will attach different weights to different values, so that the perceptions of 'problems' vary.** For example, public opinion in the UK sees change in countryside appearance as a greater problem than it does in many other nations. The difficulties which young people encounter when trying to enter farming is seen as a more major problem in France than in the UK. In Germany there is particular concern that agriculture should be given priority in land use. In Italy the threat to the tradition of family farms and family structure is keenly felt, whereas in some of the newer Member States of the EU, where much of the land had been organised into large-scale socialised farms, this attitude to family operation may be less strong (although there is often an attachment to family ownership of the land). Animal welfare is seen as less of an issue in Spain than in some more northern countries. In part these attitudes will come from the different sets of problems that each country faces, but they may also reflect differences in history, religion, political system, demography and others factors. Discussion of apparently innocuous aspects of agriculture (such as organic farming) and rural areas (such as access to housing) among representatives of Member States can reflect surprisingly large differences in attitudes, making common EU policies and any subsequent reforms hard to agree.

1.3.3 Problem filtration – which problems attract attention and action?

In a democratic society, the process of setting the broad policy aims and achieving a balance between these aims is left to the political system. While in a democracy with universal franchise everyone has a vote, this does not mean that, in practice, they each have an equal influence on which problems attract attention and policy action, together often called the policy agenda. Almost inevitably, the predominant view of the problems faced at any one time and the actions needed contains imperfections.

Sometimes individual government ministers become preoccupied with a particular line of argument (such as support for the family farm) for political or personal reasons and can give it disproportionate prominence. Government departments (or parts of the European Commission) can become committed to a particular set of problems and fail to respond to changed situations; it is often easier for a bureaucracy to keep on doing the same things than to adapt. Pressure groups exist to ensure that the problems their members face are put on the policy agenda, and often overstate their case in order to attract attention. In a more negative form, pressure groups may try to keep certain items off the agenda if they could harm their members. They will attempt to lobby national politicians, EU Commissioners and staff of the Commission and members of the European Parliament to promote their views. The politicians, bureaucrats and those groups that try to advise or influence them are termed the policy network. In a pluralist system all interests (producers, consumers, taxpayers, environmentalists etc.) will be represented by pressure groups and each will have opportunity to influence decision-makers. However in the real world, for reasons that will be explored later, some interests will be more effectively represented than others. It is usually easier for a relatively small number of individuals or firms who each have a lot to gain or lose by a policy change to band together and support a pressure group than is the case with a large and disparate group whose individual gains or losses are much smaller. The relationship between likely gains from collective lobbying and the costs of doing so are part of the explanation. Hence farmers' unions have been more active and effective than groups representing consumers. Some pressure groups have even been taken into the policy community (somewhat narrower than the policy network and consisting of those public and private groups who actually determine the policy agenda). For example, in the UK during the 1950s and 1960s the National Farmers' Union (NFU) was in effect a partner with the Ministry of Agriculture, Fisheries and Food (MAFF) in determining agricultural policy. This is an example of corporatism in operation; characteristics are that criticism of policy (in this case by farmers) is thereby muffled and it ensures that the individuals most affected by the policy are highly likely to co-operate when it is put into practice.

As will be seen later, in the past decisions about which issues EU agricultural policy attempted to address and the actions taken under the CAP were made mostly by a small policy community that shared a strong interest in promoting greater production and the incomes of farmers This community comprised agricultural politicians (national ministers responsible for agriculture), civil servants in government agricultural departments (including the European Commission's agricultural Directorate-General) and farmers' representatives (at EU level the federation of farmers' unions 'COPA'); collectively these were often called the 'agricultural establishment'. However, since the early 1990s increasing influence has been wielded by other interests, such as organisations concerned with the environment, the food quality and health lobbies, administrators concerned with rural development and so on. Consequently the policy agenda has changed.

1.3.4 When is it economically efficient to act?

Just because a policy problem has been identified does not necessarily mean that it is economically rational for the government (acting on behalf of society) to try to solve it. In principle, the decision to take action will depend on the cost to society of doing so judged against the benefit to society that results. For example, if there is a problem of poor productivity in the economy that can be traced to inadequate training and education among the workforce, the government may wish to raise standards as a way of improving the situation. Spending more on training and education, using funds raised by taxation or government borrowing, will be a cost to society, but the value of the expected gains in terms of improving national income may be greater. In theory governments should spend increasing amounts of public resources up to that point at which the extra cost is just balanced by the additional benefit (marginal cost will be equal to marginal benefit) – this will be the most efficient level of spending on training and education. To go beyond this point would cost more than the value of the additional benefits achieved and there would be a net loss to society for using the extra resources (that is, going beyond where marginal cost equals marginal benefit represents an uneconomic use of resources). Of course, the total costs of training and education may still be exceeded by the value of the total benefits, but the highest net gain (the difference between them) will be where the marginal costs and benefits are equal.

In reality there are difficulties in being able to quantify both costs and, especially, benefits from policy actions, making the identification of the optimum level of resource use hard to determine. Some benefits (such as from having an attractive countryside rather than an unattractive one) are difficult to express in monetary terms and, though techniques can be used to estimate such benefits, they can be challenged. Similarly, some of the benefits from having a more equitable distribution of incomes are non-monetary, though there may be direct benefits to national prosperity. Some benefits take a long time to materialise (the fruits of education being one), may be risky and might not happen at all if changes take place in the economy (for example, some skills can become obsolete when technology develops). On the costs side, there may be strong competition between ways of spending public funds (defence, alleviation of poverty, environmental protection etc.) so funding may never be sufficient to reach the level in any particular type of policy at which marginal costs and benefits come to be equal. Rather, society is likely to have to allocate its scarce public funds in ways that balance the benefits across a range of uses – hospitals, schools, welfare payments etc. Under these circumstances, policy decision-makers will ideally spend on each type of policy action so that the last £1 brings the same additional benefit in each use (that is, they are guided by the Principle of Equimarginal Returns). But this efficient allocation is hard to achieve when benefits are diverse in nature, with at least some of them difficult to identify or measure.

Just because the idea of an efficient policy is rather impractical does not invalidate it as a useful concept. It is especially helpful to focus on whether too little or too much is being spent on particular policy aims or on particular sectors. Sometimes circumstances change in ways that reduce the significance of a problems and governments can find themselves, for historical reasons, using too much funding in a given policy area. For example, a case can be made that support to agricultural producers is now too large when judged against the resulting benefits, and that other ways of tackling economic and social problems of rural areas should be given more resources (such as supporting village shops and rural transport schemes).

Of course, people and firms that currently enjoy the private benefits of support (higher incomes and property prices) will not favour reallocations, and they may finance pressure groups and apply political pressure in order to try to prevent change. A clear distinction should be borne in mind, therefore, between the benefits and costs to society of actions, which lies behind the economic rationale for intervention, and the private benefits to, and costs borne by, individuals. Sometimes it is justifiable to provide compensation to individuals who suffer from changes in policy because of *equity* (they might be put in a position of unfairly low incomes) or to enable a greater benefit to society (reflected in, say, a rise in national income) to be secured; this is an example of the *political economy* rationale for action mentioned earlier.

1.4 Policy formulation

The next stage is to decide on the type of action to be used to tackle the problems – policy formulation. The critical part of this stage is to decide on the objectives which public intervention is designed to achieve and which should lead to an alleviation of the underlying policy problems. Sometimes it may be decided that the best action is no action – that the problem cannot be adequately addressed given the resources that are available, or that the problem is not sufficiently serious to warrant a policy intervention, or that more problems, even more intractable, will be generated by trying to do something. The decision will involve forecasting what is likely to happen under the various scenarios of action or inaction. The responsibility for formulating objectives lies primarily with civil servants and politicians, in the case of EU agricultural policy the staff of the European Commission's Directorate-General whose proposals are adopted by the ministers of agriculture of Member States and the European Parliament (see Chapter 3).

1.4.1 Myths about reality

These civil servants and agricultural politicians will use their knowledge and skills to set policy objectives that enable the problems, identified as worth doing something about, to be tackled. Though governments will wish to be seen to be using evidence based policy (both in terms of statistics on the problems giving concern and reliable findings on how these can be tackled), frequently they will be drawing not on sound evidence but on what are termed 'myths' about reality. In this context the word 'myths' is being used in a narrow technical sense. It refers to beliefs, which may or may not be valid, about how society and the economy work in reality and which suggest ways in which changes can be made towards a 'better' state. Examples abound, and here are just a few:

- that increased national self-sufficiency in food production is desirable in order to ensure secure supplies for a country;
- that agriculture should have priority for rural land to preserve the capacity in the long term to produce food;

- that without support the incomes of farmers would be unfairly low;
- that prosperous farming is necessary for landowners to undertake adequate nature conservation;
- that the children of farmers make the best farmers and therefore should be enabled to follow in their father's footsteps;
- that a mixed rural society is necessary for a viable future;
- that keeping people living in the countryside brings economic, social and environmental benefits;
- that people born in rural areas should be able to live there as adults in order to conserve a sustainable local community;
- that monoculture, with large areas of the same crop, gives the countryside an unattractive appearance;
- that more woodland gives the nation a useful long-term resource for timber, environmental conservation and recreation;
- that hunting using dogs is the most effective way of controlling foxes.

All of these are statements about how the world is believed to function, at least by some people. Each is testable, at least in principle, though to test them may require setting criteria by which 'best' and 'necessary' might be judged. Many will be treated as self-evident and form the basis of policy action without proper scrutiny. Pressure groups will attempt to promote those myths that best serve the interests of their members (for example, farmers unions will be keen to support assertions that a prosperous farming sector is necessary for a beautiful countryside and a viable rural population). It is a role of economists and policy analysts to examine the validity of these 'myths' and thereby provide a more secure evidence base for policy actions.

1.4.2 Objectives arranged as a hierarchy

Here we must recognise some general features of objectives. First, objectives typically form a *hierarchy*. This is perhaps most simply demonstrated with personal objectives. If one's life objectives are (for the sake of argument) to keep healthy, to pass one's genes on to the next generation, to have a fulfilling job and to generally enjoy life, these can be broken down into a number of sub-objectives. To secure a fulfilling job may require the acquisition of an educational qualification, which itself can be broken down into sub-objectives (completing each year of study, further divided into completing each course, further divided into completing each assignment etc.).

An example of a generalised hierarchy for agricultural policy is shown in Figure 1.2. At the highest levels are the broad objectives of governments and of the EU; these are usually described as comprising economic goals (including economic growth, economic stability, trade promotion), social goals (for example, equity in access to and consumption of essential services, such as health and education, and social stability), national and individual security, personal freedom to control one's own environment, protection of the natural environment and cultural heritage, and so on. At the highest levels these goals overlap substantially. These broad objectives can be broken down into objectives for food supply, for land use, for defence, for the prevention of poverty, for promoting the arts, for species protection and so on. They are approached in practice using individual policy programmes (such as for the production of agricultural commodities, agri-environmental schemes, retirement incentives and so on),

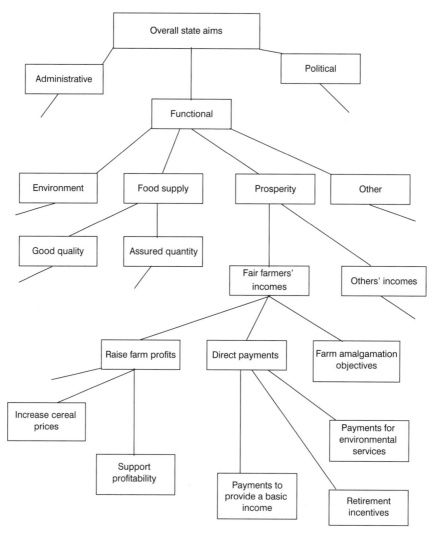

Figure 1.2   A hierarchy of objectives

each with their individual sets of specific objectives. (The EU's Common Agricultural Policy has its own set of objectives which will be covered in detail later).

Starting at the top of a hierarchy of objects enables the question to be answered 'How are the broad objectives actually put into practice?'. Alternatively, starting with the objectives of an individual policy programme (such as financial incentives for farmers to retire early) answers can be provided to the question 'What is this particular programme trying to achieve within the overall policy for the economy?'. Attempting to place objectives within a hierarchy also has the property of making more obvious the clashes which can occur between policies (discussed below), duplications and gaps. These will be important to the efficiency objectives of administrations.

Alongside these 'functional' objectives is a concern with the performance of the policy process itself, reflected in the movement towards a greater role for the assessment of policies and programmes and policies (see Chapter 11). In addition, there will be political objectives. Within the EU there are explicit commitments to greater economic cooperation and political integration. As will be seen later (Chapter 12), from the beginning of the EU (which started as three separate European Communities) there has been a strong political impetus behind the development of the joint policies for Member States. At a practical level, a government will, not unexpectedly, wish to continue in power, and in a democracy will take actions which, while tackling the 'real' problems, also enable it to be re-elected by attracting votes.

1.4.3 Testability of objectives

For policy to be efficient, it is important that objectives are both clear and testable, that is, in a form from which it will be possible to judge to what extent policy has been successful in achieving them. Politicians and civil servants may not like clear objectives, since clarity opens them up to the possibility that they can be shown to have failed in their policies and reduces their flexibility to manoeuvre. They would claim, with some justification, that changing circumstances require some room to adapt existing policies to new conditions. However, without clear, testable objectives, policy cannot be assessed satisfactorily, with the result that policies may be inefficient in their use of resources and not capable of tackling the current policy problems. The CAP has often been criticised that, while it was set up at a time (the 1950s) when there was a need to expand agricultural production, it failed to adapt its objectives adequately in the decades that followed. A closer attention to the changing problems, reflected in changed objectives, may well have lessened some of the pressing problems of today though, as will become evident from later chapters, other factors such as the way in which agricultural policy decisions are made, it is unlikely that they would have been completely avoided.

Making objectives testable will often mean that they have to be quantified. For example, if the aim is to ensure that children living in the countryside can receive schooling without excessive travelling, an objective which could be tested might be to reduce the percentage of children living in rural areas who have to travel for more than an hour each day from, say, 20 per cent to 10 per cent. But much more controversial is the CAP objective of ensuring a fair standard of living for the agricultural community. This has never been made testable (see Chapter 2). To do so would involve setting out who comprises the agricultural community (for example, does it include hired farm workers as well as self-employed farmers?) and what is a 'fair' standard of living (does this imply comparisons with other groups in society, and on what basis is the comparison to be made – income or consumption possibilities, per household or per individual?). But by failing to make this objective testable in any precise way politicians and senior administrators have left open the possibility of the CAP being expensive and inefficient. This issue is returned to later.

1.4.4 Interactions between objectives

Policy affecting agriculture and rural development is inherently a complex activity and at any one time there will be a whole array of policy objectives which the EU and national governments are attempting to pursue for their agricultures and rural areas. Even if the administration system is highly efficient, there will be interaction between these objectives. Some will be consonant with each other (such as the objectives of stable prices for farm products to help achieve a more efficient use of resources, and that of improving the stability of incomes for farmers) and mutually reinforcing, while some conflict; higher prices for cereals benefit the income of arable farmers but mean higher costs faced by livestock farmers. If agricultural policy is designed by a single administrative body (such as a ministry of agriculture), then systems should be in place so that conflicts are kept to a minimum – the construction of a hierarchy of objectives by a department should show up the more blatant conflicts. Sometimes these cannot be completely avoided, and a conscious decision has to be made to trade-off one against the other to reach a compromise.

The potential for a clash of objectives is perhaps greatest between policies controlled by separate institutions (such as different ministries of the same government, or between national and EU-level bodies). Government departments striving to achieve non-agricultural objectives can find themselves taking actions that have results that run counter to the objectives of the same government's agricultural ministry or, more rarely, reinforce them. Here are some examples:

- Setting interest rates by governments and/or central banks to regulate the general economy will have an impact on farming through affecting its borrowing costs. An increase in the rate can be very serious for highly indebted farmers, typically those who have expanded through land purchase, who may see their interest payments rise to the point that their businesses are no longer viable. Often these farmers will be the better at using farm resources and their ambitions to expand may have got them into trouble. Poorer performers may have unwittingly escaped the danger.

- Changes in the international exchange rates between currencies can have a substantial impact on the levels of product prices received by farmers. The decision by the UK in September 1992 to leave the European Community's Exchange Rate Mechanism (ERM), taken for reasons unconnected with agriculture, precipitated a rapid decline in Sterling's value against the ECU of about 15 per cent. This improved the profitability of farming in the UK because support prices (then set in ECU under the CAP) rose in terms of the national currency. This rise ran counter to the objective of agricultural policy at the time, which was to lower the prices that farmers received to prevent the accumulation of surplus output.

- Taxation policies designed to redistribute wealth may influence the sizes of farms. Because agricultural land counts as an asset on which tax may have to be paid when wealth is passed from one generation to another, parts of farms may have to be sold off by heirs in order to raise the sums required. This runs contrary to the objective of agricultural policy to restructure farms so that they become larger and thus more economically viable.

- Policies on the environment, such as the pollution of water-courses, while not being aimed primarily at farmers, can have repercussions in terms of the standards which farmers have to meet and hence reduce their ability to compete with food imported from countries with less stringent environmental legislation.

- Regional development policies which create alternative jobs in rural areas can affect the rate at which farmers lose labour to other industries and the wages which have to be paid to retain workers. Better roads and other communications, better education and training opportunities, and many other non-agricultural aspects of change in rural areas will all have an impact on farmers, their families and farm businesses.

- A ministry of education, in the interests of reducing overall costs, may wish to close small rural schools, thus making living in small villages and remoter areas less attractive to people with young families. In contrast, a government department charged with improving living conditions in rural areas and stemming the flow of families to towns will wish to make these rural areas viable by supporting facilities such as local rural schools.

- Policies on competition may result in some farmer-controlled cooperatives being ruled as illegal at a time when an objective of agricultural policy is to encourage farmers to combine their marketing operations to gain strength against large supermarket buyers. For example, the long-standing arrangements for marketing milk in the UK (with, since the mid-1930s, a single marketing board for England and Wales, virtually a monopsony in milk buying from farms and a monopoly supplier to dairies) eventually fell foul of the EU policy on competition.
- Policies which are primarily political in objective may carry implications for agriculture. For example, the enlargement of the EU by increasing the number of Member States has carried implications for the shape of agricultural policy and hence on the sort of farming carried on in existing Members. The accession of Spain and Portugal (in 1986) had an impact on farming in other Mediterranean countries and on the nature of the CAP. These were overshadowed by the further enlargements in 2004 and 2007 (twelve mostly formerly Communist-run states in Central and Eastern Europe). Again, the political decision to enlarge was a contributing factor to the reforms of the CAP made in the run-up period to these countries joining the EU (see Chapter 12).

Some of these policies with 'non-agricultural' objectives are much more powerful in their effects on agriculture and rural areas than policies which are directed primarily at these sectors. This should cause us to question whether the terms 'agricultural policy' or 'rural development policy' are very meaningful. Though useful as labels which exclude the more unrelated of government activities (such as health and safety regulations for mines), they essentially derive from the part of the public service which administer them (agricultural and rural development departments). We should not lose sight of the broader set of influences on agriculture and the countryside.

1.4.5 The conflict between equity and efficiency

Not only can there be conflicts between overt policy objectives, but there can be a less obvious conflict between the goals of policy and the efficiency with which the economy functions. To achieve a balance between the two there has to be a trade-off between equity and efficiency.

A common objective of governments is to foster the more efficient use of resources. Given certain rather heroic assumptions (including the absence of externalities), perfectly competitive markets will result in an outcome that achieves the greatest efficiency in terms of production and consumption, though this will reflect the initial distribution of income. This is why governments encourage competition, control the development of monopolies and take steps to enable resources (especially labour) to maintain their mobility. However, there may be good reasons why the market-determined, efficient pattern of resource use and consumption is not seen as 'fair'. The trouble is that modifying the pattern may well represent a shift to a less-efficient position. Furthermore, the mechanisms used to modify the pattern of production and consumption will themselves absorb resources.

As an example we can envisage a situation where low-income families might not be able to afford health care. Such a situation might well clash with the prevalent set of values of

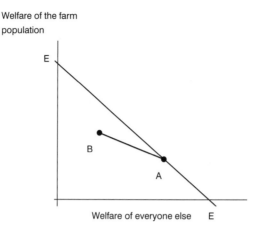

In a perfectly competitive system, competition would ensure the efficient use of productive resources. Line EE represents various efficient combinations of the allocation of a good (for example, housing) between farmers and other groups in society, depending how income was initially distributed among them. Points inside (to the left of) this line represent less efficient uses of resources. Assume initially the economy is at position A but that society wishes to move to the left from this position by applying policy that redistributed incomes to farmers from other members of society. Inefficiencies in this process mean that the best that can be achieved is to move to position B. Though equity is improved when this policy is applied, there is a loss of economic efficiency, as B lies inside the line EE.

Figure 1.3 The trade-off between efficiency and equity

society and there might be agreement, via the political system, that something should be done about this. As part of a policy programme to bring health care to these low-income people, various instruments might be employed; health care could be provided free of charge to needy cases who satisfy some form of means test, financed by a tax on the better-off, or they could be given an income supplement to pay for this care, or other mechanisms might be used. However, intervention on the grounds of 'equity' (or 'fairness') would result in a movement away from the 'most efficient' use of resources for the economy (see Figure 1.3). There is therefore a trade-off between the two which should be recognised. However, the less-efficient but more equitable pattern of resource use could be a preferable mix viewed against the overall set of values of society than what existed before.

We shall see later that a major aim of the EU's CAP has been to improve the welfare of farmers and their families, that is, to increase the market-determined level of their incomes. This is seen as an improvement in terms of equity (fairness) but it has been done in ways that reduced the efficiency with which national resources are used.

1.5 Policy implementation

Policy implementation consists of the design of programmes of action by which the objectives can be brought about and putting them into practice using policy instruments (or mechanism). Programmes and their instruments are the parts of policy which the people whose decisions are to be influenced see and feel. Examples include programmes to support farmers' incomes brought about using direct payments or raising the prices farmers receive for their production, and to maintain a rural bus network by giving grants to operators or subsidising tickets. Each programme will have its own objectives, a subset of the objectives for policy as a whole.

1.5.1 Types of policy instruments

There is a wide range of types of policy instrument that can be used. The choice will depend on a number of factors, including the total cost, the administrative problems involved, and the political acceptability of the alternatives. An exercise in options analysis should be carried out at this stage, which is a systematic review of the alternative instruments and consideration of their relative advantages and drawbacks, from which a preferred way forward may be identified. However, designers will not necessarily examine all possibilities and aim for the optimum solution; they will tend to be satisficers, that is they will look for the alternative that is adequate, or 'good enough' rather than the best, and grasp the first one that reaches this criterion. There will also be a preference for using instruments that have already been shown to work, are therefore less risky than new ones, and may be already in place to serve other objectives. The outcome is that important options may be overlooked.

Later chapters deal with the economic and other characteristics of the different form of instruments and their use within the CAP and rural policy. Here we need only to acknowledge some of the main types. Figure 1.4 shows examples of policy instruments and situations in which they have been used in agricultural and rural policy:

1.5.2 An instrument as a system

Each instrument can be envisaged as a 'system' (a set of related parts, such as a car or a cow), with inputs (financial resources, manpower, management expertise) and outputs which depend on the objective of the policy programme (such as an increase in the income of farmers). Sometimes use of the instrument will have side effects, or 'spin-offs' which may or may not be anticipated. Figure 1.5 shows the relationships. Some will be beneficial, but many are detrimental. For example, financial incentives given to UK farmers in hill areas so that they remained farming there and preserved the environment were initially paid according to the number of animals they kept. Farmers were found to respond by increasing the stocking rates, with consequent damage to the environment the payments were intended to protect. Consequently ways had to be found that countered this side effect, such as limiting the number of animals per hectare on which payments could be claimed and, later, completely removing the need to keep animals from the qualification of entitlement. As will become evident, agricultural and rural development policy contain many other instances of side effects.

Often the programme cannot achieve the objective of the policy directly. For example, if the objective of a government-financed training scheme for farmers and their workers is to raise incomes in agriculture by producing a more highly educated workforce which will be able to adapt to new technology quickly and be more productive, the final outcome of this programme will only come to fruition once the trained people are working again. A distinction must be drawn between the output of the programme (trained people), the results or impact (in terms of what happens to the incomes of the individuals and firms directly involved) and the outcome (which refers to the effect on the performance of the agricultural industry as a whole). Though the terminology is by no means standardised,

Type of instrument	Examples
Legislation	Passing laws on what land can be used for, such as for the building of houses and infrastructure (with or without compensation for the owners who find their options limited); animal welfare and pollution legislation, such as limits on the amount of nitrogen used by farmers in water catchment areas, with fines for infringement
Direct action	Public purchase of environmentally sensitive land, so that its use can be better controlled
Public provision of free or subsidised goods and services (education/ advice)	Improving the quality of farm management and hence farm output and/or productivity by providing a free advisory system; advice enabling farmers to diversify into new unfamiliar enterprises; education and training for the workforce without payment by the participants, funded by grants to training organisations and colleges; subsidies to the provision of roads and telecommunications in rural areas to aid mobility; setting up improved marketing mechanism funded from tax revenue.
Financial incentives on use of inputs	Grants for investments on farms to encourage modernisation or the restoration of historic buildings and landscape features (such as dry stone walls); tax concessions for types of investment or for firms in certain areas; subsidised interest rates on loans for certain purposes to encourage investment.
Direct payments	Income support payments, such as the EU's Single Farm Payment and Single Area Payment; special payments to farmers in disadvantaged areas to compensate for these natural handicaps; pensions; payments for management agreements on land of high environmental quality. Payments may be subject to beneficiaries complying with certain conditions (such as keeping their land in good agricultural and environmental condition, known as 'cross-compliance').
Product market intervention	Use of support buying, import restriction, quotas on production (including set-aside) to raise the prices received by farmers and hence their incomes

Figure 1.4 Examples of types of instruments and their use

the concepts are broadly accepted. In the short term the programme will have an interim (or intermediate) objective relating to outputs (for example, the training of '*x*' numbers of individuals). It is assumed that this will enable the outcome (or ultimate or final objective) of higher incomes to be obtained in the industry as a whole. Thus, it is assumed that there is a cause and effect relationship between the intermediate and final objectives (outputs leading to outcomes). Again, as will become evident, agricultural and rural development policy is full of examples.

The people with new skills may find attractive jobs outside agriculture and hence, while leaving farming, perhaps raise the productivity of the economy in general. The employment of personnel to provide the training may also improve the economic activity (jobs and incomes) in a rural locality. Though these side effects may be of little concern to policy-makers wishing to raise incomes in the farming industry, they will be of interest to evaluators of the broader impacts of the training programme. Again, agricultural and rural development policy contains many examples where side effects or spin-offs from the use of instruments are important.

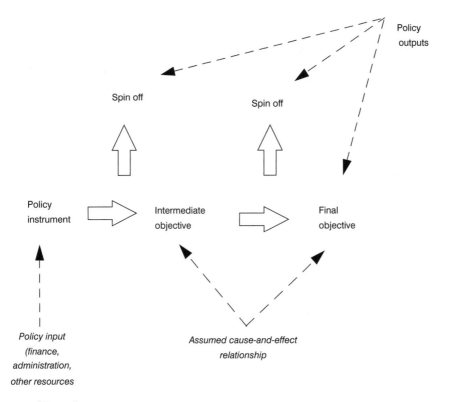

Figure 1.5   The policy programme as a system

Often there are alternative ways of administering policy programmes. For example, should they be controlled from central government or should local bodies, such as regional or district councils, be given the responsibility of running them and the finance to carry them out? Some programmes, such as support of prices of agricultural commodities brought about by taxing imports, can be best organised centrally but others, such as grants for encouraging farmers to repair historic buildings and stone walls to make upland areas appear more attractive, are probably best left to local bodies to work out the details and organise. Within the EU the Rural Development Programmes (that encourage agriculture to adapt, use agri-environment agreements with farmers to help achieve bio-diversity and landscape objectives, and improve living conditions in villages) provide for a great deal of independence of action at national and regional levels within an agreed Community framework, so that programmes are tailored to local problems and opportunities. This is an example of the principle of subsidiarity at work – taking decision-making down to the lowest effective level.

1.5.3 How policy instruments affect several objectives

Above, it was noted that policy objectives often interact – they can be consonant with each other (complementary) or conflict. Complete neutrality is probably rare. The designers of policy instruments should be aware not only of their impact on the objective at which they are aimed but also of the spin-off and secondary effects on other objectives. They will want to make instruments complementary in their action, preferably bringing synergy and, wherever possible, avoiding embarrassing situations where public money spent in one direction simply cancels out public money being spent in another.

Several ways in which an instruments can interact with more than one objective are encapsulated in Figure 1.6. Here we see what happens when there are two policy aims (giving income support to agricultural producers, and countryside conservation). For the purpose of understanding the principle it does not matter that neither is quantified. The centre of the diagram is the situation before any policy is applied. Increasing distance from the centre implies greater amounts of programme action (levels of spending etc.) Moving from the centre to the top right quadrant implies that some progress is made in both objectives. Moving from the centre to the top left or bottom right achieves progress towards one objective but away from the other. The bottom left quadrant implies that policy takes us away from both objectives. Various scenarios are described in this figure, detailed in the notes below it.

This example confines itself to two objectives. However, a more general conclusion is possible about the number of policy instruments and policy objectives (though it is not proved here). This is the Tinbergen Principle that states that, if there are a number of policy objectives, for these to be achieved there must be *at least the same number of instruments*.

1.5.4 Allowing for succession and termination

Because the objectives of policy relate to problems that are likely to change over time, maybe completely disappearing, it is to be expected that policy instruments will have to be changed or withdrawn. Hence there should be provision for succession and/or termination, or policies will suffer from obsolescence, the instruments increasingly irrelevant and the resources they use wasted. One way of doing this is to stipulate at the outset that a particular financial incentive will only be available for a given period. This will warn potential beneficiaries and also induce a culture of adaptation among administrators. Some EU support schemes take this approach (Rural Development Programmes each run for seven years, the latest covering the period 2007–13 – see Chapter 7). However, in agricultural policy there is a history of the major instruments of support continuing for decades and therefore appearing permanent. Farmers, not unreasonably, come to base their investment and production decisions on the assumption that support will continue, which makes changes, when they become unavoidable, quite difficult to make palatable to the agricultural industry. When introducing compensation for changes, politicians can sometimes appear to be deliberately ambiguous about how long such payments will be made, implying to some audiences that they are temporary while to others that there are no plans to remove them (see Chapter 6 for an example).

1.6 Policy impact

The use of instruments by policy programmes, hopefully, produces results or outcomes in line with the objectives set for the policy. In doing so, the problems which had been identified will have been eased. If the objectives have not been met at all, clearly the instruments have been ineffective and resources wasted. However, success is rarely complete and failure is rarely absolute. The process of judging the outcome in relation to the objectives and the resources used is termed evaluation. Evaluation is really part of a more comprehensive assessment process which is integrated with the policy process (as outlined in section 1.2 above) and runs parallel to it. Later Chapter 11 considers the assessment of policy in

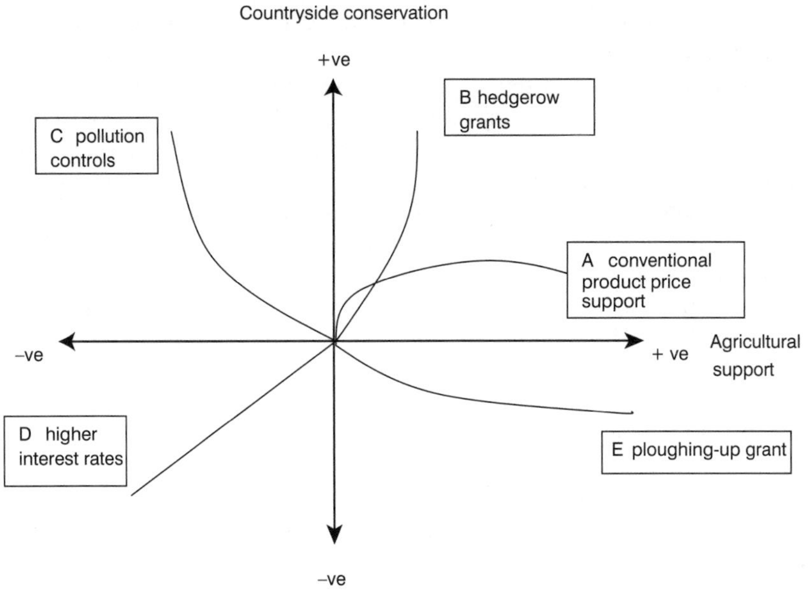

Countryside conservation

Figure 1.6 Impacts of instruments on two objectives

- Curve A represents a situation where higher prices are offered for agricultural products, which result in improved incomes for farmers. Raising prices progressively give more support. However, this instrument affects not only incomes; countryside conservation will be changed as well, but in a rather complex way. At relatively low levels of support the changed cropping pattern may be seen as good for the countryside as they produce a more tidy appearance, cause waste land to be cultivated and so on. However, this benefit fails to increase beyond a certain level and falls back as high levels of prices give incentives for farmers to undertake practices such as hedge removal, high levels of fertiliser application, heavy spraying and so on that have negative impacts on wildlife and the landscape.
- Curve B might arise where better managed hedgerows, designed to make the landscape more attractive, also happen to provide effective windbreaks, modestly increasing crop yields, animal performance and farm incomes.
- Curve C relates to something like the requirement for farmers to install and use pollution control measures. These will result in benefits to conservation, but at all levels they represent a drain on the profits which farms could make. The more pollution control, the greater the impact on profits, though the relationship is not linear.
- Curve D is not a programme which any administrator concerned with either agricultural support or conservation would willing espouse. It might happen if, say, a central bank imposed higher interest rates which had an impact on the cost of farmers' loans. These would lower farm incomes (implying less agricultural support) and farmers would therefore be even less willing to undertake conservation practices.
- Curve E is where the agricultural support uses an instrument which is harmful to conservation. An example might be subsidies for ploughing up established grassland. However, once the damage is done, repeated ploughing cannot make the situation worse.

detail. Here only some of the general points relating to evaluation as it relates to the policy cycle are mentioned.

Evaluation is not usually a simple and clear-cut process. As the name implies, it almost always involves an element of subjective judgement, though taking into account as much objective information on the performance of the instruments used as is possible. Results from evaluation form feedback to policy decision-makers and programme designers, enabling them to learn how to make improvements in future rounds of policy-making; without feedback and learning there is little point in carrying out evaluation. It also throws up additional information on the way the world works, so that new ideas about the problems which policy addresses may come to light and the validity of the assumptions about reality and the cause-and-effect relationships within the policy cycle supported or refuted.

Ultimately, the evaluator has to answer the question 'Was the benefit that came from using public resources in this way greater than the costs involved?' If the answer is no, then the exercise turned out not to be worthwhile, and should not be repeated. If the benefits outweighed the costs, then the welfare of society will have improved. As pointed out earlier, from a theoretical standpoint, public funds should be used increasingly up to the point at which the extra (marginal) benefit just balances the extra (marginal) cost. Of course, measuring both costs and benefits is not a simple matter, especially when non-monetary issues are involved (such as benefits that flow from an improved environment).

Evaluation also has some more practical problems to face. The first is to have available adequate data relating to specific policy programmes, the inputs used, the outputs and outcomes. To make this possible the decision has to be taken early in the life of a policy programme to set up the necessary administration to collect it. This systematic data collection to assist in evaluation is known as monitoring. Take as an example a government programme to encourage elderly farmers to retire from farming by offering them early pensions, the objective being to achieve a certain number or percentage of farmers in the 55–65 year age group retiring per year. The sort of information needed to evaluate this programme will include the expenditure on the policy, including administration costs. Also required will be statistics on the outputs of the programme, such as the number of people who applied and the number who actually went ahead with early retirement. We would also want to know the number of people who were eligible to apply but did not.

Apart from data availability, evaluation has to try to determine what would have gone on in the absence of the policy programme (forecasting). This should have been done by the designers of the programme (see section 1.4) but is often skipped. Continuing the example, the evaluator would want to know also how many farmers would have retired anyway; if most of the people who retired intended to do so even without the pension, the spending by the government may have been largely wasted. The real impact of the policy is the additional retirement which was caused; this aspect is often described as attempting to assess the programme's additionality. And there may be side effects that have to be considered. Perhaps the availability of the pension, by making more land available to younger farmers (who tend to have higher outputs from their farms per hectare and per person) will have created extra agricultural production, the value of which needs to be taken into account. Alternatively, by having more money to spend, incomes in the areas in which the farmers retired may have increased through the multiplier effect. This pension scheme may therefore reinforce some policy programmes and conflict with others, and the full evaluation of the incentives should take this into account. Some of these questions could possibly be answered by the use of control areas, such as parts of the country in which pensions are not offered, and by drawing comparisons with what happened before the programme was introduced. A baseline study is one which tries to establish what a situation is before a policy programme tries to change things. However, in many cases this is difficult or impossible to carry out. The evaluator will need to be aware of the problem of displacement. Displacement over time occurs if the incentives are only available for a short time; carrying on the retirement incentives example, some farmers may delay their retirement a little or bring it forward in order to benefit without having any effect on numbers retiring viewed over a longer period. Displacement over space can happen when instruments are applied in some geographical areas but not others. For example, jobs created in one location may be at the expense of jobs lost elsewhere as firms move to take advantage of the availability of financial incentives offered to help stimulate the economies of particular locations.

In view of the problems, is this evaluation stage of the policy process worthwhile? The answer must be, in most cases, yes. This is because, even though clear-cut answers cannot always be given and inevitably an element of judgement is involved, attempting to undertake evaluation will expose the more blatant examples of failure or of weakness in the logic behind policy. It will lead to a questioning of why certain policies are undertaken and the weeding out of the least effective programmes. So often a policy programme, once introduced, tends to keep going without anyone asking why, or whether it is still necessary. Unless this examination goes on, it will be difficult to stop programmes that are ineffective or which are no longer relevant to the problems of today. Without such rationalisation, it is difficult to obtain finance for new policies in areas where new and pressing needs have arisen.

1.7 In conclusion

An understanding of the CAP needs to be grounded in an appreciation of the policy process, as outlined here in Chapter 1. Problems lead to the design of policy to tackle them, the rationale for intervention being a varying mix of economic, equity or political economy considerations. Using resources in this way should produce a net gain for society, and efficiency is achieved when the marginal cost and marginal benefit are in balance. These are often hard to quantify precisely, particularly when the benefits are of an environmental sort or when the underlying problems are to do with perceived unfairness. Nevertheless, the concept is useful. But, while society as a whole should be better off as the result of policy interventions, the benefits are not evenly spread, and some individuals may be made worse off. We see this especially in the objections and obstructions from people who are benefiting from existing policies when changes to them are proposed, even if on balance the welfare of society would be improved. It might be possible for the beneficiaries to compensate the losers, but unless the mechanism exists by which the compensation is actually paid, the vested interests may prevent any change occurring

The plan of the rest of the book

This book uses the model of the policy process to promote understanding of the CAP. In accord with this, Chapters 2 to 5 are concerned with the stages of *problem formulation* and *policy formulation*. The problems relating to agriculture in the EU and the policy objectives that interventions under the CAP set out to achieve are considered in Chapter 2. Often governments have multiple objectives, and these do not always fit comfortably together as they involve potential conflicts and trade-offs. The way decisions on the CAP are made is described in Chapter 3, together with an analysis of the characteristics of that process, with Chapter 4 describing the statistical information used by CAP decision-makers as evidence. Various policy instruments are encountered; those chosen for use by the CAP are reviewed and analysed in Chapter 5. Chapters 6 to 8 focus on *policy implementation,* describing specific applications within the EU's agricultural and rural development policy, and Chapter 9 considers their relationship to trade and development. The financial inputs to these applications and the balance between them, as seen in the EU budget, are described in Chapter 10.

Progressing to the next stage, Chapter 11 considers the issues involved in assessing the *impact* of the CAP, both in terms of achieving the objectives set for it and its unintended consequences. Much can be learned from evaluating its performance so far, so that improvements can be fed into new rounds of decision-taking.

Chapter 12 stands a little outside the general sequence. Whereas the other chapters are primarily concerned with explaining the CAP as it is currently found, the final chapter puts the present policy in its historical perspective. By now it will be evident that the policy process is something that takes place over time and in a world in which economics mixes with politics. The problems that the CAP attempts to address do not remain static. As will become evident, a major influence on the present array of agricultural policy programmes is those government interventions that were set up many years ago to tackle what were then seen as problems. They still cast a heavy shadow on the present CAP. Furthermore, the way decisions are taken (the institutions and processes involved) has an impact on the outcome. These two factors – the relevance of history and the institutional structure – illustrate what is known as 'path dependency', meaning that in explaining existing policy due attention has to be given to how we got here.

Further reading

Ellis, F. (1992) *Agricultural Policies in Developing Countries.* Wye Studies in Agricultural and Rural Development. Cambridge University Press, Cambridge. (Chapters 1 and 2).

Hill, B. (2006) *An Introduction to Economics – Concepts for Students of Agriculture and the Rural Sector.* 3rd edition. CAB International, Wallingford. (Chapter 10).

Hill, M. (2006) *The Public Policy Process.* 4th edition. Pearson-Education, Harlow. (Chapter 1).

Hogwood, B.W. and Gunn, L.A. (1984) *Policy Analysis for the Real World.* Oxford University Press, Oxford.

2

UNDERSTANDING THE AGRICULTURAL POLICY PROBLEMS AND OBJECTIVES OF THE EUROPEAN UNION

Key topics

- The problems of EU countries that involve agriculture (economic, environmental, social) and their underlying explanations.
- Problems for which agriculture acts as an instrument, and those originating from the basic characteristics of agriculture itself.
- Technological progress and adjustment.
- The range of problems in EU-27, including different agricultural structures.
- Stated objectives of the EU's agricultural policy and an outline of policy in practice.

Any policy process starts from the identification of problems. Without problems there is no need for policy actions. Once problems have been recognised and formulated (the first stage of the policy process described in Chapter 1), then the most appropriate response by governments acting singly or as a community can be designed to tackle them (the second stage – policy formulation). An important step in this response is the setting of policy objectives.

This chapter is concerned with the problems that the CAP attempts to address. An understanding of their causes and nature is necessary before judging whether a particular line of action is likely to be beneficial for society at large and whether the effects brought about will be long-lasting or soon eroded. The wider problems of rural areas overlap the problems that agricultural policy attempts to tackle but take in other issues (such as difficulties of access to local education and health services). Details of the how the CAP attempts to tackle these problems, including the contribution it makes to rural development policy, are covered in later chapters.

An explanation of the EU's CAP must recognise from an early stage that agricultural policy forms part of a wider range of EU and national policies, each directed at its own set of problems. At the EU level these policies include the Common Fisheries Policy, the Common Forestry Policy, external policy (foreign and security policy), external economic and trade policy (termed the common commercial policy), regional policy, competition policy, policy for enterprise, industrial policy, transport policy, energy policy, policy on international development (aimed at helping lower-income countries), research and technology policy, environmental policy, social policy, consumer policy and health policy, and policy for Economic and Monetary Union (in 2010 the European Commission's website listed over 30 policies). Many of these other policies can have an impact on agriculture, often unintentionally. There is also cooperation between Member States on immigration, giving asylum and police activities. Conversely, agriculture can often be used to assist with solving problems that affect the whole of society. Overall, policies can be likened to a cobweb (or net). Each part of the cobweb is connected to all other parts, so that a touch will be felt throughout the web but the disturbance will be less the further from the point of contact. For example, the impact of a policy on, say, assisting the incomes of farmers by paying them subsidies linked to production will be felt to various extents in terms of land use, levels of rural employment, the environment, international trade and so on, all of which may be the subject of separate policies.

It is also worth noting that problems change. Taking another analogy, agricultural policy can be likened to a rope stretching through time. The rope has many individual strands which are interwoven and are therefore difficult to separate. Over the years some strands become less prominent as the real world changes. As we will see later (Chapter 12), the problem of ensuring a secure supply of food within the original six Member States of the (then) European Economic Community in the 1950s was fundamental in shaping the CAP at its outset. Food security in Europe became far less frequently mentioned in the 1970s onwards, as the productivity of agriculture increased and as enlargement of the EU transformed the supply situation. Currently there is a revived interest in the context of the global food debate. Other strands have risen in importance since the CAP's early days, such as concern over animal welfare, reflecting a more ethical consideration of the ways in which livestock should be treated, and the loss of biodiversity and traditional landscapes. Policy actions have to respond to these changes in balance between perceived problems. But sometimes particular strands of policy prove to be surprisingly durable, even after the problem has largely gone away, because policy interventions tend to create vested interests (benefits accruing to individuals, firms or organisations) that impede change. The main message coming from this analogy is that history is a very important factor in understanding the present shape of the CAP. an example of the path dependency mentioned in Chapter 1.

Finally in this introduction it must be recognised that policies designed to tackle one set of problems can themselves lead to new problems, for which other rounds of policy may be needed. Just as the market mechanism has imperfections that are the root cause of many problems that state intervention aims to correct (see 'market failure' mentioned in Chapter 1), in the real world where human behaviour is not fully predictable and information less than complete it is often difficult for governments to take exactly the right steps. There are always risks involved and usually a degree of 'state failure', implying situations where decisions turn out to have been sub-optimal. Hopefully Member State national governments and the EU learn from experiences in applying policy and do not make the same mistakes time-and-again.

2.1 Types of problems in which agriculture is involved

Policies directed at agriculture can be divided into two groups according to the nature of the problem they are intended to attack. First there are the policies intended to tackle general problems faced by government. When it plays a role in the alleviation of these, agriculture is being used in an instrumental way to achieve a policy aim. Second, there are the policies directed at the problems specific to agriculture, intrinsic problems which result from the economic characteristics of the agricultural industry itself. As will be seen later, often both sorts of aim are set out together in official documents, such as the 1957 Treaty of Rome which, in its Article 39, described the objectives of the CAP. But such statements are not all-embracing and in practice policy aims evolve. They are best revealed from looking at what governments and EU institutions actually do.

2.2 Agriculture's instrumental role in solving the general problems faced by society – a review of past experience

Agriculture has an important role to play in achieving many of the wider aims which governments have for their countries. The most important of these *instrumental roles* are to tackle some fundamental problems, as follows:

- the problem of ensuring that there is a secure food supply;
- the problem of achieving economic growth; agriculture has traditionally helped here by releasing resources which can be used to develop other industries;
- problems associated with the trade situation, such as the balance between total imports and exports and the international exchange value of currencies;
- problems faced in developing rural areas;
- problems of protecting the environment;
- problems of achieving good international relations and political harmony.

In each of these examples the intention is to provide benefits which are shared widely throughout society, not just going to the agricultural population or even those who live in rural areas. For example, the defence offered by a secure food supply, so that the country cannot be starved into submission by a potential aggressor state cutting off food supplies from abroad, is shared by the whole of society. Some of these aims, it could be argued, mainly concern the urban population, which forms the majority in EU Member States. It might be thought, for example, that an attractive countryside mainly benefits those people who do not normally live there but who like to visit it.

2.2.1 Food supply

Historically the most important of these general policies is that of ensuring an adequate food supply. The market mechanism, with individual producers acting in their own interests and responding to price signals, cannot be relied on to reflect adequately the national strategic view that takes into account factors such as the likelihood of the interruption of food supply from abroad because of political action or natural disasters. The importance of food security to the CAP stems from the fact that, when it was first designed, the hunger of war-time was still vivid in the memories of the statesmen concerned. The legislation of Germany formed the basis of the relevant article in the 1957 Treaty of Rome (see later), and there the need to expand agricultural production was felt particularly strongly. Even up to the early 1980s the spectre of food shortage in Europe was occasionally raised. However, the importance today of this strand of policy also stems from the fact that, once support had been set at a level necessary to prevent danger to food supply, it proved very difficult to reduce.

As with many policies, there are various ways in which food security can be brought about. One would be to keep stockpiles of food reserves, but these may be expensive to maintain (such as the refrigeration of meat), can only partly meet needs, and then only until stocks run out. Or some land and machinery can be kept in reserve, so that output can be expanded fairly quickly, though this does not get over the problem that imports of farming inputs, such as fuel, may be vulnerable to disruption. Governments may decide that, in order to safeguard food supplies in times of emergency, they wish to have a high degree of self-sufficiency in peacetime. Often this means having an agricultural industry which is bigger than would happen if free market forces were allowed to operate freely. The effectiveness of such policies is, at best, questionable.

2.2.2 Trade policy

Agriculture has often been used as a means for achieving trade policy objectives, but these have been very mixed. A founding principle of the EU is that there should be a single market for all Member States so that the benefits brought about by specialisation and exchange (that is, by trade) could be enjoyed. The CAP led the way, with a single market for farm commodities being established in the mid-1960s, only extended to most other types of goods in 1993. However, agriculture has often been used in ways that have *not* encouraged trade. In the UK its chronic Balance of Payments problem from the 1950s to the mid-1970s led to the encouragement of greater national agricultural production so that imports of food from abroad could be lowered. In the EU from the start of the CAP agriculture was protected from international competition for non-trade reasons, such as enhancing the prices that EU farmers received, and surplus production has been subsidised to be sold on the international market. These actions have had a distorting effect on the world trade in agricultural products. Much effort has been expended in the last three decades to gradually removing the distorting factors (see Chapter 9 on international trade and the rounds of negotiations to reach multinational trade agreements under the GATT and WTO).

2.2.3 Economic growth

Agriculture has often made major contributions to economic growth. The thinking behind this is basically that an expanding agricultural industry, improving its output through technical advances and by restructuring (that is, the formation of typically larger farms), soon finds that it has productive resources (mainly manpower and capital) which can be more profitably employed in other activities. This is because of the economic characteristics of its products, to which we will return later, and the effect of increased supply on product prices and on the value of resources used in agriculture. Consequently, governments will be on the lookout for ways in which resources can be transferred to other industries, with an overall net benefit. This is in line with the economic Principle of Equimarginal Returns. If there are problems to the free flow of productive factors (a form of market failure), governments will wish to ease them (see Box 2.1).

2.2.4 Rural development

Agriculture's instrumental role as an economic stimulant is seen in a more specific form in the context of *rural development policy*. Creating incomes and jobs in agriculture, or protecting them when under threat, has been viewed as one means by which the problems of the rural economy could be tackled. These problems vary widely across the EU, and areas that are relatively densely settled and near urban centres will have a different mix from those that are remote and sparsely populated. The latter include much of the hill and

---

Box 2.1 Examples of using agriculture to promote economic growth

Looking back in history, the rapid economic development in Russia following the Revolution in 1917 was seen to hinge on improving the performance of agriculture so that both labour and capital could be shifted to the heavy industries where rapid expansion was needed. The reorganisation of farming along large-scale lines, with collective farms, and the forced relocation of labour, made possible by central economic planning and an oppressive political regime, was part of this. More recently, a major contribution to the rapid growth of many continental countries of the European Community in the first two decades following its establishment in 1957 was the substantial transfer of labour out of agriculture to other industries in which it could be more productive. This source of growth was largely denied to Britain at this time because its transfer of labour had taken place in the Industrial Revolution of the eighteenth and nineteenth centuries. Consequently, when the CAP started, in the UK there was a far smaller percentage of the population engaged in farming and output per man in agriculture was already relatively high. Nevertheless, in Britain there has been constant encouragement of higher performance by the agricultural industry, partly to meet balance of payment goals but also because the benefits of its improved productivity spread throughout the economy. The main attention has centred on labour productivity. The UK government long believed that productivity could be best achieved by encouraging investment in additional capital, and from the mid-1950s to the mid-1980s gave grants to farmers for the purchase of new buildings, drainage and other capital goods. However, in the 1980s the higher levels of unemployment in the economies of many EU Member States diverted attention from the displacement of labour towards the potential of agriculture to retain employment.

---

mountainous areas of the EU (the so-called Less Favoured Areas), where problems often centre on the need to keep a viable size of population, which then can sustain rural services (schools, shops etc.). The root cause of these population changes is often what has been happening in agriculture, principally its greater productivity which means that far fewer people are required on farms, carrying consequences for the size and composition of the rural population. Non-agricultural industries can be encouraged to create opportunities (though they may be reluctant to do so if access to markets is problematic), and farms can be encouraged to diversify; this is particularly appropriate for those that are already large and can draw on management expertise and capital. However, in practice an easier solution, at least for the short term, is often to support farming. Agriculture is thus being used as a tool of social and employment policy. Rural development policy being used in this manner is dealt with in more detail in Chapter 7.

2.2.5 Environmental protection

The penultimate item in this group of general policy objectives which relate to agriculture is the environment issue. The concept of market failure is very relevant. Until the last two decades thinking among policy-makers about what agriculture produced was largely restricted to the sorts of commodities that might be classed as food for humans or animals, possibly widening to forestry products and some industrial products, such as flax. However, governments and the EU have come to recognise that agriculture also produces non-tangible outputs which are valued by the rest of society. Thus agriculture is now described as being 'multifunctional'. Some, like tourist services on farms, fall into the category of 'private' goods and can be handled by the market mechanism, though farmers may need to be made aware of the potential and trained to exploit it (that is, there is some 'imperfect knowledge' that needs addressing). However, there is now an enhanced sensitivity among EU Member States to the importance that the public attaches to the appearance of the countryside, and a willingness to pay for the conservation of its special features. This landscape/conservation character can be regarded as another output from the agricultural industry, since the land-using activities of farmers and others determine what the countryside looks like and the wildlife features it contains. Agriculture is providing a service for the non-agriculturist, through recreation or just the well-being of knowing that the countryside is 'there' and being looked after, which is valued in much the same way as its food-security role. Because of the 'public good' aspects of such features, public intervention is necessary to enable the wishes of society to be implemented, even if only partially. Reflecting the greater affluence of the population in general and the freeing up of resources for items such as vacations and hobbies, we can expect to witness an increasing role for policies which encourage farmers to use their land in ways which are consonant with the emerging ideas of what the countryside should look like and the activities which should take place there. Chapter 8 gives further consideration to the role of agriculture in pursuing environmental aims.

2.2.6 Political strand

The final item raises the issue of international relations and politics. This importance of politics in shaping the European Union and its policies can be easily overlooked by readers whose main concern is the agricultural industry and rural development. From the outset the impetus for establishing the three initial Communities that eventually became the EU (the European Coal and Steel Community, set up by the Treaty of Paris of 1951, the European Atomic Energy Community (Euratom) and the European Economic Community (EEC), the latter two set up by separate Treaties of Rome in 1957) was political. With memories of the havoc of the Second World War fresh in their minds, statesmen in Western Europe believed that, by making nations interdependent economically and politically within a larger European identity, the likelihood of future conflict would be drastically reduced (see the historical summary in Chapter 12). Agriculture was a fundamental industry, not only for the supply of food, but also, through food costs, for influencing the competitiveness of other industries. It engaged (then) a substantial minority of the working population in each of the original six Member States. It faced common problems of low productivity and the need for restructuring. When building a Community, a common policy for agriculture was a practical possibility as a starting point. For a long time the CAP dominated spending on all the common policies and still absorbs a substantial share of the EU budget (about 43 per cent of all EU spending planned for the period 2007–13: Chapter 10 gives more details). Consequently, the CAP can be seen as much more than just a policy for tackling food, agricultural and rural problems. Because Member States have been involved in developing a joint policy on agriculture, the CAP has also played a vital role in cementing the EU together, though it could not be claimed that this was the only way in which economic co-operation could have been achieved.

The early political role of the CAP in building an economic and political community has continued as other countries in Western Europe have joined (see the chronology set out in Chapter 12), though by this time the main driver was no longer food security. For Spain and Portugal the desire to underpin their newly established democracies by making them full Members was an important element of the case for accession, which of course meant participation in the CAP. The further expansions in 2004 and 2007 that produced an EU of 27 brought in countries that had rather different histories and with agricultural industries that had been restructured to include (in many of them) large scale units many times the size of typical family-run farms, but also often numerous household plots. Political will to include these countries in the EU and to share its market economy and democratic tradition was dominant, even though enlargement carried implications for the CAP and how it could be operated.

2.3 The specific problems of agriculture

The second group of reasons why the EU and Member State governments have policies for their agricultures concerns the problems peculiar to this industry. Chief among these are, first, the income problem, a term used to cover three related problems:

- the problem of *fluctuation* of incomes from year to year;
- the problem of *low incomes* in certain sectors of the industry, which become manifest in *poverty* among families occupying small farms; and
- *poor comparability* between the rewards earned in agriculture and in the rest of the economy.

Looking back at the discussion of why policy is necessary (Chapter 1), it becomes clear that the reduction of poverty is an issue of equity, though the other two contain both equity and efficiency aspects. But it is difficult to discuss incomes without also referring to another key characteristic of agriculture – its heterogeneity or diversity. Farms in the EU are of different sizes, different types and of different cost structures, so that at any one time there will be huge disparities between those which are doing best financially and those which are doing worst. Even within groups of farms of the same type, size and location there will be wide variations in performance. Thus figures which give an overall average picture of the industry will not necessarily be a reliable indication of what is happening even to the members of any one type and size group of farm. And policies which may be appropriate to some groups may be entirely inappropriate for others.

Second, there is the structural adjustment problem, again an omnibus term used to cover the difficulties which are experienced when farm operators attempt to respond to the changing economic environment in which they find themselves. Structural adjustment comes in several forms, but most important are the changes in farm size which must be made with the passage of time and the shedding of labour which must take place as the industry becomes more productive. In the pre-2004 Member States of the EU (EU-15), where farms are predominantly run as family-owned businesses with relatively small workforces, structural adjustment has principally been seen as the gradual reduction in the numbers of smaller farms as the minimum size of viable farm business has increased. The land they have given up has been typically absorbed by larger farms, so numbers in the biggest size groups have risen. The numbers of people engaged full time in agriculture has declined, though rather than exit completely, many farmers and their families have preferred to combine agriculture with some other income-generating occupation (they become pluriactive), thereby enabling an otherwise unviable unit to remain in existence and provide them with a home. The 'problem' has been that generally these changes have not been fast enough.

In the countries that joined as Member States in 2004 and 2007 (EU-12), the structural adjustment issues are rather different. Their histories up to the late 1980s resulted in many having a mix of a relatively small number of very large scale agricultural units with business forms that were nearer to companies or cooperatives and, at the other end of the spectrum, large numbers of household plots. Since the early 1990s structural adjustment has taken the form of partial dismantling of the largest units, adapting their business forms, and improving their productivity and competitiveness. Often there has been an attempt to re-establish a family-sized-farm sector. An important prerequisite for structural change involving land has been a clarification of who owns what, (that is, the system of property rights). With fewer people needed in agriculture, these countries have faced a challenge of providing alternative job opportunities and sustaining rural communities.

2.3.1 Underlying economic forces

These income and structural adjustment problems are directly related to the economic characteristics of agricultural products and the difficulties the resources used by agriculture (and principally the people who work in it) encounter in shifting to other occupations. A brief explanation of how these characteristics lead to problems is now offered. For simplicity we assume that food is the only output from agriculture.

- Basic food products typically have low price elasticities of demand at market level – that is, the quantity purchased is relatively insensitive to the price. Expressed as a graph (see Figure 2.1), this implies that the typical demand curve faced by the agricultural industry for its product is steeply downward sloping.
- In relatively affluent industrialised countries, such as EU Member States, basic food products typically also have low income elasticities of demand (sensitivity to income shifts). Again, when expressed as a graph, this means that the increased income which is available when households become better off (what happens with the process of economic growth) does not feed through to rightwards shifts in the demand curve as felt at the farm level (though more may be spent on buying processing and packaging for convenience). A rise in the size of the population will shift the curve to the right (more will be demanded at each price), but in most EU Member States this is not happening, so agriculture faces a demand curve which is more-or-less static.
- Agricultural production is subject to unpredictable variations from year to year, mainly caused by weather. These push the supply curve to the left or right to unpredictable extents (see Figure 2.1). This, when combined with a demand curve that is steep and relatively static, means that, in an unregulated free market, the impact on price movements is magnified (changes in price would be greater in percentage terms than the changes in output). Revenue from sales by farmers (price times quantity) varies greatly and can be less in a year of high yields (because price of the product is very low) than in a year when yields are low (and price is high). Because costs are, in the main, committed before the effects of weather on output are known and are therefore relatively stable over time, the income remaining to farmers (revenue less costs) will

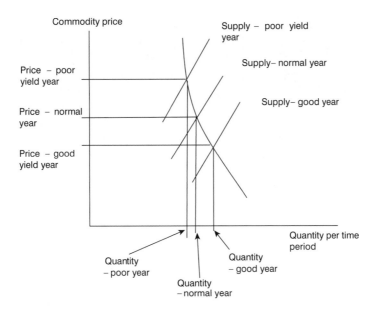

Note: the revenue to farmers is indicated by the size of the price × quantity rectangle. The revenue in the poor yield year is greater than in the good yield year. Costs of production will largely be independent of yield, since these are mostly committed in advance. Once costs have been deducted, the income (profit) in the poor yield year is likely to be greater than in the good yield year.

Figure 2.1   The problem of instability in prices and incomes

vary from year to year by a greater degree than does revenue. This is the root cause of the fundamental problem of short-term income instability faced by agriculture. Of course, some individual farmers will fare better or worse than the industry as a whole, and not all areas will be affected to the same extent.

- The agricultural industry is composed of an atomistic structure (many firms) producing virtually identical outputs (such as milk or wheat), which approximates to perfect competition. Though there is diversity in terms of farm size, even the largest are unable to have a significant effect on the overall market price, certainly when considering the whole EU market for farm commodities. This structure has a number of important consequences. Perhaps the most obvious is that there is a possibility of suffering from a poor bargaining position, such as when dealing with large buyers of farm commodities who may exploit their monopsonistic power. This can be avoided to some extent by forming farmer-controlled co-operatives. Uncoordinated production decisions are also conducive to the establishment of price cycles in an industry in which the demand curve for farm products is typically steep and in which there is a lag between the decision to expand output and that output actually coming on to the market.

- The greater significance of this structure, though, is the conflict of interest it produces between the individual and farmers as a group. The structure of the industry means that it is in the interest of individual producers to expand production if profitable technological opportunities arise, such as new higher-yielding varieties of crops, though increased supply is not necessarily in the interest of all producers because it will cause prices to fall. Innovating farmers will be able to produce more while prices are relatively high. The average farm operator is on a technological treadmill; to survive the business operator will also have to adopt the new technology, but expanding supply coming up against inelastic demand will have already started pushing product prices down. Those farmers who do not modernise will eventually find themselves facing falling prices for their products, yet doing so while operating with outdated technology and relatively high costs of production and experiencing falling incomes. The workings of the technological treadmill are illustrated in Figure 2.2. Though farmers in a single locality might agree not to adopt new technology, this would be

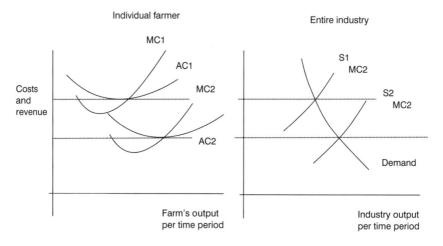

1 AC and MC curves represent the average and marginal costs of production.
2 The new technology has a lower level of costs than the old (AC2 and MC2 are lower than AC1 and MC2). In the diagram the lower costs per unit are associated with higher levels of output (the AC2 curve is to the right of the AC1 curve). This sort of technical advance is typical in agriculture; larger capacity machines require a greater output if their potential for lower costs per unit are to be realised.
3 In a perfectly competitive industry, to which agriculture approximates, competition will push down prices to a level that ensures that farms operate at the lowest points of their AC curves.
4 The industry's supply curve is composed of the sum of the MC curves of the individual farms. Anything that shifts the MC curve of any single farm to the right will also shift the industry S curve, though the effect of individuals will be tiny.
5 Innovators adopt the technique as it means that they can earn more than 'normal' profits, ('normal' profits being those just adequate to compensate for the risks involved in production).
6 When significant numbers of farmers adopt the technique, the industry S curve will move to the right, and prices will fall as output rises.
7 Falling prices will make the old techniques increasingly unviable and force all farmers to adopt the new technique eventually. Farmers incapable of adopting the new technology (often because their farms are too small) will find they are facing falling prices but are stuck with the old level of costs, so their incomes will be squeezed. They will ultimately leave the industry (fall off the end of the treadmill).
8 Innovators will have their surplus profit eroded by falling prices, so they will search for new technological advances in this or other products. The treadmill of technological advance will start on its next turn.

Figure 2.2   The treadmill of technological advance in agriculture

ineffective ultimately as it would always be in the interest of individuals to break ranks, and competitors in other areas would soon adopt and force the issue.

• The outcome is a long-term cost–price squeeze, in the sense that the prices that farmers receive for their outputs fall relative to the costs of the inputs they have to purchase. There have been short periods when this is reversed, but the trend in the EU (and other developed countries) is clear. This squeeze results in a tendency for incomes to decline, both that of the industry as a whole and, unless they adjust, at the farm level. Farmers are compelled to look for ways of countering this, such as further expansion of area, replacing labour with machinery where this enables costs to be cut, and diversifying into non-agricultural activities. In this process the smallest farms can no longer provide an adequate reward for their operators and are in the weakest position when competing with other farms for extra land. Many of them have to give up – they are unviable in the new technical and economic conditions – or when a change of generation is due, willing successors will not be found.

The combination of the above factors means that agriculture is a declining industry in all Member States of the EU, both in terms of the number of people engaged in it and its contribution to national product and income. These changes are a reflection that the price mechanism is performing its function of adjusting the economy to the new state of technology. The benefits of improved ways of producing agricultural commodities are being passed on to consumers in the form of lower prices, and productive resources which are no longer needed in farming are being released to be used in other parts of the economy. These changes are of long historical standing, but are evident from figures taken from the EU's more recent past (see Table 2.1). Table 2.2 shows that, in the 15 Member States before the EU enlargements of 2004 and 2007 (EU-15) the general pattern is that the number of agricultural holdings above 50 ha (which accounted for only 8 per cent of all holdings in EU-15 in 1997) has been rising, with smaller holdings declining in numbers. This pattern is rather obscured by the greater numbers of countries included in later years and by methodological changes that make precise comparisons between years hazardous. As the table refers to all holdings, not only those that are commercial farms, the statistics include those run as a hobby or primarily as domestic residences (whose numbers have grown) and subsistence producers in the newer Member States, factors particularly likely to affect numbers in the smallest size groups. Within countries numbers have also generally fallen; only in a few have they risen and these can be explained by exceptional circumstances (as in the break-up of the former large estates in Portugal).

But there are additional characteristics of agriculture that must be considered when reviewing its problems. They transform the process of structural adjustment from simply an economic one, of the reallocation of productive resources, to one which carries social, cultural, and environmental overtones.

• Agriculture is family-dominated, largely self-employed activity. In terms of numbers, EU farms are predominantly family-owned and family-run units, often with the family providing much of the labour. In 2007 farms in which the operator was a 'natural person' (rather than a company or similar institution) formed 98 per cent of all agricultural holdings in EU-27 (this appears to include farms run as family companies). The percentage among the older Member States (EU-15) was slightly lower (96.1 per cent) than those that joined in 2004 and 2007 (EU-12) (99.5 per cent). Overall, in 2005 farm

Table 2.1　Numbers of persons in civilian employment in the occupation group 'agriculture, forestry and fisheries', by EU Member State

	Number of persons (000)			Percentage of the total working population	
	1977	2001	2006	1992	2006
Austria		215	217		5.5
Belgium	123	78	83	2.7	2
Bulgaria		266	252		8.1
Cyprus		14	15		4.3
Czech Republic		228	182		3.8
Denmark	218	96	87	5.4	3.1
Estonia		43	32		5
Finland		140	114		4.7
France	2,013	964	977	5.2	3.9
Germany	1,589	956	844	3.2	2.3
Greece	1,084	627	533	21.4	12
Hungary		235	188		4.8
Ireland	228	120	117	13.8	5.7
Italy	3,130	1,113	982	8.2	4.3
Latvia		145	122		11.2
Lithuania		245	187		12.4
Luxembourg	10	3	4	3	1.8
Malta		3	3		1.7
Netherlands	248	238	259	4.6	3.3
Poland		2,736	2,304		15.8
Portugal	1,247	645	604	11.6	11.7
Romania		4,801	2,843		30.6
Slovakia		132	101		4.4
Slovenia		90	92		9.6
Spain	2,567	1,025	944	10.1	4.8
Sweden		114	98		2.2
United Kingdom	684	390	382	2.2	1.4
EU-27		15,662	12,564		5.9
EU-25 (excludes *)		10,595	9,468		
EU-15 (Members before 2004)		6,724	6,244		
EU-12 (Members that joined in 2004 and 2007)	13,141				5.8

(1) 'Persons employed' include all persons working for remuneration or self-employed, plus unpaid family workers. Persons employed in more than one economic sector are counted only in the sector in which they mainly work.
NB: Former GDR not included before 1991.
Source: European Commission, Eurostat (*Community Labour Force Survey* – LFS).

Table 2.2 Numbers of holdings by Member State, and by size of holding (ha), selected years

Numbers of holdings (000)

	1975	1980	1990	1995	2000	2003	2005	2007
EU (27 countries)			:	:	:	15,021	14,479	:
EU (25 countries)			:	:	:	9,871	9,688	:
EU (15 countries)			:	7,370	6,770	6,239	5,843	:
Austria		308	:	222	199	174	171	:
Belgium	106	91	85	71	62	55	52	48
Bulgaria			:	:	:	666	535	:
Cyprus			:	:	:	45	45	:
Czech Republic			:	:	:	46	42	39
Denmark	130	116	81	69	58	49	52	45
Estonia			:	:	:	37	28	23
Finland		225	:	101	81	75	71	68
France	1,209	1,135	:	:	:	614	567	:
Germany	905	797	654	567	472	412	390	:
Greece	758	752	850	802	817	824	834	:
Hungary			:	:	967	773	715	626
Ireland	228	223	171	153	141	135	132	128
Italy	2,145	1,926	2,665	2,482	2,154	1,964	1,729	:
Latvia			:	:	141	127	129	108
Lithuania			:	:	:	272	252	230
Luxembourg			4	3	3	2	2	2
Malta			:	:	:	11	11	11
Netherlands	144	129	125	113	102	86	82	77
Poland			:	:	:	2,172	2,476	2,391
Portugal		350	599	450	416	359	324	:
Romania			:	:	:	4,485	4,256	:
Slovakia			:	:	71	72	68	:
Slovenia			:	:	86	77	77	75
Spain		1,524	1,594	1,277	1,287	1,140	1,079	:
Sweden		118	:	89	81	68	76	73
United Kingdom	272	249	243	234	233	281	287	:

Numbers of holdings (000) by size group (hectares)

	1975	1980	1993	1997	2003	2005
	EU-10	EU-10	EU-12	EU-15	EU-27	EU-27
Total	5,900	5,458	6,298	6,989	15,021	14,479
1–5 ha	2,728	2,495	3,109	3,867	10,958	10,359
5–10 ha	1,044	924	1,012	929	1,526	1,585
10–20 ha	936	848	815	758	1,015	1,028
20–50 ha	867	853	859	802	835	825
>50 ha	325	339	502	599	687	691

families accounted for 93.6 per cent of the total number of people working in EU-27 agriculture and 80.7 per cent of the labour input measured in 'annual work units' (AWUs), the difference being explained by the large incidence of farmers and their families working only part-time in agriculture. On such farms personal and business wealth is closely mixed. Thus when small farms are no longer viable commercially, there will be social implications, as the need to find a new occupation for the farmer and family and, probably, a new place to live, unless a local job opportunity is available that can be taken while still living on the farm.

- The transfer of resources out of agriculture, especially labour, is often difficult. Family-operated farms are often slow to respond to price signals and income pressures, as they can absorb them, at least for a time, by adjusting their personal spending and saving patterns. In particular the occupiers of small, unviable, uncompetitive farms tend to be elderly and with little experience of other ways of earning a living. There may well be an emotional attachment to the land which makes them reluctant to leave. Whatever the cause, they suffer from occupational (and often geographical) immobility. Rather than transfer to other occupations, small farmers may struggle on, perhaps inefficient in their use of factors of production but nevertheless helping to generate the output which in turn keeps product prices low. Both among independent farmers and in the hired labour force, the most likely to shift to non-agricultural occupations are the younger and the better-educated. This means that agriculture may contain a disproportionately large number of elderly people, especially in the more remote rural areas where leaving agriculture means moving away to a town job or having no job at all. Changes in the composition of rural society may carry implications for the viability of rural communities and the culture they represent, a point considered later (Chapter 7).

- The multifunctional nature of agriculture means that there may be an environmental impact of structural adjustment. Fewer but larger farms may use their land differently from the existing pattern, affecting the biological diversity, and they may wish to increase field sizes to allow greater mechanisation, which will change landscape appearance. In contrast, where very small farms survive as hobby units, their owners may purposely aim to conserve the existing natural features, or enhance them. Often the biggest land-use changes on farms take place when one occupier succeeds another or when other major career decisions are made, such as to take an off-farm job to supplement income from the farm. Though simplistic assumptions are to be avoided, it is clear that the potential environmental implications of structural change should not be ignored.

Taking all these features of agriculture together, it is hardly surprising that there are cries in the political system for governments, singly or collectively through the EU, to do something to counter the pressures on farming to adjust, inevitable though they may be.

2.4 Aims of agricultural policy in the European Union as set out in legislation

Having identified the intrinsic problems that confront agriculture, or in which agriculture is involved in an instrumental way, and for which public intervention is deemed necessary (the *problem formulation* stage of the policy process described in Chapter 1), the next step is to examine the objectives of policy designed to attack these problems (an important element in the *policy formulation* stage). Attention is focused on the problems faced by the EU at the start of the new millennium's second decade and the objectives of its agricultural and rural development policy.

Two approaches can be used to demonstrate the situation. The first is to scrutinise the stated aims of policy, the official formulation of policy objectives as reflected in the Treaties and other agreements under which the CAP operates. This should encapsulate the collective view on what are the problems to be tackled. The second is to observe what policies are actually pursued. In practice a mixture of both approaches is used in this book. However, the official texts are a necessary starting point because they legitimise the actions of the European Commission in proposing legislation which, when approved by the other parts of the official decision-making process (described in Chapter 3). become the basis of policy actions. Without a legal base it is very difficult for progress in policy to be made.

(a) Treaty of Rome 1957 – Treaty on the Functioning of the European Union 2010

The objectives of agricultural policy (and, indeed, rural policy and other forms of collective action) have their roots the Treaty of Rome that in 1957 established the European Economic Community (EEC) (becoming operative on 1 January 1958). They have been carried forward in subsequent legislation and form an integral part of the present legal base of the CAP; the Treaty of Lisbon, which came into effect in December 2009, renamed the Treaty of Rome the Treaty on the Functioning of the European Union (TFEU) and its consolidated version (which includes agreed changes) restated the original CAP objectives. The official objectives of the CAP were set out in Article 39.1 (both Treaties), which states:

The objectives of the common agricultural policy shall be:
(a) to increase agricultural productivity by promoting technical progress and by ensuring the rational development of agricultural production and the optimum utilisation of the factors of production, in particular labour;
(b) thus to ensure a fair standard of living for the agricultural community, in particular by increasing the individual earnings of persons engaged in agriculture;
(c) to stabilise markets;
(d) to assure the availability of supplies;
(e) to ensure that supplies reach consumers at reasonable prices.

Article 39.2 states that:

In working out the common agricultural policy and the special methods for its application, account shall be taken of:
(a) the particular nature of agricultural activity, which results from the social structure of agriculture and from structural and natural disparities between various agricultural regions;
(b) the need to effect appropriate adjustments by degrees;
(c) the fact that in the Member States agriculture constitutes a sector closely linked with the economy as a whole.

Under Article 42 (both Treaties) it is possible to grant aid '(a) for the protection of enterprises handicapped by structural or natural conditions; (b) within the framework of economic development programmes.' The latter points should be noted in the context of policies to support rural areas which could be expected to suffer from the increasing competition and regional specialisation which could be anticipated to flow from a common market in agriculture.

The objectives of the Treaty of Rome/TFEU, though bearing a strong similarity to the stated agricultural policy objectives of many national administrations at the time the original was drafted, are vague and contain internal inconsistencies. For example, the second objective is imprecise about who comprises the 'agricultural community'; was the intention to ensure a 'fair' standard of living (whatever that may mean) for everyone who took part in farm production – employee and self-employed, full-time or part-time – which could imply a very large group of beneficiaries, or some narrower body, such as those whose main working time was spent as independent farmers? Or was the target group only those farmers who could exist in a higher-productivity industry, which would probably leave most of the existing farmers unsupported. There are potential conflicts built in between the assurance about the earnings of those engaged in agriculture and the 'reasonable prices' for consumers, since higher prices for farmers would (probably) mean higher prices for consumers too. In particular, the assumption that improvements in productivity could be the way in which the standard of living could be assured look rather naive in retrospect (see the earlier discussion on the implications of such improvement for incomes and the structure of the agricultural industry).

However, the real significance of the text on objectives in the Treaty of Rome/TFEU has less to do with its analysis of the actions needed to tackle the real problems faced by agriculture and rural areas, but rather more to do with their role in legitimising actions, including those of current policy. As will be evident from Chapter 3, the process by which policy is proposed and enacted depends on the Commission of the EU having a legal basis for its proposals. Without Article 39 of the Treaty of Rome much of the later body of legislation by which policy is brought about would not have been possible. Though it may be argued that the economic, technical and social conditions of the first decades of the 2000s are far removed from those of the 1950s, on numerous occasions the objectives contained in the Treaty have been re-endorsed in official documents as capable of reinterpretation in the conditions of later times and, as part of the 2010 Treaty on the Functioning of the European Union, still form the basis of new policy.

(b) Early developments from the 1957 Treaty of Rome

The 1957 Treaty of Rome specified that a conference should be held to review existing agricultural policies and to submit proposals for working out and implementing the CAP (Article 43). This took place at Stresa (Italy) in 1958. Among the issues elaborated upon was the need to closely correlate policies aimed at improving the structure of agriculture (basically, farm size adjustment) with those that affected the market for agricultural products; it appears that raising market prices was seen as a way of stimulating productivity without necessary causing market imbalance, though the newly appointed Commissioner for Agriculture (Sicco Mansholt) warned the conference of this danger of insulating farmers from market realities. The restructuring of agriculture would permit the labour and capital in agriculture to receive remuneration comparable with what they could earn in other sectors of the economy. It was taken as axiomatic that the family farm was to be safeguarded and its economic and competitive capacity raised. And it was expected that retraining of the agricultural labour force, coupled with the 'industrialisation' of rural regions would allow for a gradual settlement of the problems of those marginal farms which were economically incapable of being made viable.

In 1960 the Commission responded to requirements under the Treaty by submitting proposals for working out and implementing the CAP. These set out in detail the market and price policies to be introduced, the mechanisms of which were essentially unchanged until the radical CAP reforms of 1992. On the social aspects of the policy, the Commission merely outlined aims, without turning them into practical proposals.

Three principles emerged from early discussions which, despite their vague origins (according to Fennell 1987) since about 1960 have come to be accepted as central principles that still apply to the CAP. These are:

- **Market unity**. This implies that there is a single market for agricultural goods covering all Member States and free movement for them within it (which implies a single price, with local variations to allow for transport costs etc.) and with a single tariff regime applying to trade with third parties. When the main instrument of support was that of fixing the prices that farmers received above the free market level, market unity implied there should be a common system of marketing and common pricing throughout the Community. In practice, as will be seen later, this was not fully realised.
- **Community preference.** This means that, within the Community, the system of supporting the price of farm commodities should always operate in a way such that the purchaser should find agricultural commodities of Community origin more attractive than equivalent goods from other countries.
- **Financial solidarity.** This means that an overall view is taken of the problems to be addressed in the Community and of the resources available to meet them. Community policies are financed on a joint basis from a budget to which Member States contribute on an agreed formula. Thus there should be no concern with the balance each country achieves between the amounts contributed to the budget and the amounts received from it. This enables those areas with the greatest problems to be given the appropriate resources.

These principles have had a strong influence on the way in which the common policies, and especially the CAP, have developed. In particular, that of financial solidarity has been blamed as one factor encouraging growth in the costs of the CAP, since it has been possible for some countries or groups of countries to press for expensive forms of support to their own benefit knowing that the cost will be partly borne by all the other Member States.

Though important for marking stages in the development of other common EU policies and the process by which decisions are made, none of the subsequent major pieces of EU legislation have changed the objectives of the CAP as set out in the Treaty of Rome. However, there have been implications for the practice of agricultural policy resulting from, for example, the growing concern with the environment and attempts to move towards closer monetary union. The Single European Act (which came into force in 1987) was largely concerned with establishing a single internal market by the start of 1993. But agriculture had long been operating what was, at least in principle, a single market for farm commodities. The Maastricht and Amsterdam Treaties (coming into force in 1993 and 1999 respectively) were concerned with European political cooperation and economic and monetary union; the monetary arrangements, especially the adoption of a single currency, have had implications for the way in which agricultural policy has operated, both for those countries that adopted the euro as their national currency and those, such as the UK, that did not (see Chapter 6). The Amsterdam Treaty considered the impending enlargement of the Union to embrace countries of Central and Eastern Europe, that took place in 2004 (10 new Member States) and 2007 (two more). The Amsterdam Treaty also led to the formation of a 'consolidated' version of the Treaty establishing the European Community; this simply carried over the objectives of the CAP as set out in the 1957 Treaty of Rome (renumbered as Article 33), but this has now been superseded. The Lisbon Treaty (which came into effect in 2009) extended the role of the European Parliament in agricultural decision-making, with potentially important implications (see Chapter 3) but, as noted above, the CAP's formal objectives were not changed.

(c) Agenda 2000 *(proposed in 1997 and agreed in 1999)*

Agenda 2000, a document agreed at the highest level by Member States (the European Council), was designed to prepare the EU for the process of enlargement beyond its membership of 15 countries and to further reform the CAP. Significantly for the present purpose, *Agenda 2000* contains a restatement of the objectives of the CAP. Though these do not carry quite the weight of the objectives set out in the 1957 Treaty of Rome (and the 2010 Consolidated version of the Treaty on the Functioning of the European Union), they at least reveal how the Commission reinterpreted the earlier set in the conditions of the late 1990s. The Commission's objectives for the CAP are given as follows:

- increase competitiveness internally and externally in order to ensure that Union producers take full advantage of positive world market developments;
- food safety and food quality, which are both fundamental obligations towards consumers;
- ensuring a fair standard of living for the agricultural community and contributing to the stability of farm incomes;
- the integration of environmental goals into the CAP;
- promotion of sustainable agriculture;
- the creation of alternative job and income opportunities for farmers and their families;
- simplification of Union legislation.

These formalise the main lines discussed in various policy documents put forward in the 1990s (see Chapter 12 for details). The notion of competitiveness replaced that of productivity. Food safety, environmental concern and sustainability were incorporated, reflecting the weight now attached to these in political debate. The aim of simplification was a response to the CAP's often-criticised baroque complexity. However, there is still the commitment to the vague but potent notion of a 'fair standard of living for the agricultural community' which has been used to justify so much spending. The old link between this aim and improved productivity was removed, the assurance not now being conditional. The addition of alternative job creation for farmers and their families was a tacit recognition that support of agriculture as an activity was no longer likely to achieve for these people this 'fair standard'. Indeed, the creation of an explicit rural development component to the CAP (its Pillar 2) was a significant feature of *Agenda 2000* (see Chapters 7 and 8).

Consequently, the two official statements of CAP objectives sit alongside each other, a rather unsatisfactory coexistence.

2.5 Current policy objectives in practice

The official statements of the objectives of agricultural policy are only one element in understanding to what the CAP is trying to achieve, since policy is made in a dynamic real-world environment in which new problems are frequently turning up which require action on the part of politicians and administrators. With the passage of time quite a lot of policy will be built up in this *ad hoc* way, hopefully within the general framework set out by the grander statements of policy objectives (such as Article 39 of TFEU) but often not fitting very well and at times being inconsistent. Consequently objectives of policy need to be deduced from the actions which are taken. A useful way to group objectives observed from practice is into three:

- **Functional objectives** are those which the policy is aimed at, such as encouraging elderly farmers on small farms to leave the industry. They attempt to tackle the fundamental problems faced in the European Union, either of the *instrumental* or *intrinsic* types discussed above.
- **Operational objectives** are concerned with the way in which policy is administered, such as containing the budgetary cost of policy within agreed bounds, delivering policy in an efficient and effective way, and ensuring that the various policy measures are consistent with each other.
- **Political objectives**: it should be borne in mind that politics played a major role in the setting up of the European Communities and the transition to the European Union. The objective of greater political as well as economic integration is central to the development of the Union (see Chapter 12).

The situation in the second decade of the 2000s

The following strands of policy seem to be the most important in the minds of politicians and administrators at the start of the new millennium. This is necessarily a subjective assessment of the situation but, even if the exact balance might be contested, the broad contents would be widely agreed by commentators. Many of the strands are taken up later in this book for more detailed treatment.

Among the *functional objectives* the following are some of the most important. To some extent they overlap, so the categories should not be taken as mutually exclusive:

- **Supporting the incomes of agricultural producers.** This is the central aim of the CAP. How the term 'incomes of agricultural producers' should be interpreted is imprecise and the rationale for giving them support is rather vague, but nevertheless it exerts a potent influence. Reform of agricultural policy has always been resisted if it threatened to have an adverse affect on farmer incomes, and where reform has taken place (such as the reduction of cereal prices from 1993) this has been accompanied by additional direct payments intended to 'compensate' for the impact on income. Until recently the main instruments by which support has been given have been linked to the level of production (raised product prices or direct payments geared to past production), a system which benefited the large producer more than the small producer, even though the latter may be the main sufferer from low incomes. This form of support also retained more resources in agriculture then would otherwise have been the case; in practice this meant a greater number of farmers. Increasingly it is recognised that income support cannot come solely though agricultural production, and there has been a shift to paying farmers for their production of environmental services (such as for maintaining species diversity and traditional stone walls), encouraging farmers to make other uses of their farm resources (on-farm *diversification*) such as for tourism (accommodation) and crafts, and to enable them and their families to take off-farm jobs, by providing education and training, while still living on their farms and working them on a part-time basis (to become *pluriactive* households). However, most of the support is still given as direct payments based on previous levels of support (using various formulae – see Chapter 6) but in a way that is decoupled from current production (that is, the payments come whether or not farm occupiers produce crops and livestock for the market). The dominance of spending EU agriculture by direct payments implies that income support is still the main objective of the CAP.

- **Improving the structure of agriculture.** This term implies a range of measures which attempt to change the nature of the producing units, changes which are particularly necessary in the wake of the reforms to the way in which income support is given. They include pre-pensions to help the elderly occupiers of small farms to leave the industry, grants and subsidised interest for modernisation of capital items, payments to encourage diversification into non-agricultural activities such as farm tourism, for training to take off-farm jobs, and for the formation of co-operatives and networks so that farmers can be more effective at obtaining inputs or in marketing their produce etc. Of course, a better agricultural structure, with farms of a suitable size and farmers adequately trained, will result in better incomes for these people remaining in the industry. Such an industry can be internationally competitive and may well find itself exporting to the world market, yet not needing financial incentives from the CAP to do so.

- **Conserving the natural environment.** As the main user of land, agriculture has a particular responsibility for changes seen in the natural environment. Indeed, many environmental problems have been blamed on the support mechanisms that have induced farmers to use land in particular ways, to increase the amounts of chemicals applied which can harm water-courses and wildlife, and so on. It follows that agriculture can play a major role in reaching the EU's environmental objectives. Both restrictions on farming activity (such as legislation on water pollution) and financial incentives (for managing land using low amounts of nitrogen fertiliser, for farming in particular environmentally desired ways, for planting and maintaining woodland etc.) can be used. (See Chapter 8 for details).

- **Maintaining rural communities.** In some areas, farming is supported to keep people living and working there. Farmers in the EU's Less Favoured Areas (LFAs), now over half the total agricultural area, receive special payments with the aim of enabling them to continue and which in some areas represent a major share of their income. In addition there are aids for young farmers to set up in farming, seen as necessary in some regions where the elderly composition of the existing band of farmers means that, with the passage of time, there may be problems of farm abandonment (desertification) or very rapid structural change, with consequences for rural society and the environment (see Chapter 7).

Among the *operational objectives* are the following:

- **Restoring the market.** Until recently the main methods by which support was given to farmers to a large extent divorced them from the market. From the outset of the CAP, decisions by farmers on what to produce, how to produce it and how much, were based not on the prices in free markets but on higher, administered (supported) prices. This led to increases in farm production and imbalance in the domestic market, with farmers generating levels of output substantially in excess of demand. In attempting to solve one problem (basically, low incomes in agriculture) others have been created. Restoring the market as the indicator of what to produce and the main source of reward for production has meant 'decoupling' support and lowering administered prices nearer to free market levels, or only providing a safety net for exceptional circumstances.
- **Better market balance and less trade distortion.** This follows from the above. The aim is to move nearer that balance between, on the one hand, EU uses for agricultural commodities plus exports that are internationally competitive and, on the other, the domestic level of output plus imports that would occur in a situation of free trade. When support distorts markets and trade patterns economic costs are incurred by preventing the development of the competitively determined pattern of international specialisation and exchange. Of course, a complete removal of support that distorts markets will solve the problem. A better market balance does not preclude exports (or imports), but it reduces or eliminates those that need subsidies before they can occur.
- **Containing the budgetary cost of policy instruments.** The history of the CAP is marked by attempts to contain its cost to the EU budget, and by a tendency for costs to run ahead of the sums allowed for it. Reasons will be explored later (Chapters 10 and 12). Decisions taken since the early 1990s seem to have worked better than previous attempts at containing the growth in budgetary costs. It should be borne in mind that budgetary costs are only one form of costs; others come in the form of higher food prices, economic losses due to market distortion etc.
- **Broadening the policy base.** Until the late 1980s agricultural policy was seen as separate from policy for regional development. Changes in agriculture, to make it more productive and more competitive, were encouraged with little regard to the consequences for the rest of the rural economy; for example, there might be fewer jobs in a restructured agriculture with larger farms. From 1988 a more integrated approach was attempted. Spending on agriculture designed to improve the structure of farming was integrated with the European Social Fund and the European Regional Development Fund (though the much larger expenditure that supported production of farm commodities was not covered). Current structural policy under the CAP will be reviewed later (Chapter 7). Here it is sufficient to note that policy for

agriculture is increasingly seen as part of a more general programme of assistance for rural areas which have problems.

- **Improving the performance of policy: simplification and greater assessment.** Within the last decade or so there has been a growth in concern with the performance of policy; that is, how the outcome compares with the objectives. On its establishment in the 1960s the CAP soon became a very complex set of programmes, not well connected with each other in terms of attempting to achieve policy objectives, and with few people able to grasp the details of more than a small part. The regimes for supporting the major agricultural commodities all differed, each accompanied by volumes of regulations on how they were supposed to be applied in practice. From the mid-1990s it became clear that a simpler system would be easier to comprehend and operate. There is also an enhanced interest in a more formal assessment of the performance of policy, underlined by legal requirements to evaluate that have expanded to cover all types of policy intervention (see Chapter 11). This, together with the pressure on the budget for spending on agriculture, has sharpened policy-makers' attention on the objectives of policy. In particular, if the main *functional* aim is to support the income of farmers, does this mean all operators of agricultural holdings, or only the low-income cases, or those mainly dependent on farming for their incomes? In turn this has had implications for the way that agriculture, and in particular, incomes in agriculture, are measured and monitored.

Among the *political objectives* are the following:

- **Building a stronger EU.** The political drive behind setting up what has become the EU has already been mentioned. This is by no means fully spent. In some quarters there is still a strong desire for a more complete integration of economic and political systems though there are differing views on whether and how this should proceed. Some see a deepening of relationships between existing Member States while other prefer broadening and the bringing in of more countries to the EU. Some would prefer to move to a sort of United States of Europe, with a strong central parliament and other institutions, and others (typically that of the UK government) envisage a looser collection of countries that keep a great deal of power nationally but which agree to run common policies where this makes sense. These political objectives impact on agricultural policy. Whilst the EU enlargement to 27 Member States is now history, the accession of a large number of countries with rather different agricultural structures and rural development needs is having an impact on the way the CAP is evolving. The objective of accession of Balkan countries and of Turkey, on the agenda for some politicians, will also carry implications for the CAP.
- **Satisfying or accommodating national political objectives.** There are also matters of national political interest. Individual governments are unlikely to agree to policies which cost them something unless they also get some benefit. They will be concerned with their own domestic situations, especially when national elections are in prospect, and will press for policy moves which give them credit with their voters at home. Despite the general principle of financial solidarity, countries will keep one eye on the balance between their contributions to the EU budget and their receipts from it (see Chapter 10). Countries may be tempted to use national policy measures (for example, providing subsidised management advice to farmers or

taxation concessions) to achieve national political objectives, though there are rules and agreed EU frameworks which are supposed to ensure that such national aids do not distort the competitive positions of Member States. One way in which national aspirations can be accommodated is by applying the principle of subsidiarity, that is ensuring that policy decisions are taken at the lowest appropriate level, which is often at national or regional levels. Policies on the rural environment and rural development are obviously suited to this approach; national authorities, working within a generalised framework, are most likely to be able to establish what are the local problems and to design and apply policy mechanisms that are best at solving them.

- **International political objectives.** Good relations are needed with non-Member States, and the EU has a general policy objective of encouraging freer world trade as a way of increasing living standards and enhancing rates of economic growth. Thus securing a successful outcome to the round of trade-liberalising talks in 1993 (the GATT Uruguay Round) was an important general policy aim (see Chapters 9 and 12). The main critic of EU agricultural policy in this case was the US, and several bouts of bad relations and threats of trade barriers were encountered on the way to a final solution (which involved changes to the CAP's domestic support system). There are potential gains from an agreement to the (current) Doha Round, being brokered by the World Trade Organisation (WTO) though so far this has proved difficult to negotiate. Also aid continues to be given and trade concessions made to many of the former colonies of EU Member States (termed the African, Caribbean and Pacific (ACP)) for political and humanitarian reasons. A factor behind the trade concessions available to countries that see themselves as future members is the wish to involve them in the market economies of the west as a means of fostering the democratic process in them.

2.6 Summing up and implications

Policy-makers are grappling with a range of problems in the EU that involve agriculture. In some of these agriculture is being used as an instrument to achieve general aims (such as a safe food supply and a clean environment). But in others the problems are specific to this industry and the adjustments it has to make. Increased agricultural production coupled with a demand that does not expand at all, or very slowly, means that if markets were allowed to operate more freely, resources would be shed from this industry into other lines of activity. This is the sort of adjustment that is integral to the process of economic development and results in rises over time of the average size of farm business and the minimum viable size. To some extent this has gone on, and the numbers of people engaged in agriculture have fallen substantially in all Member States, including those that joined the EU recently with farm structures that reflect their socialised past.

Pressure to shift out of agriculture comes in the form of lower incomes in this occupation than can be earned elsewhere. The immobility of factors, particularly labour, means that the adjustment process is far slower than is desirable, with rewards more depressed as a result. Small farms, often occupied by elderly farmers, tend to persist, generating low outputs and low incomes. This situation results in calls for income support and protection of farmers from low agricultural prices. Policy-makers believe that action is needed to support the incomes of the farming community, though the nature of the need is not well established. The CAP is, fundamentally of this protective sort. However, this form of policy cannot be sustained, as the costs will continue to rise with continued technical progress, and policy reform will have to take place. Ultimately the agricultural industry has to adjust, and some farmers and their families have to exit, diversify or become pluriactive. Meanwhile, attempts to reform policy, to make agriculture more sensitive to the market, are resisted because of the impact on incomes and the personal wealth of farm operators and land owners.

Some of the current problems are, at least in part, of the CAP's own making and result from the way in which support has been given in the past. Domestic markets were distorted in ways that encouraged production and disturbed trade patterns, and agriculture was cushioned from the economic pressures that would have forced it to adjust, so its response has been muted. Further policies have been needed to deal with the problems created. Though the CAP's principal way of providing support has now largely changed to one that is decoupled from production decisions (see Chapters 6 and 12), remnants of the previous commodity regimes remain and their legacy has to be addressed.

Environmental objectives (biodiversity, landscape appearance etc.) have risen in importance on the EU's policy agenda. Modern agricultural production if unregulated has a tendency to create negative externalities, such as nitrogen pollution of water-courses and the destruction of wildlife habitats, especially if encouraged by raised commodity prices. As a response, the last decade has seen the substantial expansion of financial incentives for farmers and other instruments that use agriculture (and forestry) to achieve environmental aims. To some extent farmers may be able to retain part of their former support by persuading governments that they should be paid for providing environmental and other services.

The problems within the EU involving agriculture are thus both complex and diverse. To understand how policy attempts to tackle them in practice it is necessary to examine the process by which decisions are made. In some respects the reasons why the policies are less successful than they might be can be traced to the decision-making process, discussed next in Chapter 3.

Further reading

Ackrill, R. (2000) 'The background to government involvement in farming: the what, why and how of agricultural support policies in Europe'. Chapter 1 in: *The Common Agricultural Policy*. Sheffield Academic Press, Sheffield.

Bonnen, J. T. and Schweikhardt, B. (1998) 'Reflections on the disappearance of the "farm problem"', *Review of Agricultural Economics*, 20 (1), 2–36. See especially the annex.

Brassley, P. (1997) *Agricultural Economics and the CAP: An Introduction*. Blackwell Scientific, Oxford

European Commission (1994) *European Policy for the 21st Century*. European Economy Reports and Studies No. 4. (See Annex Chapter A – 'EC agriculture past and present' and Annex Chapter C – 'Explaining agricultural policy').

European Commission (2009) 'Why Do We Need a Common Agricultural Policy?', Discussion paper by DG Agriculture and Rural Development, Brussels.

Fearne, A. (1997) 'The history and development of the CAP'. In Ritson, C. and Harvey, D. (eds.) *The Common Agricultural Policy*. 2nd edition. CAB International, Wallingford.

Fennell, R. (1987) *The Common Agricultural Policy of the European Community*. 2nd edition. BSP Professional Books, Wagingen.

Fennell, R. (1997) *The Common Agricultural Policy: Continuity and Change*. Clarendon Press, Oxford.

Grant, W. (1997) *The Common Agricultural Policy.* St Martin's Press, New York. (see Chapters 1 and 2).

OECD (2010) *Agricultural Policies in OECD Countries: At a Glance.* Organisation for Economic Co-operation and Development, Paris.

Tracy, M. (1993) *Food and Agriculture in a Market Economy: An Introduction to Theory, Practice and Policy.* APS, La Hutte, Belgium.

Winter, A. (1990) 'Digging for victory: agricultural policy and national security', *The World Economy,* 13 (2), 170–90.

3

UNDERSTANDING THE POLICY DECISION-MAKING PROCESS IN THE EUROPEAN UNION

> **Key topics**
>
> - The institutions of the EU and the roles they play in the CAP decision-making process.
> - The passage of a piece of agricultural policy legislation through the stages between inceptionand its implementation by national governments.
> - The part played by professional associations.
> - Characteristics of the process.

3.1 Introduction

Policy does not spring instantly into being once a problem has arisen. As was noted in Chapter 1, even identifying what constitutes a problem requires someone to spot it and be concerned about it. Sometimes these persons are lone voices who, if anything is to be done, have to persuade others to join them to bring pressure to bear on public opinion and policy-makers (politicians and civil servants). This seems to be particularly the case with what might be described as 'new' problems, such as issues concerning the rural environment and animal welfare. However, more often these individuals are working within organisations, such as the public institutions (departments of central or local government) or established bodies representing the interests of particular groups (such as farmers' unions). Such institutions are important members of the policy community referred to in Chapter 1.

This chapter looks at:

- in the first section, the major institutions of the European Union (EU) and what their roles are in the development of policy;
- in the second section, the process by which policy decisions on agricultural matters are reached and the characteristics which the structure imposes on decisions.

Understanding this process helps provide answers to important questions about the CAP and rural policy in the EU. For example, why have changes in agricultural policy that most people would agree as sensible not been made until very recently? Why did the CAP persist with supporting the prices of agricultural commodities as the main way of enhancing the incomes of farmers even when this system had been widely recognised as being responsible for the production of surpluses, large pressures on the EU budget and the disruption of international trade? Why does the CAP not adopt a system of direct income payments that targets farmers in poverty, rather than one that goes to all producers irrespective of need?

Why is support for agriculture not integrated with other support for rural areas, and why does agriculture get such a disproportionately large share of the EU budget spent on it? Why are the interests of consumers not taken into greater account in decision-making?

The answers to a surprisingly large proportion of such questions lie in the structure of the decision-making process.

PART ONE – THE INSTITUTIONS OF THE EUROPEAN UNION

3.2 The main institutions of the EU

In the early stages of setting up the communities of countries that have become the EU (see the historical review of the various Treaties that did this in Chapter 12), a positive decision was taken to create some institutions that were given supra-national authority. That is, Member States voluntarily passed some powers to them as the best way to operate the common policies that form community activities. Though perhaps the best-known of these EU institutions is the European Commission, this is not really where the ultimate power of decision-taking lies. Up to the end of 2009, when the Lisbon Treaty came into force, for most agricultural matters this power remained with the Council of the EU (until 1993 called the Council of Ministers). The Lisbon Treaty gave a greater role to the European Parliament in agricultural policy decision-taking, something that it had been given in other policy areas by earlier Treaties. However, these are only three of the constellation of EU institutions which are significant in policy-making, through their various functions acting as a series of checks and balances, and which must be reviewed here. The other main bodies are the European Council (the meeting of Heads of State and Government), the Court of Justice of the EU, the Economic and Social Committee (ECOSOC), the European Court of Auditors, and the Committee of the Regions. Each is considered below in turn; a summary of the way they interact is given in Figure 3.1. There are, in addition, a raft of other, newer institutions set up with the agreement of Member States to assist in implementing EU policies, mainly by collecting and disseminating information.[1]

3.2.1 The Council of the European Union and the European Council

The Council of the EU, formerly called the Council of Ministers (and often shortened to the Council) has three main functions:

- It has been the primary decision-taking body for policy by agreeing (adopting) legal texts that set them out, though with the passage of time and successive Treaties these powers have been increasingly shared with the European Parliament. For agricultural policy, up to December 2009, when the Lisbon Treaty came into force, once the Council agreed the text of a document setting out a policy decision and this was published in the Official Journal, it became law in the EU, without any further consultation or confirmation by other EU institutions or national governments. Most past and current agricultural and rural development policy was agreed under this system. Now both the Council and Parliament have to agree on most new agricultural legislation. Despite this change, the Council alone still retains responsibility for adopting text on

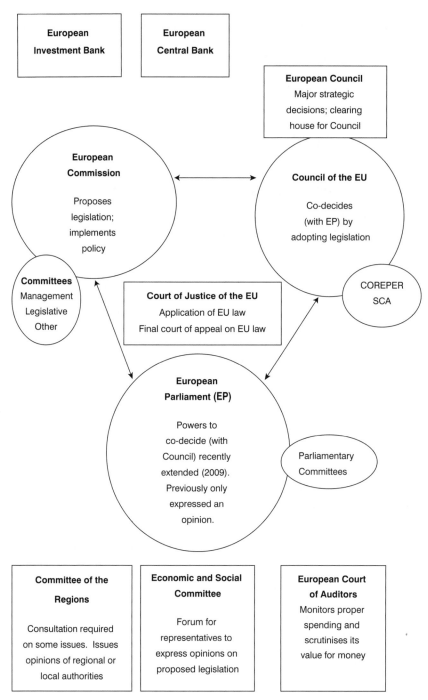

Figure 3.1   The orientation of the main institutions involved in agricultural policy decisions

fixing agricultural prices, levies, aid and quantitative limitations and on the fixing and allocation of fishing opportunities.

- It is one arm of the 'budgetary authority' (the other being the European Parliament) exercising joint control over the spending of the EU and being responsible for stages in the preparation of the annual budget.
- It is responsible for determining a mandate for the Commission to start with when negotiating international agreements on behalf of the EU and for adopting them once agreed.

Knowledge of the way that the Council reaches decisions is vital to explaining outcomes. The Council is essentially a political body; it consists of politicians (ministers) elected within their own countries who are sent to the Council as representatives of their national governments. Council decisions must be judged in the light of their political acceptability at home and the implications they hold for the national government, the ministry and the personal political careers of the ministers. Consequently, political difficulties being experienced at home, and the timing of national elections, are factors that can have an impact on decisions. They help explain why progress in tackling policy problems in the EU can at times be painfully slow and yet, at others, things can happen with unexpected rapidity if the solution is seen as politically urgent at home or if the minister needs to be seen as personally effective.

The Council comprises representatives of each of the EU's 27 Member States. The Council is chaired by a 'President', the presidency rotating on a six-monthly basis to a schedule that is agreed and published several years in advance; for that period, the country sends two representatives, one to chair (who is therefore prevented from taking a partisan role and cannot vote on decisions) and the deputy to represent the interests of the particular country. Meetings have been held behind closed doors, with only minutes and votes published, though the Lisbon Treaty intended that this should be changed. Since December 2009 when new laws are debated the Council is open to public viewing, exposing the process to greater scrutiny. The Council meets usually in Brussels but occasionally (April, June, October) in Luxembourg.

Though the singular term 'Council' is used, its composition changes according to the policy under consideration. In reality there are many 'configurations' of the council (currently 10, comprising the agricultural Council, the internal market Council, the economic and financial affairs Council and so on), on which the appropriate national ministers sit. For example, the UK representative at the agriculture Council would normally be the UK Secretary of State at the Department for Environment, Food and Rural Affairs (Defra), the member of the government with overall responsibility for agriculture, though sometimes the seat would be occupied by a junior minister in the department if the subject under discussion was their particular ministerial responsibility. National government representatives normally have their advisors in attendance (civil servants from the appropriate national ministries and from the country's permanent representation to the EU – see below). The Council has its own staff (a secretariat of about 2,500, based in Brussels) to administer meetings and arrange documentation, to draft resolutions which emerge from discussions and so on; it also services the many working groups which carry out most of the Council's work. The European Commission (see below) will be represented at Council meetings (both the full meetings and those of its committees) to put the case for its proposals, but has no rights to vote on decisions.

It is very unusual to have ministers from more than one department of government present at a Council meeting; one rare example was the joint ('jumbo') Council session of foreign and agriculture ministers held in September 1993 to ratify the Blair House agreement on agricultural subsidies and trade, negotiated between the EU and US as a step towards a more comprehensive GATT agreement (see Chapters 9 and 12). This fragmentation of policy has drawn criticism for the potential it holds for lack of coordination, for inconclusiveness and lack of practicality. Under the present arrangements it is assumed that agricultural ministers represent the balanced views of their complete governments and that other ministerial colleagues will have conveyed any concerns they may have had on the issues to be discussed to their agricultural representative. This assumption may break down if there is less than perfect communication between different departments, as seems more than likely on occasion. Where unforeseen developments occur in Council discussions, it may be necessary for ministers to delay until they have had time to consult with colleagues back at home. However, historically the agricultural Council, as the biggest spending Council, is reputed to have tended to take relatively little account of the consequences for non-agricultural issues of its agricultural decisions and has acted with greater autonomy than other Councils. Whether some of the past excesses of the agricultural Council could have been avoided if treasury ministers had been present to keep a watch on the financial implications of the decisions by agricultural ministers, is a point worthy of debate.

When a country holds the Presidency, it chairs all the Council meetings dealing with the full range of EU policies; this can put a strain on the national administrations of some smaller countries. Because this gives a degree of control of what appears on agendas of meetings, the influence of the presiding country can be substantial. Though there is a danger that the national interest of this country could be pressed home, in reality there is such awareness of this possibility that, if anything, national interests seem to be put at a disadvantage. Rather, the Presidency is seen as a way of giving direction to the Council and of achieving particular EU goals near to the heart of the chairing country, or of putting off decisions on matters which it finds nationally contentious or in which it has little concern. The President also plays a crucial role in making progress by acting as an 'honest broker' between the divergent interest of the Member States, seeing where progress is possible and what compromises might be put forward for discussion.

To reach decisions in the Council, the Treaty of Rome (1957) stipulated majority voting on most issues. Under the EU voting system, larger countries have more votes than smaller ones, though the numbers are set by agreement between Member States rather than by a simple formula linked to population. As new countries have joined, the allocation of votes has been adapted. Table 3.1 shows the allocation of votes that applied from 1 January 2007, as agreed in the Treaty of Nice (2001). A *qualified majority* is needed to carry decisions on Commission proposals concerning agricultural policy (assuming that the item has been on a Council agenda for 14 days); provision for this was made in the 1957 Treaty of Rome, and the policy areas in which qualified majority voting applies has been gradually increased over the life of the EU. Box 3.1 describes the details of a qualified majority, including the obverse concept of a *blocking minority* which can prevent legislation being adopted. Such a system allows decisions faster than if unanimity had to be reached. Also it gives room for individual ministers to gain credit at home for pursuing a policy which is popular among his own farmers but makes no sense from an EU standpoint; the minister can say that he fought for his farmers but was outvoted. This is a useful weapon in the armoury of a politician under national pressure.

Table 3.1 Votes allocated to Member States

Member State	Number of votes each 2007 onwards
Germany, France, Italy and UK	29
Spain and Poland	27
Romania	14
Netherlands	13
Belgium, Czech Republic, Greece, Hungary and Portugal	12
Austria, Sweden, Bulgaria	10
Denmark, Ireland, Lithuania, Slovakia, Finland	7
Cyprus, Estonia, Latvia, Luxembourg, Slovenia	4
Malta	3
Total	345

However, there are circumstances under which unanimity is needed (no votes against). Unanimity is required for major EU decisions such as to extend EU activities not covered by common policies previously agreed in Treaties, such as direct taxation on individuals (which in effect ensures that such tax policy remains a purely national responsibility, since it would take only one country to vote against a proposal to defeat it). Importantly, as will be seen below, for agreement in Council on *changes* to Commission proposals, including those on agricultural policy, unanimity in favour is needed (though abstentions do not count as votes against), which makes such changes difficult to achieve unless they include something to benefit each country. In (rare) situations the legislation provides for a simple majority to pass a piece of legislation.

In practice, the voting procedures have been less mechanical than the qualified majority voting system might suggest. The Council has had a preference for reaching decisions unanimously; even in circumstances in which qualified majority voting could be used; there has been a historic tendency to avoid it as this underlines differences of interest within the Council, though with the enlargement of the EU voting is now quite normal. There has also been room for compromise when countries have felt strongly on particular issues, in order to enable the work of the Council to continue. (See Box 3.2).

Two lower-level committees and one high-level meeting are associated with the Council. The first is the *Committee of Permanent Representatives (COREPER)*. This can be considered as a sub-committee of the Council that undertakes preparatory work for its meetings. Based in Brussels, its membership consists of 'permanent representatives' (or ambassadors) of Member States to the EU and their staffs; in practice there are two levels of COREPER, the higher comprising the Permanent Representatives themselves and the lower their deputies or representatives, with the latter dealing with the more technical issues. COREPER has the function of sifting and giving initial consideration to the first proposals for legislation on policy sent to it by the Commission, and has its own sets of working groups to deal with various areas of Commission work. National viewpoints can be aired and disagreements given a chance to be resolved. As such it is an important nexus of national and EU interests and between technical and political aspects of policy. Members of COREPER have substantial influence in their roles as scrutinisers of legislation and also because of their network of contacts that can be used in helping shape policy in the desired direction. Originally COREPER dealt

---

Box 3.1 Qualified majority voting

What constitutes a qualified majority has been altered as the EU has expanded. Before the accession of Austria, Finland and Sweden in 1995, out of the total of the 76 votes of all 12 Member States, 54 had to be in favour, and 23 votes constituted a blocking minority (abstentions or refusals to take part counted towards this). This meant that the four largest Member States could not together over-rule the wishes of the smaller ones; support from at least one other country was necessary. The enlargement of the Union in January 1995 to 15 countries raised the total number of votes to 87, the qualified majority to 62 and the blocking minority to 26 votes.

The 2001 Treaty of Nice, which took account of the enlargement of the EU, changed the conditions of a qualified majority to the following:

- if a majority of Member States (or in some cases a two-thirds majority) approve AND
- if a minimum of 255 votes (73.9 per cent) are cast in favour AND
- a Member State may ask for confirmation that the votes cast in favour represent at least 62 per cent of the total population of the EU.

Under the Lisbon Treaty 2009, in rules that apply from 2014, this system was simplified, to require 55 per cent of Member States to vote in favour (that is, 15 out of 27) and these should represent 65 per cent of EU population (the so-called 'double majority' rule). At least four Member States are needed to form a blocking minority. A blocking minority must include at least the minimum number of Council members representing more than 35 per cent of the population of the participating Member States, plus one member. However, between November 2014 and March 2017, any Member State may request that the current weighted voting system be applied instead of the new 'double majority' system.

The Single European Act (1986) extended the conditions under which a qualified majority could be used (in particular for legislation necessary to complete the internal market by 1992) and further steps were taken in the 1992 Maastricht Treaty, the Treaty of Amsterdam (1997) and the Treaty of Lisbon (2009). However, unanimity in the Council is still required in areas such as tax matters, social security, foreign policy, defence, operational police cooperation etc.

---

with agricultural matters but most of these are now taken by the Special Committee for Agriculture (see below).

The second committee under the umbrella of the Council is the *Special Committee on Agriculture (SCA)*, one of a range of specialist committees associated with COREPER. Its membership is made up of agricultural experts on the staff of the ambassadors and permanent representatives to the EU, and is supported by civil servants from the national government departments dealing with agriculture (Defra and the other agricultural departments in the case of the UK). The SCA is the main route for the initial consideration of policy proposals relating to the CAP. Working parties are formed on specific issues which report to the SCA, including suggested amendments. A Commission representative is present at SCA meetings

---

Box 3.2 Procedural compromises in the Council , and the 'veto'

In an earlier phase of the EU, a disagreement by France in 1965 on how the CAP should be financed led to that country operating an 'empty chair' policy in the Council, refusing to vote on proposals for institutional change and thereby paralysing progress. This resulted in the 'Luxembourg Compromise' in 1966, under which, if one or more Member States declared that a 'vital national interest' was at stake, the Council endeavoured to reach unanimous solutions to problems. When this happened other countries undertook to vote against the proposal, guaranteeing a blocking minority. Thus the declaration represented a *de facto* veto on such issues. This was sufficient for France to return to the Council. The strict legality of this compromise was never put to a judicial test. However, it was sufficiently strong for the resultant mind-set of the Council to be one of a general subsequent preference for unanimity. It was invoked little after 1982 and was last used by Greece in 1988, though it was threatened (though not followed through) by France in the discussions following the USA–EU trade deal of 1992 which needed approval by the Council. By the 1990s the general opinion seemed to be that, because of changed conditions, the declaration of a vital interest would no longer be accepted as necessitating unanimity.

In the mid-1990s when the Community grew from EU-12 to EU-15, the UK resisted the proposition to raise the blocking minority in qualified majority voting, to 27 (set on the assumption that Norway joined with Austria, Finland and Sweden). However the 27 votes in the new arrangement represented a very similar proportion of the votes available to the 23 votes in the previous arrangement. Because of concerns expressed by the UK and Spain, it was agreed that if a minority vote against a proposal of between 23 and 27 was obtained, the 'Ioannina Compromise' would be invoked. This meant that the measure became subject to a 'reasonable delay' in order to attempt to reach a consensus. The decision of Norway not to join the EU lowered the blocking minority to 26 and hence narrowed the band over which the 'Ioannina Compromise' operated.

---

to explain the proposals, and to look after the EU interest. If all points of conflict between Member States (and with the Commission) can be resolved this way, and a draft text agreed, then the proposal will be passed automatically by ministers meeting as the Council without further discussion. Where unanimous agreement cannot be achieved, ministers will be required to consider it and maybe vote on it (though it may be referred back to the SCA again by the Council).

A higher group than the Council (of ministers) is the European Council[2] (the meetings of the Heads of State and Government). This can be seen as a version of the Council but consisting of prime ministers or state presidents and is attended by the presidents of the Commission and of the European Parliament. Under the Lisbon Treaty, in 2009 the European Council was given a distinct identity of its own. It was also provided with a full-time President, elected by Council using qualified majority, who holds the post for 2.5 years (renewable once). Prior to this there had been feelings that the rotating Presidency was not satisfactory when there were many Member States, each having the experience of chairing the European Council only once every 13 or 14 years, and that a permanent incumbent could bring greater stability and continuity. Formal meetings ('summits') are held two or three times a year in the Member State currently holding the Presidency of the Council or in Brussels, though additional 'informal' summits may also take place. The European Council emerged in the 1960s as the development of the EU revealed the necessity for such meetings. The Single European Act of 1986 expressly referred to the European Council, giving it legal status, and stipulated that the President of the Commission attended in his own right. The Lisbon Treaty of 2009 took this process of institutional development a step further.

The European Council is a launch pad for major political initiatives and a forum for settling controversial matters. It deals with current international issues through European Political Co-operation (EPC), a way devised to bring national diplomatic positions into line and to present a united front. There is provision for qualified majority voting on decisions that permit it, but often the European Council will find itself dealing with issues on which unanimity is required, such as the admission of new Member States, or the location of EU institutions.

Though one might expect the European Council to deal only with the grander issues in the development of the EU (new Treaties, setting up an EU defence facility etc.), it has also acted as the last resort for agreeing difficult agricultural decisions which become blocked at Council (of Ministers) level (such as the imposition of milk quotas in 1984, which occupied it for two half-days). Heads of state and prime ministers can hardly be expected to have personal expertise in these relatively minor issues of policy implementation, though their staff will be able to brief them. However, the European Council provides a way of taking a broad view of contentious issues that cut across the boundaries that separate different policy areas, such as agriculture, trade and the EU budget. As noted above, 'jumbo', Council (of Ministers) meetings attended by more than one national minister have not been used much in EU decision-making, and this access to the very top of the political hierarchy is useful in providing final solutions.

3.2.2 The European Commission

The structure of the Commission

The Commission is the executive of the EU across all its activities. Here were are concerned with the role of the Commission in shaping and administering policy on agriculture and rural development.

At the head of the Commission is a 'College' of 27 Commissioners, one from each Member State; before 2007 there were fewer in total (17 from 1986 until the accession of Austria, Finland and Sweden in 1995, and 20 from then until 2004) but with the larger countries (France, Germany, Italy, Spain and the UK) sending two each. The Treaty of Lisbon (2007) stipulated that from 2014 the number of Commissioners was to be reduced (to 18 in an EU of 27 countries). However, concerns from a few Member States (notably expressed in Ireland during its referendum on the Treaty in the preceding June) led to a decision at the European Council meeting of December 2008 to retain the Commission's membership at 27, an arrangement likely to be written into some future Treaty (such as will be needed when a further country joins the EU).

Commissioners are appointed (not elected) by Member States for a five-year term which may be renewed. (A new Commission came into office in January 2010). The President and

Vice-Presidents of the Commission hold office by agreement of Member States. Usually national politicians of standing, the nominated Commissioners are, required under the 1957 Treaty of Rome (carried through in a consolidated form into the 2010 Treaty on the Functioning of the European Union) to leave behind their national interests when accepting the position, to be independent and to neither seek nor take instructions from any government or from any other body, a requirement which in the main seems to be fulfilled. Member States are told in the latter Treaty to 'respect their independence and ... not seek to influence them in the performance of their tasks'. Overall the Commissioners reflect the balance of the main political groupings in Europe, (Christian Democrat, Liberal and Socialist). When the UK provided two Commissioners, traditionally one was a Conservative and the other a Labour party nominee.

Each Commissioner has a portfolio of responsibilities to manage, which may be varied between Commissions. Of particular interest here is that the Commissioner responsible for agriculture has, since 1989, also looked after rural development. For assistance, each Commissioner has a private office (cabinet) of advisors (rules now require these to be of mixed nationality) and other staff who also serve as a line of communication with national governments through the permanent representations. The heads of the cabinets (chefs) meet before the weekly meeting of the Commissioners to arrange the agenda and to clear minor points. Agricultural matters are delegated to specialist groups of cabinet members aided by staff of the Commission's agricultural Directorate-General (see below). This is an example of policy 'factoring', the splitting of responsibility whereby agricultural matters are taken by a narrow group of specialists. While there may be good reason why the technicalities or degree of detail is outside the competence of other public servants, the lack of the full participation of other interests may lead to agricultural decisions which lack integration with other EU activities.

Since December 2009, when the Treaty of Lisbon came into force, the Commission has, as one of its Vice-President members, the EU's High Representative for Foreign Affairs and Security Policy. This position was created to increase the international role and effectiveness of the EU. This High Representative took over functions previously exercised by two Commissioners (those concerned with foreign affairs and security policy, and with external relations). The High Representative is appointed by the European Council, sworn in by the European Parliament, and chairs the Foreign Affairs Council at the Council of Ministers. In effect the EU's foreign minister, this person represents the EU abroad and has a diplomatic service at their disposal. No doubt the part played by this rather special member of the Commission will evolve over time, reflecting in particular interests and talents of the person appointed.

Below the Commissioners in the hierarchy comes the administrative part of the Commission, staffed by civil servants (*fonctionnaires*), some 23,000 permanent posts in total (in 2007) plus another 9,000 on other contractual arrangements (short-term consultancies, national staff on secondment etc.). These are grouped into sections (Directorates-General, or DG for short, each headed by a Director-General, and further subdivided into Directorates) that tend to undergo occasional reorganisation. Currently there are 20 DGs which deal with specific EU policies and another 26 responsible for external relations (including trade and enlargement) and services (such as translation and interpretation, the budget, and legal services which, among other activities, provide professional advice on the way in which legislation to put policy into effect is drawn up). Table 3.2 lists the DGs (as in 2010) and their areas of activity. Responsibilities of DGs and Commissioners are not exactly aligned, and a DG may be responsible to more than one Commissioner.

Table 3.2 The Directorates-General and Services of the Commission (as at 2010)

Policies

Agriculture and Rural Development	Enterprise
Climate Action	Maritime Affairs and Fisheries
Competition	Mobility and Transport
Economic and Financial Affairs	Health and Consumers
Education and Culture	Information Society and Media
Employment, Social Affairs and Equal	Internal Market and Services
Opportunities	Justice
Energy	Regional Policy
Environment	Research
Executive agencies	Taxation and Customs Union

External Relations

Development	External Relations
Enlargement	Humanitarian Aid
EuropeAid – Co-operation Office	Trade

General Services

Communication	Joint Research Centre
European Anti-Fraud Office	Publications Office
Eurostat	Secretariat General
Historical archives	

Internal Services

Budget	Internal Audit Service
Bureau of European Policy Advisers	Interpretation
European Commission Data Protection Officer	Legal Service
Human Resources and Security	Office for Administration and Payment of
Informatics	Individual Entitlements
Infrastructures and Logistics – Brussels	Translation
Infrastructures and Logistics – Luxembourg	

The Statistical Office of the European Communities (known as Eurostat and based in Luxembourg), part of the Commission, is particularly important for studies of agriculture as it is responsible for collecting, analysing and publishing a vast amount of information on the changing nature of the Member States and many aspects of their populations, economies, farms and agricultural industries. Eurostat provides much of the statistics on which policy decisions are based. This part of the Commission's activities is described in Chapter 4.

An awareness of the workings of the Directorate-General responsible for agriculture and rural development (known within the Commission as DG-Agri, formerly as DG-VI) is of major relevance to an understanding of the CAP. DG-Agri is one of the largest DGs (though in 2007 the one with most staff was the translation service). As will be seen later, it has been responsible for a major proportion of spending from the EU budget – formerly more than two-thirds of the total and even now approaching half (see Chapter 10). Its size, coverage of a wide range of expertise and budgetary weight means that, critics allege, it has tended to work alone and without close co-ordination with other DGs that may be affected by policy decisions in agriculture (trade policy, consumer or environmental affairs, social and regional policy and so on). DG-Agri is subdivided into some dozen Directorates and units responsible for various aspects of the CAP, including for the organisation of markets in crop products, in livestock products, in specialised crops and for agricultural structures (and forestry).

DG-Agri has a number of Committees that fall into two main types. The first comprises those that act with powers devolved from the Council (of Ministers) and are critical to the implementation of the CAP (Management Committees and Regulatory Committees). These were set up at the instigation of the Council but their means of operation was changed significantly by the Single European Act of 1986 that transferred some of the Council's executive competence to them, the procedures they were to follow also being set by the Council in 1987. Their memberships mirror that of the Council, with Member States being represented by specialist national civil servants delegated from their home ministries. The chair is taken by a senior Commission official. Attendance at meetings is restricted to national civil servants and Commission officials; agendas and minutes of meetings are restricted to the people responsible for the regime in each Member State. The procedure is that proposals are put before the Committee by the Commission. Opinions are expressed by the Committee, voting using the same national weights as given above for the Council votes and with a qualified majority in favour being required for the adoption of a proposal. The specific procedural rules are considered in a later section.

Within this first type are Management Committees covering the Common Organisation of agricultural markets and for certain other aspects of European Union activities. In 2008 there were 20 Management Committees, one for each major commodity and another nine dealing with other activities (such as the annual survey of farm businesses in Member States – the Farm Accountancy Data Network – and the Standing Forestry Committee). However, during 2008 the separate commodity committees were merged into one (the other nine remain). This single management committee for market regimes (Common Market Organisations – CMOs), operating with powers devolved from the Council, decides on issues such as when intervention buying shall operate (though short-term management, such as setting variable levies on imports, is carried out by the Commission alone). Previously the separate Management Committees met with a frequency which reflected the need to take decisions, usually once per month for pigs and sheep but twice a month for beef and with some almost weekly. The single committee that replaced them meets frequently (over 90 times in 2009) and deals with the various commodity markets and other issues as required.

The second form of committee with executive power, Regulatory Committees, is closely similar, although there are differences in what can happen if the committee does not give a favourable opinion of the Commission's proposal. Five Regulatory Committees currently exist (2010), but formerly there were more. Many of the activities to do with food safety and animal welfare formerly the responsibility of DG-Agri have been transferred to the DG for Health and Consumer Protection, with its European Food Safety Authority and range of regulatory committees, such as the Standing Committee on the Food Chain and Animal Health.

In addition to this type of committee that applies policy, there is a second type that is advisory to the Commission. Agricultural advisory committees were set up in 1962 at the request of the EU organisation representing farmers and were mainly focused on the management of commodity markets. Periodically these advisory groups have been reorganised as the CAP has evolved. In 2004 the committees were recast so as to appear more appropriate to the priorities of the CAP as reformed in 1999 and 2003, to take account of the EU enlargement, and to intensify dialogue with EU-level organisations representing social and economic interests. The distribution of places on the groups reflects the appearance of new European organisations in fields such as the environment, protection of animals and rural development to which the reformed CAP attaches greater importance. Currently (2010) there are some 30 such advisory groups, meeting about 85 times in the year in total.

Formerly there were parallel advisory committees on science in relation to agriculture. The Commission consulted these eight Science Committees and their Scientific Steering Committee whenever there was a legal requirement to do so, and when an issue of significance relevant to their sphere of independent and specialist expertise arose. In May 2003 the responsibilities of these committees were transferred to the European Food Safely Authority, under the supervision of the DG for Health and Consumer Protection.

The functions of the Commission

The functions of the Commission can be summarised as follows:

1 **It acts as the guardian of the Treaties.** That is, it represents the EU interest and protects and upholds the spirit of the Treaties which form its foundation. In this role it can take governments or firms to court (the European Court of Justice) for breaches of EU law (such as the British government payments to British Aerospace when it took over the British Leyland car manufacturing business, later judged to be against EU competition legislation). In this role it can take a longer-term view of where the EU is going and propose legislation to that end; an example was the push initiated by the Commission's then-President (Jacques Delors) towards completing the internal market by 1993. This pro-active role marks the Commission as being different from most national civil services, that primarily react to initiatives coming from government ministers.

2 **It drafts legislation** (principally in the form of Regulations, Directives and Decisions, described later) which then goes into the decision-making process and, if approved, eventually becomes law. The Commission is the only institution that is allowed to do this; this it termed its *sole right of initiative*. Thus, the Commission needs to be persuaded that a problem exists and that a policy needs to be put into operation before there is any chance of this taking place. Although, under the 1992 Treaty on European Union (Maastricht) the European Parliament has the right to propose legislation, the Commission is not required to comply with this request. Though the Council and, increasingly, the European Parliament are responsible for taking decisions on legislation, the Commission's role as the sole drafter of legislation in reality gives it great influence over the way that the EU develops.

3 **It acts as an executive and secretariat for EU policy.** In this role the Commission manages the EU's funds (including those for agriculture). It is responsible for implementing the legislation once officially adopted (though it should be remembered that much of the burden for this falls on the shoulders of governments and civil services in Member States which are required to operate policies at national level). It has executive powers given to it by the Council on some operational matters (such as setting taxes on imports where these form part of market intervention) and the Commission is responsible for ensuring that assessments of the impacts of proposed major policy changes are carried out.

4 **It mediates** between individual government interests and steers proposals through the Council of Ministers (and the committees which serve it). The Commission can intervene at any stage in the legislative process to facilitate agreements within the Council or between the Council and Parliament.

The Commission can also issue opinions and recommendations; these are not statutory but usually state the EU Commission's position on policy matters.

3.2.3 The European Parliament (EP)

The European Parliament (EP) consists of Members (MEPs), directly elected in each Member State to serve for a period of five years, and who elect the Parliament's own President from among their number. Currently the Parliament has 736 MEPs; the numbers from each country are given in Table 3.3. Members sit in EU-wide political groups rather than national ones. Because there is no official government and opposition, a new majority has to be built for every issue the Parliament debates and votes on.

The work of the EP takes place in Plenary Sessions and by means of standing Parliamentary Committees, comprising groups of MEPs (typically numbering 40) with a special concern with particular areas of policy. In 2010 there were 23 such committees, including the Committee on Agriculture and Rural Development. Each appoints one of its members to act as *rapporteur* on its deliberation on the legislation in hand and to write the report. When considering draft legislation, these committees can act on behalf of the full Parliament if no more than 10 per cent of their members object.

The meetings of the EP take place on a monthly cycle; only one week per month is used for a full plenary session (mostly in Strasbourg, occasionally in Brussels). Committees of the Parliament meet in Brussels in two other weeks, attended by Commission officials to respond to the questions of members. The fourth week is spent by the MEPs back in their constituencies and used for political meetings. The EP's secretariat is based in Luxembourg. This fragmentation certainly involves much regular shifting of people and paper, and probably hinders the effectiveness of the EP. There have been plans to move full-time to Brussels, though with some strong opposition from France and Luxembourg to the change; the 'Summit' of heads of state and government, meeting in Edinburgh at the end of 1992 confirmed the present arrangements.

The function of the EP, as set out in the Treaty of Rome, was to advise and supervise, although the Single European Act and subsequent Treaties have extended the areas in which it has a more active role in the making of decisions in some areas of policy. It now shares (with the Council) the responsibility for turning the Commission's proposals for new legislation into actual law in many areas of policy (including agriculture). It comments and votes on the Commission's programme of activities each year and can pass resolutions on any other matter it feels is important, indicating where future EU action should be directed. It can put written and oral questions to the Commission and Council as a way of monitoring the management of policies. At full Parliamentary sessions the Commissioner dealing with a debated issue will be present. It can commission research on policy areas. The EP is required to give assent to international cooperation and associated agreements and all subsequent enlargements of the EU (following the Single European Act). It also has power to dismiss the entire Commission by a two-thirds majority on a vote of no confidence. However, it does not have the power to dismiss individual Commissioners or to re-appoint new Commissioners. It has the right to question all persons nominated by their Member States as Commissioners (this first happened in 1995), though it is not clear what would happen if the EP were to formally reject a nominee.

Table 3.3 Numbers of MEPs elected from each Member State in the European Parliament, and political groups (2009)

Member State	Political group (see legend below)								
	PPE-DE	S&D	ALDE	Greens/ALE	ECR	GUE/NGL	EFD	NI	Total
Austria	6	4		2				5	17
Belgium	5	5	5	4	1			2	22
Bulgaria	6	4	5					2	17
Cyprus	2	2				2			6
Czech Republic	2	7			9	4			22
Denmark	1	4	3	2		1	2		13
Estonia	1	1	3	1					6
Finland	4	2	4	2			1		13
France	29	14	6	14		5	1	3	72
Germany	42	23	12	14		8			99
Greece	8	8		1		3	2		22
Hungary	14	4			1			3	22
Ireland	4	3	4			1			12
Italy	35	21	7				9		72
Latvia	3	1	1	1	1	1			8
Lithuania	4	3	2		1		2		12
Luxembourg	3	1	1	1					6
Malta	2	3							5
Netherlands	5	3	6	3	1	2	1	4	25
Poland	28	7			15				50
Portugal	10	7				5			22
Romania	14	11	5					3	33
Slovakia	6	5	1				1		13
Slovenia	3	2	2						7
Spain	23	21	2	2		1		1	50
Sweden	5	5	4	3		1			18
United Kingdom		13	11	5	25	1	13	4	72
Total	265	184	84	55	54	35	32	27	736

PPE-DE – Group of the European People's Party (Christian Democrats): S&D – Group of the Progressive Alliance of Socialists and Democrats in the European Parliament: ALDE – Group of the Alliance of Liberals and Democrats for Europe: Greens/ALE – Group of the Greens/European Free Alliance: ECR – European Conservatives and Reformists: GUE/NGL – Confederal Group of the European United Left-Nordic Green Left; EFD – Europe of freedom and democracy Group: NI – Non-attached Members

Powers of the European Parliament

The specific powers of the EP in making EU decisions vary with the context, but in terms of shaping the laws that put agricultural policy into practice, they have been quite limited. Up to the implementation of the Lisbon Treaty in December 2009 this comprised only the right to be consulted on draft legislation proposed by the Commission. By delaying its opinion the EP could hold up the process of legislation. Though being consulted meant the EP kept a constant watch on developments, the Commission could choose not to take the EP opinion into account by modifying the draft. In other words, the CAP, as we know it, is very largely the result of a legislative procedure in which the EP could only comment, the real power lying in the hands of the Council and the Commission.

In many other areas of policy the powers of the EP have been far greater, with rights to approve or reject some forms of legislation passed by the Council. It was not until the Treaty of Lisbon came into effect in December 2009 that the EP gained such powers in agriculture. It should be noted, however, that while these include a voice in setting up mechanisms that affect markets of agricultural commodities, they do not extend to adopting proposals from the Commission for fixing agricultural support prices, levies (on imports), aid to production and marketing (including to farmers operating in disadvantaged areas) and quantitative limitations (such as quotas) and on the fixing and allocation of fishing opportunities. With these exceptions, a procedure previously known as the 'co-decision procedure', now termed the 'ordinary legislative procedure', applies to agricultural legislation, so that the EP now has the power of co-decision. Under this, the Council cannot adopt a proposal that the Parliament has rejected (see Box 3.3). A compromise has to be brokered between the Council and the Parliament so that the Parliament can give its approval. The implication is that the EP now has far more power over legislation for agriculture than hitherto, equivalent to what it previously wielded over laws for the free movement of workers, the establishment of the internal market, technological research and development, the environment, consumer protection, education, culture and public health etc. How this greater participation by the only part of the EU system that is directly elected will be reflected in the nature of EU legislation will be of concern to many commentators, not least those who support this extension of what they see as the democratic principle in policy decision-making.

Extending this process to include both Council and Parliament, while increasing the democratic element in decisions, almost inevitably means that decisions will take more time to achieve. Before the 2007 Lisbon Treaty one argument for not extending the role of the EP to agricultural legislation had been that often it involved matters that were of immediate commercial concern to farmers and others involved with the agricultural industry. For example, a set of support prices agreed by the Council might take a long time to pass the further Parliamentary stages, during which period farmers would be subject to uncertainty (the EP might wish to make changes) and thus not be able to plan their production. There could be encouragement for speculators in commodity markets. However, this point has been overtaken by the shift in CAP support methods from the use of intervention in markets to a system of direct payments of pre-determined value where timing is somewhat less critical. The retention of the older system under the Lisbon Treaty for fixing agricultural prices, levies, aid and quantitative limitations reflects these concerns.

Another factor for not extending co-decision earlier to agricultural matters might have been the unwillingness of national politicians (in the form of the Council of agricultural ministers

---

Box 3.3 The European Parliament's role in the EU's 'ordinary' legislative procedure

The Commission submits a legislative proposal both to the Parliament and Council. At the 'first reading' Parliament adopts its position (which may include modifying the text) by majority vote. If the Council approves the Parliament's wording, using its own voting rules, then the act is adopted. If not, it adopts its own position (again using its own rules) and passes it back to Parliament, with explanations. The Commission also informs Parliament of its position on the matter.

At the 'second reading', the act is adopted if Parliament approves the Council's text or fails to take a decision. The Parliament may reject the Council's text by an absolute majority vote (in which case the legislation fails to become law) or modify it, adopting it again by absolute majority, and pass it back to the Council. (Absolute majorities imply more than 50 per cent of all possible votes, including absences and abstentions, whereas simple majorities only apply to numbers actually voting). The Commission gives its opinion once more. In line with the Council's voting rules, where the Commission does not accept the amendments to its text, the Council must act unanimously rather than by majority.

If, within three months of receiving Parliament's new text, the Council approves it, then it is adopted and becomes law. If it does not, then the Council President, with the agreement of the Parliament President, convenes the Conciliation Committee, composed of the Council and an equal number of MEPs (with the attendance of the Commission as a moderator). The committee draws up a joint text on the basis of the two positions. If within six weeks a common text cannot be agreed, then the legislation fails. If the committee approves the text, then the Council and Parliament (acting by simple majority in this 'third reading') must then approve the compromise text. If either fails to do so, the act is not adopted.

---

and European Council) to see power over decisions on the CAP (which remains a policy of central importance to the EU and commands a major share of expenditure) gravitate to the EP. This would imply shifts in the balance between EU and national government authority, and between the agricultural ministers and the EP, that were politically resented in some Member States. The fact that governments were willing to agree to the changes contained in the Lisbon Treaty implies that there has been a downward shift in the priority given to agriculture by Member States, with enlargement and the growth of other common policies carrying an increased weight of emphasis.

The third main area of EP power is that of budgetary approval. The EP acts as one arm of the 'budgetary authority' of the EU (the other being the Council), and the EP and Council interact in a way similar to the 'ordinary legislative procedure' to reach an agreed position. Consequently the EP has the authority to reject the draft budget (which includes spending on agriculture). The Lisbon Treaty gave the EP equal rights to those of the Council over all areas of the budget; up to 2009 the EP had relatively limited power over 'compulsory expenditure' (spending which is the inevitable consequence of the Treaty, accounting for some 70 per cent of the budget and largely made up of CAP expenditure) but more over 'non-compulsory expenditure' (such as social and regional funds, research and some administration costs).

In practice, it seems that so far the last of these (budgetary power) has been the most effective tool the EP has possessed, since failure to approve the budget causes administrative problems for the other EU institutions and their policies, including the CAP. However, in 1999 the threat of dismissing the entire Commission (over the issue of improper behaviour by one Commissioner that the EP was unable to displace) was sufficient to cause the whole Commission to resign. How the EP uses the additional powers remains to be seen.

3.2.4 The Economic and Social Committee (ECOSOC)

ECOSOC was established by the Treaty of Rome and must be consulted on specified areas of legislation (including agricultural legislation) and elsewhere if the Commission or Council thinks necessary. From 1972 it has been able to have a 'right of initiative' whereby it can bring matters which concern its members to the attention of the other institutions of the EU. It consists of 'councillors', representatives of special interest groups in the EU (Group I – employers and managers, Group II – workers and trade unions, Group III – various other interest groups covering small businesses and the self-employed, bankers, academics, consumers etc.). These people are nominated (not elected) for terms of four years by national governments, but are subject to approval by the Council. They are expected to serve in personal capacities and not as delegates for the bodies or nations from which they come. Farmers can be represented as part of both groups I and III.

ECOSOC is subdivided into sections responsible for particular fields of interest, including ones for agriculture, for regional development and for the protection of the environment (also covering public health and consumer affairs). ECOSOC has no statutory powers other than a right to be consulted on relevant legislation. As a non-elected body of experts, its opinions appear to be relatively free from political motivations and to be of quality, thus bringing influence to bear on the Council and Commission decisions indirectly.

3.2.5 The Court of Justice of the European Union (CJ)[3]

The Court of Justice of the EU is the supreme judicial authority on EU legislation. Based in Luxembourg, the Court consists of a group of 27 judges (including one from each Member State, though this is not mandatory), assisted by eight advocates-general. Judges are appointed for six years and elect a President from among themselves. For the most serious cases all judges may sit together, though subsets of them tackle many issues. Following powers given under the Single European Act and to reduce the workload, the Council set up the Court of First Instance to hear and determine cases falling under certain classes of action, including competition cases, with a right of appeal to the full Court. The Lisbon Treaty changed the court's name (the higher body was previously known as the European Court of Justice) and relabelled the Court of First Instance as the General Court.

In short, the CJ is concerned with the clarification and application of EU law – to ensure that the law is observed. Where there is only national legislation on an issue, the CJ holds no authority, though because of the increasingly complex relationship between national and EU legislation there may be a dispute about whether a particular case is covered by EU law or not.

Actions take two main forms. *Direct actions* involve disputes between two parties and the court has a normal judicial function. For example, the Commission may take action against a Member State for infringement of the relevant Treaty or legislation which flows from it, and the CJ can order the country to comply, and fine it for not doing so. Action can also be taken against EU institutions; on occasion, when the Council failed to set agricultural prices for a particular year, the Commission went to the Court to establish that the Council was failing in its responsibilities under the EEC Treaty, thereby empowering the Commission to take action on prices which it felt to be in the best interest of the EU. Member States, individuals and companies can also use the CJ.

Requests for *preliminary rulings*, the other main form, are made by national courts when the interpretation of application of EU law is unclear. These rulings form the main workload of the CJ and are binding on national courts. There is no higher authority on EU law than the CJ so there is no further appeals system.

3.2.6 Other European Union institutions

The European Court of Auditors is headed by one auditor from each Member State. Set up in 1977, its functions are, first, to perform the normal auditing roles of examining the accounts of all revenues and expenditures of the EU's institutions. It looks after the sound financial management of the EU by assisting the Council and EP in exercising their budgetary powers. However, it also carries out 'value for money' studies of the policies of the EU, so that not only are the funds absorbed by the policies properly accounted for, but that the objectives of the policy are scrutinised in relation to the resources they absorb. Reports have been made on hill farming, food aid, the disposal of the European butter surplus and so on. One (unpublished) report on the EU's Farm Accountancy Data Network (FADN) was highly critical of the system of collecting information from farms, and the report on the use of quotas in the milk sector concluded that the system did not meet its objectives of improving the balance between supply and demand in this sector and that some Member States had not implemented the scheme as intended. Among the EU institutions, this critical look at the performance of policy seems to be unusual.

The Committee of the Regions (CoR) (Brussels) was set up in 1994 under the Maastricht Treaty with responsibilities extended by the Amsterdam Treaty. Member States appoint representatives of regions and local authorities to serve for four-year periods of office. The Treaties require this Committee be consulted whenever new proposals are made in specified spheres (including education, culture, public health, and economic and social cohesion, employment policy, social policy, the environment, vocational training and transport) that have repercussions at regional or local levels. Agriculture is not on this list. Outside these areas, the Commission, Council and European Parliament have the option to consult the CoR on issues if they see important regional or local implications to a proposal. The CoR can also draw up an opinion on its own initiative, which enables it to put issues on the EU agenda. Though it is not directly relevant to the main instruments with which the CAP has operated, the increasing part played by the Structural Funds in rural areas suggests that it may become more important as policy is disaggregated to national and regional levels.

The European Investment Bank (EIB) is an institution with its own legal identity, established under the 1957 Treaty of Rome, which has as its board of governors, ministers nominated by Member States and a board of directors nominated by the Member States and the Commission. Its function is to finance infrastructure investment projects which contribute to the balanced development of the EU, mainly to regions in which the European Regional Development Fund is active. Its funds are contributed by Member States.[4] Associated with the EIB is the European Investment Fund, established in 1994 and concerned not with lending but with investing in venture capital and in guaranteeing loans, particularly for small and medium enterprises.

PART TWO – THE DECISION-MAKING PROCESS ON AGRICULTURAL POLICY

3.3 Stages in the decision-making process

As noted above, proposals for legislation (which are necessary for any form of EU action) can only come from the Commission. Three main types of legislation emerge from the decision-making process of the EU:

- **The Regulation** lays down rights and obligations that are binding in every respect and applicable in all Member States. It is implemented nationally as agreed collectively. An example is the Regulation adopted by the Council that enables EU funds to be spent on rural development over the period 2007–13 (Council Regulation 1698/2005). However, a Regulation can give the Member States the option of doing something (such as setting up a grant scheme to assist young farmers to enter the industry) without making the action compulsory.
- **The Directive** states an objective but leaves the means of implementation to national governments. This will mean that national legislation has to be enacted to enable the objective to be pursued. In the UK schemes of the early 1970s part-funded by the EU for the modernisation of farms, the provision of socio-economic advice (on non-farming occupations) and pre-pensions were all the result of Directives.
- **The Decision** is binding only to those mentioned, usually a Member State but also possibly an association, company or individual.

Both Regulations and Directives are published in the (daily) Official Journal of the European Communities (the OJ). The Decisions may appear in the OJ for information, but the official procedure is to notify the Permanent Representative of the particular Member State or the person or firm involved.

Before tackling the details of the process by which decisions are made on the legislation needed to bring agricultural policy into effect, it is helpful first to have an overview. Figure 3.2 outlines the decision-making process that applied to agricultural policy up to when the ratified Lisbon Treaty came into force (December 2009) and thus which has shaped most of the CAP as it now exists. In short, proposed legislation, drafted by the Commission, was sent to the European Parliament (EP) and the Economic and Social Committee for their 'opinions' which had to be considered by the Commission (though this did not necessarily lead to revisions in the proposals). Then the proposed Regulation was submitted to the Council for debate and acceptance by voting, a positive decision leading to the legislation being formally 'adopted'. In the case of agricultural legislation, once the Council adopted the Regulation and it was published in the Official Journal of the European Union in all the official languages, it immediately became law. This system (though without the need for the EP to express an opinion) is still in place for Commission proposals for fixing agricultural prices, levies, aid and quantitative limitations that form part of managing the market for agricultural commodities.[5]

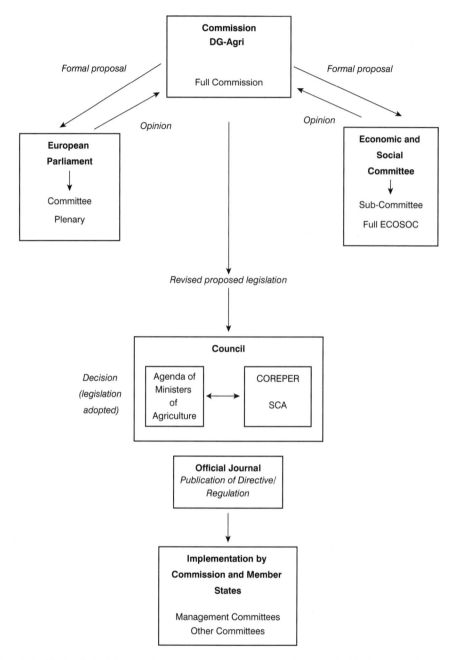

Figure 3.2 The basic decision-making process on proposals for agricultural legislation before December 2009

As noted above, since December 2009 the flows are rather different for agricultural legislation outside these exceptions, with a much greater role for the EP. Now the proposed text of legislation has to be agreed by both the EP and the Council, according to the steps outlined in Figure 3.3. With the EP starting the process by first considering the legal text drafted by the Commission (its 'first reading'), then passing it to the Council, there is the possibility of two rounds of exchange (the EP's 'second reading'). If a text cannot be found that is acceptable to both, a committee from both attempts to negotiate something that both can adopt (the EP's final approval being its 'third reading' of the legislation). If a compromise cannot be reached, the legislation fails to become law. As generally it is not in the interest of any party for this to happen, there will be considerable pressure for a conciliated outcome; on the assumption that there is a real need for policy action to benefit the EU as a whole that is captured in the Commission's proposals, neither Council ministers nor MEPs will want to be seen to be standing too resolutely in the way of reason.

Once proposed legislation has been adopted by both the Council and Parliament it is published as law in the Official Journal. The Commission then assumes responsibility for putting that law into effect. Member States will be required to set up mechanisms by which adopted policies can operate. For example, under the CAP Regulations each country needs to have a system for making subsidy payments to farmers, including checking on the validity of claims and avoiding fraud. If support is given to the prices received by farmers by actions such as buying into public intervention stores, national governments will be responsible for carrying this out.

Because understanding decision-taking is central to understanding the CAP, it is worth examining the various stages in greater detail. Some duplication of material is inevitable.

3.3.1 Initiation in the Commission

Suggestions for policy actions will come from a variety of sources, including pressure groups (such as farmers' unions and environmentalists), national governments, the EP, the other EU institutions and, not least, the Commission itself through its role as guardian of the Treaties and as needs emerge in the policies that it administers. In the past there was a regular annual process by which new support prices for agricultural commodities were proposed, though now the balance has shifted to longer-term actions (such as systems for setting up direct payments, or rural development schemes that typically last some 7 years). On such strategic developments it is common for the Commission to publish discussion papers drawing on the best available information and statistics and to hold conferences in order to publicise its thinking on issues and to stimulate public debate and gauge opinion of options; for example, relating to the shape of the CAP after 2013, a conference was held in 2009 and a Commission 'communication' issued in 2010 (*The CAP towards 2020: Meeting the food, natural resources and territorial challenges of the future*). Often pressure groups (such as COPA, the EU-level representative of farmers unions) will attempt to influence proposals by putting papers to the Commission, setting out its interpretation of the real policy needs and the steps that the Commission should take.

When the time comes to propose legislative texts for policy action, the relevant section of the Commission's DG-Agri will form an initial draft which will be discussed within the DG and with the agricultural Commissioner. Soundings will often be taken from national governments, other DGs, and independent experts in these early stages. It is also useful for

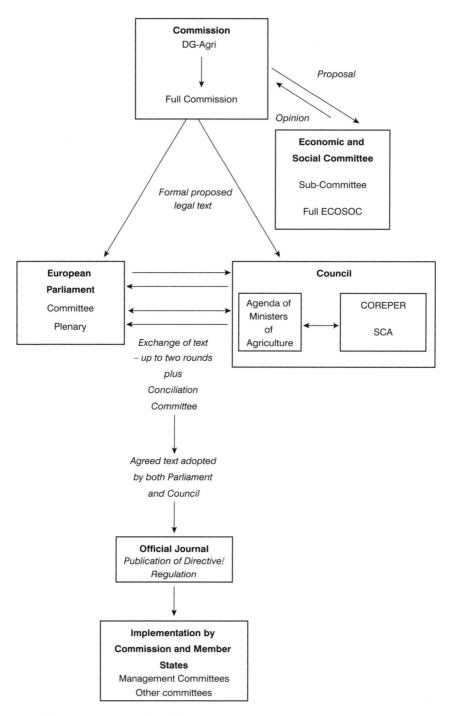

Figure 3.3 The basic agricultural decision-making process after December 2009 (excluding fixing agricultural prices, levies, aid and quantitative limitations)

Community-level pressure groups (of farmers, fertiliser manufacturers, the food industry, consumers etc.) to be drawn into discussion of draft legislation and their reactions assessed, as the rejection of a proposal here may indicate that it will also be unacceptable to the Council, since these same pressure groups and their national equivalents will be lobbying their national ministers at home.

After taking these soundings, DG-Agri will agree the text of a proposed Regulation with the Commissioner for agriculture and his *cabinet*. After scrutiny by the legal service to ensure that it is technically satisfactory as a draft law, it will be put up for consideration by the full Commission, either by placing it on the agenda of one of the Commission's regular meetings or by a written circulation procedure. If no objections are raised by other Commissioners (the *cabinets* will be influential in spotting these) then it is assumed that general agreement has been given by the entire Commission. If there are objections, discussion will take place until objections are resolved and the proposed Regulation is adopted (passed) unanimously, or if voting is necessary in a meeting of the full Commission, by simple majority. It then becomes the collective responsibility of the entire Commission (that is, individual Commissioners should not dissent from it, at least not in public). Minor proposals can have a simpler process, and power of approval can be delegated to a single Commissioner. The way that proposals emerge from the internal process in the Commission is illustrated in Figure 3.4.

The Commission proposal for a Regulation is then published in the Official Journal. This may engender reactions from within the Commission's other DGs and from interest groups concerned with these areas of policy. These will be noted by DG-Agri. The Commission may choose to modify its proposal or to leave it intact. The proposal will then be sent to the Council, which in the case of agricultural legislation is formed of the ministers responsible for agricultural departments in national governments, and the EP.

3.3.2 Procedure in the European Parliament on agriculture legislation

The European Parliament's role of co-decision on agricultural legislation only dates from December 2009, though it has been required to provide official opinions since the outset of the CAP.[6] As pointed out above, this extended role does not apply to fixing agricultural prices, levies, aid and quantitative limitations. A system of delegation to an agricultural specialist committee is in place. Initial consideration of the Commission's proposals for legislation is undertaken by the EP's Committee on Agriculture and Rural Development. If the Committee can accept the proposal without amendments, it can be passed back to the Commission as the EP's official response (the result of the EP's 'first reading' of the draft legislation). This is then fed to the Council for its first deliberation. The Committee may propose amendments, and the Commission may be asked to change the text, which it may be willing (or not) to do. In the event of at least one-tenth of the Members objecting to any particular amendment, the amendment will be put to a vote at the Committee's next meeting. A report and resolution is passed to the plenary session for voting.

When the Council has considered the EP's first reaction to the proposals and communicated the outcome, the specialist Committee debates the new text. It again makes a report on whether the text should be accepted, rejected or amended, and tables a resolution to be voted on by the plenary session, being adopted by absolute majority.

In the event of no agreement being reached on a text by the EP and the Council, the conciliation procedure is set in motion, with representatives from both forming a conciliation

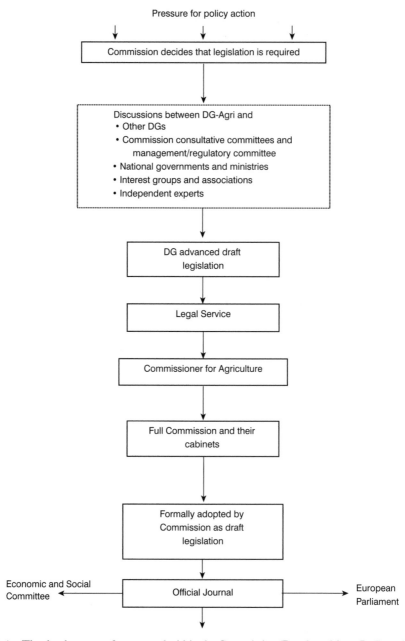

Figure 3.4 The development of a proposal within the Commission (Developed from R. Fennell (1987) *The Common Agricultural Policy of the European Communities*)

committee (see Box 3.3). Once a text has been worked out, this cannot be altered by the EP. The specialist agricultural committee is by-passed, and a resolution is voted on, by simple majority, by the EP's plenary session. If a majority is achieved, the legislation has been adopted; if not, it fails to become law.

This account of what happens in the EP is rather bald. It is rather too early to make the EP's procedure the subject of observations on its characteristics given to Council (see below) which reflect a half-century of activity. Furthermore, the balance between those parts of CAP decision-making in which the EP has the right of co-decision and that where it still has not (fixing agricultural support prices, levies, aid and quantitative limitations) has not yet emerged fully.

3.3.3 Procedures in the agriculture Council on legislation

When proposed agricultural legislation reaches the Council, its Secretariat will decide whether it should first be looked at by the COREPER or the SCA or both. If, on the basis of the views of the experts on these committees representing Member States, the proposed legislation is acceptable, agreement is given at this level. The item then appears as on the agenda of a subsequent full agricultural Council for routine formal adoption as an uncontested 'A' item, and the Regulation becomes law without further discussion by ministers. In effect, laws are made by agreement between civil servants acting on behalf of ministers. If an agreed position cannot be reached at the committee level, the item is put on the agenda (as a 'B' item) for discussion by the ministers who form the agricultural Council at a meeting at which the Commission will be represented. It is thus not surprising that publicity surrounds the contentious issues that dominate Council meetings; the things on which Member States can easily agree are settled earlier.

What goes on in the meetings of the agricultural Council is essentially undocumented since, before the changes made by the Lisbon Treaty, the public were not admitted and verbatim transcripts not published. Reliance had to be placed on leaks from those who were there. These were often sufficient to enable a picture to be built up which helped explain the rather unexpected outcome of some of these meetings and the ways in which what started out to be diametrically opposed views could turn into compromises which enabled European Union legislation on agriculture to go forward.[7]

First, there is the matter of voting in the Council. The weightings used and the votes for a qualified majority were given above. In principle, qualified majority voting can be used to decide on the acceptability of proposed legislation on most aspects of agricultural policy. In practice, things have worked out rather differently, because such a system is not necessarily the best at achieving what is in effect a joint goal of the rotating Presidency of the Council and of the Commission – the aim of enabling legislation to pass successfully through this stage of the decision-making process. Qualified majority rules are no help to either institution if they fail to result in a decision; failure to reach a qualified majority means that the proposals do not progress, necessitating a time-consuming rethink of the policy.

It is also important to recall that, while the voting rules allow qualified majorities for the approval of Commission proposals on agricultural legislation, there is a requirement that *changes* to Commission proposals (as compared to their approval or rejection) require unanimity. In the decision-making process that existed up to December 2009, and still does for the treatment of proposals from the Commission on agricultural support prices, aids and quantitative restrictions, discussion in the agriculture Council could result in the Commission being asked to modify its proposals, which it might do, allowing majority voting. If the Commission was *not* willing (and this has often been the case) unanimity rules applied and efforts among Member States were directed at achieving this by reaching a solution that all the ministers can support.

In reality, many of the decisions by the agricultural Council, particularly those in the past on support prices for agricultural commodities, have covered a bundle of issues and have been political compromises of national interests. Given the rules on voting (and in any bargaining situation the rules are very important), a need for unanimity to modify Commission proposals would be expected to lengthen greatly the time needed to reach agreement. However, the ability to trade-off items in an overall package added flexibility. The steps to this position of unanimous acceptance of a package could involve hard bargaining and brinkmanship, since an objection by one Member State, even the smallest, could prevent agreement. 'Log-rolling' is the term describing where ministers side with each other in return for a similar favour later; political actors believe that if they restrict their competitive behaviour, other actors will do so too, a pattern similar to that found in oligopoly in a market economy. Alliances can be forged between countries which have no direct interest in particular policies; for example, country X which grew no wine but had many sheep could offer not to vote against a part of the proposal which mentioned wine if country Y, which had virtually no sheep but a lot of vineyards, would undertake to support a change to the sheep regime which X would have liked. Essentially, what was being forged were alliances, usually temporary, and these must have carried some reward for each member.

Such an *ad hoc* process was likely to result in a bundle of legislation which departed substantially from what the Commission considered was the best policy. Some of the compromises involved changes in the proposed legislation, the full implications of which were impossible to foresee without careful analysis and recourse to models used for their calculation. At the end of a long meeting, often extending far into the night, and with a deadline for a decision dictated by some budgetary or related procedural reason, such careful consideration was impossible. Consequently, any bad policy mistakes needed to be corrected in the next round of legislation.[8] Though 'log-rolling' and deadline-meeting probably play a smaller part in decisions on agricultural policy now than when the CAP was dominated by the annual setting of support prices, they have left a legacy that has to be unpicked by the process of reform.

A case could be made that the system of voting has produced a general tendency for increases in spending under the CAP, as Member States which were net beneficiaries from the European Union budget usually could outvote the net payers. And because costs are put against the overall budget rather than the contributions to the budget made by individual countries (see Financial Solidarity, mentioned in Chapter 2), agricultural ministers may have favoured forms of support which predominantly benefited their own farmers, knowing that the costs were borne disproportionately by other countries. As in a restaurant, there will be an incentive to order the most expensive dishes if the bill is to be split equally among the diners, since some of the burden of paying is passed to those who choose the cheaper dishes. Though such tendencies were talked about in the early days of the CAP, there is no hard evidence for such behaviour in the recent past.

3.3.4 Decision-making delegated from the Council

For certain types of legislation, such as details of implementing rural development schemes, the agricultural Council has delegated responsibility to the Commission. Much of the detail of policy implementation is dealt with in this way and covered by Commission Regulations. The Commission is also empowered to take detailed decisions on short-term matters (such as on the level of export subsidies, that might be varied daily) within general frameworks and rules set by the Council. Also some powers are passed down to Management and Regulatory Committees, chaired by the Commission, on which national Member States are represented. Decisions on legislation proposed by the Commission are taken by votes, using the same weights as in the Council. Depending on the number of votes in favour, a 'favourable opinion' or an 'unfavourable opinion' is possible, with a 'no opinion', falling between these two. An unfavourable opinion in a Management Committee can be overturned by the Council. When a Regulatory Committee fails to reach a favourable opinion, a more complex system involving the Council operates, but the Commission cannot take a decision, even a provisional one, without the involvement of the Council. Figure 3.5 shows what happens at committee level.

3.4 Influences on policies and decision-making – the role of farmer pressure groups

The EU institutions described above are major actors on the stage when it comes to agricultural policy. However, their views of the problems that exist (problem formulation) and their decisions on the means by which policy should attempt to address them (policy formulation and implementation) are not taken in isolation (see Chapter 1 on stages in the policy process). They are influenced by other institutions and interest groups. The structure of the Commission, Parliament and Council means that there are good opportunities for ideas and opinions to be fed in by outside bodies; thus the policy-making process itself is not a closed system but one which is quite permeable to inputs from other actor-organisations within the policy network. It can be argued that, among these other actors, one group – the unions representing farmers – carry such influence in determining the shape of policy (at least in the past) that they really form part of the policy community, the core decision-making group. It is appropriate to consider here how their power arose, how it was used, and why it appears to be waning.

There is plenty of evidence suggesting *prime facie* that farmers and groups acting on their behalf have managed to influence the policy-making process strongly in their own interest. Agricultural policy is often criticised for being synonymous with policy *for* farmers rather than a policy *about* agriculture conducted for the benefit of society in general. Similarly, ministries *of* agriculture frequently are seen, and see themselves, as ministries *for* farmers. Even the bureaucrats in these departments appear to have some proprietorial interest in farming. Though the CAP has a number of objectives, and the interests of consumers is mentioned specifically (Chapter 2), in practice it is primarily directed at supporting the standard of living of farmers. When reform of the CAP is contemplated for the benefit of society at large, it is often blocked on the grounds of the harm it might do to the incomes of farmers. In some countries (such as France) governments that pursue policy changes which appear to diminish the fortunes of the farming community find themselves paying a large political price in terms of economic and social disruption.

How can the influence of such a small group on the process of policy-making be so large? How do they bring their influence to bear? Factors that help explain the situation include history. In the past farmers may have been very important to governments keen to expand domestic food production, and there is likely to be residue in the minds of politicians (in a sense 'farmers are important now because they were always important'). Once a system of financial support is in place, it can be difficult to demolish it because of objections from beneficiaries, so today's pattern of expenditure on agriculture is shaped by history – another

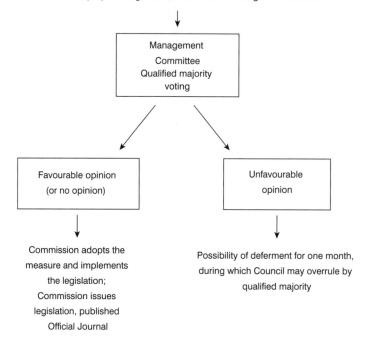

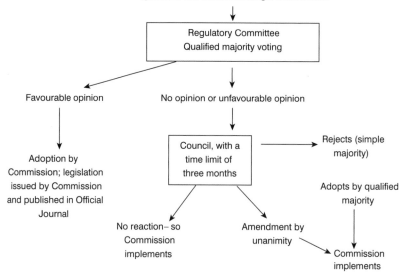

Figure 3.5   The legislative process within Committees

example of path-dependency (see Chapter 12). Today their prominence is also linked with the fact that, as occupiers of much of the land area, they are important to the delivery of environmental objectives, and receive much financial support to do so (see Chapter 8). Another factor is the role of farmers in political systems. Though the votes exercised by farmers and their families are not numerous when compared to the total in most Member States, nevertheless in some countries (for example, Germany) the characteristics of the electoral system and tradition of coalition governments mean that the farming vote may be critical in a few key constituencies; change here could mean a change of minister and perhaps of government. In such a situation, the national agricultural minister in the Council will be keen to protect the interests of his farmers, which may mean giving support for all farmers. Allied to this, in some countries farmers and landowners may be disproportionately important in the mechanisms of particular political parties; in the UK, farmers have been prominent committee members of the local Conservative Party machine in rural areas, ensuring that their interests are acknowledged among senior politicians. Ministers of agriculture often have been farmers and landowners or have had close family links with the land, so that personal and political motives become mixed.

But without doubt a major reason for the prominence of agriculture within current EU policies is the effectiveness of the farmers' unions widely recognised as having been some of the most effective of EU pressure groups. They operate both nationally and through the EU-level associations of national unions, COPA (the Committee of Professional Agricultural Organisations in the EU). Officially the Commission only deals with recognised EU groups, not with their national members. A similar two-level structure is found in other interest groups involved in the food chain, including those representing suppliers of inputs (such as fertilisers), food processors and distributors, and consumers. In the earlier years of the CAP, farmers' pressure groups exercised great power. However, their grip over the policy agenda has loosened. In part this reflects the emergence of situations in which pressure cannot achieve results. For example, when faced with a binding EU balanced budget rule or international trade agreement rules, both of which have applied since the early 1990s, the opportunities for farmers' pressure groups to further the interests of their members by opposing CAP reform are severely constrained – the counter-forces have been simply too strong. This decline in influence has also coincided with the growing awareness that the support of farm production does not deliver the environmental and social objectives that are increasingly important to the rationale for the CAP. Other forms of support, given to people who are not farmers, may have to be considered. In short, the dominant ideology in the EU towards agricultural policy has shifted. Nevertheless, pressure groups acting on behalf of farmers, landowners and related parts of the food chain are far from being a spent force.

Before turning to how pressure groups attempt to influence decisions it is worth reviewing the forces behind their establishment and continued existence. Changes here help explain today's relatively diminished influence of farmers' unions within the EU.

3.4.1 The formation and maintenance of pressure groups

Whether or not a pressure group is formed is dependent on a number of factors, important among which are the extent to which proposed policy change affects the potential members, and on how easy it is to organise. (An *interest group* shares a common interest, such as steam traction engines societies or stamp collecting circles; a *pressure group* takes a more active role in attempting to influence a decision, often both pointing out a problem and offering solutions that, if adopted for public action, will benefit their members). Only a brief explanation can be offered here. Nevertheless, this should be sufficient to demonstrate that an understanding of their existence and mode of operation is important in explaining agricultural policy.

Farmers typically respond vigorously to proposals which affect them negatively. Most have a lot to lose. In the long-term cost–price squeeze that they face, and increasing pressure on incomes and the need to restructure, their efforts to make a living will be frustrated. Many individuals cannot easily transfer their resources from agriculture to other activities because of factors such as age, education and lack of appropriate skills (their 'exit' is blocked), and there is often a strong intrinsic bond with land and farming. The consequence is strong political pressure ('voice'). This combination of 'exit' and 'voice' will be experienced especially when there is a realistic threat that policy reform will undermine the existing level of support. Farmers will realise that they can achieve more by acting together than as individuals and will band together as groups who share common interests.

Against the potential benefits of membership must be set the costs, since pressure groups will only function if the perceived benefits for the individual members are greater than the costs. The largest farmers with most to lose find it worthwhile to spend considerable time, effort and money in this activity (described in economic theory as 'rent-protection'); typically farmers' unions are set up through the efforts of the proprietors of large farming concerns and the administrations of farmers' unions are dominated by them, though they may rely heavily on arguments based on the impact on small farms for which greater public and political sympathy can usually be elicited. These farmers alone would see it worth their time and expenditure to try to influence policy; these are termed the 'privileged' (sub-)group and are in a position to offer incentives (such as membership fees scaled so that smaller farmers pay less) to increase the coverage of the group, and hence its effectiveness. Without this encouragement and incentive structure the smaller farmer might see himself too small to achieve any impact and thus would normally do nothing; he would form part of the 'latent' (sub-)group in the membership.

Once set up, acting collectively as an organisation to obtain information on the nature of proposed changes and assessing their impact reduces the costs for each individual, swinging the balance between the costs and benefits of membership in favour of keeping the pressure group in existence; in the UK, the NFU headquarters regularly gives briefings to its area representatives on policy proposals which are then passed on to members. Costs of maintaining a pressure group can be lowered by the group running a related business (such as insurance) using the same network of communications. This also keeps the officials and members in regular contact and helps build loyalty to the organisation, since leaving will imply loss of insurance cover and the need to seek alternative arrangements. This helps to reduce the 'free-rider' problem; farmers who do not belong to the pressure group or contribute to the costs of its operations but who nevertheless benefit from the changes to agricultural policy it secures. In this circumstance there will be a tendency to opt out of paying for membership, but the insurance cover link ensures the payment of the basic membership fee as a part of the package.

Pressure groups will be more successful if their membership is relatively homogeneous and if their coverage of the potential membership is high. Farmers' organisations will have difficulty in representing both cereal producers and livestock rearers in discussions over proposals to change the price of cereals because of conflicting interests. Differences in farm size, tenure, political affiliation and religion within the membership will complicate the task of a pressure group, and break-up may occur. Enlargement of the EU has increased the range of types of farmer whose interests have to be represented by COPA, so that it can no longer speak with a single clear voice.

Nevertheless, pressure groups of farmers are far easier to organise and maintain than, for example, pressure groups of consumers because the potential benefits (such as avoiding the costs of policy change) are greater than the costs to the farmer, they are less numerous (so that the costs of communicating within the group is less), and the group is relatively homogeneous. Consumers, on the other hand, might expect small amounts of individual benefit to flow from membership of a pressure group to reform agricultural policy, so that, relative to the costs incurred, membership of consumer groups is generally not attractive. This suggests that most will fall into the 'latent' category, so that the coverage of consumers by pressure groups acting on their behalf is small. Consumers are also a very heterogeneous group and, because of the complexity of the agricultural policies they face, will not necessarily have coherent and well-focused opinions, so that it is not always clear in which direction the pressure group should try to influence decisions. In short, in situations where, overall, society would benefit from a change of policy which improved the lot of the consumer at the expense of the farmer, it is unlikely that pressure group action will cause reform in this direction.

3.4.2 Relationships between pressure groups and decision-makers

As noted in Chapter 1, a pluralist view of the way that pressure groups operate is that all sections of society which wish to influence policy are free to set up groups to act on their behalf. These will compete for the ear of the decision-makers and policy will be the product of this competition between interests. Some groups will have more power than others, and this will depend on the social position of the group (landed gentry with family connections in parliament are more likely to be listened to than the underclass of the permanently unemployed), the extent to which it is organised and the skills and qualifications of the leaders (good information and slick presentation will often win over well-meaning incompetence, even if the latter holds the stronger case), the size of the organisation, the level of finances and the degree of mobilisation (is everyone affected lined up behind this group?). Where no pressure group exists to represent a particular fraction of society, policy-makers will perhaps encourage one to be set up (users or consumer groups, for example) or will be aware that there is such a gap and will make allowances. Perhaps other departments in the administration will take on the role of representatives of non-represented sections (such as health departments representing the consumer interest in agricultural food scares).

An alternative view of pressure groups is that of corporatism. This is where the pressure group is taken into the policy-making circle (that is they are incorporated into it), forms a close liaison with the state machinery and, as a trade-off, finds itself partly responsible for implementing the policy which it helped to design. Where a single union represents farmers and the union is strong, the interests of both government and pressure group can be served by this close alliance. Consultation by the policy-makers with 'the industry' in the form of farmers' groups may give enough of a feel as to whether their proposals are workable. Farmers' unions who agree to policy initiatives will be expected to exercise control over their members to secure compliance with the policies (acceptance of negotiated agreements, not to criticise the results and to contain the objections which some of its members may have). The pressure group will be able to introduce ideas into policy proposals early (experience suggests that this results in a greater likelihood of the ideas taking root and being applied) and they will be well placed to bring influence to bear throughout the stages of the policy process.

Which pressure groups are let into the circle (the 'policy community') which determines the policy agenda will depend on the government, and its decision will reflect the basic ideology operating at the time. If the approach, attitudes and proposals of a pressure group match those of the government, the group is more likely to be let in. If farmers' unions have managed to persuade policy-makers that farmers are economically vital to the welfare of the nation and that other aspects of the rural economy and rural land use are insignificant, then only the farmers' representatives will be let into the circle. Consumer groups, environmentalists and so on will be left out and their protestations at the policies which are being pursued will fall on deaf ears. If, however, circumstances change and the vital nature of agriculture to the nation starts to be questioned (for example, when food shortages start to change into food surpluses) and others are eventually successful in persuading governments that there are real environmental problems or whatever, the power of the farmer representatives will be undermined and other pressure groups may find themselves being included in the agenda-setting group.

In CAP policy-making, while the representatives of farmers (in the form of COPA) have regularly and frequently consulted with the Commission, there has not been a similar level of contact with BEUC, the consumers' group. However, the influence of COPA seems to have declined markedly. Explanatory factors include the broadening of policy CAP objectives to include environmental and social aims (particularly under the CAP's rural development Pillar 2), recognition that farmers' unions cannot adequately reflect the diversity of EU agriculture (which includes not only family farms run on a 'professional' basis but also hobby farms and large corporate units), that farming is usually a minor activity in rural areas, and that other interests (environmental, social, cultural, animal welfare etc.) need to be publicly acknowledged and listened to. A reflection of this is that some EU environmental pressure groups (including EU-based sections of Friends of the Earth and the World Wide Fund for Nature) have received payments from EU funds where the Commission felt that the interests of the organisation corresponded with what the EU was attempting to achieve and where they provided a mechanism for important information gathering.

The role of pressure groups should not be overstated. Frequently governments develop policy for reasons of their own and not as the response to pressure groups. Certainly the European Commission, when proposing policy, is to some extent acting independently to implement the objectives stated or implied in the Treaty of Rome and subsequent legislation. Sometimes actions are taken that happen to do what pressure groups want, but for their own motive rather than through pressure.

3.4.3 Exercising influence

Pressure groups can bring their influence to bear in a variety of ways, and the method used will reflect the stages through which legislation passes. The procedure once adopted by COPA is instructive (see Figure 3.6). This shifted the point of pressure to the stage at which crucial decisions were being taken. Though the details have now changed (importantly, the additional responsibility given to the European Parliament), the principle is of universal validity.

At the early phase, when the legislation was being proposed and drafted, it was important to bring pressure on the Commission. COPA was a member of the Commission's

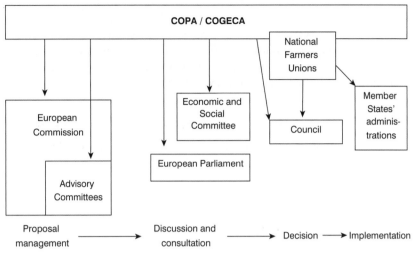

Figure 3.6 Paths used by COPA to influence agricultural policy decisions (Source: after a COPA briefing paper 1993)

Advisory Committees set up as a forum in which the various interested parties could discuss proposals. In addition, the open-door attitude of the Commission meant that there could be a network of contacts between staff of the pressure groups and their equivalents in the Commission hierarchy, ranging from the presidium of COPA meeting the Commissioner for agriculture to the exchange of letters, documents and phone calls further down the staff ladder. In these discussions the consequences of proposed policy changes for the agricultural industry could be articulated in terms which highlighted the interests of farmers and spelt out the wider consequences (social, environmental, political), again in a partial way which was intended to steer decisions in the interest of farmers. Aspects of changes which were beneficial to farmers would not be mentioned or were played down. Guidance could be offered to administrators on what options were available in a way that steered them towards the mechanisms which operated to the greatest favour of farmers. Once the Commission was agreed on a proposal the focus of the pressure group's attention switched to the European Parliament, its members, committees and secretariat, and to the Economic and Social Committee (on which farmers were represented). After these institutions had given opinions, COPA would, through its contacts in the Commission, urge acceptance of changes contained in the opinions which were to the advantage of its members. Next, the pressure group tried to influence the Council (of Ministers) in both direct and indirect ways. Papers might be sent to the Council and meeting sought with its President or the whole Council, though the main way in which this body was influenced seems to have been by the national members of EU institutions lobbying their individual ministers. Finally, again through national unions, the governments of individual Member States could be alerted to the flexibility that might exist within the legislation for alternative interpretations and ways of application that might be to the particular advantage of their farmers (such as the choice of support mechanism).

Clearly, following the application of the 'ordinary legislative procedure' to agricultural decision-making from December 2009, the details of how pressure groups can bring their influence to bear has changed from the above example. More opportunities have arisen to lobby the Parliament and, especially, the MEPs who form its specialist committee on agriculture and rural development. The Committee of the Regions might be another route on issues on which it has to be consulted. However, the essential message remains the same; exercising influence is an activity that explores all potential opportunities and shifts its focus as the decision-making moves through its various stages.

3.5 Characteristics of agricultural decision-making

Finally in this chapter, what we have seen so far on the structure of CAP decision-making enables a number of observations to be made that concern the outcome of those decisions.

3.5.1 Policy – a process through time

Policy rarely takes the form of a one-off activity, after which the policy problem is solved. This is especially true for agricultural policy in the EU, where for most of the last 50 years policy has operated continuously. For the most expensive parts of the CAP (that now constitute Pillar I) there has been no termination date or strategy for succession (replacement of the policy), though there has been evolution from the support of commodity prices, then to forms of direct payments based on production and now to the (decoupled) Single Payment Scheme (see Chapter 6). Only in the relatively small area of rural development is there a system of funding that runs for a given period (seven years at a time), after which the policies and schemes that put them into practice have to be renewed and refinanced. When policies have no built-in end the policy decisions of today are particularly dependent on the policy decisions taken in previous years, and today's decisions carry implications for what follows. As was pointed out earlier, many of the actions seen in the CAP (such as the introduction of quotas in the milk sector, and set-aside schemes for cereals) can be interpreted as attempts to correct, or at least counter, the results of previous policy.

Although policy may be a process though time, this may not have much sense of direction. In the past the major CAP decisions were taken by ministers on an annual basis – the yearly determination of the support prices for agricultural commodities. In the fluster of reaching compromise agreements on prices there were bound to be loose ends, but remaining problems and side effects of policy could be dealt with the next year. Short-term agreements do not necessarily add up to a coherent long-term policy. Though there was general agreement on the direction in which the structure of farming should change and some structural adjustment policies were in operation, these were minor in terms of spending. Since the mid–1990s there has been a welcome general move towards longer-term planning.

The more general lesson is that we cannot understand the present state of the CAP unless we are aware how we got here – history matters (see Chapter 12).

3.5.2 A bureaucratic and political process

It is an elementary but none-the-less critical observation that, in the sort of society that exists in the EU (liberal democracies with market-based economies), there is no omniscient central authority that knows the full extent of the problems that exist and which organises the appropriate actions to tackle them from the wide range of possible alternatives. If this were true, this rational actor (who might be a beneficent dictator) would be able to balance all the economic, social and environmental objectives of policy in a perfect way and we hardly need be concerned with the way that this was achieved.

Rather, in the EU, the policies that emerge are the result of the actions of individuals and organisations, each bringing their own sets of values and objectives which become mixed with the underlying 'real' policy problems and condition their responses to them. For example, a DG of the Commission, in addition to the issues of the sector for which it is responsible, will also see an expansion of its budget as a goal to be pushed for, since control of more funds means greater power and prestige both for the department and for the personnel who run it. Departments will look for ways of expanding the policies they control, perhaps to the extent of finding 'problems' where none exist. Politicians will be looking for policies which will enable them to be re-elected, optimising the number of votes these policies can attract, even if they know that these are expensive and cannot be maintained. Appealing to the sensitivity of the public on issues such as preserving family farming or a high degree of self-sufficiency in food supply may win votes, even if the rationale of such actions is questionable. Consequently the outcome may be very different from what the perfectly informed and all-wise beneficent dictator might devise. In this real world we need to use various aspects of public choice theory to explain the outcome, an approach which takes on board the fact that policy-making involves many individuals and organisations pursuing their own ends, which may or may not lead to the implementation of policies which are effective at tackling the underlying 'real' problems. It is clearly wrong to assume that the democratic political process works perfectly as a way of signalling the presence of problems and as a way of prioritising and balancing competing problems.

On the demand side of policy, for voters to gain information and signal their desires to politicians will involve them expending time, energy and money, and for many these costs will outweigh the value which the individual attaches to the benefits from policy action. On the supply side of policy, politicians and public servants will have to judge whether any action is worth their effort. The instigators of policy and the people who make the decisions on behalf of society may not share the same ideas about what constitutes a problem or what should be done about it, so there can be frustration at what appears to be inaction ('Why can't someone do something about it') or unfair action ('Why is there support for farmers and not support for small shop-keepers in financial difficulties?'). Understanding policy has to take account of the bureaucratic and political processes which the making of policy decisions involves in the real world.

3.5.3 Policy factoring and power fragmentation

No one part of the bureaucratic and political machine can deal with all the problems over which action is thought necessary. Policy is therefore subdivided (or factored) to make it manageable so that, for example, agricultural ministries, ministers and DGs of the Commission specialise in dealing with agricultural problems. This also means that power to act is broken up between departments. In this situation, each constituent organisation views problems from its own perspective and has its own priorities, with a consequential tendency to only look at parts of problems and to lose sight of the whole. A good example is the staff who are primarily concerned with managing the markets of particular agricultural commodities; they seem often to disregard the higher aims of the CAP. Also, where an area of policy straddles the responsibilities of several parts of the administration, there is a tendency for this to be neglected. Rural development is a good example; before the *Agenda 2000* reform of the CAP it was split between agricultural policy, regional policy and environmental policy, with relatively small quantities of resources devoted to it. Since *Agenda 2000* the primary responsibility has been given more overtly to DG-Agri and rural development now forms a core activity of the CAP (its Pillar 2),

3.5.4 Sectoral isolation

It is clear that decisions about the policy for agriculture are made primarily by people and institutions that have a particular concern with this industry. What is put on the policy agenda and the outcome of deliberations has been controlled by a 'policy community' (or 'agricultural establishment') consisting of civil servants in agricultural parts of the European Commission and governments of Member States, national ministers of agriculture (who also have tended to have been farmers or landowners), and the representatives of farmers. As noted above until relatively recently, this policy community did not extend to other interest groups (representing the interests of consumers, environmentalists, other industries) and of other parts of government with legitimate interests in agricultural policy. Conflicts and trade-offs with other goals looked after by other parts of the administration tended to be ignored or given little weight.

This isolation is breaking down. What goes on in agricultural policy is now heavily influenced by external factors such as budgetary pressure and international trade rules, and it is hard to act in isolation in such circumstances. There is also recognition among politicians that there are now few votes to be gained by supporting agriculture (from those in the industry and those who think that support is a good thing) and many more in putting forward 'green' policies. Other actors are being allowed to appear on the policy stage – to shift from simply being part of the 'policy network' to becoming part of the 'policy community' that actually draws up the policy agenda. However, the former strength of the agricultural establishment is by no means fully dissipated.

3.5.5 Policy lags and administrative inertia

As noted above, policy is a process that extends over time. While the problems involving EU agriculture have changed, the basic shape of the CAP has not, though there has been some evolution since the late 1990s. Concerns about an adequate food supply and a fair standard of living for farm families do not carry the weight that they did in the CAP's early years. The problems faced today are much more to do with the natural environment in rural areas, the appearance of the countryside, food quality, and the social and economic difficulties faced by residents of rural areas, of which farmers only comprise a small and decreasing fraction (see Chapter 2).

Why does the policy agenda tend not to adjust while problems change? Part of the explanation is that any intervention builds up vested interests among beneficiaries that will be difficult to erode. For example, if farmers have become used to receiving subsidies, they will resist attempts to take them away as their incomes are likely to suffer. Politicians may not wish to challenge them, even if a net benefit to society could be demonstrated, because to do so might undermine their power base.

Another explanation is that any bureaucracy finds change inconvenient. Once a system or standard procedure has been set up, it is usually easier to keep it running than to change, since this results in a cost in terms of time and other resources to learn how to manage new policies and instruments. The larger the number of people who have to be consulted in any change, the greater the cost and therefore the stronger the preference for maintaining the *status quo*. Change also implies uncertainty, and bureaucracies are by nature risk-averse. Change will also often mean that parts of the administration find their resources reduced, and this will run counter to the interest of the institutions under threat; they will therefore oppose the policy change. The personal and professional careers of bureaucrats, especially those with most power near the tops of organisations, will be frequently strongly linked with the fortunes of their departments, so a reduction in institutional power is seen as a personal threat to be opposed. Often the position which an administrator holds will govern his attitude to a particular policy issue (encapsulated in the jibe 'where you stand is where you sit').

3.5.6 An incremental approach to change

Given the characteristics of the institutions which administer policy, and the fact that policy is linked in time, it is not surprising that, when problems change, the response in the policy process tends to represent only small changes on what has gone on before. This *incrementalist approach* is relatively low-risk (assuming that previous policy has been working relatively smoothly) and involves little alteration in the procedures operated by administrations. An example was the annual tinkering with support prices for farm commodities in the period before the CAP reforms of 1992 that left intact the basic market intervention mechanisms. This approach may end up with the policies being no longer appropriate to the real problems which have emerged and with the administration only being prepared to consider incremental changes rather than a radical revision of policies, which the situation demands.

3.5.7 Crises ease radical changes

The history of the CAP is punctuated by crises, often of a budgetary sort (when the continuation of existing policies have threatened to take CAP costs beyond their permitted limits) but also where agriculture has got in the way of the achievement of urgent higher level EU goals (such as reaching international trade agreements or the political aim of enlarging the EU). Crises can be a threat to the *status quo* of the institutions involved in agricultural policy-making. These are the times at which radical revisions in both policies and the administrations which run them are contemplated.

A budgetary crisis in agriculture causes other parts of the public service, especially budgetary authorities, to take an interest in agricultural policy matters. Normally these other departments will be content to leave agricultural policy matters to the agricultural 'specialists'. A budgetary crisis in agriculture, however, is a threat to non-agricultural departments as their own programmes in other policy areas may be endangered (more for agriculture means less for social policy spending etc.). These unfamiliar departments start to become actors on the agricultural policy-making stage. There may be talk of integrating agricultural policy with other policies (general social policy on poverty, since why should farmers have a policy special to themselves?) and amalgamating the agricultural DG with others (forming a part of a general administration for industry, or a new regional department for rural areas of which agriculture would only be a part?). Though some civil servants and ministers may see such developments as new career opportunities, and therefore to be supported, on balance the reaction is more likely to be one of resistance, accompanied by an attempt to salvage as much of the present arrangement as possible. From an administration's viewpoint, crises are therefore unwelcome. So if a radical reform of policy will avoid a catastrophic crisis, it should be considered seriously.

Unfortunately, the CAP history shows that when crises have threatened, the declaration of schemes for reform have usually been accompanied by an increase in the funds available, often cloaked as necessary to overcome the short-term problem but, in effect, making more resources available on a permanent basis and therefore dissipating the need for change.

Many of the features of agricultural policy-making will be recognised as highly relevant when, in Chapter 12, we look at the history of the CAP and the various attempts at its reform. They are instrumental in explaining the slowness and ineffectiveness of such changes as have been introduced. Part of the continuing problems associated with the CAP are thus not the result of deliberate obstruction but rather the outcome of the process of decision-making and of the structure of the institutions that are involved in it.

Further reading

Recent information on the workings of the EU institutions and the process of decision-making is available on the website of the institutions (www.europa.eu.int). The views from the Commission and Parliament are somewhat contrasting.

Addresses of relevance include the following (all have the prefix http://):

consilium.europa.eu/ (Council)

ec.europa.eu/ (Commission)

europarl.europa.eu/ (European Parliament)

curia.europa.eu (Court of Justice)

eca.europa.eu (Court of Auditors)

eesc.europa.eu (Economic and Social Committee)

cor.europa.eu (Committee of the Regions)

See also

AgraEurope (regularly updated) *CAP Monitor* (introductory sections).

Averyt. W. (1977) *Agropolitics in the European Community: Interest Groups and the CAP.* Preager, New York.

Fennell, R. (1987) *The Common Agricultural Policy of the European Community.* 2nd edition. BSP Professional Books, Wageningen

Hill, M. (1997) *The Policy Process in the Modern State.* Prentice Hall/Harvester Wheatsheaf, London

Kunst, G. (2010) 'EU institutions and decision-making process'. Chapter 2 in Oskam, A., Meester, G. and Silvis, H. *EU Policy for Agriculture, Food and Rural Areas.* Wageningen Academic Publishers, Wageningen.

Meester, G. and van der Zee, F. (1993) 'EC decision-making, institutions and the Common Agricultural Policy', *European Review of Agricultural Economics*, 20 (3), 131–50.

Moyer, H. W. and Josling, T. E. (1990) *Agricultural Policy Reform: Politics and Process in the EC and USA.* Harvester Wheatsheaf, London.

Nello, S.S. (1984) 'An application of public choice theory and the question of CAP reform', *European Review of Agricultural Economics*, 11 (3), 261–83.

Petit, M. (1985) *Determinants of Agricultural Policies in the United States and the European Community.* Research Report 51. International Food Policy Research Institute, Washington, DC.

Robert Schuman Foundation (2007) 'The Lisbon Treaty: 10 easy-to-read fact sheets'. December 2007. Online at www.robert-schuman.eu.

Stocker, T. (1983) 'Pressures on policy formation'. In Burns, J., MacInerny, J. and Swinbank, A. (eds) *The Food Industry: Economics and Policies.* Butterworth-Heineman, London.

Swinbank, A. (1989) 'The Common Agricultural Policy and the politics of European decision making', *Journal of Common Market Studies*, 27 (4), 303–22.

Swinbank, A. (1997). 'The CAP decision-making process'. In Ritson, C. and Harvey, D. R. *The Common Agricultural Policy*, CAB International, Wallingford.

Tracy, M. (1993) *Food and Agriculture in a Market Economy: An Introduction to Theory, Practice and Policy.* APS, La Hutte, Belgium.

Tracy, M. (1996) *Agricultural Policy in the European Union and Other Market Economies.* APS, La Hutte, Belgium.

Wallace, H. and Wallace, W. (1997) *Policy-Making in the European Union.* Oxford University Press, Oxford.

Wilson, G.K. (1977) *Special Interests and Policymaking.* Wiley, London.

Winters, L. A. (1987) 'The political economy of the agricultural policy of industrial countries', *European Review of Agricultural Economics*, 14 (3), 285–304.

Winters, L. A. (1993) 'The political economy of industrial countries' agricultural policies'. In Rayner, A. J. and Colman, D. (eds) *Current Issues in Agricultural Economics*. Macmillan, London.

4

EVIDENCE-BASED POLICY

Information and statistics for policy decisions

Key topics

- Types of evidence, and the role of statistics.
- Information systems and data systems.
- Gaps in the evidence, and implications for policymaking.
- The main sources of statistics on EU agriculture and rural areas.
- Ways of measuring incomes of farms and farmers.
- Aggregate and microeconomic accounting systems.

4.1 Introduction

The CAP cannot be adequately understood without an appreciation of the information on which the decisions of agricultural policy are based. This chapter looks at this basic information, and in particular the economic statistics on this industry, and how this matches the requirements of the CAP's objectives.

Information comes in many forms, and much of EU policy-making would claim to be evidence-based; the implication is that this improves the quality of decisions and the effectiveness and efficiency of the actions taken. Some of this evidence is historic; for example, what instruments have worked well in the past and which have proved to be failures. Some will be behavioural, such as scientific findings on the ways that farmers and their families respond to different incentives. Some will come from economic modelling, such as how trade of non-EU countries is likely to be affected by changes to the CAP. Research and evaluation studies contribute to the evidence base that policy-makers can draw upon.

But a type of evidence of particular importance to public policy is official statistics. While the output of research studies from universities and institutes can be useful in helping define a policy problem, policy-makers will tend to attach particular weight to figures coming from official (that is, government or EU) institutions, such as ministries of statistics or the Statistical Office of the European Communities (Eurostat). A well-organised society will have available regularly produced statistics on the more important aspects of its public life – statistics on economic, social, environmental and other parameters by which its progress as a society can be monitored.

Reliable statistical information can benefit all stages of the policy process described in Chapter 1. It can help to identify where problems exist and the extent of those problems, and to indicate whether the instruments of policy are being successful in tackling them. In the absence of reliable statistics it is difficult to formulate clear and testable policy objectives and to design an efficient means of reaching them. Thus, the demand for statistics is generated by the need to make decisions on policy problems.

A central issue in the provision of statistics is that of quality. Policy-makers require statistics that are pertinent, reliable, impartial, accurate and timely. Another desirable feature is that they should be comparable internationally, not only among Member States of the EU but in a more widespread way as trade and other agreements require statistics by which situations in countries across the world can be monitored.

However, too much emphasis must not be placed on having perfect information (if, indeed, such perfection is meaningful). Often policy-makers have to take decisions on the basis of information that they know to be incomplete. At the highest level, it is often said that ministers in the EU Council (see Chapter 3) do not want too much information about particular problems, since statistics constrain their room for political manoeuvre, and without this wriggle-space, agreement on some decisions could never be reached. There is also the point that information which is very detailed is often difficult to interpret by non-experts. Nevertheless, these caveats do not undermine the general principle that important decisions require evidence that has adequate statistical foundations, even if these statistics need simplifying and digesting by bureaucrats before they are passed to politicians.

The statistical needs of agricultural policy in the EU are becoming increasingly diverse as the policies themselves evolve. In the early years of the CAP the main concern was with generating an increasing amount of food from the EU's own resources in order to give a secure supply. In such a situation there was an obvious need for information on the quantity of food which was being consumed, how this compared with dietary needs, the volume of production from domestic agriculture, imports and exports in food material and so on. Governments were interested in what land areas were being assigned to each crop, the yields obtained in animal and crop production, and the resources used (energy input, fertiliser use, labour required). Attention focused on spotting potential problems of lack of supply in relation to utilisation. Crises of some sort give impetus to obtaining such information; wartime has proved to be a surprisingly good period for making advances in statistics since then there is an imperative that resources are used where the need is greatest.

As was seen from Chapter 2, there has been a shift of emphasis in agricultural policy away from production issues. Today, there is a strong concern with the rural environment, the provision of public goods and with broader issues of rural development. Information on biodiversity, air and water quality, and the welfare of rural residents (their jobs, incomes, access to services and living conditions etc.) is in increasing demand. However, the main thrust of the CAP is that of supporting the incomes of farmers and their families. As will become clear later, a case can be made that on this central issue EU statistics are woefully inadequate. Partly as a consequence, the CAP has found itself using resources highly inefficiently and, as a by-product, generating unwanted surpluses of agricultural commodities and environmental damage. However, not everyone would benefit from better statistics in this area, and there is resistance in some quarters for providing more transparency. And to fill these gaps it is necessary to face some critical questions which go to the core of the rationale of agricultural support.

4.2 General theory of information systems

In explaining the changing statistical needs of CAP policy-makers and the observers of agricultural policy, it is worth bearing in mind the essentials of an 'information system'. This can be characterised as having three essential components:

- a data system, which generates the raw material;
- the necessary analysis to transform data into statistical information;
- the decision-maker, who incorporates this information into decisions at various stages of the policy process.

These components are shown in Figure 4.1 which presents an overall information framework. This forms a useful basis for examining the role of existing statistics in serving the needs of agricultural policy.

Statisticians will be required to analyse the data they collect, generating statistics (such as average incomes per farm) and to present the outcome of this analysis to policy decision-makers as information. Such high-level policy staff rarely make use of raw data and may not even be fully conversant with what the statistics mean; they cannot be expected to be totally familiar with the methods by which the figures have been obtained, including the limitations imposed by the sources of basic data or the strength of the inferences that can be drawn from the figures. Some digestion and interpretation by experts are usually required, and this is what turns the statistics into information. Only then can policy-makers use it as an input to their decision-taking.

The provision of statistics is an activity that requires professional skills, not just in the planning, design and collection of the data and its analysis but also in the design of statistics and their interpretation. This will involve a good deal of interaction between statisticians and the potential users of the statistics (shown in the top part of Figure 4.1). Statisticians will require, on the one hand, an appreciation of the needs of policy-makers (the main driver, shown in bold) and to have this some years before the users themselves do (since data systems will take some time to set up). On the other hand, statisticians require an ability to remain free of undue influence from policy-makers. In particular, politicians will wish to show that their policies have been successful and are likely to encourage statisticians to use figures to demonstrate this success, including the revision of methodology to bring statistics into line with their preferences (unemployment figures seem to be particularly subject to this type of manipulation). Some statistics may be unwelcome and their publication would not be encouraged by politicians embarrassed by a demonstration that policy problems were not being addressed satisfactorily. Policy-makers are not the only users of statistics, and statisticians must also bear in mind the other types of user (policy analysts representing alternative stakeholders, such as opposition politicians, newspapers, consumer groups etc.). By increasing the store of knowledge available to society in general in the form of publicly available statistics, the statistician is providing what is, in part, a 'public good'. Consequently, statisticians must be capable of exercising a degree of independence and objectivity from government control. It is to this end that the provision of statistics is often given to a specialist department of statistics separate from ministries or departments responsible for policies (examples include Eurostat in the EU and the UK's Office for National Statistics). However, it must be conceded that in many EU countries responsibility for agricultural statistics is primarily in the hands of ministries of agriculture, which carries a potential for a lack of statistical independence.

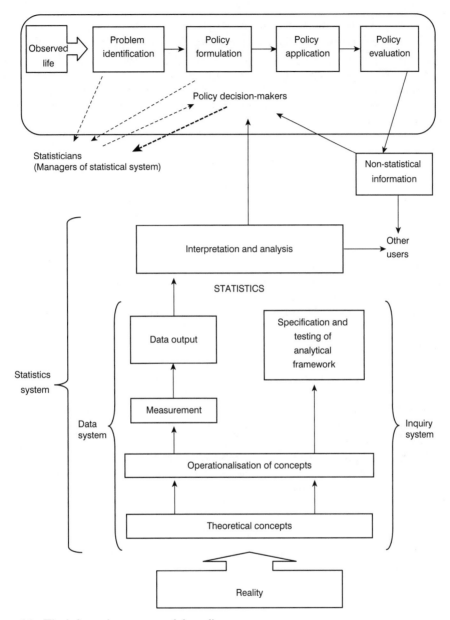

Figure 4.1   The information system and the policy process

The collection and analysis of data (the *data system*) forms only part of the larger information system needed to service policy shown in Figure 4.1. In parallel with the direct servicing of policy there is generally a system of scientific inquiry (the *inquiry system*) which is designed to test the basic assumptions of the data system and its interpretation and analysis. Though civil servants who are concerned with generating statistics are often the most familiar with the details of their methodologies, they are also usually preoccupied with the difficulties of getting results calculated and making them available to users, often publishing to a regular timetable. They may well not have the resources to reflect on the suitability of their statistics for the purpose to which they are put, or the validity of the assumptions that lie behind them. This is where academics, outside commercial consultants or specialist review groups from elsewhere in the government service can be useful. They can ask the awkward questions that ultimately cause revisions in the provision of statistics, and thereby lead to an improvement in their quality and to the chance of better policy decisions based on them.

4.2.1 Stages in the data system

A property of any data system, without which its utility is reduced, is its ability to reflect the aspects of the real world to which policy relates. There are three distinct steps which must be taken before data can be produced which purport to represent reality. In the terms used by the US agricultural economist and statistician Bonnen (1975, 1977), these are: (a) 'conceptualisation'; (b) 'operationalisation' of the concepts (definition of empirical variables), and (c) measurement, meaning the actual collection of data.

Concepts central to policy (such as 'standard of living' or 'biodiversity') often cannot be measured directly, and for the information system to be practical it is necessary to define proxy indicators (substitute measurable entities, such as the income of farmers or numbers of farmland wild birds) which are as highly correlated with the object of enquiry as is possible. The choice of indicator will be governed by the objective for which the measurement is taking place. Sometimes there will be a trade-off between desirability and practicality. For example, consumption expenditure might be theoretically preferred as a means of operationalising the concept of standard of living but, because measurement is difficult to carry out, some form of income measure may be an acceptable substitute. While biodiversity ideally would involve counting all wildlife in an area, cropland bird numbers are far easier to assess and they reflect in an acceptable way the general state of biodiversity. Often there is a temptation to use indicators simply because the information exists, but this is likely to result in ineffective and inefficient policy actions. The starting point should be the object of policy that the information system exists to serve.

4.2.2 Conceptual obsolescence

If the data system is flawed, all the subsequent steps in the information system will be undermined. The data system can fail – in the sense that it does not produce high-quality statistics on which decisions can be based – for two main reasons. One is inadequacy in the collection mechanism, such as faults in the size and representative nature of samples, and reliability of data entries. This is the aspect to which most attention has been paid by statisticians.

However, perhaps more important is a failure in the link between the concepts employed and the problems in hand. Maybe the initial process of conceptualisation is poor, or the link weakens over time; the term 'conceptual obsolescence' is used in the latter context. Conceptual obsolescence may occur when the nature of the real world changes or if the needs of policy shift. The result is that the statistics in use no longer represent the aspect of reality that policy-makers need to know about, and statisticians find themselves using concepts and operational forms which belong to previous circumstances. For example, they may continue to publish bird numbers as a proxy for biodiversity when environmental concerns may have moved more towards countryside appearance. Statisticians, when trapped in obsolescence, cannot provide the new forms of information yet continue generating the old for which there is reduced demand and relevance; this represents a waste of skills and other resources. It provides another example of the 'path dependency' first mentioned in Chapter 1.

It is not difficult to provide explanations for why conceptual obsolescence can occur. Analysis of the behaviour of bureaucracies indicate a tendency to prefer the *status quo*. Changes to established procedures commonly involve resource costs (as doing things in a new way involves planning, maybe having the old and new going along in parallel until the new is shown to work) and risks (since new procedures involve a step into the unknown). Frequently changes will be opposed by groups or individuals who see their interests threatened, such as those whose livelihoods have come from conducting regular surveys in a particular way. Countering conceptual obsolescence will have to overcome this type of institutional inertia and devise a new pattern of interest which is conducive to change. Often substantial changes are accepted only when the very existence of the bureaucracy is threatened. Managers of statistical systems will need to be constantly vigilant and plan to ensure that their outputs are appropriate for current policy problems.

4.2.3 Costs and benefits from statistics

In the real world, public statistics – like most forms of information – require resources to produce and thus cannot be considered as free to the national economy (in contrast to the artificial assumptions of perfect competition where information is costless). Society therefore needs to consider how much to spend on its statistical system.

It is not unreasonable to assume that improvements in statistics (quantity and quality increases) will become increasingly expensive to make as the least-cost opportunities for doing so are exhausted first, so that the marginal cost of the supply of statistics rises. Conversely, it is reasonable to assume that, in each particular area of policy, the benefits brought about by having better statistics (in terms of more effective, efficient or economic policy actions) face a decline as the more obvious improvements are made first. This (admittedly simplistic) view suggests that society will wish to spend more on statistics up to the point at which the marginal cost of improving statistics is just balanced by the marginal policy benefit resulting from them. This is represented in Figure 4.2.

Managers of statistical systems will have to ask themselves whether the costs of more and/ or better statistics in each of the various policy areas are balanced by the benefits they bring. In practice, the benefits will be reflected primarily in the demands made by policy-makers (politicians and civil servants) for information; they will want statistical improvements on topics they see as important, even though this may leave some areas of statistics inadequately developed as far as other users are concerned. Managers will need to balance the 'public interest' with that of politicians, not always easy to achieve when politicians are usually important in agreeing to finance statistics.

Even this elementary analysis enables some insights into what happens when, for example, a policy area such as concern with the environment grows in political importance. As the perception of the value of environmental statistics increases, the marginal benefit curve in Figure 4.2 will shift to the right; the logical outcome is that more statistics should be provided. If the marginal cost of statistics falls (such as by developments in remote sensing of crop yields by satellite), the cost curve drops and more and better statistics can be provided in that particular topic. Because managers of statistical systems will not only be concerned

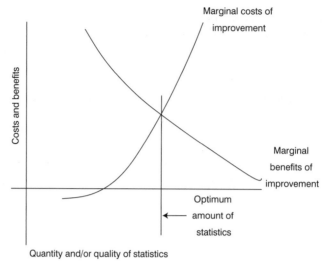

Figure 4.2 Marginal costs and benefits from statistics

with the marginal costs and benefits of spending resources in each class of statistics, but also with balancing the spending across the various classes, it is likely that cost falls in one area will not only lead to better statistics in that area but also a switching of some resources to statistical improvements in other areas, an example of application of the principle of equi-marginal returns. In such management decisions, a good deal of subjective judgement will be required, as the benefits from improved statistics are hard to quantify and, as already pointed out, commitments to developing statistics often have to be made in advance of the need for them becoming fully apparent.

4.3 Key statistics for EU agriculture

The Commission collects and publishes a large array of statistics on many aspects of life in the EU. Eurostat, based in Luxembourg, is mainly responsible for this activity although, as will be shown below, some agricultural statistics are handled by DG-Agri in Brussels. Typically, these statistics are at least annual (some quarterly) and figures are shown for individual Member States and for the EU as a whole. Almost entirely, the data are drawn from national statistical systems (Eurostat collects very little data itself), though presented by Eurostat in ways that are harmonised across all Member States. Published statistics are grouped into various 'Themes', depending on subject area. Currently these are:

- Theme 1 – General and regional statistics;
- Theme 2 – Economy and finance;
- Theme 3 – Population and social conditions;
- Theme 4 – Industry, trade and services;
- Theme 5 – Agriculture and fisheries;
- Theme 6 – External trade;
- Theme 7 – Transport;
- Theme 8 – Environment and energy;
- Theme 9 – Science and technology.

For the present purpose, attention will centre on statistics about agriculture (Theme 5), although information on trade in agricultural commodities, on the environment, regional development etc. will also be of concern to CAP decision-makers.

Within Eurostat's agricultural statistics (Theme 5) there are separate series on:

- crop production (for each main crop, giving land use, areas, yields and production, organic production, supply balance sheets and/or external trade);
- animal production (for meat, eggs and poultry, and milk and milk products, giving physical details of domestic production, including organic production, and supply balance sheets and/or trade);
- prices of agricultural products (producer selling prices in absolute and index forms) and of the inputs purchased by farmers;
- structural characteristics of agriculture, as revealed in the periodic Farm Structure Survey (now biennial). Statistics are published on the structure of agricultural holdings (such as their numbers broken down by area, economic size, type of farming, whether in a Less Favoured Area etc.), their land use, stocking patterns, and the labour found on them (including the ages of their operators, whether the operator is full-time on the holding or part-time, and whether the operator has another gainful activity). Organic production forms part of this structural information;
- the economic accounts for agriculture and for forestry, from which are developed Eurostat's indicators of the aggregate income from agricultural activity in the EU and in Member States (see below);
- accounts for the income of the agricultural households sector (now discontinued).[1]

In addition to the statistics coming from Eurostat, DG-Agri has developed its own series in certain areas, particularly on matters of immediate concern to the management by the Commission of commodity markets. DG-Agri publishes its own series on market prices of agricultural commodities, on stocks held in intervention stores, and on results from the Farm Accountancy Data Network (FADN). The latter gathers data annually from a sample of farms across Member States drawn to represent 'professional' or 'commercial' producers. The FADN provides a wealth of detailed information on both the physical and financial aspects of the farm as a business, including both its current productive activities and its capital position (loans outstanding, net worth etc.). Among the results are several measures of profitability and income (described below). The FADN is linked with equivalent national surveys found in all Member States (such as the Farm Business Survey in the UK and the National Farm Survey in Ireland).

A summary of agricultural and rural development statistics appears in the European Commission's annual report *Agriculture in the European Union – Economic and Statistical Information* and *Rural Development in the European Union – Economic and Statistical Information*. Eurostat also publishes *Europe in Figures – Eurostat Statistical Yearbook*. All are available electronically as free downloads. The Commission also requires Member States to supply a prescribed list of statistics on a wide range of indicators on the agricultural, economic and environmental conditions in their rural areas when submitting their draft Rural Development Programmes for approval; these too are available on-line at the Commission's rural development website.

4.4 Economic statistics required to service agricultural policy

The statistics outlined above enable a detailed picture to be painted of the changing circumstances of agriculture in the EU and its Member States, more comprehensive than for any other industry or for any other aspect of life in the Union. For example, they can be used to demonstrate the shift in average farm size (strictly, size of agricultural holding), with reductions in numbers of smaller farms and increases among the largest size classes, the reduction in the quantities of labour used in agriculture, changing patterns of land use by the various crops and types of livestock and the quantities produced, and the incidence of other gainful activities found among farmers. They enable the fall in the prices that farmers receive for their output relative to the costs they face for the inputs used to be traced, and thus the extent of the cost–price squeeze on the income earned from agriculture to be monitored. The diverse structure of farm businesses (by economic size, farming type and performance) can be described and their environmental impact monitored (using agri-environmental indicators such as intensity of stocking measured by the average number of animals per hectare). All these are important to various aspects of agricultural policy; they are in line with the axiom that in a well-designed statistical system the statistics that are generated should be determined primarily by the sorts of problems that the policy is attempting to tackle and be capable of casting light on the success of the policy at reaching the objectives that have been formulated.

Similarly, official statistics for rural development cover a wide range of aspects of the CAP's Pillar 2, though there is some overlap with agricultural statistics to reflect the role this activity plays in the economy and environment of those areas classed as rural. However, it should be noted that EU statistics for rural areas only cover topics that are addressed by the CAP's rural development activities (see Chapters 7 and 8). For example, housing and access to services – both major problems in many rural areas – are omitted. Pillar 2 accounts for only about one-fifth of CAP spending, so attention here will focus on Pillar 1, which is concerned with direct payments to farmers and market regulation.

If statistics are, in principle, policy-driven, it is worth recalling what are the CAP's main objectives, as these will determine what statistics policy-makers need. Agricultural policy in the EU and, indeed, most industrialised countries, has for at least the last three decades been primarily concerned with the incomes of farmers. As noted in Chapter 2, there are other strands within the diffuse fabric of policy, some of which have been of greater importance in the past than now – food security, balance of payments, improvements in efficiency of production and marketing. New strands have emerged and risen to prominence more recently – including concern with employment creation or protection, with the maintenance of the rural economy, with the environmental impact of farming practices and the conservation of landscape and wildlife, and with animal welfare. But the strongest strand, and the one which has proved the most hard-wearing in its resilience to attempts to reform agricultural policy, to make it less costly in the economic and budgetary senses, less distorting to patterns of production and trade and more equitable in terms of the distribution of benefits and costs, has been the issue of agricultural incomes. A good case can be made, then, that statistics on the incomes of farmers and their families are central pieces of information which should receive particular attention both by policy-makers and by any attempt at explaining the present shape of the CAP. As will become evident, there is a remarkable gap here that needs to be explained. While in the EU and in many other OECD countries, statistics on agricultural production and the rewards earned from it are well developed, the situation is far less satisfactory when it comes to the central issue of assessing the well-being of the agricultural community. Shortcomings in this area have major consequences for the way that agricultural policy is conducted and help explain the present nature of the CAP.

When the objectives of the CAP were discussed in Chapter 2, it was noted that the 1957 Treaty of Rome (Article 39) refers to 'ensuring a fair standard of living for the agricultural community', a phrase that was repeated in the 1997 restatement of the Commission's view contained in its *Agenda 2000* document. This has become interpreted as the 'income objective'. With the success of the CAP in achieving, even over-achieving, most of its other original aims, the concern with incomes has come to dominate agricultural policy-making.

Quite what is meant as the policy goal for living standards is by no means clear, though it is usually interpreted not in terms of consumption of goods and services, but rather in terms of income, which implies the ability to consume or save. Within the income strand, three components are often implied:

- **prevention of poverty** among the agricultural community, which is usually interpreted as having an income above a given minimal level;
- **securing a comparable position** for farm families *vis-à-vis* people belonging to other socio-professional groups in society. The inference is often made that agricultural households are typically in a disadvantaged income position and that governments must act to narrow the gap between farmers and non-farmers. This raises the problem of with which other groups the comparison is to be made;
- **inherent variation of farming prosperity** may cause farm households to face particular problems in their living standards from year to year as the result of a dependence on the weather.

Radical revisions of the CAP have been opposed and rejected on the grounds of the unacceptable impact they would have on the livelihoods of farmers. Though primarily thought of as affecting absolute income levels, presumably implying that more farmers would find themselves in poverty, reforms could also impact on comparability and variability. It might be anticipated that statistics would be available on all three of these, but in practice this is not the case.

Hence it is important to understand how statistics on incomes in agriculture are calculated in the EU, the units to which they relate and the items covered. If the information used does not closely match what is needed to service the policy aim in hand, then decisions will run the risk of being incorrect and policy actions inappropriate and potentially wasteful of public resources. For example, if EU decision-makers use statistics on the rewards from farming, which may be available, as a proxy for the income of farmers and their households, data for which may not currently exist, they will omit anything coming from other sources (wages, profits, welfare benefits and pensions, property income etc.). These other sources are particularly significant to the family among occupiers of small farms. Evidence from the US and elsewhere clearly shows that a low income from farming is not a safe indicator that the household's total income will be low. What statisticians measure should be dictated by the objective that policy is attempting to achieve. In the EU a mismatch has arisen between income statistics and the CAP's principal aim – the 'fair standard of living of the agricultural community' – resulting in much support spending not going to those households in need. The rest of this chapter is given over to this issue of how income is measured and contrasting this with how it should be measured if spending on the CAP's declared aims were to be respected.

4.5 Case study – Different approaches to accounting and concepts of income in agricultural statistics

In discussions of the state of agriculture there is a common failure to distinguish between overlapping but distinctly different views of what agriculture is. The first views agriculture as an activity (at aggregate and microeconomic levels) of producing agricultural commodities. The second looks at agriculture as a collection of institutional units that operate farms[2] (land holdings that engage in agricultural production). In agriculture the main institutional unit (at least numerically) is the household that runs a farm as an unincorporated business (sole trader or partnership), though members of such a household may also have other sources of income (from wages, other business profits, investment income, pensions etc.). For some households, agricultural production may be so small or insignificant (gardens, hobby farms etc.) that they are not included in statistics as agricultural holdings. The other main form of institution in agriculture is the company (corporation), in which the farm business has its own legal status. The government and charities are other types. The way that the activity of agricultural production is split among the types of institutional units is shown in Figure 4.3.

Economic accounts can be drawn up for the activity of agricultural production. They can also be drawn up for groups of institutions; households that run farms as unincorporated businesses companies and other institutional forms. Thus, incomes can be looked at from two standpoints:

- The first approach is to view income as the return (or reward) from a productive activity. Agricultural income in this context represents the reward remaining to the owners of the factors of production used in the production of agricultural goods and

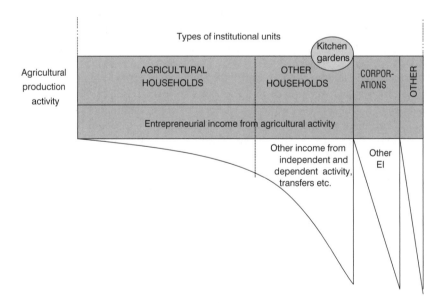

Figure 4.3   Relationship between institutional units and agricultural production

services. Measurement can be at the aggregate level (national agricultural activity) or at the level of the individual 'farm business' (microeconomic level).

- The second approach is to consider incomes that accrue to institutional units. As in agriculture the most important of these from a policy perspective are households, we are talking about the personal incomes of individuals and households that can be spent on consumption and on saving. Only part of this will come from farming. When measuring personal income it makes sense to take the household as the unit over which measurement is made, since the incomes and expenditures of farmer and spouse are usually pooled, and this may also extend to others living in the same house. All farming households can be considered together – the agricultural household sector of the economy – or as individual units, in which situation distributional issues can be explored. Particular interest is usually attached to the proportions of households having incomes that fall below some designated poverty level and the characteristics which are associated with being in poverty (such as size of farm, age and education of farmer, region, and so on).

In an ideal world, information would be available to policy-makers and analysts on both the incomes from agricultural production activity and on the personal incomes of farmers and their households. In the real world of the EU, however, the personal income approach is by far the worse served in terms of official statistics.

4.6 EU statistics on incomes as a reward from agricultural production

4.6.1 Measures of the aggregate income of the agriculture branch of the economy in the EU and Member States

Incomes from agricultural production for each Member State and for the EU as a whole are monitored using three indicators derived from the aggregate Economic Accounts for Agriculture (EAA). The EAA forms part of the system of national accounts for the EU and for each Member State, for which there is an agreed basic methodology (the European System of Integrated Economic Accounts – ESA). The aggregate accounts for agriculture both contribute to estimates of how this activity contributes to the national economy (that is, to national income of gross national product) and are the basis of monitoring performance of the agricultural industry alone, such as its productivity and the income it generates.

The Economic Account for Agriculture is drawn up for the agricultural 'industry'. The main characteristics may be summarised as:

a the 'industry' account covers all agricultural products (of which there is an internationally agreed list) irrespective of what type of unit produces them. However, the output from domestic gardens is not now covered if these are too small to be included in the Farm Structure Survey, though subsistence production on household plots in the Member States that joined the EU in 2004 and 2007 is included;

b non-agricultural goods and services which might be produced from farms are excluded (except where they are inseparable in data sources from the production of agricultural goods and services, such as where retail farm shops or snow-clearing are run as part of farm businesses);

c the value of output is estimated from a variety of sources, but principally from data on the physical area of crops and numbers of livestock, combined with estimated yields and multiplied by appropriate prices found from market and other surveys;

d the values of inputs, such as feedstuffs and seeds, are derived principally from statistics on sales from other production branches to agriculture, something possible because of the unambiguously agricultural nature of many of these inputs. Again, the main form of data is quantity multiplied by average prices.

The advantage of this form of accounting approach is largely one of timeliness; the information is more quickly to hand than if reliance were to be placed on surveys of sets of farm accounts, and for policy-makers rapid estimates are important. Provisional estimates can be made before the end of the calendar year to which they relate, with revisions made as more recent data become available. Also the sources will be consistent with information provided for other calculations within national accounts. From examining the figures in this account, published annually, it is possible to trace what is happening to the value of production, to inputs, to the cost of labour faced by agriculture, and so on.

The structure of the EAA is shown in Figure 4.4. The first part of the EAA, down to net value added at basic prices, is fairly uncontentious. Net value added represents the return to the complete resource base in agriculture (all the labour, land and capital in the industry) after correcting for taxes and subsidies linked to production. It is common to all national accounting systems in OECD countries and represents what this industry contributes to the national economy. Aggregate accounts for agriculture usually go a step further and distribute the value added between the owners of factors. Payments made to owners of land and capital who are not farmers (in the form of rents and interest) and costs of hired labour are deducted. What is left is the reward to the farmer and the unpaid members of his family (mainly the spouse) for the use in agricultural production of their own physical and managerial labour and the capital and land they own; this residual is termed Entrepreneurial Income.

Based on the EAA, Eurostat has developed three indicators to monitor how the aggregate income from agricultural production changes over time. The first (Indicator A) is calculated by adding in subsidies not already included, to give net value added (NVA) at 'factor cost', deflating (to take out the effect of inflation), dividing it by the amount of labour engaged in agriculture expressed in annual work units (AWUs) (to take into account that there is a falling quantity of labour among whom the rewards have to be shared), and expressing it in index form. In view of the significant amount of part-time activity found among family members (pluriactivity, or multiple job-holding), it is important that the labour input to farming is expressed in terms of full-time labour equivalents. Indicator B is calculated in a similar way; in this case Entrepreneurial Income is divided by the amount of non-paid labour (hired labour costs will have already been deducted). In some Member States (particularly Germany) there are problems in measuring labour input, so Indicator C is simply Entrepreneurial Income. Within the macroeconomic income monitoring system of the EU, NVA/AWU (Indicator A) has been the main indicator employed and is still the most widely quoted and features in the influential *Agricultural Situation in the European Union* annual report. It is usually considered the most statistically reliable of the three, partly because some countries have lacked until recently some of the information necessary to calculate the other Indicators. However, it is self-evident that, except in very particular circumstances, Indicator A represents a concept which is far removed from the personal income of farmers and their households. Apart from

	Sales of farm crops, horticulture, livestock and livestock products
plus	Value of physical change in output stocks and work in progress (closing stocks minus opening stocks)
plus	Own consumption
plus	Subsidies on products
minus	Taxes on products
equals	Output at basic prices
minus	Expenditure on intermediate consumption goods and services (bought from other industries
equals	Gross value added at basic prices
minus	Depreciation
equals	**Net value added at basic prices**
plus	Other subsidies on production
minus	Other taxes on production
minus	Rents paid
minus	Interest paid (including loans for land purchase)
minus	Wages and salaries paid (compensation of employees)
equals	'Entrepreneurial Income'

From the above three indicators are derived

Indicator A: Index of the real income of factors in agriculture per annual work unit

Net value added at basic prices
    plus Other subsidies on production
minus Other taxes on production
    = Net value added at 'factor cost'
deflated and divided by total labour input in annual work units, and expressed as an index

Indicator B: Index of real net agricultural entrepreneurial income, per unpaid annual work unit

Entrepreneurial Income, deflated and divided by the labour input of unpaid labour in annual work units, and expressed as an index.

Indicator C: Net entrepreneurial income of agriculture

Entrepreneurial Income, deflated and expressed as an index or in absolute form

Figure 4.4 Framework of the EU's aggregate economic account for agriculture (Source: derived from Eurostat (1997) *Manual of Economic Accounts for Agriculture and Forestry* Rev.1)

ignoring interest, rent and paid labour costs, which may be considerable, it excludes any income accruing to farmers and their families from sources other than farming and makes no allowance for the amounts taken by taxation and other forms of involuntary spending. It would be wrong therefore to interpret it as representing the personal incomes of farmers and their families. Even using it as a proxy for developments in personal incomes over time is suspect, since the existence of multiple income sources means that it is possible for the total income situation of farmers and their households to be improving while their incomes from farming are declining, and vice versa. Nevertheless production-based indicators have often been misused in this way, probably because they were published and no other measure nearer the policy needs was available.

4.6.2 Microeconomic farm accounts surveys and their income results

The official source of farm-level information on incomes from production in the EU is the annual survey of accounts of individual farm businesses, known as the Farm Accountancy Data Network (FADN), or its French acronym RICA. For historical reasons, FADN is supervised not by Eurostat but by the Commission's DG-Agri.

FADN was established in 1965 'with the specific objective of obtaining data enabling income changes in the various classes of agricultural holding to be properly monitored' (Commission 1982 VI/308/82-EN, p. 6). The justification for it was rooted in policy, in that '... the development of the Common Agricultural Policy requires that there should be available objective and relevant information on incomes in the various categories of agricultural holdings and on the business operation of holdings coming within categories which call for special attention at Community level.' (EEC Regulation 79/65).

FADN collects data from almost 86,000 (2010 – EU-27) farm businesses annually, selected from a population of about 6.4 million farms in the EU. FADN is not a single survey but is an amalgamation of national surveys carried out by Member States. Ways of collecting the data vary, but there is a fundamental harmonised methodology which applies to the concepts of income employed and, increasingly, to the selection of the sample. The orientation towards 'professional' (or 'commercial') farms means that very small farms are excluded. Consequently, while the FADN's field of observation covers at least 90 per cent of all agricultural economic activity, it represents just under half of all the holdings found in the EU (in 2007 there were some 7.3 million commercial holdings, taken as 1 European Size Unit (ESU) (a measure of economic size) and larger, and a further 6.4m below this size, many of them being subsistence producers and almost half of them located in Romania). The threshold for inclusion varies according to the size structure of holdings in the countries concerned, being 2 ESU in Portugal at one extreme to 16 ESU for the Netherlands.

The income concepts used in FADN relate to the farm business rather than to the farmer or his family. Consequently, income from non-farm sources (other than forms linked to farming such as grants and interest subsidies) are not taken into account. Neither are personal outgoings on tax or other compulsory payments deducted. Some of the national accounts surveys contributing to FADN collect this information, but FADN itself does not request that this additional data be supplied.

Until recently the main income measure has been Farm Net Value Added (Farm NVA), expressed per farm or per AWU (that is, per full-time person equivalent working on the farm). This Farm NVA measure, when expressed per AWU, corresponds to the Community's main macroeconomic concept (Indicator A), though there are differences of detail that prevent direct comparison. As with the macro-indicator, the reason why Farm NVA per AWU is used without distinguishing between farmer labour and hired workers seems to be one of interpretation of the intentions of Article 39 of the Treaty of Rome as relating to all agricultural workers (employed, self-employed and family help). It seems highly unlikely that such a measure when applied in countries with significant quantities of hired labour (such as the UK) at group average level can adequately provide this information.

More recently greater attention has been given to Family Farm Income, per farm and per Family Work Unit. This concept corresponds with Entrepreneurial Income, as it is derived from Farm NVA by deducting interest payments, rent payments and the costs of hired labour. It is the reward to the farmer and his family remaining for the use of their own land, capital and labour inputs to agricultural production.

It appears that the aggregate income figures are the more significant in contributing to the background against which policy decisions are made and are the ones that take priority in official policy documents. The reason has been largely to do with timing; macroeconomic estimates can be available at or soon after the end of the calendar year to which they relate. In contrast, the FADN survey-based results are inherently rather historic by the time that they are gathered, calculated and published. FADN figures are used as a way of exploring issues seen to be of lower political imperative. Rather surprisingly, little formal comparison has been made between the income patterns emerging from the two sources.

4.7 Measures of personal income at the macroeconomic and microeconomic levels

Despite their origins in attempts to find measures of income that were relevant to the aims of agricultural policy, the EU's activity-based income indicators at industry and farm levels (EAA and FADN) are not capable of use in answering the central agricultural policy questions 'What are the standards of living of the agricultural population', and 'Are they fair'. They cannot help with responses to 'How many farm families fall below the level which would be considered acceptable, and where are they – on what types and sizes of farm and in which regions?' or 'Is the standard of living of farmers better or worse now than in the past, and how do farmers compare with other socio-professional groups in society?'

Official statistics which reflect the overall income situation of the agricultural community are currently totally absent at the EU level, though there is a growing body of research evidence at farm household level. In the early 1990s, Eurostat developed a macroeconomic measure of personal income of agricultural households that enabled a little light to be shed on some of these issues. These *Income of the Agricultural Households Sector (IAHS)* statistics related to an entire sector of households that were classified as being agricultural (on the basis that self-employment in agriculture was the main income source of the head of household). Such aggregate calculations only gave a single figure for each Member State each year. The income concept was net disposable income (as defined in Figure 4.5).

The results, though not fully harmonised, suggested the following important information:

- The number of agricultural households (defined as those where the main income of the head of household came from farming) was substantially smaller than the number

(1) Net operating surplus (or income) from independent activity
    a)   from agricultural activity
    b)   from non-agricultural activity
    c)   from imputed rental value of owner-occupied dwellings
(2) Compensation to members of agricultural households (wages) as employees, from agricultural and non-agricultural activity
(3) Property income received
(4) Non-life insurance claims (personal and material damage)
(5) Social benefits (other than social benefits in kind)
(6) Miscellaneous inward current transfers

(7) Total resources (sum of 1–6)

(8) Property income paid (rent and interest if not deducted in calculating 1 above)
(9) Net non-life insurance premiums
(10) Current taxes on income and wealth
(11) Social contributions
(12) Miscellaneous outgoing current transfers

(13) Net disposable income (7 minus 8 –12)

(14) Social transfers in kind
(15) Net adjusted disposable income (13 plus 14)

Figure 4.5   Definition of net disposable income (Eurostat's IAHS statistics)

of households where there was *some* income from farming, and generally smaller than the number of agricultural holdings. Where data existed over time, absolute numbers of agricultural households had been falling, in some instances very rapidly.

- On average, households with an agricultural holding but where farming was *not* the main income source of the reference person appeared to derive little income from self-employment in agriculture.
- Agricultural households (defined as above) in all countries were recipients of substantial amounts of income from outside agriculture. Though typically about a half to two-thirds of the total comes from farming, there were large differences between Member States and some between years.
- The total income of agricultural households was more stable than their income from farming alone. Non-agricultural income (all types taken together) was less variable from year to year than was farming income. Disposable income seemed to be less stable than total income, but the relationship between the two depended on a variety of factors, including the way that taxation was levied.
- Countries differed in the share of income taken from agricultural households in taxation and other deductions, so the same average total income figure could imply different levels of disposable income in different Member States. Within individual countries, agricultural households tended to pay a lower share of their total income as taxes and social contributions than the all-household average.
- Agricultural households had average disposable incomes per household that were typically higher than the all-household average, except for Portugal where they were noticeably worse off. The relative position was eroded or reversed when income per household member or per consumer unit was examined (Figure 4.6).

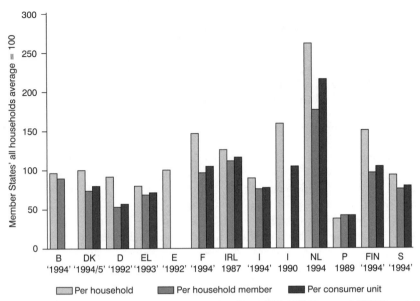

Figure 4.6 Net disposable income per unit by Member State (EU-15)[3] (Eurostat's IAHS statistics)

These findings were very much in line with OECD studies that have drawn on microeconomic data on the income of farm families that include important contributions from the US and Canada where surveys of farms and tax returns filed by farmers are available for analytical purposes.

This EU series of statistics was suspended by Eurostat in 2002 on the grounds that the results were not of high quality, not fully harmonised and had gaps in coverage in terms of years (the most recent data were often rather old). Preference was expressed by the Court of Auditors and the Council for a new system, based on microeconomic methodology (that is, using surveys or other household-level data sources). Such an approach could provide answers to many of the important policy questions facing the CAP, including the number of low-income farm families and the types and sizes and regions in which they were found. A feasibility study carried out in 2007 found that few EU countries have accessible data sources by which the distributional aspects of farm household incomes can be explored. Data sources vary widely, although they tend to be of three forms – farm accounts surveys, household budget surveys and tax records. Surveys of farm accounts in EU Member States tend to restrict their field of interest to the income from the farming activity alone; this is true of the EU's Farm Accountancy Data Network though some countries collect data on other income sources that they use for solely national purposes. Household budget surveys are held typically only every five to seven years; in northern Member States there are few agricultural household cases and in southern ones the quality of income data is not good. Taxation records are not a useable data source on incomes in the many EU countries where farmers are taxed on a flat rate rather than on their actual incomes or where farmers are poorly covered by the tax net. Consequently, among the EU countries only four – Denmark, the Netherlands, Finland and Sweden – can be described as reasonably well provided with microeconomic data on the overall income situation of agricultural households. Nevertheless, this study found that data collection was a practical proposition at a cost that formed little more than a fifth of one per cent of the budgetary costs of the CAP, which did not seem to be an over-ambitious improvement in the performance of agricultural policy that might result from using better income statistics.

4.8 Cause, persistence and implications of using inappropriate income indicators

The present unsatisfactory situation stems from the fact that the conceptual framework of the present information systems carrying out income measurement (both macroeconomic and microeconomic), and much of the data collecting procedures, were established a half-century or more ago. Then there was a strong requirement to know about the level of agricultural production and the extent to which this met food supply needs, the resources used, and how much farming contributed to the national economy. Even in the early years of the CAP it was probably safe to assume that most farmers producing significant amounts of produce were full-time and had few or no other economic activities. The income of farmers corresponded more-or-less with that from agricultural production, and measuring the latter gave an acceptable approximation for the former. But this is clearly no longer the case. There is wide and increasing awareness that the income of farmers comprises much more than their profits from farming, though we do not have a system across the EU to provide reliable statistics on their household incomes. Historical developments have led to the official monitoring systems of incomes in European agriculture being conceptually out-dated and informationally inadequate.

In this example of conceptual obsolescence, there has been little political or bureaucratic pressure within the EU to make the income position of agricultural households more transparent, though this may be changing as interest in agricultural policy reform gathers pace. Those who might have something to gain – mainly those representing non-farmers – have lacked the expertise and impetus necessary to effect change. Farmers and their representatives have had an interest in maintaining the information vacuum; as members of the 'policy community' they had a vested interest in keeping information of an 'unhelpful' nature from appearing, since this might have an eventual effect on the policy agenda. There is evidence to show that in many EU countries agricultural policy acts as a transfer mechanism of income from the relatively poor (consumers) to the relatively rich (farmers), with a disproportionate benefit accruing to the largest farmers whose incomes could not justify support on grounds of social equity. Pressure groups working for farmers tend to be dominated by the more successful and larger farmers, and the personal prospects of these would not be well served by a major change in the income support system. They could hardly be expected to promote actively a more detailed disclosure of the personal incomes of the farming community that harmed their interests.

What may not be immediately apparent is that the provision of fuller information on the income position of farmers may also be against the interests of the agricultural bureaucracy and politicians. Agricultural departments are unlikely to accept easily changes which involve a reduction in their power and influence. And there is the added dimension that the national interest of countries like the UK could be harmed if a more transparent farmer income situation led to a reduction in the sums it could draw from the EU budget while leaving its contributions unaltered. It is noticeable that, even in countries where some information on the total income of farm households is well established (for example France, the Netherlands, Denmark, and the USA and Canada), it has not figured prominently in discussions of agricultural policy. For whatever reason, this uncomfortable information has been effectively marginalised.

Perhaps what is feared most by the current agricultural policy community (and this must include parts of the agricultural bureaucracy) is the exposure of the lack of uniqueness of poverty in agriculture and questions about the need for a special income support system for farmers when a general welfare safety net exists for everyone else. Are not poor farmers just households with low incomes who happen to occupy farms? However, to recognise this is to expose the weakness of much of the case for continuing the present level and forms of support to agriculture. To be seen to be giving special treatment to poverty in agriculture is to open the floodgates of comparison with the way in which many other groups in society have been treated, some of whom could assemble a far more pressing case for assistance from public funds than could farmers. The lack of reliable statistics effectively keeps such questions off the policy agenda and thus serves the interests of many elements in the agricultural policy community.

The causes of poverty among farmers, where it is found, may have an agricultural base – their farms may be too small or producing a commodity which has undergone a price decline – but the means of relieving their poverty need not be organised through support of agricultural production. Indeed, measures such as Single Farm Payments will be economically inefficient as they benefit the un-needy more than the needy, and they may also be ineffective, as the sums given to small farmers will be small (see Chapter 6). In the past such blunt instruments may have been the only practical way of bringing relief to a wide spectrum of distressed agriculture. However, there is little reason for perpetuating a system linked to agricultural production if preferable alternatives are available or can be developed at reasonable cost.

The absence of adequate information on the incomes of farmers does not stop agricultural policy from being implemented or reform from taking place. Rather, it means that decision-makers have a very imperfect picture against which to operate. A good case could be made that the present woeful lack of statistics on farm household incomes has imposed considerable costs on the rest of the economy that finds itself supporting a policy that is patently inefficient at helping those farmers most in need. Partly as a consequence, the CAP has found itself using resources highly inefficiently and, as a by-product, generating environmental damage and unwanted surpluses of agricultural commodities that have distorted international trade. However, not everyone would benefit from better statistics in this area, and there is resistance in some quarters for providing more transparency. Questions about the performance of policy interventions are carried further when evaluation of the CAP is considered in Chapter 11.

Further reading

Commission of the European Communities (1982) *Indicators of Farm Income*, Working document of the Services of the Commission, VI/308/82 EN (0082d)

European Commission (2010) 'Agriculture in the European Union – economic and statistical information'. Available online at http://ec.europa.eu/agriculture/agrista/2010/table_en/2010enfinal.pdf

European Commission (2010) 'Rural development in the European Union – economic and statistical information'. Available online at http://ec.europa.eu/agriculture/agrista/rurdev2010/ruraldev.htm.

European Council (1965) Regulation No 79/65/EEC of 15 June 1965, OJ L 109, 23 June 1965, p. 1859

Eurostat (2002) *Income of Agricultural Households Sector: 2001 Report*. Theme 5. Eurostat, Luxembourg.

Eurostat (2010) *Europe in Figures – Eurostat Yearbook 2010*. Eurostat, Luxembourg. Available online at http://epp.eurostat.ec.europa.eu/portal/page/portal/product_details/publication?p_product_code=KS-CD–10–220.

Eurostat (annual). *Income from Agricultural Activity* (formerly called *Agricultural Incomes*). Theme 5. Eurostat, Luxembourg.

Gardner, B. L. (1992) 'Changing economic perspectives on the farm problem', *Journal of Economic Literature*, 30, 62–101.

Hill, B. (1999). 'Farm household incomes – perceptions and statistics', *Journal of Rural Studies*, 15 (2), 345–55.

Hill, B. (2011) *Farm Incomes, Wealth and Agricultural Policy*. 4th edition. CAB International, Wallingford.

Hill, B. (2008) 'Some economic aspects of public statistics – Presidential Address', *Journal of Agricultural Economics*, 59(3), pp. 387–420.

OECD (2003) *Farm Household Income: Issues and Policy Responses*. OECD, Paris.

OECD (2005) *Policy Brief: Farm Household Income – Towards Better-Informed Policies*. Organisation for Economic Co-operation and Development, Paris.

OECD (2007) *Information Deficiencies in Agricultural Policy Design, Implementation and Monitoring*. Organisation for Economic Co-operation and Development, Paris.

Offutt, S. (2002) The future of farm policy analysis: a household perspective – Presidential Address, *American Journal of Agricultural Economics*, 84 (5), 1189–1201.

UNECE (2005 and 2007) *Handbook on Rural Household Livelihood and Well-being: Statistics on Rural Development and Agricultural Household Income*. Hill, B. and Karlsson, J. (eds). (web-based (2005) and printed (2007) editions.) United Nations Economic Commission for Europe, Geneva. (On FAO website, an updated on-line edition available from late 2011).

5

UNDERSTANDING THE INSTRUMENTS USED TO IMPLEMENT THE CAP

Key topics

- Instruments used to implement policy are categorised.
- They include legislation (controls), direct income payments, financial incentives, and market intervention.
- Economic and financial analyses are made of the main forms of intervention (direct payments, support buying, quotas, subsidies on production etc.) used in the CAP.

5.1 Introduction

In Chapter 1, which outlined the policy process, it was shown that the actions to achieve the objectives of the CAP are taken using *policy instruments*. Sometimes the terms *policy mechanisms* or (confusingly) *policy measures* are used to described the instruments and the way they work, though *measures* is more properly reserved for the legislation that enables instruments to be used (the Regulations often comprise sections labelled as Measures). These instruments attempt to alter what would otherwise happen, to bring about changes which improve the situation as seen by policy-makers. A wide range of types of policy instrument can be used. The choice will depend on a number of factors, including the nature of the change intended, the instrument's budgetary cost, the administration problems involved, the political acceptability of the alternatives etc. The purpose of this chapter is to review briefly these instruments and their characteristics, taking each singly and concentrating on the impacts likely to be felt once the various decision-makers involved have had time to adjust to their introduction.

The CAP currently uses a wide range of instruments. There is not enough space here to cover every one in detail. Rather, attention is focused on those which are of the greatest practical importance to the CAP now and in the foreseeable future. The review is in general terms; later chapters will describe more precisely support mechanisms for farming production, for the provision of environmental services and for rural development. This approach is taken because, with the passage of time, the details of the instruments used in the CAP can be expected to change as policy problems shift and as administrative and political aims evolve. However, the basic characteristics of each instrument, the subject of this section, remain stable.

It should be borne in mind that, at any one time, there will be an array of instruments in operation aimed at the agricultural industry and related sectors (especially forestry and those parts of the food chain nearest farming). No attempt is made at this point to evaluate the overall impact of the instruments operating together – that is, the effects of the entire CAP – in terms of budgetary cost, impact on economic efficiency etc. This is left for the later chapter on policy assessment (Chapter 11).

Agriculture and rural areas are affected by the CAP and its instruments, but they also feel impacts from other policies, both EU and national. Some of these influences can be substantial. EU environmental policy on cutting down pollution of water-courses or lowering the emission of greenhouse gases can impact on farming in a major way by placing constraints on land use. Some of these non-agricultural policies may be primarily national in nature rather than part of EU activities. For example, taxation of income and wealth, including on intergenerational transfers of property, which is still very much left in the hands of Member States, can impact on the structure of land ownership and farm businesses, and on farm size. Any such influences cannot be attributed to the CAP. Conversely, instruments that belong to the CAP can impact on other policy aims; for example, aids to improving the productivity of agriculture may lead to the loss of jobs in farming, which may worsen rural unemployment. The main focus here is on the instruments of policies that are specifically directed at the EU agricultural industry and closely related sectors by the CAP. For the purpose of a more complete explanation it is helpful also to cover those used by national policies where the Member States still retain authority and where these instruments might be taken up by the CAP on some future occasion.

5.2 A typology of instruments

Instruments used by the CAP and other EU policies that impact on agriculture can be categorised in many ways. One basis, of particular concern to the CAP, is according to the *extent to which they rely on distorting market prices* for agricultural products to achieve their goals. Another closely related criterion is the extent to which they influence the decisions by farm operators to produce commodities (their degree of *coupling* – see Box 5.1). Another is according to their degree of targeting, either geographically (for example, support may be

---

Box 5.1 'Coupled' and 'decoupled' instruments

Attention has been drawn by analysts to the impact that instruments can have on the decisions that farm operators make to produce commodities. Raising product prices to improve farmers' incomes is a prime example, as the rational response by farmers to the incentive of higher prices is to increase their output. The instrument and the decisions are 'coupled', or linked together. This distortion of decisions and markets leads to inefficiencies and is particularly unwelcome when there is a surplus of production relative to demand. Consequently, policy-makers have tried recently to switch support to forms that are 'decoupled', in the sense that they do not influence farmers' production decisions. An example is direct income payments to farmers, made whether or not they generate any production. In reality, there will always be some degree of 'coupling', as some farmers may decide to stay in the industry rather than quit. So a 'decoupled' form of support is one that is relatively less distorting on farmers' decisions.

Source: Based on text from the OECD

---

universal or only available to farms in hill and mountain areas) or according to characteristics of the farmer (grants for training may be open to all applicants or restricted to those meeting certain eligibility tests). Analysis soon shows that borders between types of instrument are often blurred because almost all interventions have some effect on prices of agricultural commodities, and markets ensure that instruments targeted at one region or type of farmer have knock-on effects in others. Nevertheless, in explaining the array of instruments used by the CAP it is helpful to review them in approximate order according to the degree to which they distort the market for agricultural commodities to achieve their goal. On this basis, they can be grouped as follows:

5.2.1 Group 1 – Legislation, education and designation

This group comprises three elements in the institutional framework within which other policy instruments work. Public policy has to be based on laws, and all actions undertaken in the CAP, of whatever type, are founded on the EU Treaties and law (regulations, directives etc.) derived from them, as agreed by the Council (increasingly in co-decision with the European Parliament – see Chapter 3) or by committees of representatives or the Commission using powers devolved to them by law. These EU laws exist alongside national legislation, particularly on matters where no EU policy applies.

Legislation is used as a direct way of achieving some policy aims. This group includes EU laws on:

- health and safety at work on farms (exposure to hazardous chemicals) and in the food industry (such as hygiene in slaughter houses);
- animal welfare, including transport conditions of live animals;
- protection of wildlife.

Though not part of the CAP, national legislation affecting agriculture and rural areas is used, for example, in the form of:

- controls of development (house-building etc.) on agricultural land;
- protection of buildings worthy of conservation, or of landscape features (such as individual trees).

Legislation is used in situations where policy requires everyone to comply with some minimum standard and often involves what may loosely be termed 'rights'. Health and safety legislation implies that employees have a right not to be endangered by their employment. Protection of wildlife and planning controls stem from the notion that society in general has rights over the environment (natural diversity and landscape) which individual landowners should not be allowed to erode. Animal welfare legislation can be taken to imply that animals have rights, though quite how this translates into human welfare and rights is often left rather vague. Often legislation is concerned with defining and clarifying these 'rights' of individuals and of society, and with setting up mechanisms by which these 'rights' can be defended.

Legislation has the advantage that, once in place, the direct cost to the EU budget (and to national exchequers where there is joint financing) is confined to ensuring that the laws are complied with (sometimes referred to as 'policing'). However, this is not the entire economic cost, since those who feel the impact of the laws (in the CAP's case principally rural land users such as farmers and foresters and other businessmen in the food industry) are forced to take steps which incur them in costs (such as in meeting minimum animal welfare standards). These costs are reflected as shifts in the supply curves of the goods and services produced by these people, with usually some increase in the prices paid by the final consumer and reduction in the quantity bought, thereby imposing some economic cost on the purchaser. On the other hand, the consumer will benefit in terms of the assurance of safer food, a cleaner environment, satisfaction that food is produced in humane ways etc. at which the legislation is aimed.

This group also includes the provision of education through a programme of free information and advice from publicly funded bodies, a *people-centred activity* which, for example, will make them aware of countryside features and enable them to harness the resources to protect valued characteristics (educational programmes often have a broad impact, spreading far beyond the topic studied), and training, a *job-centred activity* aimed at improving technical performance, for example in the safe use of chemical crop sprayers. In the EU, education is largely a national responsibility in terms of implementation, but the CAP legislation contains measures that enable EU funds to be used to support schemes that provide vocational training for people who work in agriculture and forestry (see Chapter 7). The demarcation between education and training is not precise; training in business skills for members of farm families (which, as they are not specific to agriculture, could also be used in setting up non-agricultural businesses) might also be educational in that these skills may facilitate the acquisition of information on all manner of subjects, lead to empowerment and so on. As far as the agricultural use of education and training is concerned, the CAP targets farmers, farm workers and others in rural areas who have control of or use rural resources. Though largely decoupled from production decisions, there is some link with the level of agricultural output, in that better educated and trained farmers and staff are likely to be more productive.

Official *designation* under EU legislation of certain geographic areas, as (in the UK) Less Favoured Areas (LFAs), Environmentally Sensitive Areas (ESAs), Nitrate Vulnerable Zones (NVZs), or Natura 2000 sites (see Chapter 8) can be, in part, educational, in the sense that making people aware of what is around them may result in them being more sensitive about actions which might harm such areas. A similar role exists for national designations, such as the UK's Areas of Outstanding Natural Beauty or conservation areas in towns and villages, or listed status for historically important buildings. However, designation also has an important administrative role in that it is linked to the ability to apply instruments in a selective way using public funds. For example, farmers in certain designated parts of the country may be provided with financial incentives (see below) to, say, repair stone field boundaries, something not available in non-designated areas.

5.2.2 Group 2 – Direct income payments

The essential feature of this group is that payments are made to recipients because of what they do (in the sense that they occupy agricultural land, or undertake some other selected rural activity) and where they do it. The purpose of these payments is linked to a policy objective, in the case of the CAP principally income support of the recipients. Apart from the fact that the people who receive support are involved in agriculture, there is no direct link with the markets for farm commodities. Although the amount paid may depend on some initial farm characteristic (such as farm size, or to payments they received in the past), once that base has been established, the sum paid is not linked with changes in the volume of output; the payment is essentially *decoupled* from current production decisions.

Examples of direct income payments under the CAP include:

- **The Single Farm Payment – SFP (or, in some Member States, Single Area Payment – SAC).** Since 2005 or 2006 (depending on the country) each holding has received a direct payment calculated in ways described in Chapter 6. The SFP/SAC is conditional on farm occupiers respecting certain husbandry and environmental standards, an example of *cross-compliance* between agricultural and environmental policy (see Box 5.2). The key point here is that, other than occupying some agricultural land, there is no requirement to produce anything. The payment is thus largely *decoupled* from decisions about what crops to grow or animals to keep, and how much output to aim for.
- **Payments to farmers in mountain and other disadvantaged areas (Less Favoured Areas – LFAs)** to improve their incomes and hence keep them farming these areas. Payments are intended to compensate for the adverse natural conditions such operators encounter. Conditions may be attached (such as maximum permitted stocking densities, this latter being a further example of *cross-compliance* between agricultural and environmental policy. Chapter 7 gives more consideration to such payments.

Another category worth noting is *tax concessions*. Most Member States offer concessions to their farmers and landowners on the taxes they pay on incomes and/or capital. Examples of special treatments include not being taxed on actual income but on a per-hectare basis (which usually works to the advantage of farmers), averaging over a run of years (which means that the farmer avoids having to declare occasional peaks in income that might attract high tax rates), exempting farmland from capital taxes or using special low valuations rather than market prices to calculate liabilities. These arise from national policies on taxation, though they are allowed under EU rules. Such treatments mean that farmers pay lower amounts of tax than they would if in another occupation and thus have improved post-tax incomes, so these concessions can be put under the same heading as direct income payments.

Though direct income payments are usually thought of as being essentially decoupled from decisions on production which farmers make, this is a *matter of degree*. Some influence can probably be detected in all circumstances, and this increases with the length of period

---

Box 5.2 Cross-compliance

Cross-compliance is a technique to enable an instrument to pursue more than one objective. It makes a main use conditional on meeting conditions related to a secondary use. Examples include direct income payments being conditional on observing environmental standards, and retirement incentives being dependent on the land released by retiring farmers being made available to younger ones. However, cross-compliance may not be the most efficient way of achieving a given aim. The economist Jan Tinbergen established a principle that implies the number of instruments must be at least as great as the number of objectives.

under consideration. There may be some indirect impact on production decisions by enabling farmers to consider more risky enterprises, knowing that the direct payments provide a safe core income. Direct payments probably also keep some farmers in business who otherwise would quit production, though the direction of influence on industry-level output is by no means obvious. On the one hand, the higher the direct income payments, the greater the numbers of farmers who would stay in business. On this basis there would be a positive relationship between payments and production. But what if the land of uncompetitive farmers leaving the sector were to be taken over by more efficient operators, typically larger farmers looking for ways to spread their fixed costs? This sort of structural change could easily result in an expanded total output and a negative relationship between the level of direct payment and the volume of output (smaller direct payments leading to higher output). Hence it is safer to describe direct income payments as *relatively decoupled* compared with some other forms of policy instrument discussed below and to remember that only relatively short-term conditions are being contemplated.

5.2.3 Group 3 – Financial incentives to modify the use of resources in agriculture

The key aspect of this group is that it is hoped that financial incentives will cause people, through the pursuit of self-interest and without legal compulsion, to take certain actions in their use of resources which policy-makers wish to encourage as being in the EU interest. Often there will be some impact on the market for farm commodities, though in an indirect way. Examples used by the CAP include:

- grants for part of the cost of capital items in which policy-makers wish to encourage greater investment (such as in pollution-control equipment, in tree planting, in developing diversification on farms);
- pre-pensions to encourage farmers to retire early, thereby removing their labour from agriculture and allowing their land to be transferred to other holdings. The outcome is that the remaining farms can be of a size that is viable in the current period and (medium-term) future;
- payments for making management agreements with agencies of the national government, so that land is used in ways which are environmentally preferred;
- payments to farm operators who agree to leave field margins uncultivated to generate environmental benefits;
- access agreements with national governments, so that farmers and foresters allow greater public use of their land, with the social benefits that this brings, in exchange for an annual fee;
- financial support for the formation of groups (such as co-operatives) to improve the bargaining position of farmers when faced with small numbers of large buyers, thereby obtaining higher prices for the members. Also under this heading could be included the encouragement for farmers to make inroads into processing their produce, capturing some of the value added which other businesses currently enjoy, and to develop new markets, such as for organically produced food and local branded foods. The formation of groups or associations is often part of this attempt to extend farmers' business interests further along the food chain. These all represent changes to the present use of resources.

Some general features of instruments in Groups 2 and 3 should be noted. First, the costs of such payments to farmers have to be paid out of a budget financed by the public purse; that is, they are a direct burden on the taxpayer. As budgets have to be prepared in advance, some assessments need to be made of the likely expenditure, but this may have to be expanded if claims are greater than expected, or the incentives will need to be rationed (perhaps using a points system or put on a first-come-first-served basis) or suspended once the money has run out, usually until the next financial year. Under the CAP, while direct income payments are very largely funded out of the EU budget, for the financial incentives in Group 3 it is usual to employ joint financing, meaning that contributions come from both the EU budget and national budgets, though the proportion often varies according to the type of payment and status of the area in which the payment is made.

Second, these payments are administratively burdensome, much form-filling and correspondence taking place between the public body responsible for them and each individual farmer who applies for payment. The EU requires each Member State to set up an agency which is responsible for checking applications from eligible farmers, making payments, monitoring expenditure and checking for fraud. These administration costs are a form of transaction cost faced by the national government (and ultimately taxpayers) that are necessary to make the system work. So too are the costs incurred by the farmer in finding out the availability of such payments (costs of information) and in applying for them. Transaction costs borne by recipients are made particularly irksome if the payments are risky; this can occur if they are discretionary (rather than automatic) and dependent on meeting tests of eligibility (see below) and of cross-compliance requirements that are complex and can be failed through minor technicalities.

Third, the greater use of direct payments to farmers and incentives has raised the transparency of support. *Transparent* means that the payments are clearly visible, such as cheques paid from the government to individual farmers. Details of payments have been made publicly available, though the legal position seems to be settling to one where, in the future, what individuals receive will not be disclosed, though payments to companies (including farms run as corporate businesses) and similar institutions (charities, trusts etc) will be published annually. This visibility has already attracted adverse publicity in the media and political criticism, making such payments vulnerable to change, reduction and, perhaps, termination. For example, large sums are now widely known to be paid to prominent individuals who are clearly not in any financial plight (including the UK's HM the Queen and the former Governor of the Bank of England), making the CAP difficult to defend as one intended to avoid unfairly low standards of living among the agricultural community.

Fourth, because of the greater transparency, policy designers are forced to confront policy performance and the efficiency and effectiveness with which public funds are used. Political criticism will highlight the question of what the instrument is trying to achieve. For example, payments to farmers in LFAs formerly had the aim of inducing people to continue to live in these areas, but it is now clear that many more effective ways than supporting farming can be found to achieve this objective (such as grants to local service providers and shops, creating non-farming employment etc.). Consequently, the present set of payments refocuses on the contribution these payments can make to the environment and countryside through preventing land abandonment (see the aims of Rural Development Programmes outlined in Chapters 7 and 8).

Fifth, and closely related to the question of performance, is the issue of targeting. This implies being clear who the policy is really being aimed at – the target group – and whether the instrument is being effective and/or efficient at reaching this group. Often policy-makers will have only had an imprecise idea of who the target group should be, illustrated by the failure of the CAP to be explicit about the nature of the 'agricultural community' whose standard of living policy it is supposed to ensure as being fair (see Chapter 2). Any support that goes to people who are not part of the target group is a waste of resources and a source of inefficiency, and poor targeting poses difficulty to attempts to minimise this waste; we might term this impact deadweight. At the level of individual policy programme involving direct payments, administrators will wish to apply tests of eligibility to receive payments as a way of improving targeting. In most cases this will be fairly straightforward – a pre-pension intended for holders aged 55 years and over should not be paid to someone younger – though there is always the possibility of fraud. But even what appears a clear eligibility test needs probing; why is the age of 55 chosen, and how does it relate to general old-age pensions in Member States? Sometimes eligibility tests seem rather arbitrary, and possibly misguided. To take an interesting but rather dated example, under Regulation EEC No 797/85,[1] grants for improvements to effluent and waste handling, and restoration of hedges, walls and banks were restricted to farm operators who spent more than half their time farming (that is, a minimum of 1,100 hours) and where more than half their income came from farming. In the UK it was felt that the restrictions were not in the national interest either in terms of the real aim of the policy programme to improve the environment (as it excluded the many UK farms, some very large, that were operated by people whose main income and occupation was off the farm) or in terms of budgetary implication, since funds could not then flow back from the EU budget to the UK. Consequently the administering institution in the UK undermined the attempt at targeting by being willing to accept applications in the names of farm managers where the owner of the farm business failed to meet the time and income conditions.

5.2.4 Group 4 – Intervening in the market for agricultural commodities and inputs

Historically, this group has been by far the most important in terms of the amount of spending on support of agriculture in the EU, though now it is much reduced. In 1993, before the programme of CAP reforms agreed in 1992 took effect, instruments used to intervene in markets for plant and animal products absorbed 84 per cent of total agricultural expenditure. Changes to the CAP in the 1990s and 2000s have reduced the importance to only about 6 per cent of spending in 2009, the major role now being taken by more direct payments (69 per cent) (see Chapter 10).

The immediate purpose of market intervention is to increase the profitability of farm production. However, the underlying aims have always been mixed, and the mixture has changed over time. While in the early days of the CAP the greater profitability was in part to encourage a greater volume of farm output, from about the late-1970s the main purpose was to support the incomes of farmers. Market intervention comes in two main types, which are:

- **Product price support** (that is, raising the prices which farmers receive for their products). The principal instrument by which this has been achieved has been support buying by national agencies, using funds provided by the EU to keep prices up on the domestic market. In essence, farmers have been guaranteed a buyer for their output. In its simplest form, support buying ensures that a rise in supply does not produce a subsequent fall in market prices. Other instruments include taxes on imported commodities (so that foreign supply is constrained and prices on the domestic market raised); making up the difference between the market price and a higher price that the CAP wishes to support by using top-ups (called deficiency payments); giving a bonus (or bounty payment, or subsidy) per unit of production (e.g. for each animal produced or area cropped), thereby in effect raising the price received by producers. A detailed analysis of each instrument is given in the Appendix to this chapter. Higher product prices cause farmers to receive higher profits on the quantities they would produce in the absence of support and to *expand production*, thereby earning additional profits on this extra output. Quantitative restrictions (quotas) on imports and/or on domestic production also result in farmers receiving higher prices for the reduced quantity on the market; though they sell less, this is usually more than compensated for by the extra price per unit (so that revenue rises). Even if the value of sales is little changed, the lower volume of production will mean that costs are reduced, so that the profit left to the producer will rise.

- **Lowering input costs.** There are many examples where farmers are relieved from paying the full costs of some of the inputs they use. Under the CAP, subsidies are no longer provided for the use of fertiliser or other variable inputs. However, many instances exist as part of national policy programmes that are permitted within the framework of the CAP. Examples include subsidies to the use of glasshouse heating fuel in the Netherlands and concessions in the level of excise duty on fuel for tractors in the UK (where farmers also escape the business rates tax which are paid by other industries on their business assets). Many EU countries (though not the UK) operate systems of subsidised interest on loans for farming purposes. The provision of advisory services free or at subsidised rates also is a form of input subsidy, at least to the extent that farmers would otherwise pay for this advice.

A feature of support to agricultural commodity prices is that, generally, the instruments used are administratively convenient because they usually avoid the need for direct contact between the institution administering the support and a very large number of individual farmers (a major exception is farm-level milk quotas).[2] For example, the European Commission delegates the responsibility for administering taxes on grain imports to national governments. These have customs officers at ports (of which there are likely to be a relatively small number with merchants allowed to import and export agricultural products). In a situation where domestic supply is inadequate to meet market demand, by imposing taxes on imports of grain, the prices which domestic farmers receive are raised automatically. Intervention in domestic markets can be similarly administratively simple; powers will be delegated to single national authorities to buy grain into intervention if market prices fall to prescribed levels. Again the need to contact every farmer in the country is avoided. Because no direct payments are generally made to individual farmers, this form of support is far less transparent than those described above and is therefore less likely to attract media and public attention. For these two reasons, in the past, farmers' unions and government ministries of agriculture have tended to favour this form of support.

However, they can be ineffective in benefitting low income farmers. Under a system which raises product prices, the amount of support which any farmer receives is related to the amount of production he generates. If the aim is to support the income of farmers to ensure that they have a fair standard of living, then the greatest amount of support will miss this target group comprised primarily of small farmers and, instead, go to the larger producers.[3] The amount received by farmers who do not need the support but who get it is an example of impact deadweight.

This form of support distorts the prices which would result in a freely competitive market, driving a wedge between the farmer and fundamental economic forces and leading to economic inefficiency, which is another form of deadweight loss. Higher prices retain productive resources in agriculture which, under a competitive market system, would find their way into other uses. This implies a loss of efficiency to society. The international pattern of production and trade is also distorted, with a loss in the economic benefits which international specialisation and trade, in the direction indicated by comparative advantage, would bring. There is not space here to explore this point in detail, but analysis can show that the overall gains to farmers brought about by instruments that distort markets are smaller than the losses suffered by groups that bear the costs of the instruments (typically taxpayers and consumers). There is also a blunting of the longer-term pressure for farmers to look for improvements in productivity, felt in a competitive market economy as a downward pressure on prices to which they have to respond. When farm output prices are supported this spur to the adoption of technological advance is relaxed, leading to a loss in efficiency in the longer term (loss of dynamic efficiency).

Many of the instruments used to support the prices received by farmers also mean that the burden is passed to consumers as higher food prices and to other users of agricultural commodities as higher input prices. Though the price of the basic food material will be only one of the elements contributing to the amounts consumers pay across the counter, and this will vary between types of food purchased, higher prices paid by food processors for their raw material will usually be reflected in the prices they charge, and these will be passed down the wholesale and retail stages in the food chain. In turn this means that the amount which farmers can sell will be reduced. For commodities which are used as animal feeds (such as cereals) there will be a search for cheaper alternatives (such as manioc, which is imported from Asia). Thus, higher commodity prices for farmers are likely to result in a cutback in consumption (or utilisation) and thus an imbalance (or 'disequilibrium') in the markets.

Where production is stimulated, but utilisation remains the same or falls, surpluses can arise, the disposal of which presents a major problem. The EU has at various times been faced with 'mountains' of grain, frozen beef, chilled butter, and 'lakes' of wine, vivid labels for accumulating stock in public and private storage facilities. Various methods can be used to reduce these stocks, each of which carries problems (see Box 5.3).

Reflecting their many disadvantages, instruments of support that raise market prices for agricultural commodities have been largely abandoned by the CAP in favour of direct payments. The process started in earnest in the 1992 reforms (the MacSharry Reforms) and has been continued to the extent that now there is very little direct market intervention, though provision exists for it to be used in emergency situations (see Chapter 6 for details). The main pressures in this process have come from the budgetary cost of such a support system and the political will to conclude successful negotiations in freeing up world trade, to which agricultural support systems have been a major impediment (see Chapter 9 on trade and Chapter 12 on the stages of reform). However, market price support has left a potent legacy. The distortions to the working of free markets built up many vested interests that have had to be bought off or compensated. Important among this compensation is the current

Box 5.3 Ways of getting rid of an accumulated surplus of agricultural commodities

- **Destruction (e.g. burned, dumped or let rot) or denatured in some way.** Though a relatively cheap method of disposal, public opinion is hostile to such practices, as consumers find themselves paying substantial amounts for food identical to that which they see being destroyed.
- **Subsidised use for industrial purposes.** Wine can be distilled and used for industrial alcohol, and small amounts of cereals can be used in similar ways in the chemical industry, though these actions are only attractive if heavily subsidised.
- **Discretionary sales.** Some can be sold at very low prices to selected groups in society (e.g. Christmas butter for pensioners and to charities, including educational establishments), though there is a danger that this will undermine the 'normal' market for the product.
- **Food aid.** Some can be given as food aid to developing countries, though the types of food in surplus probably will not match the needs of the recipients, either from a dietary or cultural points of view, or their ability to handle the material (no frozen food storage facilities). The wisdom of food aid, other than as emergency relief, is also now widely discredited.
- **Preferential sales to assist international relations.** Closely similar to the above, such sales carry political dangers. For example, stocks of surplus EU butter and beef in the 1980s were sold at low prices, to the USSR as a way of improving relations. However, such sales to nations that were then often identified as 'hostile' by the public aroused heavy criticism in the press when EU citizens were having to pay much higher prices, causing problems in domestic politics.
- **Subsidised exports to the world market.** This is the option which causes the greatest objections from other countries. To be able to sell commodities in storage onto the world market, exporting firms have to be given a subsidy, termed an export restitution, for each unit sold, equal to the difference between the internal EU price and the world price (plus a margin to cover transport etc.). When the volume of farm products exported in this manner is substantial (as was often the situation with EU cereal exports), the world price is depressed as the supply on the world market increases. Consequently, the amount of export subsidy had to be increased. Other countries exporting to the world market object because their earnings fall and their traditional outlets are lost, to the subsidised EU goods. This will be particularly damaging to developing countries heavily dependent on export earnings though others that are importers of the commodities in question may benefit from lower world prices. Countries such as the US that are capable of applying retaliatory actions may threaten to use tax on other commodities imported from the EU, which will be against the EU's interest.

system of Single Farm Payments to EU farmers which is, in essence, a means of giving them the sort of support they were receiving under the former CAP regimes for commodities, but in an uncoupled and less-distorting form.

A complication to instruments under the headings of Groups 2 to 4 above is that, where incentives or prices are set under the CAP, they are done so in terms of the EU currency, the euro (€). However, for these sums to be put into practice they must be expressed in local currencies. With the adoption of monetary union in 1999, the national currencies of the 11 participating countries are locked to the euro (the *Euro-Zone*). However, for the other Member States, changes in the exchange rates will affect the coefficients used to convert euro support prices into national currencies and hence the level of support as seen by farmers in these countries. For example, a rise in the value of the pound sterling against the euro will lead to a reduction in the level of support payments made to UK farmers, a change that happens independent of agricultural policy and the problems it attempts to address. The rates at which currency conversions are made, and the mechanisms lying behind these rates, are collectively referred to as the *agri-monetary* system. Though not designed as an instrument of agricultural policy, in practice the manipulation of the agri-monetary system was used by governments as a means of influencing the prices received by their farmers. Chapter 10 deals with the financial aspects of the CAP, including agri-money.

5.3 Analysing instruments of policy

From points touched on in the above discussion, it is clear that policy instruments can be analysed from four broad perspectives:

- **The economic perspective** is concerned with the effects on markets for agricultural products and inputs, the gainers and losers from any changes which the instrument brings about (principally the welfare implications for agricultural producers, consumers of these products and taxpayers) and the impact on the economic efficiency with which resources are used.

- **The budgetary perspective** is concerned with something narrower, the payments from and receipts into the EU and national budgets arising from the instrument. National budgets are financed by taxpayers, and the EU budget is made up largely of contributions from the national budgets of Member States. If tax systems are progressive (that is, people with higher incomes pay a greater proportion of that income as tax than do those with lower incomes), the burden will fall mostly on those best able to pay. However, predictability and controllability may be seen as more important than the overall cost. Treasuries will like instruments that raise revenue for them and be cautious about instruments that cost them money.

- **The administrative perspective** looks at an instrument from the point of view of how easy or difficult it is to implement. Administrators have a tendency to prefer the status quo, or at least to model new instruments on those which already exist and work, as these will require similar activities and functions to what is currently in place. The administration will have limited staff and resources; it will have its own priorities and goals independent of those of the policy instrument. From this perspective, there will often be a preference for an instrument which is easy and cheap to operate, even if this means that the policy objectives are less than fully met.

- **The political perspective** looks at the pressure on decision-makers in the policy process to use or to avoid using a particular instrument, and on the sources of that pressure. The perceptions of these pressures can sometimes change with surprising rapidity depending on circumstances. For example, the political judgement of the acceptability of direct payments by the agricultural industry changed markedly before their introduction as part of the CAP reforms of 1992, so that the move to the present system of Single Farm Payments was a relatively small step.

As part of understanding the CAP, recognition must be made that, in the real world, when choosing a policy instrument, economic rationale is often overridden by budgetary, administrative and political factors linked to the history of how the present situation was reached (another example of path-dependency). For example, if the main objective of the CAP is to protect the living standards of farmers by improving their income situation, economic rationale suggests that, if we were to start afresh, the most cost-effective way of achieving this aim would be to, first, identify precisely where the living standards are unsatisfactorily low by actually measuring disposable incomes (the main determinant of what households can spend on their standard of living or save), and then to give direct income payments (supplements) to those farmers with unacceptably low incomes. However, this action would be difficult administratively because, for historical reasons, adequate information on the overall incomes of farmers and their families is not available throughout the EU (see Chapter 4). If this system cost more to the EU budget, decision-makers would not welcome it at times when the overall budget was under heavy pressure. And there are political issues. If payments to farmers can be interpreted as welfare handouts, they become more easily compared with other social payments in society; they are therefore more vulnerable to reform and reduction, something which farmers' unions will be keen to avoid. However, if the payments are perceived as rewards for providing environmental services (protecting biodiversity, conserving the landscape etc.) they may be far more acceptable to all parties. A danger is that dressing up an existing payment as something else, for example by imposing environmental cross-compliance conditions to the EU's Single Farm Payment system, is likely to be an inefficient way of achieving the environmental objective.

It should be noted that often several instruments are used together. For example, support buying into intervention as a way of increasing the prices received by EU farmers needs to be combined with a control of imports, or the EU would find itself facing an impossible task as foreign supplies flood in. Ways will be needed to dispose of accumulating surpluses, of which subsidies to exporters to enable them to be sold on the world market has been a major mechanism. Similarly, it is futile to impose quotas on domestic (EU) producers, with the intention of raising prices, without at the same time controls being placed on imports.

To help understand the effects and impacts which can be brought about by a CAP policy instrument, a useful checklist of questions is given in Box 5.4. These can be answered in the detailed treatment of instruments contained in the Appendix to this chapter and with the information on the regimes for individual commodities given in Chapter 6. Two examples may be useful at this point. A direct income payment (such as the CAP's Single Farm Payment), if fully decoupled, should not have any effect on the market for agricultural commodities or the food chain, and there is unlikely to be any impact on the market for inputs, though the price of land may be affected if payment is dependent on occupying land. There should not be any direct impact on the pressure for efficiency because the full force of the market remains, though if the payments provide a prop to the agricultural activities

---

Box 5.4 Checklist for a policy instrument

What happens to the following?:
- the markets for agricultural commodities, including
  - market prices and the quantities of products demanded from the market by consumers, or otherwise utilised;
  - prices received by domestic (EU) farmers (which may be different from the market price) and the quantities they supply;
  - prices paid by food consumers or other users of agricultural commodities;
  - the balance between demand and supply for each agricultural commodity on the domestic (EU) market, and especially any accumulation of surplus;
  - knock-on effects between the markets for single agricultural products;
  - the markets for inputs used by farmers, and in particular the likelihood of costs rising or falling in response to changes in demand by farmers for these inputs (as reflected in supply elasticity);
  - the markets for food processors and distributors;
- stability of prices and incomes experienced by EU farmers;
- the pressure for domestic farmers to become more efficient;
- the distribution of benefit between farmers of different sizes, types and regions (price rises give greater benefit to those farmers that produce most, and farmers on some types of farm may benefit by more or less than others);
- the price received by foreign (world) farmers and the quantity they supply to the EU;
- stability of prices and quantities on the world market;
- the pressure for efficiency among foreign farmers;
- the EU's balance of trade in the agricultural commodity, and the related change to the balance of international payments and the related exchange rates;
- the distribution of the cost of the instrument (between consumers, taxpayers, rest of the world);
- the cost to the EU and national budgets and any revenue raised by the instrument;
- the markets for non-agricultural commodities, and the consequential whole-economy effects of any one instrument;
- the administrative feasibility of the instrument and the transactions costs involved, both those of the administrators and of the potential recipients,
- the political acceptability of the instrument to the various members of the policy community; any side effects, and their compatibility with the aims of other policies (environment, social etc.).

---

of some poorly performing farmers who otherwise would quit the industry, there could be a negative influence. The cost unambiguously falls on the taxpayer (who provides the EU budget with funds). There may be administrative difficulties (a detailed system of eligibility tests and payments is needed), and political implications depend to a major extent on how the SFP is explained and justified.

In contrast, the system of quotas as applied to milk producers in the EU, with each agricultural holding receiving an allocation but limiting the volume it can produce, is designed to restrict the quantity coming onto the market. In theory this alone could keep prices up as long as imports are controlled, but in reality quotas have been used in combination with support buying. Assuming the price farmers receive is above the free-market level, the larger the level of production permitted by the quota, the greater the benefit to the quota holder, so that larger farmers (with more quota) receive the bulk of the support. Consumers face higher milk prices, the burden falling with disproportionate weight on the shoulder of poorer consumers (for whom milk purchases take a larger share of their disposable income). The quota itself becomes an asset that has value in the balance sheets of farm businesses so, once created, they are difficult to dismantle. They tend to lower the incentive for higher efficiency because better performers cannot expand output beyond their allocated quota, though in practice this can be eased by allowing quotas to be traded between individual holdings. Administratively they are demanding, requiring a system to allocate them initially, to police them (checking that farms only produced up to their permitted quantity) and to allow transfers. But from a political perspective, and despite having many known undesirable features, quotas had attractions. In 1984 politicians and the industry faced a crisis in the dairy sector that meant that something had to be done quickly to stem escalating production volumes and costs of support. Quotas were preferred to the alternative, which was a very large cut in support prices. Although initially seen as a short-term expedient, they have proved difficult to remove. Their planned termination in 2015 is not certain.

5.4 The OECD's estimation of support

The OECD has developed a methodology that brings together estimates of the value of support arising from the various instruments used in agricultural policy into a single indicator (or rather, a range of indicators). Figures are published annually for its member countries, the EU being treated as a single unit in these tables as the CAP applies throughout its territory. Though concern remains with the level of support, today there is particular interest in the changing balance between the various ways in which it is given, with a general move towards decoupled payments and less distortion of markets. Here there is space only to give a brief mention of what is covered, and reference should be made to the OECD documentation for details of the methodology and access to the results.

The main focus of interest when looking at instruments of the CAP is in the Producer Support Estimates (PSEs). These give an indication of the amount of effort put into supporting agriculture in various ways; this is a measure of what is absorbed by the policy, in contrast to the outcome, such as an increase in income or other changes that the support is targeted at. The main contributing elements in building up the PSE are the values of:

- **Market price support**, estimated on a commodity by commodity basis and then summed. It corresponds to the difference between, on the one hand, what purchasers of the commodities have to pay as the result of the use of instruments that generate higher prices for farmers and, on the other, what their expenditure would be if they purchased the same quantity at the price the commodity could be bought for if imported (that is, the market price differential times the existing quantity). This represents an economic transfer from consumers of the commodity to producers;
- **Budgetary and other transfers**, which includes direct payments to individual farmers (such as under the Single Payment Scheme – see Chapter 6 – and for agri-environment management agreements – see Chapter 8). In principle, this group

also covers the value of all tax concessions (revenue forgone) given to farmers and landowners, though in practice this is confined to the value of the lower fuel duty that is found in many countries. Collectively this group is referred to as transfers from taxpayers.

PSEs are expressed in absolute amounts (in euro for the EU, though for international comparisons they are also expressed in US dollars). Thus a PSE of €1 billion represents the monetary value of the gross transfer from consumers and taxpayers as the result of the policy instruments used to support agriculture. PSEs are also expressed as a ratio of the value of gross farm receipts; a %PSE of 20 per cent means that the estimated value of transfers to individual producers is equivalent to 20 per cent of gross farm receipts. A %PSE cannot by definition be higher than 100 per cent, at which level all farm receipts come from policy measures, with no returns from the market. It does not necessarily follow that if the support instruments were removed, farm revenue would fall collectively by 20 per cent, as there would no doubt be adjustments in domestic and international markets; this illustrates the importance of recognising that PSEs are estimated in current world market conditions.

Other transfers and coefficients are calculated, including support provided collectively (such as advice services for farmers financed from the public purse) and the monetary value of transfers to consumers (which will normally be negative but where individual instruments can confer a positive element to them). The Total Support Estimate brings these all together (the PSE transfers to agricultural producers individually, support provided collectively as well as subsidies to consumers) and eliminates any double-counting. When expressed as a percentage of a country's gross domestic product (GDP) it gives an indication of the financial cost to (or burden imposed on) the economy of the policy measures supporting agriculture.

It is worth noting that PSE estimates do not cover all policy instruments; some form of transfer to agricultural producers has to be present, so a Regulation to change farmer behaviour in the interest of the environment will not appear, although if the legislation enables compensation payments to be made, these will be included. Forestry and fishing are not covered, nor are any general policy measures not specifically targeted at agriculture (such as the availability of business training courses not specific to people engaged in agriculture). Neither do they differentiate as to the reason why support is given; while in the past the main purpose can be assumed to have been to increase the incomes derived from farming, today the objectives of many schemes are environmental or social, with any impact on income being incidental.

As well as its regular *Monitoring and Evaluation Report*, the OECD also makes its estimates available on a public database showing the detailed breakdown of the main forms of support provided by the EU (and other countries) for a run of years, together with a range of indicators. Detailed methodological documentation is available and an account given of data sources and approaches used for individual commodities and in each country; most of this is available on the OECD's website.

5.5 In conclusion

This chapter has considered the way in which the EU has implemented policies relating to agriculture. It is clear that all the instruments used require public resources to make them work, though some need more than others. The main resource mentioned has been financial, but other forms of input are also involved (such as labour to administer and deliver policies).

Some of the resource implications are not felt directly in public spending but by consumers who are required by some instruments to pay more for their food and thus support farmers through distortions in the markets for agricultural commodities. Many of these issues will be met again in Chapter 11 where there is an attempt to evaluate the CAP.

Further reading

Buckwell, A. (1997) 'Some microeconomic analysis of CAP market regimes'. Chapter 7 in Ritson, C. and Harvey, D. (eds) *The Common Agricultural Policy.* 2nd edition. CAB International, Wallingford.

Colman, D. and Roberts, D. (1994) 'The Common Agricultural Policy'. Chapter 4 in Artis, M. J. and Lee, N. (eds) *The Economics of the European Union,* Oxford University Press, Oxford.

Hill, B. (2006) *An Introduction to Economics: Concepts for Students of Agriculture and the Rural Sector.* 3rd edition. CABI, Wallingford. (Chapter 10 ' Government Policy for agriculture and the rural sector').

OECD (2006) *Decoupling: Policy Implications.* Organisation for Economic Co-operation and Development, Paris.

OECD (2009) *Agricultural Policies in OECD Countries: Monitoring and Evaluation Report 2009.* Organisation for Economic Cooperation and Development, Paris.

OECD (2010) *Agricultural Policies in OECD Countries at a Glance 2010.* Organisation for Economic Cooperation and Development, Paris.

OECD (2010) *OECD'S Producer Support Estimate and Related Indicators of Agricultural Support – Concepts, Calculations, Interpretation and Use (The PSE Manual)* [Summary available on OECD website www.oecd.org as 'Introduction to the OECD producer support estimate and related indicators of agricultual support']. Organisation for Economic Co-operation and Development, Paris.

Ritson, C. (1977) *Agricultural Economics – Principles and Policy.* Crosby Lockwood Staples (Granada), London. (Chapter 8).

Stevens, J. (1993) *The Economics of Collective Choice.* Westview Press, Boulder, CO (Chapter 2).

Annex to Chapter 5

Market analysis of some CAP policy instruments

To understand the way in which instruments work, simple graphical representations of the economic impact of each on the market for an agricultural commodity are useful. Figures 5.A1 to 5.A6 present static, partial equilibrium analyses of the major instruments that are or have been used by the CAP, starting with direct income payments and progressing through a range of market intervention instruments. The term 'static' is used, because only the final situation brought about by the instrument is considered, not the steps by which this change occurs (which would constitute a more 'dynamic' approach). The analysis is 'partial' because it only considers one commodity at a time and ignores impacts on the market situations of other commodities or of the wider economy (which would be a 'general' equilibrium approach).

In assessing the use of each instrument, it is assumed that the instrument is applied to a 'free-market' situation of a single commodity in which the demand within the EU for the commodity, the supply from EU farmers and the supply from abroad (from the world market) interact to determine the price on the EU market and the amount imported or exported. Other assumptions are made in the interest of simplicity. Among the most important of these are that:

a   the demand for the agricultural commodity in question is relatively inelastic; that is the quantity demanded from the market is not greatly affected by price, so that a 1 per cent change in price is associated with a less-than-1 per cent change in quantity demanded. This produces a relatively steeply sloping demand curve;

b   the supply of the agricultural commodity from domestic (EU) producers is relatively price-inelastic in the short term. Again, this produces a domestic supply curve that is relatively steeply sloped;

c   the supply of the commodity that can be bought from the world market is infinitely elastic at the world price. That is, the amount which traders from the EU buy from or sell to the world market does not affect the world price. This assumption enables the world supply curve to be drawn as a horizontal line in the graphs below. We have already noted that the EU can depress world prices by selling subsidised exports on the world market, so the fragility of this simplification must be borne in mind.

The notes attached to the diagrams raise the main issues associated with each instrument. They echo the checklist given in Box 5.4. For a more formal approach to the analysis of the welfare changes they bring about see Ritson (1977) and Hill (2006).

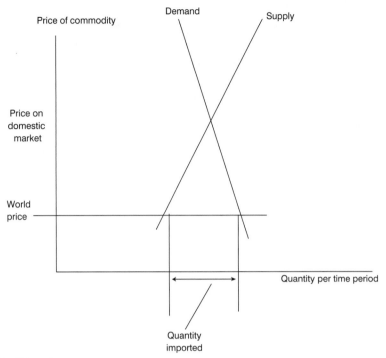

Figure 5.A1   Direct income payments

Notes:

1   This diagram assumes that supply comes both from domestic (EU) producers and from the world market, and that the EU is a net importer.

2   If there were no imports, the price EU farmers would receive for their produce would correspond to the intersection between the supply and demand curves. With imports allowed, the price in the EU is the same as the world market price, because no one will pay more for domestic production than for imports. EU farmers receive, in essence, the world price and produce, the quantity corresponding to this price on their supply curve. The gap between this quantity and the total demanded is made up by imports.

3   If a direct income payment is paid to farmers, as long at this is fully decoupled (that is, is not related to the amount that farmers produce and does not influence their production decisions) it will have no effect on the supply curves for agricultural commodities from domestic (EU) producers. The basic demand and supply relationships are not changed.

4   Pressure on domestic farmers to become more efficient is maintained, and they have to be internationally competitive.

5   Food prices to consumers reflect world prices, which are as low as international competition allows.

6   There is no distortion of international markets, and foreign suppliers who are competitive are able to sell to the EU market.

7   But direct income payments are relatively complex to administer, needing detailed contact between government and individual farmers, systems to validate and make payments, and are susceptible to fraud.

8   The cost falls on the EU budget, and thus on taxpayers.

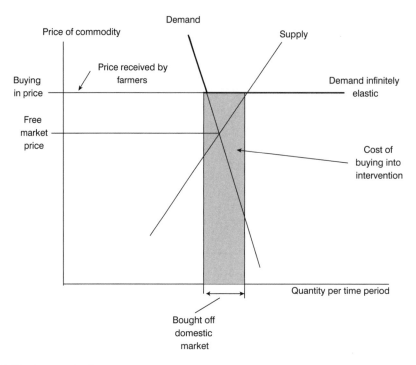

Figure 5.A2 Support buying

Notes:
1 When an agency of the European Union buys a commodity from the market, a new kinked demand curve is created which is infinitely elastic at the buying-in price, that is, any quantity, large or small, will be bought in at the intervention price.
2 The supported price being higher than the free-market price, output from domestic farmers increases as they respond to the incentive. However, the amount taken from the market by consumers/utilisers of the commodity (other than the support buying agency) will contract.
3 Accumulating stocks of the commodity in the hands of the intervention agency have to be disposed of. Selling them on the world market will involve subsidising their export, but this may be the least politically objectionable action; alternatives are burning, let rot, giving away, discretionary sales etc.
4 Support buying will only be effective if imports are controlled, usually by import levies.
5 Consumers of food find themselves paying higher prices, a regressive change because lower-income consumers are affected proportionally greater than higher-income consumers. Higher food prices are inflationary.
6 Domestic farmers find the pressure on them to become more efficient is relaxed.
7 The cost of buying into intervention falls on the EU budget, and hence on taxpayers.
8 Support buying is administratively relatively quite simple, as the purchasing agency need only offer to buy at the supported price and need not have details of each individual producer of the commodity.

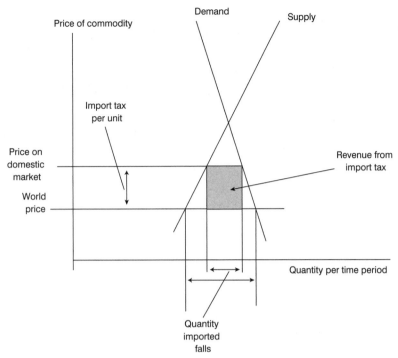

Figure 5.A3   A tax on imports

Notes:

1   A tax on imports can only work to raise domestic prices if there are some imports to tax. The free-market situation (before a tax is imposed) is one in which the EU is an importer of the commodity. The price in the EU is the same as the world market price, because no one will pay more for domestic production than for imports.

2   A tax on imports has the effect of raising the supply curve for the commodity from the world market by the extent of the levy, thereby raising the price that EU farmers receive.

3   As a result, home farmers expand their supply, but the amount demanded will shrink. In consequence, imports of the commodity are reduced. This will have an effect on the demand for foreign currency, tending to bid up the international value of the home currency.

4   A levy will raise money for the budget of the EU.

5   Domestic prices can only be raised to the point at which no imports occur (where the domestic D and S curves intersect). To raise prices further, some other instrument will need to be used, such as support buying.

6   Food prices to consumers are raised, a regressive step which may be inflationary.

7   Pressure on domestic farmers to become more efficient is relaxed.

8   Relatively simple to administer.

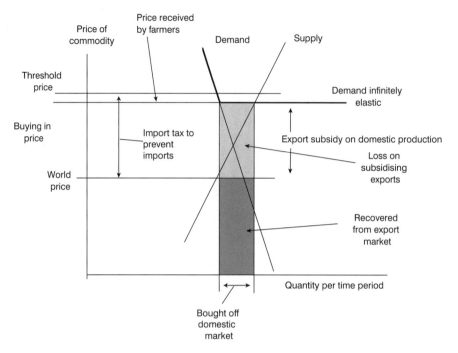

Figure 5.A4 A combination of an import levy and support buying (This builds on the features of the two preceding diagrams; the combination applied to several major agricultural commodities, including cereals, beef, and wine)

Notes:

1 In the example, support buying is used to maintain a price for EU farmers higher than could be achieved by an import tax alone.

2 The import tax is, in essence, a way of preventing the supported domestic market from being undermined by cheaper imports. The tax raises the price of potential imports to the threshold price, which is above the support buying price and the price on the domestic market, so imports are not worth buying.

3 In the example, the use of the two instruments has changed the EU from being an importer of the commodity into an exporter.

4 Exports have to be subsidised, with the cost being borne by the EU budget. These exports can depress the world price (not shown here) and be a cause of dislocation of international trade, including the use of retaliatory action by other exporters.

5 The system works to the disadvantage of consumers because they pay higher prices, the burden being felt more keenly by the low-income members of society.

6 Pressure for improved efficiency among EU farmers is relaxed.

7 The support is administratively attractive, as there is no direct contact with individual farmers.

8 The support is not 'transparent' so keeps a low political profile

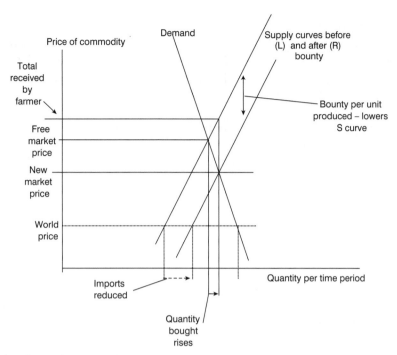

Figure 5.A5   Production bounty (such as a subsidy payment per head of animal or per ha of crop) or a subsidy on an input to production

Notes:

1 A bounty (subsidy payment linked to production and paid directly to farmers) lowers the supply curve by the extent of the bounty.

2 When there are no imports (solid lines in the diagram) the shift in the supply curve pushes down market price. Consequently, the final price the farmer receives is less than the original market price plus bounty; it is the new lower market price, plus bounty.

3 The benefit of the bounty is thus in part passed on to the consumer in the form of a lower market price, the extent depending on the elasticity of demand.

4 In practice, this form of support was often combined with support buying, for example in the beef regime, where the suckler cow premium was used to encourage extensive beef production while intervention buying prevented the decline in market price that otherwise might result.

5 When imports are allowed, and price on the domestic market is determined by world prices, the subsidy's effect is to leave prices unchanged but to reduce imports

6 A subsidy paid to farmers which reduces the cost of an input to production (for example, grants for new buildings) also shifts the supply curve in the same direction as does a production subsidy. However, the extent of the shift will depend on the elasticity of supply of the input. The subsidy increases farmers' demand for the input. However, if the suppliers of the input cannot (or will not) increase their output, in the short term, the additional demand simply results in higher prices for the input, and the farmers end up paying the same net price for the input, and the supply curve of the commodity is unchanged. All the benefit goes to the supplier. However, the more elastic the supply of the input, the greater the proportion of the benefit that goes to the farmers, and the more the supply curve of the product is shifted to the right.

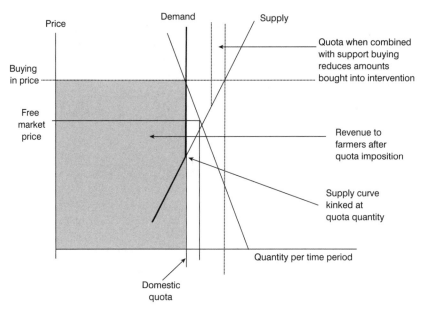

Figure 5.A6 Quota on domestic production

Notes:

1 By imposing a quota on the maximum amount that EU farmers are permitted to produce (which may be fixed at national, regional or farm level) at a quantity that corresponds to less than the free-market situation, a new supply curve is created, kinked at the quota quantity (see diagram in solid lines).

2 By reducing supply, the market price is raised to the point at which the quota-restricted supply curve intersects the demand curve. Where the demand curve is steep (price-inelastic demand) the smaller volume of output will be more than compensated by the higher prices, so revenue will increase. Costs of production will fall with a lower output, so incomes should improve.

3 Consumers are faced with higher prices on the market, regressive and potentially inflationary.

4 Pressure for producers to become more efficient is relaxed, both because of higher product prices and, if quotas are applied at the farm level, because the more efficient cannot expand unless they can obtain more quota.

5 Quota systems have to be administered and policed. Questions arise, such as at what level should quotas be imposed (e.g. national, regional or farm level?); how should quotas be allocated, and should they be given to farmers (which is tantamount to giving the farmers a capital asset free) or sold to them?; should they be tradable and, if so, should this be possible across national boundaries; how should new entrants be treated for the system to be equitable; what should happen if quotas are exceeded?

6 The dotted lines illustrate the situation with the quota on milk production in the EU. The quota quantity corresponds to a volume greater than that at which demand and supply would be at equilibrium in a free market. The imposition of a quota system was largely to contain the rapidly expanding level of output and thus to contain the amount which had to be bought into intervention and the cost of doing so. Similarly, in the beef market, there are, in effect, regional quotas for the 'special premium' payable on young male animals; the main form of support, however, is intervention buying of beef.

6

UNDERSTANDING THE SUPPORT OF AGRICULTURE IN THE EU

Pillar 1 of the CAP (direct payments and market support)

Key topics

- As preparation for understanding the present support system, an outline is given of the commodity regimes before the 2003 Mid-Term Review and their implications for production, land use, trade and structural change.
- The transition to the present Single Farm Payment/Single Area Payment system is described.
- The features of the CAP's Pillar 1 are described, comprising direct payments and remaining elements of market support.

6.1 Introduction

Nothing demonstrates better the speed with which changes having been taking place in the CAP over the last decade or so than the way in which support is given to agriculture. As was described in Chapter 2, reforms to the CAP agreed by the European Council as part of *Agenda 2000* divided support from the EU budget to agriculture into two Pillars. The first, or Pillar 1, includes direct forms of support to farm operators and the cost of interventions in markets for farm commodities. It accounts for some three-quarters of all spending on EU agriculture and is thus by far the thicker of the two Pillars.[1] Over four-fifths (84 per cent) of Pillar 1 spending takes the form of an annual payment to farm operators under the Single Payment Scheme (see below), the remainder being evenly split between market support and other forms of direct aid (8 per cent each). Thus, the Single Payment Scheme accounts for approaching two-thirds (62 per cent) of all spending from the EU budget on agriculture. Spending under Pillar 1 is wholly funded by the EU budget, with no direct contribution from national government budgets. The slimmer second Pillar (Pillar 2) is made up of what is called 'rural development' spending, which includes EU support provided to the cost of schemes organised on a national basis (but based on EU legislation) that cover a mix of economic aims (including farm adjustment and some improvements in village living conditions) and environmental aims where agriculture can be instrumental in improving and conserving biodiversity and landscape. Chapter 6 deals with Pillar 1 of the CAP, and Chapters 7 and 8 with Pillar 2.

In explaining the present situation, some mention of how it has come to be is unavoidable (though the historical perspective is mostly reserved for Chapter 12). The CAP's objectives when it was established by the 1957 Treaty of Rome included the aims of providing a secure supply of food, improving productivity and ensuring a fair standard of living for the agricultural community (see Chapter 2). Between the early 1960s and the early 1990s, the

CAP attempted to achieve these objectives mainly by raising the prices received by EU farmers for what they produced. This was brought about by intervening in the domestic markets for agricultural commodities in the EU and by protecting these markets from international competition. These interventions were arranged as Common Market Organisations (CMOs), one for each major commodity, also often called 'commodity regimes'. In addition, there were some measures to assist structural change, though these took only a relatively small share of resources spent on agriculture from the EU budget.

An explanation of the CAP written before 2005 would have included a detailed account, commodity by commodity, of the CMOs (beef and veal, milk, wine, sugar and so on), concentrating on the regimes that consumed the largest amounts of public expenditure in their support of prices of farm commodities on domestic EU markets. In the mid 1990s there were some 19 CMOs covering three groupings of agricultural commodities – crop products, livestock products and 'specialised crops'. These CMOs were typically highly complex arrangements designed to keep the prices that farmers received above what they might otherwise have been (for which the price on international markets was often assumed the reference level) built up over a number of years, and each CMO differed from all others. Practitioners and commentators tended to specialise and become expert in a small number of CMOs, but it was hard to become highly proficient in understanding them all. Because of a fundamental reform to the CAP made in 2003/2004 and implemented in 2005 and 2006 with the introduction of the Single Payment Scheme, the present situation is much simpler, many of the earlier forms of CMO support having been rolled up into the Single Farm Payment. However, it is not satisfactory to ignore completely the CAP arrangements as they were before 2005. They have left a legacy of problems the current CAP has to confront, and remnants of the previous CMOs remain.

6.2 Key elements of the CAP before the reform of 2003

CMOs were highly complex arrangements whose purposes were to intervene in commodity markets. They differed in detail, depending on the commodity, but often used similar instruments. The economic analysis of instruments was covered in Chapter 5, especially the Appendix that reviewed a series of the most important ones. Our present concern is their legacy and what remains of them.

The three main approaches used to raise prices for farmers up to the CAP changes of 2003/4 were as follows:

6.2.1 Protection of domestic markets from international competition (often called 'external support')

In the absence of any market intervention, the prices received by farmers in the EU would have corresponded with the price on the world market, as no-one would be prepared to pay more for domestically produced agricultural commodities if they could be obtained cheaper by importing. A tax on imports gives this protection (shown in Figure 5A.3).

Before the 1994 GATT Uruguay Agreement the principal form of import tax was a *variable levy* that made up the difference between the commodity's price on the international market and a threshold (or minimum import) price below which the commodity was not allowed into the EU (see Box 6.1 and Figure 6.1). This threshold price was set at a level that sought to ensure that producers received a closely related 'target price', determined politically,

Box 6.1 CAP institutional support prices

In early decades of the CAP, policy-makers had in mind a target price for each commodity (though the label was not applied consistently); how they came to a decision on this price is not at all clear but market balance was one major determinant. Following the 1993 GATT Uruguay Round Agreement the concept of a target price was officially abandoned. However, there was clearly still some less formal target level of prices implied for each commodity at which the various forms of support were aimed.

The intervention price was the level at which the official intervention agencies (or others acting on their behalf) started buying the commodity (or 'withdrawing' it); in effect they put a floor in the market, though this was not entirely a level one because of restrictions on the time period over which the agencies were allowed to be active. Also there were variations from place to place caused by differences in transport costs and other national variations. In the pre-1993 GATT conditions this intervention price was set somewhat below the target price but was thereafter determined independently. The price which farmers actually received from selling their produce was expected to be close to this intervention price, given that each farmer was free to strike a good or bad deal in the market, though it would reflect variations in transport costs etc.

To prevent goods being bought on the world market by traders and sold straight into intervention at the higher supported price, a tax (tariff) was imposed on top of the world price importers paid for the commodity. In the situation before the 1993 GATT agreement, this was a variable levy, calculated not only to mop up the difference between the world price and the intervention price, but going much further and raising the price of imports almost to the level of the target price. Thus the frontier threshold price or minimum import price (corresponding to the price the importer had to pay for the commodity on the world market plus the import levy) provided a defensive boundary for the prices set under the CAP; it was set just a little lower than the target price to reflect the cost of transport from the ports to internal parts of the EU where there was the greatest deficit of the commodity and thus the highest local price. As the world price went up and down, adjustments were made in the levy (reduced or increased respectively) to ensure that the cost of potential imports always corresponded to the threshold price. In the 1993 GATT agreement the variable levy was transformed into a fixed tariff, so changes in world prices were subsequently mirrored in the price at which the commodity entered the EU (frontier entry price). Basically, the new system gave less external protection when world prices were low, though there were emergency powers ('safeguards') to raise import taxes in extreme circumstances where the volume imported exceeded given levels or import prices fell below a certain level.

To dispose of the commodity taken into intervention stores or from the domestic market an export restitution (subsidy) was paid out of the EU budget. This corresponded to the difference between the internal market price (which would be closely related to the intervention price) and the world price. In practice the amount of subsidy was usually determined through a tendering system for would-be exporters.

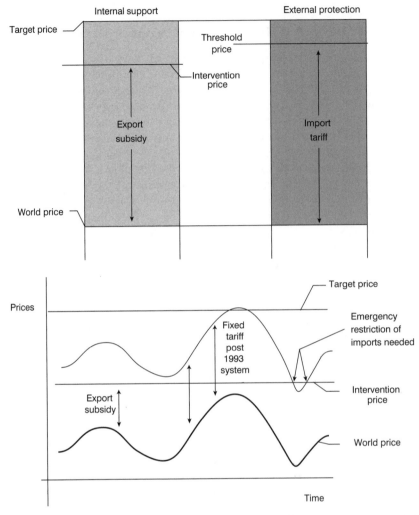

Figure 6.1 The CAP's intervention in agricultural commodity markets: upper – before 1992; lower – after the 1994 GATT agreement

intended to give EU producers a satisfactory return and help them achieve the CAP's aim of a 'fair standard of living'. This 'target price', sometimes given other names depending on the commodity, was set as part of the CMO by a mix of decisions by the Council and by the Commission using powers delegated to it (see Chapter 3). Use of this variable import levy meant that EU farmers were insulated from developments on world markets. If world prices for a commodity fell or rose, the import levy would be adjusted accordingly. Thus, both the production patterns of domestic farmers and the structure of the industry were prevented from reacting to world market signals. International markets and trade were also often distorted, and this became a source of political friction between countries. Under the 1994 GATT Uruguay Round agreement, these variable levies underwent 'tariffication', that is, were made fixed rather than variable, so that changes in world prices were better reflected in domestic prices, albeit at a higher absolute level.

Less commonly used was a restriction on the quantity of a commodity that could be imported that also helped restrict total supply on the EU market and thus kept prices up.

6.2.2 Support of domestic markets

The principal way of doing this was by intervention buying (by national bodies acting on behalf of the EU and using EU funds) into storage (see Figure 5A.2). Though this did not apply to all commodities, it was an important element in the CMOs for cereals, beef, milk products and wine. There was provision for selling accumulated intervention stocks (and commodities that would otherwise have been taken into storage) onto world markets by offering subsidies ('export restitutions') to firms willing to tender for them. In effect, these subsidies compensated exporters for the difference between EU prices and lower world prices. Such subsidised exports were politically sensitive as they enabled EU exports to undercut unsubsidised exports and had price-lowering impacts on international markets, both characteristics carrying implications for non-EU countries that depended on their export earnings; these made such subsidies a major issue in international trade negotiations.

Other ways of supporting domestic markets included quantitative restrictions on domestic supply:

- For some commodities (notably milk and sugar) a system of quotas applied that restricted domestic production, the purpose being to constrain supply on the internal EU market. This was done to maintain domestic prices above the level that would otherwise have resulted, and also to limit the costs of support buying of the commodity and of subsidising the disposal of stocks (see Figure 5A.6).
- From 1988, a system was introduced by which land was set-aside from production, initially on a voluntary basis but later (1992) made a requirement for the receipt of direct payment support for arable crops. Again, there were connotations both for market prices and support costs.

6.2.3 Direct payments related to production

Payments per hectare of some crops (notably cereals, oilseeds and protein crops) and per head of animals (mostly beef and sheep) were introduced from 1992 as part of the process of switching support away from mechanisms that relied on raising market prices to achieve CAP aims. They were annual and not time-limited. Initially at least, these payments were intended to be compensation, set in advance, for the lowering of institutional support prices which were expected to result in farmers receiving lower revenues from their products, though in practice this did not happen because other factors impacting on world markets kept prices up. Later, payments per animal were also converted to a per hectare basis. (See Figure 5A.5).

CMOs were in a continuing state of flux in their detail and underwent reforms periodically. Some CMOs had all three types of CMO mechanisms operating; for example, cereals had intervention buying with export refunds, variable import levies and forms of direct payment. These were often known as *heavy* regimes and the degree of control of the price which EU farmers received was quite high. These attempted a two-pronged attack at enhancing the prices of farm commodities; they both controlled the external supply of commodities and,

---

Box 6.2 Quantitative restrictions on support by CMOs (as at 2000)

- Cereals and oilseeds: compensatory (direct) payments for cereals and oilseeds were calculated on each farm's arable base area, with no payment for additional area that the farmer chose to grow.
- Sugar beet areas were controlled through the issue of contracts that were in turn related to each country's national quotas.
- Milk had (and still has) delivery quotas at the farm and national levels, with guide prices reduced if aggregate production exceeded certain levels.
- Beef: the 'special' premiums for young male beef animals were payable for not more than 90 animals per holding in each of the age categories specified and were reduced if the regional totals exceeded those in a base year (1990, 1991 or 1992); premiums on suckler cows were restricted to the number of premiums paid in a base year.
- Premiums on sheep were paid at the full rate up to limits (1000 ewes per producer in LFAs and 500 animals in other areas) and the extra payment in LFAs was subject to an individual limit per producer.

---

where that was not sufficient, they also supported the internal market by various means, usually by support buying.

At the other extreme were the *light* regimes CMOs such as for pigmeat, and eggs and poultry where there was only modest protection against very cheap imports. If the internal balance of supply and demand pushed down prices of these commodities, there was little if any attempt to bring into play internal measures to raise prices. The lightest of all was the CMO for flowers and ornamental plants, which was hardly more than a price monitoring exercise.

Another feature of the CMOs was that many, particularly the heavy ones, eventually had some form of limit on the quantity of production for which support was given (see Box 6.2). This had two impacts. The first was to contain the overall cost of the support; agricultural support costs tended to expand rapidly, and frequently the CAP found itself pushing at the spending ceiling set for it. The second was to discourage levels of production which generated surpluses on the domestic market that had to be disposed of. By not offering support for production in excess of given levels, the lower prices that resulted would, it was hoped, act as a disincentive to increases in aggregate output. They would also help boost demand, the two effects combining to reduce surpluses in need of disposal.

In addition, the CMOs often contained some automatic price reductions to discourage expansion; for example, the support prices for fresh fruit and vegetables were lowered if the amount which had to be withdrawn from the market exceeded given quantities, and the olive oil intervention price was similarly lowered if production exceeded set amounts.

6.3 The transition to the present system

While the previous system of CMOs had prices set by the Council and Commission (institutional prices) to which farmers responded, a series of reforms has taken place which, in essence, has largely restored the market as the main driver for decisions on farms, though there remain vestiges of the former interventionist system that should not be overlooked. Several milestone reforms can be identified (considered in detail in Chapter 12). The reforms of 1992 (often known as the MacSharry Reforms after the Commissioner principally responsible) which marked the beginning of dismantling the system of price support also introduced direct payments together with certain other 'accompanying measures' concerned with agri-environment, early retirement and forestry. The *Agenda 2000* package of changes, agreed by the Council in 1999, among other things further scaled down market price support (with the intention of reducing it to a safety net), increased direct payments as a partial compensation, and introduced Pillar 2 of the CAP (market support to producers and direct payments then being labelled Pillar 1). The 2003 Mid-Term Review (MTR) of *Agenda 2000* was in reality more in the nature of a package of policy changes than a progress review and is sometimes referred to as the 'Fischler Reforms'.[2] This MTR, together with some additional clearing-up done in 2004, ushered in the main features of the present system, as applied from 2005 (or a year or two later, depending on the country). The 2008 CAP Healthcheck marginally adjusted the new approach. Further change is expected for the period 2014 onwards.

It is worth noting the extent to which the cuts in support prices accumulated over the reforms for some of the major commodities (Table 6.1). According to figures from the European Commission, for wheat and beef, the cuts in the MacSharry and *Agenda 2000* reforms essentially reduced internal support prices to world market levels (though this can only be indicative), though for butter and sugar there is still a substantial margin despite changes in these two regimes announced since 2004.

Some reforms are quite recent. Consequently, EU agriculture is still in the process of adjusting to them. When these have worked through it is likely that the patterns of production and land use will take forms similar to what might have been had the market interventions not taken place, though path-dependency (the fact that how we got here affects the outcome), the remnants of market support and other strands of policy mean that the adjustment will not be complete. In particular, the structure of the industry (farm sizes, degree of pluriactivity etc.) will be expected to take a substantial time to adapt, and there are impediments (many less to do with the CAP but more to do with national legislation on issues such as land ownership and taxation) that prevent easy adjustment. Nevertheless, it is clear that support to producers is mostly given now in ways that distort markets far less than previously.

Table 6.1   EU decisions on cuts in commodity support prices, and world market prices

Commodity	MacSharry price reductions 1992	Agenda 2000 price reductions	MTR 2003 price reductions	EU price 2004 €/tonne	World market price €/tonne
Wheat	30%	15%	0	100	100
Beef	15%	20%	0	1,560	1,500–2,000
Butter	0	0	25%	2,464 (in 2007)	1,400
Skimmed milk powder			15%	1,747 (in 2006)	1,700
Sugar	0	0	33%	632 (421 in 2007/8)	250

Source: CEC (2006) European Commission *Scenar 2020*. p73

6.4 The present system of support

The main features of the present system of support under the CAP's Pillar 1 (direct payments and market support) were introduced at the CAP's 2003 Mid-Term Review (MTR). These are:

6.4.1 The Single Payment Scheme (SPS) and its Single Farm Payment and Single Area Payment

The main current form of support, accounting for more than four-fifths of budgeted spending under Pillar 1 in 2011, are payments under the Single Payment Scheme (SPS). EU-15 Member States could operate the SPS from 2005 though they could delay this unto 2007 (only Malta chose this last year); new Member States had up to 2009 to introduce it. Called the Single Farm Payment (SFP) or the Single Area Payment (SAP) depending on context (see below), this is an annual payment to producers, administered by national authorities but funded wholly by the EU, that was seen, initially at least, as replacing the support they had received from the previous range of separate commodity regimes (crops, beef and sheep, with milk introduced in 2004, subsequent reforms expanding the list further[3]).

The SFP/SAP is not directly linked to how much the farm currently produces. Rather, it reflects past amounts of subsidies received by farmers. Thus the SFP/SAP is very largely 'decoupled' from the production decisions of farmers, which in principle are now made in the light of market prices and costs. This is unlike the former system under which support provided incentives to produce (first in the form of raised prices and latterly as direct payments per hectare of certain crops or per animal of certain types). Legislation adopted by the CAP's decision-making procedure (see Chapter 3) determines the size of the SFP/SAP and it is the responsibility of national governments to set up payments agencies and the paraphernalia of applications, checks of eligibility, making the payments, monitoring and preventing fraud. Box 6.3 shows the Commission's description of the Single Payment Scheme.

Options within the Regulations allowed alternative formulations of SPS payments. In essence the choice was whether payments to individual holders were to be based on what they received in the past (the 'historic model', using the average level of subsidies claimed in livestock and arable sectors during a 2000–2002 reference period), or on a standard rate per hectare calculated at regional level (the 'regional model', using the eligible area declared by each farmer in his/her Integrated Administration and Control System (IACS) return, or two 'hybrids' of these, and whether this system was allowed to change over time or was fixed ('dynamic', implying a movement from the historic to the regional model, or 'static'). The term Single Farm Payment (SFP) is used when the 'historic model' is used, whereas Single Area Payment (SAP) is applied when the 'regional model' is used. The 'historic model' SFP was chosen by most EU-15 countries, an important factor being that this preserved the pattern of benefit; adopting the regional model would have meant that some land areas used for production on which no subsidies were previously received now became eligible while others, those previously in receipt of production-linked subsidies, would see them diluted. SAPs were chosen by a few EU-15 countries and are used in Member States that acceded to the EU after 2003. Obviously farmers in the latter were not in receipt of the previous types of direct payments in the reference period 2000–2002 so the 'historic' model could not be applied to them. What their farms receive involves sums specified in the Accession

---

Box 6.3 The Commission's description of the Single Payment Scheme (SPS)

The 2003 reform of the CAP introduced a new system of single farm payments (income support) and cut the link between support and production (decoupling). The SPS replaces most of the direct aid payments to farmers previously offered.

The main points to note are:

- All farmers may apply for direct payments.
- The single payment is an annual income payment to farmers that is based on their entitlement over the 2000–02 reference period (with the exception of the new Member States).
- Farmers may receive direct payments provided that they maintain their land in good agricultural condition and comply with the standards on public health, animal and plant health, the environment and animal welfare (cross-compliance).
- Farmers who fail to comply with these requirements face reductions in direct payments.
- Farmers are free to decide what they want to produce in response to demand without losing their entitlement to support.
- All Member States should introduce the single payment scheme by 2007 at the latest (with exception of the new Member States, which have until 2009 to introduce the scheme).

Source: Commission (2006) Factsheet – 'Simplification of the Common Agricultural Policy'

Agreements for these countries that were paid at uniform amounts per eligible hectare of agricultural land. Which countries selected which options and the years these became operational is shown in Table 6.2. Most EU-15 countries opted for the historic mode, and most started using the SPS from 2005.

Payments of SFPs are conditional on the observance of certain conditions ('cross-compliance'). These link with the respect of standards of environment, food safety, human, animal and plant health, and animal welfare, as well as the requirement to keep all farmland in good agricultural and environmental condition (GAEC). These conditions are seen as contributing to the environmental aims of the CAP

6.4.2 Other direct aid and market support

Together these other forms of support under Pillar 1 account for less than one-fifth of the total budget cost (16 per cent, equally split, in the 2011 draft EU budget). These provide for limited elements of the previous 'coupled' system to remain in force according to the national preferences of Member States, with the rationale that this is necessary to counter the abandonment of production (which may be a danger in some circumstances)[4]. Consequently a proportion of the previous arable payments and livestock premiums may still be paid, though the intention is that this arrangement will terminate in 2012. Currently (2010) the maximum varies between commodities; for example for cereals it is 25 per cent but for suckler cow 'premiums' it is 100 per cent. Some countries have not retained any of

Table 6.2 Overview of the implementation of the SPS (SFP/SAP)

	Historic	*Static hybrid*	*Dynamic hybrid*	*Flat rate*
2005	Austria (milk 2007)	Denmark	Germany	Cyprus
	Belgium (milk 2006)	Luxembourg (milk	UK (England)	Czech Republic
	Ireland	2006)		Estonia
	Italy (milk 2006)	Sweden		Hungary
	Portugal (milk 2007)	UK (Northern Ireland)		Latvia
	UK (Scotland)			Lithuania
	UK (Wales)			Malta
				Poland
				Slovakia
				Slovenia
2006	France		Finland	
	Greece (milk 2007)			
	Netherlands (milk			
	2007)			
	Spain			

AgraCEAS Consulting Ltd – personal correspondence, and Balkhausen and Bause (2007)

these 'coupled' direct payments (Ireland, Malta and the UK). France and Spain, in contrast, have chosen to keep the SFPs coupled to production as much as possible in all agricultural sectors. Consequently, France still applies a wide range of direct payments ('premiums' on beef animals, sheep and goats, olives, hops, some fruit and vegetables and, importantly, 25 per cent of its arable payments). In addition, countries are allowed to apply the 'Article 69 provision' which enables Member States to grant additional payments (funded from national aid entitlement 'envelopes') to their producers 'for the purposes of encouraging specific types of farming which are important for protection or enhancement of the environment and of improving the quality and marketing of agricultural products' (Art, 69 of Regulation (EC) No 1782/2003). These payments, however, must not exceed 10 per cent of each country's overall national aid entitlement. Rates of aid under this scheme have to be lower than any specific 'coupled' aids payable in the beef, sheep, and arable sectors. Spain, in addition to maximising the possibility of maintaining 'coupled' payments, has also decided to apply Article 69 in the case of beef and milk, cotton, tobacco and sugar, though France has not gone down this route. Of the Member States that joined the EU in 2004 and 2007, some have chosen to retain parts of their entitlements specified in their Accession Agreements in coupled form, and some apply Article 69 provisions.

6.4.3 Modulation

This is a convenient point at which to mention another aspect of the SPS system – the use of *modulation*. This is a mechanism by which a percentage of funds is transferred from Pillar 1 support to provide additional resources to Pillar 2, implying a reduction in what is available to support the SPS (see Chapters 7 and 8).[5] The notion of a systematic and mandatory modulation was introduced by the 2003 Mid-Term Review. Though the modulation percentages applied to Pillar 1 are small (a low level of compulsory modulation – 3 per cent in 2005, increasing to 5 per cent in 2007 – but with Member States able to use a higher level up to a maximum of 20 per cent), they can be significant in several countries to the amount of funding available to rural development, especially in the light of the additional funds from national budgets that co-financing triggers. A small slice of Pillar 1 can make a relatively large contribution to spending on rural development within the much slimmer Pillar 2. However, modulation also carries distributional implications. Firstly, the system makes provision for exempting certain producers by the application of a 'franchise', the size threshold below which the SPS entitlements are not scaled back. In effect, this means that small producers are exempt. These additional resources are made available to rural development, which may be targeted at particular groups of farmers. The effect is that some farmers may be net beneficiaries of the process of recycling funds (withdrawal by modulation and reintroduced by Rural Development Programme (RDP) schemes) while others are net losers. Secondly, there are redistributions between countries, though the legislation ensures that at least 80 per cent of the funds raised by modulation in each Member State remain in that country.

To sum up, support to EU agriculture is now organised very largely in the form of the Single Payment Scheme that makes Single Farm Payments/Single Area Payments. But elements of the coupled system remain. In addition to the opportunity to retain coupled payments up to a maximum set out in legislation, there are vestiges of the former CMOs relating to several commodities (see Box 6.4). As part of a move towards simplification, in 2007 the 21 separate commodity regimes (Common Market Organisations – CMOs) were replaced by a single CMO, the new arrangements coming into effect mostly in 2008. This has also meant that the work of the specific management committees has been taken over by one single Management Committee for the Common Organisation of Agricultural Markets (see Chapter 3). However, sight should not be lost of the fact that payments under the Single Payment Scheme dominate, accounting currently for more than four-fifths of the Pillar 1 total.

6.5 How important are SFPs and other direct payments to farmers?

It is not easy to assess the importance of SFPs to farmers in the EU. Whether a farm remains a viable independent unit will reflect not only its earnings from agriculture but what other sources of income are available to the family or company that operates it. Many farms, particularly small ones, would not be capable of surviving without these outside resources, and often they form part of the long-term strategy of their operators, who see the combination of two or more activities as acceptable and often desirable. It would be instructive to explore the extent to which income from the production and marketing of farm commodities, subsidies – especially the Single Farm Payment – and off-farm income react with each other. However, the point has already been made that information on off-farm income is not generally available in EU Member States, and the official measures of farmer incomes ignore it. Nevertheless, it is possible to make observations from data relating only to farming activity that have interesting implications.

Table 6.3 draws on data from the official Farm Accountancy Data Network (FADN) that carries out annual surveys of the accounts of farms large enough to be considered as commercial operations. Figures are averages per agricultural holding (which approximates to the average single farm business). Various ratios can be calculated of the relative size of SFP or SAP to the level of business activity, though for reasons already given, caution must be exercised before drawing conclusions about dependency. The fourth column shows for each country the ratio between the average value of output of FADN farms and the value of subsidies they receive; this will be mostly as SFP or SAP but will include any residual

Box 6.4 Vestiges of market intervention (as at 2010)

The Single CMO Regulation (EC) No 1234/2007) covers elements of support through market interventions for apiculture, bananas, beef and veal, cereals, dried fodder, eggs, ethyl alcohol, flax and hemp, fruit and vegetables, hops, live plants, milk, olives, pigmeat, poultrymeat, processed fruit and vegetables, rice, seeds, sheepmeat and goatmeat, silkworms, tobacco (raw), and wine. Some provisions are of a transitional nature and some more of a reserve in case of market imbalance.

The most significant vestiges of market intervention are:

Milk: to enable milk quotas to expire by April 2015 with a 'soft landing', quotas are to be increased by 1 per cent every year between 2009/10 and 2013/14. (For Italy, the 5 per cent increase was introduced immediately in 2009/10). In 2009/10 and 2010/11, farmers who exceed their milk quotas by more than 6 per cent have to pay a levy 50 per cent higher than the normal penalty. For butter and skimmed milk powder, limits on intervention stocks are 30,000 tonnes and 109,000 tonnes respectively, beyond which intervention will be by tender.

Cereals: Intervention is set at zero for barley and sorghum. For wheat, intervention purchases will be possible during the intervention period at the price of €101.31/tonne up to 3 million tonnes. Beyond that, it will be done by tender.

Assistance to sectors with special problems (so-called 'Article 69' measures): Member States may retain by sector 10 per cent of their national budget ceilings for direct payments, for use for environmental measures or improving the quality and marketing of products. Under the 2008 CAP Health Check changes, the money no longer has to be used in the same sector; it may be used to help farmers producing milk, beef, goat and sheep meat and rice in disadvantaged regions or vulnerable types of farming; it may also be used to support risk management measures such as insurance schemes for natural disasters and mutual funds for animal diseases; and countries operating the Single Area Payment Scheme (SAPS) system became eligible for the scheme.

Other measures: A series of small support schemes will be decoupled and shifted to the SPS from 2012. The energy crop premium has been abolished.

Options to retain coupled direct payments: Though full decoupling is the general principle from 2005 onwards, Member States may maintain some product-specific direct aids alongside the SFP/SAP where this is justified in order to avoid production abandonment or severe market disturbance as a result of moving to this system. Member States may apply a limited number of options, at national or regional level. Examples are;

1 Cereals/other arable crops: 25 per cent of the arable component of the SPS may be retained to continue existing coupled per hectare payments;
2 Beef: Member States may keep up to 100 per cent of the suckler cow premium and up to 40 per cent of the slaughter premium coupled (there are other options);
3 Sheep and goats: 50 per cent of premia can be granted as coupled payments;
4 Olive oil: up to 60 per cent decoupled – remainder paid via coupled payments to maintain land under olive oil trees for environmental reasons;
5 Cotton: 35 per cent has to remain coupled.

Sugar: The CMO for sugar was reformed in 2006; minimum beet prices for growers are set. A quota system is still in place, but quotas are to be reduced, with a payment from a 'restructuring fund' for holders who voluntarily renounce quota, financed by a levy on sugar producers. Following an initial disappointing response, from 2007 growers who renounce quota get an additional payment, paid retroactively to avoid penalising those who have already given up their quotas. Beet growers can apply directly for aid from the restructuring fund, up to a certain limit. There is provision for supporting private storage and export subsidies.

Table 6.3 Average values per holding (€) 2006 in the Farm Accountancy Data Network

	(a) Total output	*(b)* Current subsidies *(less taxes)*	Ratio output to subsidies *(a)/(b)*	Farm Net Value Added	*(c)* Family Farm Income	Balance of FFI and subsidies *(c) less (b)*
Austria	62091	22466	3	33788	27690	5224
Belgium	180788	20244	9	78,254	55,178	34,934
Cyprus	23557	3613	7	8364	5470	1857
Czech Republic	272673	59214	5	94026	23826	−35388
Denmark	241612	27114	9	86968	19222	−7892
Estonia	67915	16085	4	25697	14229	−1856
Finland	65974	40621	2	27664	17941	−22680
France	125776	25864	5	51574	30230	4366
Germany	179763	33757	5	69794	34350	593
Greece	18307	5997	3	14281	12449	6452
Hungary	49648	9950	5	18076	7930	−2020
Ireland	35270	17646	2	21159	16722	−924
Italy	51359	6161	8	29514	23952	17791
Latvia	34859	12161	3	15731	12490	329
Lithuania	25316	8202	3	12530	13976	5774
Luxemburg	170,574	45,608	4	54,295	40,916	−4692
Malta	55531	10410	5	25840	22691	12281
Netherlands	324187	13242	24	112397	49253	36011
Poland	23282	4683	5	10706	9087	4404
Portugal	21224	4943	4	11119	8834	3,891
Slovakia	368455	96843	4	10241	−101158	−198001
Slovenia	15504	4,082	4	4,592	3,668	−414
Spain	38790	6340	6	25421	21374	15034
Sweden	129100	34295	4	33696	10048	−24247
UK	206642	45939	4	80595	36113	−9826
EU	63110	11849	5	29483	19702	7853

Source: FADN data, European Commission.

direct payments that have not been decoupled. These subsidies are not included in the value of output, though the effect of any market operations (such as milk quotas) that raise market prices is reflected in output. The main lesson is that in the Netherlands, SFPs (with other direct payments) are exceptionally small in relation to output derived from the market – only one twenty-fourth of their size. It might be concluded that the overall prosperity of agriculture there could survive a cut in direct subsidies relatively easily. No doubt this reflects the types of production found in the Netherlands, with horticulture and dairying predominating in which direct payments have been very small historically. In most countries, market output was about four or five times the size of direct subsidies. At the other extreme, in Ireland and Finland, they were about half the size of the value of output. This suggests an unequal dependency on Pillar 1 payments.

Another way to approach the issue is to compare the Family Farm Income (FFI) figure with the level of subsidy. FFI represents what is left to the farm operator after the costs of bought inputs (such as fertiliser) and paid wages, interest payments on borrowings and rent have been deducted. Importantly, in this calculation, the value of subsidies has already been included as a source of income. The difference between FFI and the amount of subsidies received gives some indication of the dependence of the average holding in that country on the subsidy. Put crudely, if subsidies were suddenly cut off, what FFI would remain? The final column in the table shows that in 11 Member States the average holding would have a negative income without direct payment subsidies, with very large losses in Slovakia and the Czech Republic. On the other hand, in Belgium and the Netherlands there would still be a sizeable positive income.

Of course, this analysis is very broad-brush. Figures vary from year to year, and farms of different types and sizes within the same country can display marked disparities. The sudden cancelling of subsidies is implausible, and even if it did take place, very soon farmers would make all sorts of adjustments to protect their income positions, as they have demonstrated in the past. Nevertheless, the analysis suggests that there are different degrees of exposure to direct payments, and thus it is unwise to make sweeping generalisations on the dependency of EU farmers on this form of support.

6.6 Payments under the Single Payment Scheme – characteristics of the main tool of support

Instruments of policy can be viewed from several perspectives (Chapter 5), and the SPS is no exception. Economic analysis would include looking at the impacts of SFP/SAP on the incentives to produce and subsequent effects on output levels and market prices, while budgetary analysis would take a narrower perspective and concentrate on the costs to public spending. Political analysis would consider the gainers and losers when the SPS was introduced and how they affect power and influence and, consequently, decisions on public policy.

In theory, the SPS provides support to farmers in a different way from the former system. When the CAP worked primarily through intervening to raise market prices of farm commodities, this provided an incentive for farmers to produce more, use more inputs, use their land more intensively and bring into cultivation land that would otherwise have been left idle (two effects often referred to as 'extending the intensive and extensive margins of cultivation'). Also, because support was not spread evenly across commodities, the pattern of production was distorted. Aid given as direct payments linked to the volume of production (numbers of hectares or animals) acted in much the same way. In particular, land use changes often carried environmental implications arising from greater fertiliser and agro-chemical use – with attendant run-off and pollution – and loss of natural habitats (i.e. land uncultivated or only lightly so wildlife could be sustained).

The combination of the SPS and market prices largely undistorted by intervention mechanisms avoids many of these incentives. Farmers now respond to price signals that are the product, in principle, of demand from users of agricultural commodities interacting with the willingness of producers to supply, which reflects their marginal costs of production (recall Figure 5A.1). Economic theory suggests that the rational farmer would base decisions on what to produce, how much to produce and how to produce it on market prices alone. What the farm operator receives as SFP/SAP would not be taken into consideration in reaching such decisions, as this would be received irrespective of the types and quantities of farm commodities produced.

With the introduction of SFP/SAPs as a replacement for the previous support system, as market prices fell, production would be expected to drop back, land to be less intensively farmed, a change in the mix of commodities produced to take place, and so on. In reality this may not have happened, at least in the short term, because of the legacy of the previous system. Firstly, SFP/SAPs are relatively recent and may not be perceived by farm operators as decoupled, at least for some time. They might be regarded as part of the rewards from production, though this is likely to fade progressively. Second, many of the rational adjustments to new market conditions may be substantial (such as setting up a non-farm enterprise, or shedding staff, or a family member taking an off-farm job, buying or selling land etc.), and these take time. Some of them may only come about when a farm is passed from one generation to another. Third, changes are not always symmetrical, in the sense that, while high commodity prices can lead quickly to intensive farming and the removal of hedges and wildlife, reversing the changes may take a long time and some landscape features may have been permanently destroyed. There was no shortage of estimates of what the expected results of changing to SFPs would be, not least of which was the impact assessment undertaken by the European Commission itself. However, the evidence of actual impacts is still quite thin. In short, the full impacts of the SFP have yet to emerge.

Another aspect of the SPS that reflects the past system of support is the distribution of budgetary transfers. SFPs that are based on historic receipts of subsidies retain a very similar pattern of who gets how much. Under the previous system, larger producers received the greatest sums as coupled direct payments (and, before that, the benefits from price support); they now receive the biggest SFPs and they account for the bulk of total spending. A flat-rate system (the 'regional model') enables producers whose crops or livestock did not carry payments before to benefit now, at the expense of the others. There are some adjustments brought about by the modulation system that slightly readjust this distribution (such as exempting very small producers from having their SFPs modulated to provide extra resources for Pillar 2) but these do not shift the pattern fundamentally. Farmers clearly do not receive Pillar 1 support according to need, in terms of what would be necessary to bring low-income households up to some income level that would give them a 'fair standard of living', as set as a CAP objective both by the 1957 Treaty of Rome and *Agenda 2000*.

Information on how much individual beneficiaries receive as CAP subsidies has been published (though without distinction between what is received under Pillars 1 and 2), with results that critics of the current policy are quick to seize upon. This was made mandatory under the 2005 Financial Regulation, although a ruling by the European Court of Justice on the legal basis has prevented results being made public from November 2010. As a consequence, the data have been removed from the Europa and national websites, though this may be temporary until a way of presenting the data that meets certain discloser conditions is devised.[6]

Nevertheless, the information that was released showed, as might be expected from the history of payments, a very skewed pattern, with a relatively small number of very large payments accounting for a substantial proportion of total spending, and large numbers of small payments. For example, in the UK in 2008, the recipients of the five largest sums accounted for just over a third (36 per cent) of the total of €3,755 million. An analysis by Oxfam has identified as major recipients of Single Farm Payments many land-owning members of the aristocracy and industrialists, few of whom are likely to be experiencing standards of living that the rest of society would deem to be unacceptable. Furthermore, the largest sums often go to companies rather than individuals. Continuing the UK example, the two largest recipients in 2008 were Tate and Lyle Europe (€828 million) and Nestlé UK Ltd (€197 million), for comparison, the average paid was €12,517 per farm. There is also considerable doubt whether some of the beneficiaries are members of the 'agricultural community' at which CAP support is intended to be directed. A careful scrutiny of lists of recipients for 2008 (by the website http://capreform.eu/2009-data-harvest/) has found infants, people in their 90s, an accordion club (Sweden – €59,585), a billiard club (Denmark – €31,515, a payment for beer and soft drinks), a Juri High School alumni society (Estonia – €44,884), Ons Genoegen ice skating club (Netherlands – €162,444), the Sint Maarten amateur football club (Netherlands – €354,566.62) and Schiphol Airport in the Netherlands (€98,864.33). As in previous years, a number of banks and horse riding clubs were among the beneficiaries. Such findings might be expected to make payments under the SPS politically vulnerable.

At the other end of the spectrum there are large numbers of CAP beneficiaries who are paid only small sums. A previous Commissioner (MacSharry) claimed that some 80 per cent of agricultural payments then went to 20 per cent of farmers (the largest ones); though this applied to the system of payments before CAP reform, it seems likely to still apply. According to figures from the Commission, some 82 per cent of farms received €5,000 or less in 2008, though in several (including the UK) the proportion was much lower (Table 6.4).

Finally, it should be noted that, though usually labelled as 'decoupled', SFPs and SAPs are not completely independent of production. If they were, farmers could sell their farm businesses, move away, take non-agricultural jobs or retire, and still receive their annual payment. Instead, to be eligible they have to remain as occupiers of agricultural land and to keep it in good condition, though this need not be the same holding as they had in the base period and they need not produce crops and livestock on it. This provides an incentive to stay in agriculture, even if only nominally so, perhaps by remaining the legal occupier of a holding but leasing it out on a short-term basis to other farmers. If this final link with land were to be broken, it is likely that some structural change would be seen in the statistics as those who wished to sell found themselves no longer constrained, but at least part of this would result from the regularising of arrangements that were previously informal. In most EU Member States there are probably enough taxation advantages to land ownership to prevent an outflow of farmers at a rate that would cause social problems in the countryside.

6.7 The future of Pillar 1 support

It is now certain that support to agriculture under Pillar 1 will continue for at least another decade. While the remnants of market interventions may shrink, direct payments made under the SPS will remain in some form or other. This tells us much about the forces that shape the CAP and the dynamics of bringing about change in it.

Since the start of the period covered by the current Financial Perspective (2007–13) discussions have been taking place on what shape the CAP should take from 2014 onwards. As a reformulated version of direct payments that were themselves a legacy of the compensation made for reforms of the CAP in 1992, it would be hard to justify the continuation of

Table 6.4 Distribution of benefits from CAP direct aid under the EAGF by Member State (2008)

	% of farms benefiting from direct aid under the EAGF		
	With aid ≤ € 5 000	*With aid ≤ € 20 000*	*With aid ≤ € 100 000*
Austria	62.95%	95.82%	0.06%
Belgium	45.37%	78.59%	0.33%
Bulgaria	93.55%	97.56%	0.23%
Cyprus	98.69%	99.90%	0.00%
Czech Republic	69.56%	86.21%	5.00%
Denmark	51.19%	76.53%	2.27%
Estonia	91.91%	97.72%	0.11%
Finland	47.37%	92.73%	0.06%
France	31.53%	63.22%	1.28%
Germany	47.96%	80.28%	1.60%
Greece	83.73%	98.48%	0.01%
Hungary	91.71%	97.80%	0.38%
Ireland	42.28%	87.16%	0.21%
Italy	89.01%	97.83%	0.19%
Latvia	97.98%	99.59%	0.03%
Lithuania	97.92%	99.63%	0.04%
Luxembourg	23.40%	61.17%	0.53%
Malta	98.31%	99.81%	0.00%
Netherlands	49.50%	77.99%	0.34%
Poland	98.41%	99.75%	0.03%
Portugal	90.50%	97.33%	0.31%
Romania	99.18%	99.76%	0.01%
Slovakia	83.74%	90.79%	3.20%
Slovenia	98.22%	99.90%	0.02%
Spain	75.96%	93.85%	0.37%
Sweden	62.74%	87.63%	0.51%
UK	46.17%	72.84%	2.83%
EU-27	82.48%	94.31%	0.35%

European Commission – Indicative Figures on the Distribution of Aid, by size-class of aid, received in the context of direct aid paid to the producers according to Council Regulation (EC) No 1259/1999 and Council Regulation (EC) No 1782/2003 – Financial Year 2008.

SFP/SAPs so long after the events that triggered them have faded into history. A case can be made that such compensation should have been time-limited, but it was not. A rationale response would be to terminate them at the end of 2013 or phase them out, starting then. Historically, farmers have shown themselves to be adept at responding to economic changes, given a reasonable period of notice; an announcement a few years before ceasing payments should be sufficient to avoid economic waste. However, it is clear that the SFP/SAP system will not be dismantled in the near or medium future.

Payments under the SPS seem to generate no obvious benefit to society. Their costs fall on the EU budget, and payments can be seen clearly going to beneficiaries who are often of higher income and of higher wealth than the rest of society that finances them. Nevertheless, they have become a familiar part of the economic landscape of EU agriculture and an important source of income to farm operators. While it would be hard to justify their use if they did not already exist (another example of path dependency) the reality is that it is not possible for political reasons to withdraw them completely.

In 2007, in early discussions on the future of the CAP beyond 2014, the then Commissioner for Agriculture (Mariann Fischer Boel) indicated that the SPS and associated payments would be unlikely to survive in their present form. This produced a predictably angry response from farmers' representatives. Since then, the Commission's position has changed; there is now an assumption that SPS payments will continue.

The rationale for the introduction of SPS direct payments has been displaced by a rationale offered for their continuance. For at least a decade direct payments have usually been mentioned in Commission documents without their origins as compensation being made explicit; whether this was deliberate to prepare the ground for a possible change in rationale is open to debate. In a Communication of November 2010 to the Council and European Parliament, which outlined options for the CAP for the period after 2013, the Commission states that SPS payments are seen as providing 'basic income support' (see Chapter 12). The implication is that they are needed in order for farmers to deliver basic CAP objectives of a secure supply of quality and diverse foods produced sustainably and 'in line with environmental, water and animal welfare ambitions'. However, no convincing evidence is presented by the Commission for why intervention is needed to ensure food security, or why annual payments are to be preferred to more targeted interventions that might focus on delivering environmental and other non-market services. Mention is made of relatively low incomes in agriculture (based on average factor earnings), but this ignores other evidence that suggests the incomes (and wealth) of farm households compares rather well with other groups in society (see Chapter 4).

While the validity of the Commission's view might be challenged, there seems little enthusiasm among most EU governments for terminating or phasing out SPS payments. What is far more probable is that they will be modified (such as changing the allocation between Member States) and some relabelling may take place, such as calling SPS payments 'for providing basic services'. Part of the sums involved may be transferred to alternative mechanisms that are more politically defensible, such as agri-environmental schemes (see Chapter 8) and, possibly, schemes to stabilise the incomes of farmers and their families (though the basic data required to do this is lacking – see Chapter 4). The first could be seen to bring benefits to society at large by providing public goods in exchange for the payments. The latter could be seen to bring benefits to the agricultural industry itself (assuming the data gaps could be filled), plus some possible efficiency gains that might increase national income. Political, rather than economic, drivers will dominate such developments.

Further reading

European Commission (2006) *Scenar 2020 – Scenario Study on Agriculture and the Rural World.* European Commission, Brussels.

European Commission (2009) *Preparing for Change: Update of Analysis of Prospects in the Scenar 2020 Study Final report.* European Commission, Brussels.

European Commission (2010) Communication from the Commission to the European Parliament, the Council, the European Economic and Social Committee and the Committee of the Regions. 'The CAP towards 2020: Meeting the food, natural resources and territorial challenges of the future'. Brussels, 18 November 2010, COM(2010) 672 final.

Jongeneel, R., and Brand, H. (2010) 'Direct income support and cross-compliance'. Chapter 9 in Oskam, A., Meester, G. and Silvis, H. (eds) *EU Policy for Agriculture, Food and Rural Areas.* Wageningen Academic Publishers, Wageningen.

Hill, B. (2006) *An Introduction to Economics: Concepts for Students of Agriculture and the Rural Sector.* CABI, Wallingford. (Chapter 10, 'Government policy for agriculture and rural areas').

Moreddu, C. (2011) 'Distribution of Support and Income in Agriculture', OECD Food, Agriculture and Fisheries Working Papers, No. 46, OEC, Paris, Online at http://dx.doi.org/10.1787/5kgch21wkmbx-en

OXFAM (2004) *Spotlight on Subsidies.* Oxfam Briefing Paper, January 2004. Oxfam, Oxford

Silvis, H. and Lapperre, R. (2010) 'Market, price and quota policy: half a century of CAP experience'. Chapter 8 in Oskam, A., Meester, G. and Silvis, H. (eds) *EU Policy for Agriculture, Food and Rural Areas.* Wageningen Academic Publishers, Wageningen.

Swinbank, A. (1997) 'The new CAP'. Chapter 5 in Ritson, C. and Harvey, D. R. (eds) *The Common Agricultural Policy.* CAB International, Wallingford.

UNDERSTANDING THE SUPPORT OF AGRICULTURE AND RURAL DEVELOPMENT IN THE EU

Pillar 2 of the CAP

Key topics

- CAP and rural development.
- What is a rural area – OECD/EU definitions of rurality.
- Problems of rural areas – economic, social and environmental.
- Agriculture's role as a provider of incomes and jobs, and user of natural resources.
- The rural development policies of the EU – aims, objectives and programmes.

7.1 Introduction – CAP and rural development

As explained in previous chapters, the *Agenda 2000* package of policy reforms introduced a split of support under the CAP into Pillar 1 (which deals with commodities, markets and direct payments to farmers) and Pillar 2, which is often labelled as the 'Rural Development' but which in reality deals with public expenditure of three main types:

- **Assistance to agricultural adjustment.** This comprises assistance to farms to adjust their structure to better cope with the economic and technical conditions faced by the agricultural industry (used in the broad sense to embrace farming, horticulture and forestry). This includes grants or loans for the modernisation of capital equipment, financial assistance to encourage elderly farmers to leave the industry (thereby enabling their land to go to farms that need to grow in size), help to younger people to set themselves up (thereby improving the age structure of farming), vocational training to improve skills, aids to food marketing and processing, better integration of farming in the food chain etc. The end result should be a smaller industry (in terms of numbers of independent farms) but one where the remaining businesses are internationally competitive and thus viable. Though the number of people working on farms may go down, the earnings and living standards of those on the remaining holdings will improve and their jobs become more secure.
- **Development of non-agricultural activities in rural areas.** This includes support to the creation of non-agricultural economic activities in rural areas (jobs and incomes), such as tourism, small-scale manufacturing and food processing, and services. Most of these will be undertaken by individuals and firms that are not primarily in agriculture, though farmers may also play a part by diversifying their businesses on the farm or elsewhere in the rural locality. There can also be assistance to enable rural communities to have a better quality of life by access to public facilities (such as

village halls or lighting) or to build up their capacity to help themselves by establishing networks (social capital) that enable them to better access what is available. Of course, farm families, as a part of rural society, can benefit from these broader opportunities and amenities.

- **Agri-environmental schemes.** Payments to farm operators and landowners to use their land in ways that deliver environmental benefits and landscape appearances that the EU wishes to encourage. Two sorts of payments are found, those of a recurrent nature (such as those made annually in return for farmers agreeing to leave field margins uncultivated to encourage wildlife) and those related to specific investments, such as the repair of stone field walls or cattle shelters in hill areas. These may carry implications for the number of jobs and incomes on farms and in rural communities, since farm operations may be necessary to keep fields in certain biological conditions and contractors may need to be engaged for some processes (building, fencing, tree planting etc.). But these are incidental to the environmental aims of the spending.

This chapter deals with the first two of these, which are the economic and social aspects of the CAP's Pillar 2. The third concerns agriculture's role in conserving the environment (often the term agri-environment is used in this context). In some countries (and especially the US) policy instruments for this last category would not be seen as part of rural development (which is concerned primarily with the economy) but rather to do with environmental policy. But in the EU the history is rather different, and the way that agriculture contributes to achieving environmental aims is seen as part of the CAP's rural development Pillar. In reality it is so important that this book devotes a separate chapter (Chapter 8) to it, concentrating here on the general framework of Pillar 2 support and the non-environmental aspects of rural development.

Even among the economic issues tackled by the CAP's Pillar 2 there is debate whether the first listed above (assistance to agricultural adjustment) should be treated as part of rural development. Agriculture is only one activity of many carried on by residents of rural areas, and usually not a major one in terms of the income it generates for them. Nevertheless, the way that the CAP has developed – and in particular the fact that under *Agenda 2000* actions that were not clearly direct income payments or linked to agricultural commodity markets were all lumped together in Pillar 2 – means that in the EU context, interventions to help farm operators adjust to changing economic and technical conditions are seen as falling firmly within the CAP's contribution to rural development. While there is a link between changes on farms and the broader jobs market and income situation, these are dependent on many other and usually more powerful influences. Here is another example of path-dependency; the inclusion of agricultural adjustment within the rural development pillar of the CAP is a result of how the policy has come into being.

Despite this, the importance of agricultural adjustment should not be under-estimated. Almost from the start of the CAP there has been a realisation that structural change in agriculture is a necessary and on-going process. In particular, in the 1960s, the industry needed to be reorganised into fewer but larger and more modern farms and many of the people working in agriculture needed to be moved to other sectors or retired. Moreover, it was also recognised that change would not happen sufficiently quickly by itself. An economic case existed for facilitating adjustment by the provision of financial and other assistance; the anticipated benefits would likely be greater than the value of the resources used. In 1968, the EC Commissioner for agriculture (Sicco Mansholt), proposed an ambitious restructuring that included the provision of socio-economic guidance for those who wished to retrain for other industries or who wished to start non-agricultural enterprises on their farms (such as tourism). Eventually these led to the relatively modest response of Directives in 1972 that enabled EU funds to be used to support national schemes for farm modernisation, vocational training, early retirement and (in 1977) improved marketing (European Commission, 1990). It was also recognised that in the mountains, hill areas and other 'Less Favoured Areas' (LFAs) farming was a key factor in shaping the social fabric and environmental character of these areas but that the continuation of farming was threatened. Under a Directive of 1975 (Dir. 75/268) special forms of support ('compensation' for the natural handicaps faced) could be paid, 'in order to ensure the continuation of farming, thereby maintaining a minimum population level or conserving the countryside'. As will become apparent, the legacy of these early forms of intervention are still with us today in the form of schemes with many of the same broad aims and sharing the same basic rationale run as part of Rural Development Programmes (see below).

But we should not assume that the CAP's Pillar 2 is the only EU policy that is directed at solving the problems of rural areas or that it is the most important. Another is EU regional policy. The EU has long held the principle that the regions that are lagging behind should be assisted to share in the EU's collective prosperity. Many of these happen to be relatively rural in nature. The Treaty of Rome, and subsequently the Single European Act and the Maastricht Treaty, committed the Community to be active in the promotion of economic and social cohesion; this meant that the EU could not tolerate the impoverishment of rural areas outside the mainstream of national and community life. If rural areas were poor in the sense of income levels, jobs, access to education and training, cultural activities and so on, then policies should be introduced to help. This could apply to rural parts of individual Member States or to whole regions (such as Northern Ireland). Within EU regional policy those areas that have incomes per head (GDP/head) below 75 percent of the EU average have been designated for targeting (called Objective 1 area). The European Regional Development Fund (ERDF) was set up in 1975 to support national aid for regions with development problems. With enlargement to 27 countries the areas designated for EU support as Objective 1 areas have shifted towards the new Member States. The interventions that attempted to stimulate economic development there have been primarily directed at the non-agricultural parts of the economy, though farmers may have benefited because they happened to be businesses situated in regions designated for special assistance.

Allied to this, the European Social Fund (ESF), set up under the 1957 Treaty of Rome, has aided actions against long-term unemployment and for the professional integration of persons under the age of 25 years by vocational training, accompanied if necessary by vocational guidance and recruitment premiums for newly created stable employment and aid for creating independent businesses.

Historically the main concerns of both the ESF and the ERDF were with where the greatest problems were concentrated, predominantly the urban areas suffering from unemployment and industrial decline. Development in rural areas has not been high on their agendas.

An idea of the relative importance of Pillar 2 spending in relation to Pillar 1 and other structural fund spending (mainly regional policy) is given in Figure 7.1, which relates to the period 2000–06. In all the EU-15 countries shown, rural development spending was obviously small in comparison with Pillar I and with what was made available in regional and other structural policy interventions. So care must be taken not to over-estimate the role that the CAP's contribution to rural development makes.

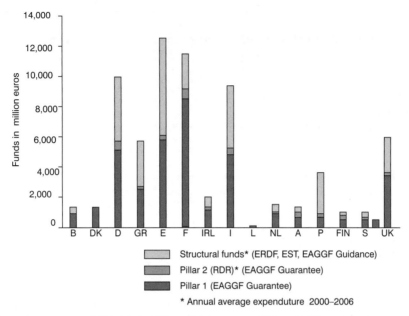

Figure 7.1 Comparison of EU aids for Pillar 1 CAP payment, Pillar 2 RDR, and the Structural Funds in EU-15 Member States (from LUPG, 2002)(2000–06)

7.2 Understanding what is rural – the EU definition of a rural region

A complicating issue when discussing rural development is what is meant by the term rural area. This is capable of a range of interpretations and alternative classifications are possible, though for present purposes we use the system adopted by the European Commission, which is based on OECD methodology that takes low population density as the critical feature of rural areas (see Box 7.1). This classifies quite large geographical areas (corresponding in the UK to counties or groups of counties) as Predominantly Rural (PR), Intermediate Regions (IR) or Predominantly Urban (PU). Nevertheless it should be acknowledged that this is not always satisfactory. In densely populated countries such as England, the countryside is often dotted with settlements and land is farmed intensively up to the edges of towns and often within their boundaries. Yet, because the unit chosen is too large, according to the EU classification, England does not have any predominantly rural counties or regions even though there is an undeniable concern at national level with the problems experienced by people living in the English countryside and with what goes on there. Consequently, for situations like England, a much smaller-scale (finer) approach to defining what is a rural area is needed, and a national classification system is in place that reflects this. In contrast, situations where there are large expanses of extensive agricultural or forestry land use and only the occasional small village may find a large geographical unit adequate and the EU classification system satisfactory.

Regions classed as Predominantly Rural account for just over half (53 per cent) of the territory of EU-27, a little more in the older Member States (EU-15) at 55 per cent than in the newer Member States (EU-12) at 43 per cent. A little less than a fifth (17 per cent) of both the population and total employment is found in these PR regions, with a somewhat small share of economic activity (12 per cent of gross value added) (all figures relate to 2005 and,

Box 7.1 OECD methodology to define rural areas, adopted by the EU

The OECD methodology is based on population density. It has a two-step approach:
    First, local units (e.g. municipalities) are identified as rural if their population density is below 150 inhabitants per square kilometre.
    Then, regions (e.g. NUTS 2 or NUTS 3, in the UK corresponding to counties or local authorities or groups of them), are classified in one of the three categories:

- **Predominantly Rural region (PR):** if more than 50 per cent of the population of the region is living in rural communes (with less than 150 inhabitants / km^2);
- **Intermediate Region (IR):** if 15 per cent to 50 per cent of the population of the region is living in rural local units;
- **Predominantly Urban region (PU):** if less than 15 per cent of the population of the region is living in rural local units.

But:
- if there is an urban centre greater than 200.000 inhabitants (in EU) representing no less than 25 per cent of the regional population in a 'predominantly rural' region, it is re-classified as 'intermediate'
- if there is an urban centre greater than 500.000 inhabitants (in EU) representing no less than 25 per cent of the regional population in an 'intermediate' region, it is re-classified as 'predominantly urban'.

An 'urban centre' in Europe is defined as a local unit LAU (e.g. municipality) with a population density above 150 inhabitants per km^2 and total population above 200,000 inhabitants.
    Characterisation of the rural character at regional level, where most of the statistics are available, allows drawing easily a picture of the different types of areas at national level.
    As for the first step, the method requires information on population and areas at local level, the characterisation can only be made with a long periodicity (in general every 10 years when a population census is made).
    The OECD methodology is the only definition of rural areas internationally recognised. However, the results of this methodology are sometimes considered as imperfectly reflecting the rural character of areas, particularly in densely populated regions. The methodology is therefore sometimes adapted or replaced by another approach.

Source: Taken and adapted from Commission (2008) *Rural Development in the European Union: Economic and Statistical Information*

when regions are classified, using NUTS 3 territorial units – which correspond in England to areas generally smaller than counties comprising groups of local authorities). The relative importance of rural areas varies between Member States, and there are differences in the political imperative of taking actions to alleviate problems. The Netherlands and UK, with 2 per cent or less of their populations living in areas classed as Predominantly Rural (according to OECD criteria and using NUTS 3 classification) in 2005, can be expected to take a rather different view from Sweden (49 per cent), Slovenia (57 per cent) or Ireland (71 per cent) (See Table 7.1).

7.3 Problems faced by rural areas

Rural areas, by definition, are relatively sparsely populated. They are also often remote from major centres of population and poorly served by transport links. These characteristics bring some economic disadvantages. Firms located in rural areas (including farms) find themselves separated from their main markets and facing relatively high transport costs. Rural residents may not be able to obtain well-paid occupations locally and will face long commuting journeys. Where this is impractical they may need to migrate to towns, and those who go tend to be the more able, the relatively young and the enterprising, leaving an imbalance in the countryside. The delivery of public services (health, education etc.) and commercially operated facilities (buses, trains etc.) is more expensive per person in remote and sparsely populated areas, so there is a tendency for rural residents to receive poorer provision and to have poorer access to them, especially people who have low incomes or who in other ways do not have much choice. On the other hand, there are undeniable positive aspects to living in the countryside, including a more pleasant and less crowded environment that may attract visitors and tourists with money to spend and settlers looking for the qualities of rural life, which may include a more cohesive society. Thus, the balance of problems and advantages faced by rural society depends to a substantial extent on where the individual is within that society. Public policies are very much to do with taking the broad view and what is best for society as a whole, which usually means paying special attention to the interests of the disadvantaged (those facing income or employment problems, housing difficulties, those needing better skills etc.), though there will also be situations where aid to the relatively well-off can be justified (such as investment grants to operators of rural businesses) because they create employment and incomes in rural areas.

Several characteristics of rural areas in the EU are important to note. The first is their heterogeneity in terms of characteristics and of the problems they face, a feature that the enlargement to EU-27 has further stretched. This implies that any EU-wide policy for rural areas has to be capable of reflecting a range of needs and solutions. As will be seen below, in practice, Member States are allowed a wide degree of flexibility in how they tackle rural problems, though this is done within a single framework that applies across the EU.

Second, a feature shared by rural areas in the EU is that, although agriculture as an activity is more important in rural regions than in urban ones, its contribution to the total economy is still relatively small when assessed at NUTS 2 or NUTS 3 level. Even in areas classified as Predominantly Rural in EU-27, the primary sector (agriculture, forestry and fishing but also including mining) only accounted for 5.5 per cent of gross value added generated by the economy when measured at NUTS 3 level in 2005, and it was only more than 10 per cent in PR areas in four countries (Bulgaria, Estonia, Greece, Lithuania, and Romania)(see Table 7.2 from European Commission, 2008). This has substantial relevance for policy, as support

Table 7.1 Relative importance of rural areas in EU-27

	Percentage by type of rural area – NUTS 3							
	% Territory in rural areas 2005				*% Population in rural areas 2005*			
Country	% PR	% IR	% PU			% PR	% IR	% PU	
Austria	78.5	20.2	1.3		46	30.8	23.2	
Belgium	23.4	18.1	58.5	excl. 2/44 NUTS 3	3.6	9.4	87.0	excl. 2/44 NUTS 3
Bulgaria	36.6	62.2	1.2		24.9	59.2	15.8	
Cyprus		100.0				100.0		
Czech Republic		99.2	0.8	excl. 2/14 NUTS 3	5.0	83.5	11.5	excl. 2/14 NUTS 3
Denmark	n.a.	n.a.	n.a.		n.a.	n.a.	n.a.	
Estonia	20.9	71.4	7.7		10.5	76.6	12.9	
Finland	92.2	5.5	2.2	excl. 2/20	53.1	21.1	25.8	excl. 2/20
France	48.3	47.2	4.4	2 003	16.8	53.6	29.6	
Germany	35.6	43.9	20.5	excl. 14/429 NUTS 3	13.0	28.8	58.2	excl. 14/429 NUTS 3
Greece	73.9	23.2	2.9		36.8	27.3	35.9	
Hungary	58.0	41.5	0.6		41.4	41.8	16.8	
Ireland	98.7		1.3		71.9		28.1	
Italy	23.6	48.9	27.5	excl. 8/107 NUTS 3	9.3	36.8	53.9	excl. 8/107 NUTS 3
Latvia	56.2	43.4	0.4		39.1	29.2	31.7	
Lithuania	32.7	52.2	15		19.8	55.4	24.8	
Luxembourg		100.0				100,0		
Malta			100.0				100,0	
Netherlands	3.5	37.8	58.7	excl. 2/40 NUTS 3	1.4	17.0	81.7	excl. 2/40 NUTS 3
Poland	n.a.	n.a.	n.a.		n.a.	n.a.	n.a.	
Portugal	69.7	21.7	8.6		21.2	26.7	52.1	
Romania	54.7	45.2	0.1		40.9	50.2	8.9	
Slovakia	32.2	63.6	4.2		25.4	63.4	11.2	
Slovenia	70.4	29.6		2 000	57.6	42.4		
Spain	45.8	40.1	14.1	excl. 10/59 NUTS 3	13.8	38.2	47.9	excl. 10/59 NUTS 3
Sweden	90.1	8.3	1.5	2 000	49.4	29.8	20.8	
United Kingdom	13.3	59.9	26.8	excl. 7/133 NUTS 3	2.0	28.4	69.6	excl. 7/133 NUTS 3
EU27	52.6	37.6	9.7	excl. Denmark, Poland	16.7	37.1	46.2	excl. Denmark, Poland
EU15	55.1	33.4	11.5	excl. Denmark	14.4	33.7	51.9	excl. Denmark
EU12	42.5	55.1	2.4	excl Poland	30.2	56.4	13.5	excl Poland

The following regions are excluded from their respective national totals and therefore from the EU aggregates: for Belgium, part of the province of Liège; for Czech Republic, Jihovychod; for Netherlands, Acterhoek and Arnhem-Nijmegen; for Finland, Satakunta and Pirkanmaa; for Germany, Sachsen-Anhalt and part of Thüringen; for Italy, Sardegna; for Spain, Canarias and Baleares; and for UK, North Eastern Scotland and Highlands and Islands.

The following regions are excluded from their respective national totals and therefore from the EU aggregates: for Germany, Sachsen-Anhalt and part of Thüringen; for Italy, Sardegna; for Spain, Canarias and Baleares; and for UK, North Eastern Scotland and Highlands and Islands.

% OVA in rural areas 2005				% Employment in rural areas 2005			
% PR	% IR	% PU		% PR	% IR	% PU	
34.9	34.3	30.9		n.a.	n.a.	n.a.	
2.6	7.4	90.0		2.8	7.4	89.8	p-excl. 2/44 NUTS 3
19.1	49.9	31.0		21.4	58.6	20.0	
	100.0				100.0		
4.2	71.7	24.0		4.6	78.6	16.8	
38.1	24.2	37.7		40.5	26.1	33.4	
6.4	85.3	8.3		9.2	79.5	11.4	
44.0	20.4	35.6		48.6	20.6	30.8	
13.3	47.7	39.0		15.9	51.5	32.6	
9.7	22.5	67.8	p – excl. 14/429 NUTS 3	10.8	24.3	64.9	excl. 14/429 NUTS 3
28.1	23.0	48.8		34.4	28.2	37.4	
28.4	35.7	35.9		37.3	37.6	25.1	
59.2		40.8		67.2		32.8	
6.8	32.1	61.1	excl. 8/107 NUTS 3	7.4	33.7	58.9	excl. 8/107 NUTS 3
24.3	18.3	57.4		38.5	25.8	35.7	
13.4	50.6	35.9		18.8	54.1	27.1	
	100.0				100.0		
		100.0				100.0	
0.9	14.7	84.3	p	1.1	14.2	84.7	p
n.a.	n.a.	n.a.		n.a.	n.a.	n.a.	
16.6	22.6	60.8		20.7	26.7	52.6	
30.4	50.0	19.7		39.2	51.0	9.8	
20.4	52.2	27.3		22.5	58.0	19.5	
48.6	51.4			53.9	46.1		
10.6	33.7	55.7	excl. 8/59 NUTS 3	11.8	34.5	53.7	excl. 8/59 NUTS 3
43.0	28.0	29.0		46.3	29.6	24.1	
1.1	23.4	75.5	excl. 7/133 NUTS 3	n.a.	n.a.	n.a.	
12.0	29.7	58.3	excl. Poland	17.0	35.6	47.4	excl. Austria, Poland, UK
11.7	28.7	59.6		14.9	31.5	53.6	excl. Austria, UK
20.3	53.7	25.9	excl. Poland	27.4	55.5	17.0	exc. Poland

The following regions are excluded from their respective
national totals and therefore from the EU aggregates: for
Belgium, part of the province of Liège; for Germany, Sachsen-
Anhalt and part of Thüringen; for Italy, Sardegna; and for
Spain, Canarias and Baleares.

Table 7.2 Structure of the economy (% GVA by branch) – 2005

Country	% GVA by branch by type of area – 2005 – NUTS 3									MS value (National Accounts)			Notes
	(1) PR			(2) IR			(3) PU						
	% primary sector	% secondary sector	% tertiary sector	% primary sector	% secondary sector	% tertiary sector	% primary sector	% secondary sector	% tertiary sector	% GVA in primary sector	% GVA in secondary sector	% GVA in tertiary sector	
Austria	3.5	37.6	58.9	0.9	31.8	67.3	0.3	18.6	81.1	1.6	29.4	69.0	
Belgium	3.4	22.3	74.3	2.3	23.6	74.1	0.7	24.2	75.1	0.9	24.1	75.0	
Bulgaria	19.1	30.3	50.5	11.3	33.7	55.0	0.4	21.8	77.8	9.4	29.4	61.2	
Cyprus	2.8	19.5	77.7	2.8	19.5	77.7				2.8	19.5	77.7	
Czech Republic	8.6	48.8	42.6	3.5	44.2	52.2	0.2	18.1	81.7	3.0	37.9	59.1	
Denmark	2.9	28.6	68.5	1.7	23.9	74.4	0.2	15.0	84.8	1.4	25.0	73.6	
Estonia	12.0	36.2	51.8	3.2	25.5	71.3	1.7	52.4	45.9	3.6	28.4	68.0	
Finland	5.2	34.8	60.0	2.4	37.5	60.1	0.4	23.7	75.9	3.0	31.3	65.7	
France	5.4	24.9	69.8	3.0	23.2	73.8	0.4	16.2	83.4	2.3	20.7	77.0	
Germany	3.0	32.4	64.6	1.8	33.1	65.1	0.4	27.7	71.9	0.9	29.0	70.2	p – excl. 14/429 NUTS 3
Greece	10.3	31.5	58.2	5.3	26.0	68.7	0.4	15.0	84.6	4.3	22.2	73.5	
Hungary	8.8	32.0	59.2	4.9	38.7	56.4	0.2	20.3	79.5	4.3	30.2	65.5	
Ireland	3.2	44.0	52.8				0.2	23.7	76.1	2.0	35.7	62.3	
Italy	4.1	25.2	70.7	3.4	27.1	69.5	1.3	26.7	72.0	2.2	26.9	70.9	excl. 8/107 NUTS 3
Latvia	9.4	29.9	60.7	7.1	23.6	69.3	0.6	17.5	81.9	4.0	21.6	74.5	
Lithuania	11.1	37.7	51.2	7.0	36.2	56.8	1.8	26.9	71.3	5.7	33.1	61.3	
Luxembourg				0.4	15.7	83.8				0.4	15.7	83.8	
Malta							2.7	22.5	74.8	2.7	22.4	74.9	
Netherlands	5.9	26.1	68.1	3.3	33.2	63.4	1.9	21.4	76.7	2.1	23.9	73.9	
Poland	n.a.	n.a.	n.a.	n.a.	n.a.	n.a.	n.a.	n.a.	n.a.	4.5	30.7	64.8	p
Portugal	7.8	26.4	65.8	4.7	27.8	67.5	0.8	22.9	76.3	2.8	24.5	72.6	
Romania	15.8	33.2	51.0	9.5	38.5	52.0	0.1	29.7	70.3	9.5	35.2	55.3	
Slovakia	7.1	36.3	56.6	4.4	41.8	53.8	0.8	25.5	73.7	4.0	36.2	59.8	
Slovenia	3.9	40.2	55.9	1.2	26.7	72.1				2.5	33.2	64.2	
Spain	9.9	30.1	60.0	4.5	33.0	62.5	1.2	28.7	70.1	3.2	30.0	66.8	excl. 8/59 NUTS 3
Sweden	1.7	33.4	64.9	1.1	28.6	70.2	0.1	18.3	81.6	1.1	27.7	71.2	
United Kingdom	n.a.	n.a.	n.a.	n.a.	n.a.	n.a.	n.a.	n.a.	n.a.	0.9	23.1	76.0	
EU27	5.0	31.5	63.5	3.1	28.8	68.1	0.8	24.2	75.0	1.9	26.2	71.9	excl. Poland, UK
EU15	4.6	31.2	64.2	2.9	28.0	69.1	0.8	24.3	74.9	1.9	26.1	72.0	excl. UK
EU12	10.4	34.9	54.6	5.2	37.7	57.1	0.5	22.4	77.1	4.9	32.3	62.9	excl. Poland

Data sources differ at regional (Economic Accounts) and national (National Accounts) levels. The following regions are excluded from their respective national totals and therefore from the EU aggregates: for Germany, Sachsen-Anhalt and part of Thüringen; for Italy, Sardegna; and for Spain, Canarias and Baleares.

to agriculture is therefore unlikely to be a suitable way of influencing the broader economy of these rural regions to a significant extent. On the other hand, these primary industries are very important to issues that involve landscape and the natural environment. Agriculture and forestry represent 78 per cent of land use in the EU-25, ranging from 50 per cent in Malta to 95 per cent in Poland. A considerable part of the agriculture area is located in regions where conditions are difficult for this activity, for instance in mountains. 'High nature value farming' systems cover more than 10 per cent of the agricultural area in most Member States (and more than 30 per cent in some of them – Greece, Portugal, Spain).

Another feature is that many of the economic and social problems found in rural areas are also seen in non-rural areas of the same country (deprivation of various kinds, low income and employment opportunities, lack of affordable housing, poor access to services etc.). The causes are not particularly linked to the characteristics of rural areas, such as land use or low population density. This raises the issue of whether policy interventions that are unique to rural areas are appropriate (either because of their causes or because of their delivery mechanism) or whether they are best tackled by general policies (transport, education, health, housing, alleviation of poverty, taxation etc.) that may contain special provisions for any peculiarities of rural situations (see Hill *et al*, 2005).

Finally, it should be noted that Pillar 2 of the CAP exists alongside other EU policies (especially regional policy) and national and sub-national interventions. What is experienced on the ground is a mix of all these, and the mix varies geographically even within the same country. Attention here focuses on the CAP's contribution to rural development at EU level, since this is both the focus of this book and provides a consistent framework for most of the spending explicitly directed at rural areas in Member States, and national measures have to be consistent with EU policies. However, the significance of purely national interventions (land use planning, social security payments etc.) to many aspects of conditions in rural areas should not be underestimated.

7.4 The role of agriculture in providing solutions to problems of rural areas

Given that supporting agriculture, a small and declining sector of the economy in most rural areas, is incapable of stimulating in a major way incomes and jobs of rural residents as a whole, the economic role played by Pillar 2 is bound to be narrower and more specialised. The Commission's 1988 paper *The Future of Rural Society* made a very broad analysis of the types of rural areas found in the EU, the sorts of problems they faced, and policy action appropriate to the problems, including the role for agriculture. This analysis is still largely valid. Three types of rural areas were highlighted:

- **Areas faced with the pressures of modern life on rural society** (into which much of Southern England would fit). In the Commission's analysis, the main issue here was how to keep the countryside intact from an environmental point of view, not only so that it can fulfil its function as an ecological buffer but also to provide it with new and lasting scope for development as an area for recreation and leisure for town dwellers. The aim of policy was thus less one of stepping up the pace of economic development in these rural areas and more one of environmental protection and of allowing these areas to take full advantage of the growing demand of urban dwellers for green spaces. Agriculture was involved in this policy insofar that it was encouraged to be competitive (by farm restructuring) and by encouragements to lower intensity of its farming systems.

- **Areas in rural decline.** This is the classic model of declining rural populations, ageing among those left, depletion of rural services, economic isolation among non-agricultural businesses, limited credit opportunities. The policy actions to be taken included the encouragement of diversification on farms and in the rural economy generally, improved marketing, provision of training facilities, improved infrastructure (roads and telecommunications especially, though these are part of regional rather than agricultural policy).
- **Extremely disadvantaged areas** such as some mountain and hill areas, or islands, which are relatively inaccessible, sparsely populated and suffer natural and structural disadvantages. For them, agriculture was likely to remain the main economic activity. Support of farming, of services and aid to any other businesses found there, was likely to be needed permanently. The environment and cultural values of the population should be protected, and opportunities for new business ventures supported (such as integrated forestry and production of timber products).

This typology can be traced in the background to much of current thinking in terms of rural development, in that a flexible approach is applied in EU policy that allows policy interventions to be tailored to the problems of specific rural areas, and environmental issues are closely bound in with economic ones. However, it should also be noted that this analysis only gives the support of agricultural production a prominent role as a policy mechanism in the third – extremely disadvantaged – areas. Elsewhere the emphasis is on agriculture as a provider of environmental and recreational services and on helping farming to diversify.

7.5 Previous attempts to align the CAP with rural development

There has always been awareness in parts of the European Commission of the need to take a view of issues in rural areas that went broader than agriculture. In recognition of the problems of policies administered along sectoral lines, with separate parts of the bureaucracy being responsible for agriculture, for education and training, for industrial development and so on, and with poor cross-links and abilities to switch funding according to need, there have been historic attempts at taking an integrated approach. Integrated Development Programmes were initiated in the early 1980s in selected areas – such as the Luxembourg province of Belgium (1981) and the islands to the north of Scotland (1981), the Lozère in France (1981), and Western Ireland (1980). The Commission also helped finance pilot studies of integrated rural development, such as in the Peak Park experiment in the UK. The Integrated Mediterranean Programmes (IMPs), initiated in 1985, in Greece, southern France and Italy were put in place to enable these countries to cope with the enlargement of the Community to include Spain and Portugal and the increased competition it brought. These areas suffered from classic development problems – underdeveloped agricultures, difficult natural conditions, difficulties in marketing their produce, extensive Less Favoured Areas, unemployment, small and medium firms employing low levels of technology, other industries in crisis, tourist industries which were large but created socio-economic imbalance, and poorly organised administrations. IMPs were multi-annual programmes (maximum length seven years), covered all sectors of the economy, and were intended to be consistent with other Community policies, including the CAP. The IMPs involved coordinated assistance from the various Community Structural Funds (European Regional Development Fund, European Social Fund, and the Guidance part of the European Agricultural Guidance and Guarantee Fund), and contributions from national governments. By and large the experience with these integrated development programmes was not a happy one; the Commission later concluded that these attempts were 'sometimes badly adapted, badly coordinated and not always mutually consistent' (European Commission, 1988). A critical issue was the difficulty of coordinating spending; the lead tended to be taken by the Fund with the most money available and the attempt at integration hit rocks of institutional self-interest.

The year 1988 proved to be a pivotal date in the evolution of development policy for rural areas in the EU. As part of an agreement which put a limit on CAP commodity support spending and introduced stabilisers, a commitment was made to double the size of the Structural Funds by 1993 and to 'reform' them so that they worked better together. Five objectives were identified, of which the first and fifth are of particular importance in the context of rural development (Objective 2 was concerned with assistance to areas suffering industrial decline, such as coalfields, by the ERDF and ESF, and Objectives 3 and 4 with measures to counter unemployment issues by the ESF). Areas designated to receive support under Objective 1 were regions that were lagging behind economically, many of which were rural in nature. The problems of rural development in these regions were intended to be tackled as part of the overall strategy for these regions. Objective 5(a) was concerned with assisting agriculture to adjust in all areas and 5(b) was intended to tackle rural development problems in designated areas that fell outside Objective 1 regions (see Box 7.2). It is worth noting that all Member States where rural development was not already covered by Objective 1 status had at least one Objective 5(b) area – suggesting that political considerations were not ignored in allocating assistance. Later, Objective 6 was introduced to support development in the special conditions found in the extreme north of the EU, brought in when Sweden and Finland acceded in 1995. Of the total committed from the Structural Funds (ECU 60.315 billion for the period to 1989–93, including ECU 1,150m transitional and innovatory measures), almost two-thirds was to be spent on Objective 1, 6 per cent on 5(a) and only 5 per cent on 5(b).(The ECU or European Currency Unit, was in use as the EU's unit of account from 1979 to January 1999, when it was replaced by the euro).

Under the agreement with Member States, spending from the Community Structural Funds was only expected to part-finance schemes, the remainder coming from Member States. EU funding for Objective 1 support was within the range 75–50 per cent of total costs, and Objective 5b in the range 50–25 per cent. There was a set procedure for applications and operation of support for these objectives. Member States put forward plans to the Commission (Regional Development Plan in the case of Objective 1 and Development Plan for Rural Areas for Objective 5b). The Commission after consultation agreed a *Community Support Framework* with the Member State. This led on, in most cases, to an *Operational Programme*, again put forward by the Member State and then approved by the Commission. Thus the ideas on what was needed were settled at local level – the principle of *subsidiarity* – and there was a *partnership* between the EU, national and regional bodies. Although this could be a strength, it could also be bureaucratic and a weakness. At least some of the funding was applied to pre-existing national schemes as a way of continuing them.[1]

The balance between spending on the various objectives and the designation of areas suggests that, in the Commission's view, the problems of the first type of rural area identified

Box 7.2 Structural Fund objectives relating to rural areas, as established in 1988

Objective 1: the development and structural adjustment of regions whose development was lagging behind (funding came from all three Structural Funds – ERDF, ESF, EAGGF). Objective 1 regions were selected essentially according to macroeconomic criteria, principally where the per capita GDP of the region was less than 75 per cent of the EU-15 average. Areas designated for assistance included the whole of Greece, Ireland (both the Republic of Ireland and Northern Ireland) and Portugal, and parts of Spain, France, and Italy. These regions together accounted for 38 per cent of the total area of the Community and 21 per cent of its total population. Many of the regions designated under this objective were rural in character. The main axes of development, as reflected in the regional plans by Member States, were;

- support to agriculture (improvement of natural and structural production conditions, quality policy, restructuring and development of traditional products such as olives, wine, cereals, improving living conditions of rural communities, development of water supplies, farm tourism);
- development of basic infrastructure (transport and communications etc) paying attention to environmental protection;
- development of other sectors, tourism, environment, human resource development (vocational training in all sectors and at all levels).

Objective 5: with a view to reform of the CAP:

(a) speeding up the adjustment of agricultural structures (EAGGF). This covered aid to farm investment, farm diversification, vocational training, LFA payments, set-aside, payments to farmers in ESAs, extensification and land diversion, pre-pensions, aid to young farmers, improvements to marketing structures etc. These payments were 'horizontal', i.e. available throughout the EU (assuming that national governments passed the required legislation to adopt them). Such spending was related to rural development in so far as, in many areas, the fortunes of agriculture and of the rural economy were seen as linked.

(b) promoting the development of rural areas outside those designated for Objective 1 status (EAGGF, ERDF, ESF). Assistance was offered for diversification on and off the farm, encouragement of small and medium enterprises (including tourism), training in agriculture and other sectors, improvement of infrastructure etc. Criteria for selecting areas for 5(b) included a high share of agricultural employment in total employment, a low level of agricultural income, and a low level of socio-economic development assessed on the basis of GDP per inhabitant. In practice, designation criteria were flexible and included peripherality and low population density. Areas designated 5(b) areas together accounted for 17.3 per cent of the land area of EU-12 and 5.1 per cent of the population of the Community. However, because funds were allocated on a per capita basis, it appears that more densely populated regions were allocated more money than remoter and more sparsely populated ones which frequently had greater needs of structural improvement. The main types of spending under this head that were proposed by Member States in their plans were on agriculture (development of agricultural products which were not in surplus, support for research and the creation of advisory services); forestry; development of other sectors of the economy (especially small and medium enterprises); tourism (including farm tourism); environment; and human resource development (training programmes to support the other development priorities).

in the 1988 FRS – areas in economically developed regions suffering from urban pressure – received very limited attention and only benefited from sorts of assistance to farmers (under Objective 5(a)) that were already generally available. Nothing more was to be directed by the EU at non-farmers, whose needs arguably were greater.

In addition to spending under the five Objectives, there were a number of Community Initiatives. Though the sums were not large in comparison with those of the above Objectives, they gave the Community a more direct handle on rural development. The most important in the rural development context was LEADER (Links between Action for the Development of the Rural Economy), the first phase of which ran from 1991–94 and used ECU 442m from EU funding (out of the Structural Funds), ECU 347m from Member States and ECU 366m from local economic operators. Operated in Objective 1 and 5b areas, LEADER offered direct finance for joint development initiatives launched by local communities, and experiences were networked between projects. LEADER actions supported rural tourism, processing of farm goods, small and medium-sized enterprises and rural crafts, and development support and training. Subsequent rounds of this initiative have carried the concept forwards (LEADER2, LEADER+ and now Axis 4 of Rural Development Programmes for 2007–13). In contrast to the 'top-down' system of development by designating areas for assistance, the LEADER approach to rural development is often labelled as 'bottom-up' as it enables Local Action Groups (LAGs), comprising mixes of local government and non-governmental organisations such as voluntary associations, to identify problems, propose solutions and implement them using contributions from EU funding. Moreover, there is an emphasis on developing the capacity of communities to be resourceful in helping themselves ('endogenous' development) by cooperation, networking, accessing funding etc. (that is, to build social capital).

Subsequently, the 1992 MacSharry Reforms to the CAP introduced a number of 'compensatory measures' of relevance to rural development. These included schemes for conservation of the environment, afforestation and early retirement for farmers. Implementing these involved Member States designing schemes operated on a national basis, passing national legislation to make them operational and providing part of the finance from their own budgets.

7.6 Present system of Rural Development Programmes under the CAP's Pillar 2

The present way that the CAP contributes to rural development thus has a rather complex history. Certain features from past experience had proved beneficial, such as the ability to tailor policy interventions to suit local circumstances, the notion of applying a plan over a run of years, and the ability to have a package of interventions that could work together and, potentially, create synergy (a combined impact that was greater than would be expected from independent interventions). There are negatives to consider as well, in particular that some schemes (particularly management agreements to achieve agri-environmental ends) carry long-term financial commitments and eat into budgets for new actions. Part of the legacy is a complicated funding arrangement that has only recently been resolved.

The present way of operating support for rural development under Pillar 2 really started with the first Programming Period that ran from 2000–06 and has been continued, relatively little altered, into the subsequent 2007–13.

7.6.1 Rural development in Programming Period 2000–06

The *Agenda 2000* agreement that recognised rural development as the CAP's Pillar 2 also involved a further reform of the Structural Funds (with a reduction in the number of Objective areas to three); Objective 1 (less developed regions, with GDP per head less than 75 per cent of the Community average, and including former Objective 6 regions); Objective 2 (areas confronted with restructuring problems and including all territorially based objectives, including rural development not covered in Objective 1 regions); Objective 3, education and training systems in other areas. The total EU funding was limited to €195 billion over seven years (2000 to 2006 inclusive) plus €18 billion of Cohesion Funds. Funds for accession countries were allocated from 2002 (they joined the EU in 2004), of which a small part was for agriculture (a third in the first years, falling to about a quarter in 2006).

To implement Pillar 2, a Rural Development Regulation (RDR) was passed by the Council of the EU (Council Regulation 1259/1999) that provided financial support to national schemes by the EU's agricultural fund (EAGGF). Its various Chapters provided support for a menu of 22 measures, falling into the following broad groups:

- investments in agricultural holdings to meet certain objectives;
- assistance to entry and exit of individuals, and vocational training;
- agriculture in Less Favoured Areas (such as uplands);
- agri-environmental schemes and organic farming methods;
- improving marketing and processing of products originating on farms;
- afforestation;
- measures in various forms to improve the quality of life in rural areas.

Of these, the agri-environmental schemes were obligatory, but Member States could select others according to their requirements. The only measure proposed voluntarily by all EU-15 countries was support in Less Favoured Areas (Commission, 2006a). Some Member States proposed close to the full menu (Germany, Italy, Spain and France) whereas others proposed only very few (Portugal, Greece and Ireland, though these countries may have applied and financed schemes not chosen from the menu in other ways).

The 1999 RDR also specified reporting arrangements and the process to be used for evaluation (including *ex ante* evaluation, baseline study, mid-term and *ex post* evaluations), who should carry them out, and a timetable (see Chapter 11). Later detailed implementing Regulations were issued by the Commission, such as the setting of Common Evaluation Questions and selection of indicators.

While the 1999 Rural Development Regulation marked a significant shift of policy under *Agenda 2000*, in practice it was largely an amalgamation of previous legal instruments (it brought together nine different pieces of legislation which in some instances had been initiated in the 1970s) under a new heading. However, the new rhetoric of 'integrated rural development' was reflected in a more systematic way of looking at the problems of rural areas and their solution. Member States were required to submit Rural Development Plans for approval; this included a statement of the conditions in their rural areas (agricultural, economic, social, environmental), a SWOT analysis (strengths, weaknesses, opportunities, threats), details of the proposed national schemes for each Chapter in the Regulation, and a financial statement covering the planning period 2000–06 (how EU funds were to be used and in which year, and how much would come from national budgets). Given that the

Council Regulation was issued in 1999 for a set of programmes that were intended to start on 1 January 2000, the timetable was exceedingly tight. As a result, the schemes proposed reflected an accumulated legacy of past policy interventions, largely focused on adjustment by farms, with relatively little that was to do with broader issues of rural development. Critics have judged their aims and objectives to have been complex, not fully coherent and difficult to translate into testable form (Bradley, Dwyer and Hill, 2006) Such a situation made evaluation difficult.

Planned expenditure from the EU budget for the period was €64.4 billion. The allocation of funds was made first to Member States, at levels that reflected their previous spending on these sorts of measures rather than a reassessment of need. For the period 2000–05 the largest amounts were allocated to Spain, Germany, Italy and France. Where countries used more than one RDP (such as the UK, with separate programmes for England, Wales, Scotland and Northern Ireland) a second, sub-national, allocation had to be made nationally. Spending per hectare varied widely among EU-15, with Luxembourg's level being about eight times that of the UK. The scope of the RDR was somewhat expanded at the time of the Mid-Term Review of *Agenda 2000* in 2003. More funds were made available and some new measures added to promote environment, food quality and animal welfare and help farmers meet EU production standards starting in 2005.

Allocation of spending within RDPs was severely constrained by commitments under earlier rounds of policy implementation; for example, in the UK, agri-environment agreements made under previous schemes that predated the RDR of 1999 typically ran for 10 years, and the funds available in the 2000–06 programming period had to bear their costs. Therefore the sums available for new schemes were severely compromised.

In terms of the balance of spending between broad groups of measures, for 2000–05 the picture was dominated by spending on agri-environment schemes and support to farming in Less Favoured Areas; it seems that together these items accounted for just under half of the total from the EU budget. It is also abundantly clear that both the list of actions and expenditure were heavily dominated by schemes directed at farmers and landowners. Only the RDR's last Chapter (comprising Article 33 of the Regulation) was concerned with the broader aspects of rural areas, the quality of life of the people living there (most of whom would not be farmers), and this absorbed probably not much more than 10 per cent of spending.

The reason why there is still a problem in describing how much was spent on what is that, because of history, the way in which funding was provided was highly complex. For some interventions, the source of finance differed according to whether actions were carried out outside or inside areas given Objective 1 status. By the Commission's own admission, the complexity of funding streams made it difficult to report on the actual public spending on the various chapters of the regulation (and on the contributions from EU and national funds and, where appropriate, by beneficiaries themselves). Such funding mechanisms will be of little concern to most observers now.

Many (though not all) of the types of action permitted under the RDR were paralleled among countries that were not EU Member States in 2000 but acceded in 2004. This provision was by means of the SAPARD programme (Special Pre-accession Programme for Agriculture and Rural Development) initiated in 1999 (Malta and Cyprus were not included). Actions not covered included support for farming in Less Favoured Areas, and assistance to setting up young farmers and the early retirement of older ones. For the remaining years of the 2000–06 programming period, finance was provided under the Temporary Rural

Development Instrument (TRDI). Grants for investments in processing and marketing, rural infrastructures and on farms were the main types of action funded.

Also within this programming period mention must be made of LEADER+, a third-generation example of rural development initiatives based on Local Action Groups (LAGs). Although the sum allocated to it (some €5 billion) was relatively small, it could claim to take perhaps the most fundamental approach in promoting basic rural development. It was structured around 'three actions'; (a) integrated territorial rural development strategies of a pilot nature based on a bottom-up approach and horizontal partnerships; (b) inter-territorial and transnational cooperation; (c) networking of all rural areas, irrespective of whether they were beneficiaries of LEADER+, and all rural development actors.

Finally, within this period, the 1996 First European Conference on Rural Development (the Cork conference) established some important features that were to be incorporated into future policy. They included the use of an integrated approach (multisectoral and multidisciplinary, territorially targeted); diversification (of the rural economy); sustainability (of landscape, biodiversity, cultural environment etc.); the principle of subsidiarity (a bottom-up approach); simplification; programming; finance (co-financing and involvement of private sector and banking); management (technical assistance to local administration); and the need for evaluation and research (this must take place and involve stakeholders).

7.6.2 Rural development under programming period 2007–13

For the programming period 2007–13 rural development activities at EU level are enacted under Regulation 1698/2005, agreed in September 2005. This has given rise to a number of Rural Development Programmes (at national or sub-national level, according to the preferences of each Member State) that, after agreement with the Commission, become the basis by which EU funds can be used to support (partially) various schemes ('measures') operated by Member States to promote agricultural adjustment, the quality of life in rural areas, environment and landscape conservation, and build up the capacity of communities to develop endogenously.

In line with recommendations made at the Second European Conference on Rural Development in Salzburg (12–14 November 2003), the Regulation aims to reinforce rural development policy and simplify its implementation by:

- Introducing a new strategic approach for rural development with a clear focus on EU priorities (such as the Lisbon and Göteborg goals, principally to do with economic growth and environmental sustainability respectively), and targeting the wider rural population, i.e. going beyond the agricultural sector. This strategy has been set out for the EU as a whole in a Community Strategy document, adopted by the Council in February 2006. The rhetoric claims that this strategic approach attempts to;
    - identify and agree the areas where the use of EU support for rural development creates the most value added at EU level;
    - make the link with the main EU priorities (Lisbon, Göteborg) and translate them into rural development policy;
    - ensure consistency with other EU policies, in particular in the field of cohesion and environment;
    - accompany the implementation of the new market-oriented Common Agricultural Policy and the necessary restructuring it will entail in the old and new Member States.

- Strengthening the bottom-up approach – Member States, regions and Local Action Groups will have more say in attuning programmes to local needs.
- Introducing a single funding and programming instrument for rural development, the European Agriculture Fund for Rural Development (EAFRD). Pillar 1 will continue to be funded from the European Agricultural Guarantee Fund. This EAFRD now also funds rural development aspects of programmes in Objective 1 areas. Transitional arrangements are in place for areas that have lost Objective 1 status following the EU enlargements of 2004 and 2007 (the new Member States now constituting most of the regions lagging furthest behind the Community economic average). But, as before, financial commitments entered into during the 2000–06 programming period are retained into the 2007–13 period, reducing the ability to design policy *ab initio*.
- Reinforcing control, evaluation and reporting, and dividing responsibilities more clearly between Member States and the Commission.

Under the new strategic approach, rural development policy is to be focused on three core objectives, that all Member States should pursue:

1 increasing the competitiveness of the agricultural and forestry sector through support for restructuring;
2 enhancing the environment and countryside through support for land management;
3 enhancing the quality of life in rural areas and promoting the diversification of economic activities through measures targeting the farm sector and other rural actors.

For each core objective, key actions are suggested across four Operational Axes which are:

- Axis 1: Improving competitiveness of farming and forestry
- Axis 2: Environment and countryside
- Axis 3: Improving quality of life and diversification of the rural economy
- Axis 4: the LEADER approach

As in the previous programming period, the Regulation specifies the sorts of schemes ('measures') that Member States can use in each of the four Axes. These are shown in Box 7.3; details for Axes 1, 3 and 4, which relate to the socio-economic aspects of rural development, are shown in detail, but measures for Axis 2 are held over for consideration in the next chapter. Member States each draw up their own Rural Development Programme. This has to reflect the Community Strategy for rural development and be tailored to the specific problems and opportunities of their individual national or regional situations. From the menu of measures those appropriate to circumstances can be selected and national schemes designed that implement support. The process of drawing up a RDP and having it approved is described in Box 7.4.

To ensure a balanced strategy, a minimum of 10 per cent of each country's national envelope has to be spent on Axis 1, 25 per cent on Axis 2 and 10 per cent on Axis 3, a prescription that (in theory) still leaves Member States or regions substantial flexibility to meet their specific situation and needs. The EU co-financing rate is a maximum of 50 per cent (75 per cent in convergence regions) for Axis 1 and 3 and 55 per cent (80 per cent in convergence regions) for Axis 2. For afforestation, the co-funding rate is 80 per cent in LFAs and 70 per cent in other areas, i.e. 20 per cent higher than in the 2000–06 period. EU-15

Box 7.3   Measures under the four Axes of the 2005 Rural Development Regulation

Axis 1 – Improving the competitiveness of the agricultural and forestry sector

Measures

Support targeting the competitiveness of the agricultural and forestry sector shall concern:

(a) measures aimed at promoting knowledge and improving human potential through:
- (i) vocational training and information actions, including diffusion of scientific knowledge and innovative practises, for persons engaged in the agricultural, food and forestry sectors;
- (ii) setting up of young farmers;
- (iii) early retirement of farmers and farm workers;
- (iv) use of advisory services by farmers and forest holders;
- (v) setting up of farm management, farm relief and farm advisory services, as well as of forestry advisory services;

(b) measures aimed at restructuring and developing physical potential and promoting innovation through:
- (i) modernisation of agricultural holdings;
- (ii) improving the economic value of forests;
- (iii) adding value to agricultural and forestry products;
- (iv) cooperation for development of new products, processes and technologies in the agriculture and food sector and in the forestry sector;
- (v) improving and developing infrastructure related to the development and adaptation of agriculture and forestry;
- (vi) restoring agricultural production potential damaged by natural disasters and introducing appropriate prevention actions;

(c) measures aimed at improving the quality of agricultural production and products by:
- (i) helping farmers to adapt to demanding standards based on Community legislation;
- (ii) supporting farmers who participate in food quality schemes;
- (iii) supporting producer groups for information and promotion activities for products under food quality schemes;

(d) transitional measures for the Czech Republic, Estonia, Cyprus, Latvia, Lithuania, Hungary, Malta, Poland, Slovenia and Slovakia concerning:
- (i) supporting semi-subsistence agricultural holdings undergoing restructuring;
- (ii) supporting setting up of producer groups.

Axis 2 – Improving the environment and the countryside: *Measures described in Chapter 8*

Axis 3 – The quality of life in rural areas and diversification of the rural economy

Measures

Support under this section shall involve:

(a) measures to diversify the rural economy, comprising:
  (i) diversification into non-agricultural activities;
  (ii) support for the creation and development of microenterprises with a view to promoting entrepreneurship and developing the economic fabric;
  (iii) encouragement of tourism activities;
(b) measures to improve the quality of life in the rural areas, comprising:
  (i) basic services for the economy and rural population;
  (ii) village renewal and development;
  (iii) conservation and upgrading of the rural heritage;
(c) a training and information measure for economic actors operating in the fields covered by Axis 3;
(d) a skills-acquisition and animation measure with a view to preparing and implementing a local development strategy.

Axis 4 – LEADER

Definition of the LEADER approach

The LEADER approach shall comprise at least the following elements:

(a) area-based local development strategies intended for well-identified sub-regional rural territories;
(b) local public-private partnerships (hereinafter local action groups);
(c) bottom-up approach with a decision-making power for local action groups concerning the elaboration and implementation of local development strategies;
(d) multi-sectoral design and implementation of the strategy based on the interaction between actors and projects of different sectors of the local economy;
(e) implementation of innovative approaches;
(f) implementation of cooperation projects;
(g) networking of local partnerships.

Measures

The support granted under the LEADER Axis shall be for:

(a) implementing local development strategies (as referred to above), with a view to achieving the objectives of one or more of the three other axes;
(b) implementing cooperation projects involving the objectives selected under point (a);
(c) running the local action group, acquiring skills and animating the territory as referred to in Article 59.

Box 7.4 The process of drawing up a Rural Development Programme for the period 2007–13

As with the previous period, the process of achieving agreement to financial support is one of seeking Commission approval in advance. Regulation 1698/2005 sets out the organisational background for the 2007–13 programming period, including a timetable for the submission of the various stages for design, approval, and evaluation.

First, Member States had to provide a National Strategy Plan (NSP) which described the overall problems and objectives for rural development, and was to be consistent with the EU-level Strategy adopted in February 2006 (though in draft form late in 2005). The Commission released guidelines on the construction of this NSP on 16 November 2005 (European Commission, 2005). These guidelines alluded to a stakeholder consultation on the NSP, although it was unclear whether this was mandatory.

The next phase was for Member States to draw up a Rural Development Plan that elaborated the NSP and reflected consultations with stakeholders. The Commission issued specific guidance to the contents of any proposed RDP: Annex 2 of the draft Implementing Regulation, dated 27 October, 2005 (European Commission, 2005), prescribed the structure and contents of an RDP in detail, including the consultation process. A detailed SWOT analysis should be carried out at the implementation level to help inform the focus of the RDP, and it had to form part of the RDP. Although there was ultimately no requirement to carry out a Strategic Environmental Assessment (SEA) in respect of the RDP, the Commission had suggested that such an assessment would be required; this also involved a consultation process.

The plan sent for approval had to contain descriptions of the schemes chosen to make it operational. The 2005 Regulation set out a menu of types of schemes that could be supported financially (given in Annex 2), a list that was similar to that of the previous Regulation. The draft RDPs had to include an account of the alternatives considered and why the chosen schemes were the preferred options.

The RDP had also to contain evidence that an *ex ante* evaluation had been carried out (see Chapter 11).

Draft RDPs were to be submitted to the Commission at the beginning of June 2006. Though the concept of a strategic plan and environmental assessments preceding the RDP, together with their consultations, was laudable, in practice the process was beset with problems of timeliness that undermined its design (see Agra CEAS 2005) (including the issue of voluntary modulation that released funds from Pillar 1 to rural development uses and that for countries such as the UK were highly significant to what actions could be financed). Consequently, by the end of May 2007, RDPs for only two Member States (Czech Republic and Sweden) had been approved, for programmes that were intended to start on 1 January (five months earlier), though many other Programmes were approved later in 2007. Thus the start of the programming period 2007–13 contained echoes of the lack of an adequate lead-in period that beset its predecessor.

Member States have to reserve a minimum of 5 per cent of national programme funding for LEADER (Axis 4). This approach should be incorporated into ways of achieving the three main objectives and also plays an important role in terms of improving governance and mobilising the endogenous development potential of rural areas. In particular, the building of local partnership capacity, the promotion of private–public partnerships, the promotion of cooperation and innovation and the improvement of local governance are looked for. While there are clear opportunities for applying the LEADER approach when designing schemes to improve the quality of life in rural areas, it remains to be seen how much this is realistic for those belonging to Axes 1 and 2. Also under Axis 4 is support to establish at national and international (EU) levels rural development networks to assist all aspects of implementation, evaluation and exchange of best practice.

Beyond the minimum shares of spending on each Axis that the Regulation imposes, Member States may choose to allocate resources according to their particular circumstances, although what is available is constrained by commitments to previous schemes (which may last for up to 10 years) that have to be respected. Particular 'measures' may not be used if countries think they are inappropriate; for example, neither England nor Wales have chosen to introduce schemes for early retirement of elderly farmers or for assistance to young entrants, on the grounds that they are not likely to represent good value-for-money in these countries when compared with other calls on funding. When all RDPs are aggregated, for the EU as a whole, almost half of all public spending (EU budget and national contributions) on the CAP's rural development activities in the period 2007–13 is projected to be on schemes directed at the environment and landscape, and only 12 per cent on the quality of rural life and diversification (Figure 7.2), though there are wide differences between RDPs and Member States. The Commission's 2008 report on rural development provides a detailed breakdown by type of intervention (Commission 2008). At EU-27 level, the most important categories in spending from the EU budget are agri-environment payments (22 per cent), modernisation of agricultural holdings (11 per cent), and Less Favoured Areas payments (7 per cent in mountain areas and another 7 per cent in other areas) (Figure 7.3). Axis 2 gets

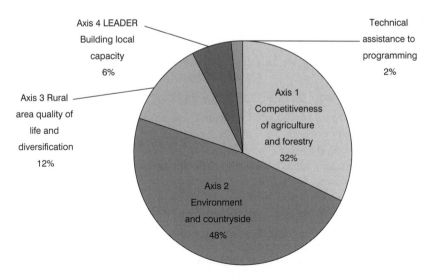

Figure 7.2   Planned spending from EU and national budgets on rural development 2007–13 (Source: Hill and Blandford (2008) based on data from the European Commission)

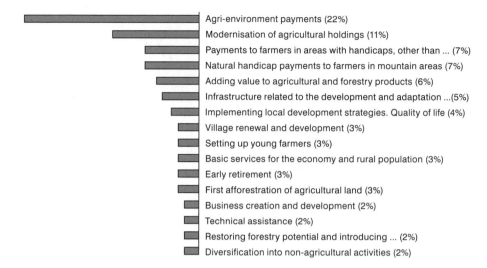

Figure 7.3   Planned spending from EAFRD by main type of scheme, 2007–13 (Source: European Commission (2008) *Rural Development in the European Union – Statistical and Economic Information.*)

therefore the lion share. The first ranked measure belonging to Axis 3 is 'implementing local development strategies. Quality of life', which correspond to Axis 3 measures implemented via LEADER. It is followed by 'village renewal and development' measures (3 per cent).

7.7 Comments on EU activities for promoting rural development under the CAP's Pillar 2

Finally, in coming to an understanding of the CAP and rural development, it is worth noting that the EU's approach to rural development has a number of characteristics and embedded assumptions that need drawing out. These may impinge on the ability of the actions directed at promoting rural development to achieve their aims, and to do this in an efficient way.

7.7.1 Many problems in rural areas are outside the influence of EU-level RDPs

The list of concerns of people living in rural areas stretch way beyond those that Rural Development Programmes are designed to tackle. A case study that compared different types of area in England (reported in Countryside Agency, 2004) found that the features which residents felt most needed improvement, shared equally by rural and urban communities, were facilities for teenagers, affordable housing, public transport and highway maintenance, with job prospects following after. Compared with urban residents, rural residents saw more need to improve public transport (a particular problem in the more rural of the areas), and facilities for shopping and leisure. In contrast, rural residents saw a smaller need in terms of crime (reduction), education service, a range of social features that reflected the general vibrant nature of rural communities (such as community activities and events), and environmental features that are associated with lower-density living (less need for easing traffic congestion or improving access to the countryside). The CAP's Pillar 2 policies for rural development do little or nothing about these issues, though general regional development policy for Objective 1 areas (which are now concentrated in the new Member States) can help. In EU-15 countries these concerns have to be picked up primarily by national policies.

Related to this, there seems to be under-recognition that the problems of rural areas are strongly affected by the conditions of the economy in general. In modern economies the links between the rural and urban are strong. Consequently, if there is a general problem of unemployment in the wider economy and a lack of growth, this will be felt in rural areas. In such circumstances it is highly unlikely that actions specifically aimed at rural development, and in particular the agricultural sector, will achieve more than very marginal results.

7.7.2 Relationship between EU and national and sub-national policies

Most countries have policy actions organised and funded nationally that are closely contiguous with, perhaps even overlap, those funded from the EU. Examples include the provision of vocational training for people in agriculture and other land-based industries (where a recent study has shown that other public funding in England in the first few years of the twenty-first century outstripped that coming from the England RDP's Vocational Training Scheme some twenty-fold or more), taxation concessions to encourage young people to be successors on farms, publicity for tourism in rural regions and grants for the provision of tourist accommodation, the planning system to control land use and maintain attractive landscapes etc. The CAP's Pillar 2 rural development policy and the performance of its measures and schemes must be seen against this complex web of other policies and interventions.

7.7.3 Simplistic view of poor living conditions in rural areas

There is a long-held assumption that socio-economic conditions in rural areas are sufficiently unfavourable that action is justified. The European Commission's evidence to the UK House of Lords inquiry (on the European Community's rural development policy as revealed in the 1988 FRS document) throws light on this. Its representative (Graham Avery) commented 'There is an obligation for the public authorities, through European, national and regional action, to intervene in such a way that those who live in rural areas do not suffer permanently from handicaps compared with urban dwellers'.

But, in reality, rural residents may not 'suffer' in the way implied. Recent evidence in the European Commission's analysis of statistical and economic information on rural areas (2006 and 2008) points to the dangers of making simplistic assumptions about the handicaps rural residents and firms face. Despite any migration from the countryside of young people, the age structure of the population did not vary significantly between types of rural area within Member States, though there were differences between countries. Unemployment rates (including long-term unemployment) were in general higher in rural areas than in urban ones, though there are several countries in which unemployment rates were lower in rural areas (Estonia, Germany, France, Latvia and Portugal). In many countries the level of education was lower in rural areas than in urban ones, but this pattern is not consistent. While at EU-25 level income per inhabitant (using an indicator based on GDP measured at the place of work) was around a quarter less in rural areas and generally increased from Predominantly Rural to Predominantly Urban areas, there is some evidence (for example, in Wales, see Agra CEAS 2005) that incomes measured at the household level may be higher in rural areas because of income from property, social benefits, private pensions and transfers between households. Indeed, on many economic and social indicators (crime, forms of deprivation etc.) in the UK, rural areas are superior to urban areas (summarised in Hill *et al.* 2005).

7.7.4 Multiple objectives of EU policy and the difficulty of testability and trade-offs

Even if consideration of rural development policy is confined to activities under the RDR, the problems tackled are a complex mix. Some are socio-economic (mostly focusing on farmers but with some interest in the wider economy and population) and some problems are environmental or to do with animal welfare. In such circumstances there is no simple way in which an optimum balance between objectives can be known, and the allocation of resources to the various streams will be a matter of political judgement and administrative compromise. Frequently the objectives of interventions are not in a testable form, and even those that are may not be supported with much logic and can be disputed. Indeed, the socially optimum level of any single line of activity is hard to determine. For example, what should be the level of education of farmers, or the number and size of farms kept operating in hill areas for environmental and social reasons? In the absence of a sound rationale and testable objectives the task of evaluating the policy is made difficult (see Chapter 11).

7.7.5 Spending on agriculture still dominates but is not an appropriate lever

Perhaps the most significant feature of EU spending directed at rural areas is the fact that, despite the changes that have taken place, most of the assistance still goes via support to agriculture. This is even more true of activities to promote economic development under Pillar 2 of the CAP. Mechanisms to target other economic agents based in rural areas seem to be weak. Perhaps this is simply a reflection of the political reality that it has been impossible to scale down support to agriculture rapidly. However, accumulating evidence supports the view that there are likely to be more efficient ways of achieving socio-economic policy aims for rural areas.

Chapter 7 has not attempted to cover the environmental aims of Pillar 2, where the case for using agriculture as a instrument to achieve biological and landscape objectives is far more robust. The next chapter tackles this issue.

References and further reading

Agra CEAS (2006) *Ex-Ante Evaluation of the Wales 2007–13 Rural Development Plan*. Welsh Assembly Government, Cardiff.

Blandford, D. and Hill, B. (2008) 'Directions in rural development policy – lessons from both sides of the Atlantic'. *EuroChoices*, 7 (1), 6–11.

Bradley, D., Dwyer, J. and Hill, B. (2006) 'Assessing the performance of the CAP's Second Pillar – A UK perspective on experiences in evaluating EU rural development programmes'. Paper to the joint meeting of SFER and Agricultural Economics Society, Paris.

Countryside Agency (2004) *The State of the Countryside 2004*. Countryside Agency, Cheltenham.

European Commission (1985) Commission of the European Communities (1985b), *Perspectives for the Common Agricultural Policy*, COM(85)333, Final. The Commission, Brussels (also published as Newsflash 33).

European Commission (1988) *The Future of Rural Society,* COM(88)501, Final/2, The Commission, Luxembourg.

European Commission (1990) *Agriculture and the Reform of the Structural Funds – Vade Mecum.* Green Europe 5/90. Commission of the European Communities, Brussels.

European Commission (2005) *Establishing the National Strategy Plan: Guidance Template* (VI/197/396/05).

European Commission (2006) *Rural Development in the European Union: Statistical and Economic Information.* Report 2006, DG-Agri, Brussels.

European Commission (2008) *Rural Development in the European Union: Statistical and Economic Information.* Report 2008, DG-Agri, Brussels.

European Commission (2008) *The EU Rural Development Policy: Facing the Challenges.* European Commission, Brussels.

Hill, B. with contributions from Campbell, D., Carter, C., Gamble, B., Hibbs, J., Lee, B., Meadowcrot, J., Morris, J., North, R.D., Rickard, S., Stockdale, A. and Withrington, P. (2005) *The New Rural Economy – Change, Dynamism and Government Policy.* Institute of Economic Affairs, London.

Hill, B. and Blandford, D. (2008) 'Parlons graphiques: Where the US and EU rural development money goes', *EuroChoices*, 7 (1), 28–29.

Land Use Policy Group (2002) *Europe's Rural Futures – The Nature of Rural Development II.* Report by Janet Dwyer, David Baldock, Guy Beaufoy, Harriet Bennett, Philip Lowe and Neil Ward. World Wildlife, London.

OECD (2003) *The Future of Rural Policy: From Sectoral to Place-Based Policies in Rural Areas.* Organisation for Economic Co-operation and Development, Paris.

OECD (2005) *New Approaches to Rural Policy – Lessons from around the world.* Organisation for Economic Co-operation and Development, Paris.

OECD (2006) *Coherence of Agricultural and Rural Development Policies,* Diakosavvas, D. (ed.) Organisation for Economic Co-operation and Development, Paris (especially Chapters 1, 8 and 14).

OECD (2011) *OECD Rural Policy Reviews: England, United Kingdom 2011.* Organisation for Economic Co-operation and Development, Paris.

Terluin, I., Strijker, D. and Munch, W. (2010) 'Economic dynamic in rural regions'. Chapter 18 in Oskam, A., Meester, G. and Silvis, H. (eds) *EU Policy for Agriculture, Food and Rural Areas.* Wageningen Academic Publishers, Wageningen.

Woods, M. (2005) *Rural Geography.* Sage, London.

8

UNDERSTANDING THE CAP AND THE ENVIRONMENT

The environmental part of Pillar 2

Key topics

- Background of EU environmental policy.
- The environmental externalities of agricultural activities, both positive and negative.
- Internalisation mechanisms.
- The implications of support to production.
- Using agriculture as an instrument to achieve environmental and landscape objectives.
- Rural development and the environment.
- The agri-environmental part of the CAP's Pillar 2.

8.1 Introduction

As was seen from Chapter 7, the bulk of spending under the CAP's Pillar 2, which focuses on rural development, goes on agri-environment and closely related schemes such as payments to farmers in Less Favoured Areas, conversion to organic production and planting of forests, with only a relatively small amount used for socio-economic purposes. Agri-environmental spending has grown over the last two decades and is likely to do so in the future. This is because the much more expensive Pillar 1 of the CAP – and in particular the Single Farm Payment – seems destined to be transformed, at least in part, into some form of agri-environmental payment when the present financial package under which it operates runs out at the end of 2013. Indeed, a dominant – perhaps the major – plank in the argument for continuing financial support to farmers is the contribution that agriculture makes to the environment.

Agri-environmental schemes use agriculture and forestry in an instrumental way to achieve environmental aims. They must be seen against the larger background of the EU's overarching concern with environmental issues, rather as job creation and income generation under rural development programmes must be viewed against regional policy and the pursuit of economic growth, competitiveness and employment (see Chapter 7). The EU's general environmental policy is in the care of its own Directorate-General (DG-Environment) which performs functions similar to those undertaken by DG Agriculture and Rural Development for agricultural policy.

In view of the current importance attached to the role that agriculture can play in the conservation of biodiversity and the appearance of the countryside, it is perhaps surprising that the environment was not mentioned in the 1957 Treaty of Rome, where the objectives of the CAP were set out in Article 39 (see Chapter 2). But growing concern with what was happening in the environment, such as deterioration in the quality of water and air and the incursion of noise, led to its inclusion and progressive expansion in subsequent EU Treaties. The Single European Act (1986) established the principle that environmental protection should be considered in all new Community legislation, and the Treaties of Maastricht (1992) and Amsterdam (1997) made sustainable development a core EU objective. Reflecting this, the *Agenda 2000* agreement included a revised set of objectives for the CAP that included two that are directly relevant here. These were the 'integration of environmental goals into the CAP' and the 'promotion of sustainable agriculture'.

Concern with the environment and sustainability now permeate all EU policies. In 2001 a meeting of the European Council in Göteborg agreed the EU's first Sustainable Development Strategy (the Göteborg Strategy), which added an environmental component to the 'Lisbon Agenda' on employment economic reform and social cohesion, with attention focused on combating climate change, sustainable transport, addressing threats to human health, and the responsible use of natural resources. In 2005 the European Commission proposed a Strategy on the Sustainable Use of Natural Resources used in Europe, the objective of which is to reduce the environmental impacts associated with resource use and to do so in a growing economy. The notion of tightly linking the environment with other policies has been carried forward in the 2007 Lisbon Treaty and the Europe 2020 Strategy.

In pursuit of its environmental aspirations the EU has an Environmental Action Plan (EAP). EAPs were first introduced in 1972. The current EAP, with an operating period 2002–2012, identifies four priority areas for action:

- climate change;
- nature and biodiversity;
- environment and health;
- natural resources and waste.

The EAP promotes full integration of environmental protection requirements into all Community policies and actions and provides the environmental component of the Community's strategy for sustainable development. Monitoring is carried out by the European Environment Agency (EEA), a body set up by an EU Regulation in 1990 that contains, in addition to EU Member States, several other countries (Iceland, Liechtenstein, Norway, Switzerland, Turkey) and six 'cooperating' countries in the western Balkans, all of which have close environmental ties with the EU. The EEA also fosters environmental collaboration at a global level.

In terms of climate change, the EU took a prominent part in the negotiations that led to the two United Nations climate Treaties (the UN Framework Convention on Climate Change (UNFCCC) in 1992 and the Kyoto Protocol in 1997). Reducing the emissions of Green House Gasses (GHGs) is seen as a way of mitigating global warming. Under the Kyoto Protocol, the 15 countries that were EU members at the time are required to reduce their collective emissions in the 2008–2012 period to 8 per cent below 1990 levels; the EU has offered to go beyond this. Production of renewable energy from farming and forestry, which may substitute for other forms, is part of its strategy. In this respect, forestry's role is currently about nine times more important than agriculture's at EU-27 level, though there are marked differences in this respect between countries (Table 8.1).

Under the protection of biodiversity and preventing further losses, the EU has built up over the last 25 years an extensive network of 26,000 protected areas in all the Member

Table 8.1   Basic agri-environmental indicators EU-27

	UAA classed as Natura 2000 area (%)	Territory classed as nitrate vulnerable zone (%)	Risk of erosion (loss of land from water) (t/ha/ year)	UAA used for organic farming (%)	Production of renewable energy from agriculture (kToe)	Production of renewable energy from forests (wood and residues) (kToe)	Greenhouse gas emissions (1000 t of CO_2 equivalent)
	2009	2008	2004	2007	2007	2007	2007
Austria	11.4	100.0	0.46	11.5	363.7	3930.0	7949
Belgium	7.3	67.8	1.07	2.4	155.3	649.0	9621
Bulgaria	22.0	53.1	0.56	0.3	7.7	709.0	5030
Cyprus	1.5	6.8	–	1.5	1.1	11.0	761
Czech Republic	6.4	39.8	1.31	8.2	86.3	1948.0	7838
Denmark	4.9	100.0	2.29	5.1	135.7	1441.0	10072
Estonia	5.5	7.5	0.16	9.7	0.0	731.0	1333
Finland	0.9	100.0	–	6.6	33.5	7149.0	5530
France	8.2	45.6	1.55	1.9	1028.5	9234.0	95728
Germany	9.1	100.0	0.89	5.1	4382.8	10578.0	51479
Greece	14.2	24.2	5.77	7.0	86.0	1005.0	11298
Hungary	14.5	45.8	0.41	1.8	27.0	1146.0	9477
Ireland	3.1	100.0	0.11	1.0	7.9	169.0	17748
Italy	10.3	12.6	3.11	7.9	390.3	1707.0	37211
Latvia	6.6	12.7	0.11	8.1	16.9	1532.0	2059
Lithuania	3.8	100.0	0.33	4.5	32.6	732.0	4251
Luxembourg	11.0	100.0	0.54	2.7	10.0	16.0	711
Malta	5.8	100.0	–	0.2	0.9	nd	70
Netherlands	4.6	100.0	0.08	2.5	163.0	524.0	18423
Poland	10.7	1.5	0.67	1.8	148.4	4550.0	35040
Portugal	18.5	3.7	4.59	6.3	164.9	2808.0	7638
Romania	9.6	6.7	0.44	0.8	31.0	3304.0	19550
Slovakia	16.3	33.5	1.29	6.1	55.4	484.0	3245
Slovenia	22.3	100.0	0.87	5.9	13.3	429.0	2082
Spain	15.5	12.6	2.41	3.9	343.3	4206.0	46426
Sweden	4.3	15.0	–	9.9	116.2	8441.0	8431
UK	3.0	38.7	0.31	4.1	139.2	784.0	43216
EU-27	9.9	40.9	1.52	3.9	7940.6	68 218.0	462217

European Commission (2009) *Rural Development in the European Union. Statistical and Economic Information.*

States covering some 18 per cent of the EU's land area. Known as Natura 2000, this is the largest network of protected areas in the world. It comprises two types of sites; Special Areas of Conservation (SACs – known more recently as Sites of Community Importance) are those designated under the 1992 Habitats Directive, and Special Protection Areas (SPAs), designated under the 1979 Birds Directive. In 2008, SACs accounted for 13 per cent of the territory of EU-27, ranging from 31 per cent in Slovenia to 7 per cent in the UK; SPAs covered 10 per cent of EU-27 (with a high of 25 per cent in Slovakia and lows of 3 per cent in Ireland and zero in Bulgaria). Taking the two together, the countries with the highest incidence of Natura 2000 sites on their agricultural areas (in contrast to their territories, which are larger) in 2009 were Slovenia and Bulgaria, each with 22 per cent, and the lowest was Finland, with barely 1 per cent (Table 8.1). There may also be national designations that must be complied with.

Of course, these protected areas can only achieve so much, and agriculture (especially organic forms of production, which currently account for 4 per cent of the farmed area), forestry and other land-using industries are expected to play a part.

Air and water quality carry health implications and impact on multiple aspects of the environment. Water quality and the prevention of pollution of water-courses has been the subject of legislation, of which the 1991 Nitrates Directive and the 2000 Water Framework Directive are important to the agriculture industry because they may impinge on how farmers use their land (see Box 8.2).

It is worth noting that the initiation and management of these policies are outside the CAP and its decision-making process. Nevertheless, agriculture and forestry are influenced by them. For example, farmers of land that lies within areas designated under the Nitrate Directive as Nitrate Vulnerable Zones (NVZs) find themselves facing mandatory restrictions whose purpose is to contain nitrogen pollution of water by reducing the loss from agriculture, though the extent to which these curb farmer decisions will vary from site to site. Again there are large differences between Member States; 10 classify the whole of their agricultural areas as NVZs, whereas in another five the figure is less than 10 per cent (Table 8.1). In addition, there may be restrictions as part of River Basin Management Plans and other schemes under the Water Framework Directive.

As will become apparent, there are sound arguments for intervening in the market mechanism to encourage certain farming (and forestry) practices for environmental purposes and to discourage others. Whether this is something that should be organised through agricultural policy (as happens in the EU through Pillar 2 agri-environment schemes) or though more general environmental policy (as in the US) is a matter for debate. Whichever approach is taken it must be borne in mind that interventions taken under the CAP to achieve environmental aims must be put in their broader context of EU environment policy, just as the socio-economic actions under rural development policy had to be seen against the aims and instruments of EU economic and regional policy (Chapter 7).

However, when trying to explain why the CAP of today has a strong environmental flavour it is difficult to escape the smell of *ex post* rationalisation. Some of the ways of assisting farmers that now carry labels of environmental justification are little different from those formerly used to give income support. Though the motive has been repackaged, in practice the impacts may be surprisingly similar. Thus, it pays to be sceptical.

8.2 The rationale for intervention – environmental externalities

When the justification for policy action was discussed in Chapter 1, one form of market failure on which a case for intervention could be based was the presence of externalities. These are the outputs from production and consumption (some negative, some positive) that are disregarded by producers or consumers in their decision-making, who just consider their private costs and benefits. The market mechanism is not good at taking externalities into account. By failing to do so the market does fails to ensure the optimum use of resources from society's standpoint (the point at which the marginal social cost of any action equates to the marginal social benefit) (see Figure 8.1). In some circumstances the uncorrected market would produce volumes of production or consumption above the social optimum, while in others it would result in too little.

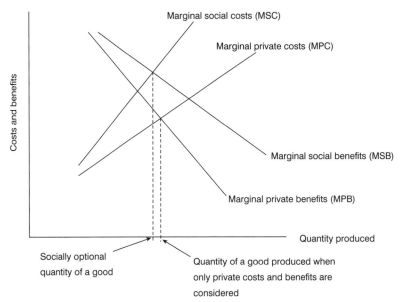

1 The optimum amount of any activity from society's standpoint is where marginal social benefit coincides with marginal social cost, in contrast to the optimum from the point of view of a producing firm, which equates marginal cost and marginal revenue in the interest of maximising its profit.

2 In this example the socially optimal quantity of the good is less than that which would result from the consideration of private costs and benefits only. However, the socially optimal quantity under other sets of conditions can be greater. For example, if in the above diagram the MSC line were very close to the MPC (implying there were little negative externalities from production) or if the MSB line lay at a higher level (implying greater social benefits).

3 It is possible to envisage situations where the MSB lies below MPB, e.g. where external diseconomies of consumption are involved, or where MSC lies below MPC, e.g. where unemployed productive resources exist so that more of the good can be produced without sacrificing the output of any other good.

Figure 8.1. Divergences between private and social marginal costs and benefits arising from the production and consumption of a good

Examples of negative externalities are the pollution caused to local water supplies by effluent from silage made by farmers who fail to take care to prevent it, or the use of insecticide spays which, in addition to controlling harmful pests on crops, kills butterflies that are part of the natural biodiversity and much appreciated by many people. Sometimes these negative externalities can be tolerated by the ecosystem if carried out by a few individuals, but if the practice is widespread the environment may be unable to absorb the pollution and serious harm may result. When negative effects arise, they represent costs to society of the activities (silage-making or crop production) beyond those borne by the farmer. These costs come in many forms, such as perhaps the expense to consumers of buying bottled water, the loss of pleasure in seeing butterflies, and the cost to taxpayers of attempts to restore environmental damage. The implication is that activities that cause negative externalities need to be cut back to achieve the social optimum.

Society has a range of instruments at its disposal to correct for such negative externalities (see Chapter 5 for an analysis of their performance), including legislation prohibiting the pollution of water-courses (backed up by fines or imprisonment), setting 'standards' such as limits on the use of chemicals that farmers must respect if they are to keep other benefits ('cross-compliance'), and taxes that raise the cost of potentially harmful fertilisers to raise their costs and lessen their use, and subsidies to producers who agree not to use them (such as payments to farmers who agree to adopt organic practices). Where the responsibility for causing damage can be attributed to an individual or firm and rights are well-defined, the legal system often provides for compensation to be extracted, though this is impractical for many forms of environmental harm. There are both more interventionist instruments (such as taking vulnerable sites into public ownership) and ones that are less so (such as educating landowners about the importance of the biological features found on their land, or designating areas as being of outstanding natural beauty. Each has its own advantages and disadvantages, and characteristics such as certainty (or not) of impact, political acceptability, administrative feasibility, budgetary cost, and burden on those affected. Each mechanism will almost always involve costs to society (directly or indirectly), and policy-makers will have to decide not only which is the most suitable approach to use (e.g. legal restrictions or voluntary incentives) but also how the balance between (marginal) costs and benefits turns out, though they are unlikely to be able to do this in any precise way. Box 8.1 explains a conceptual approach to balancing marginal costs and benefits. Sometimes the case for intervention is clear-cut (banning the heavy use of nitrogen fertiliser in drinking water catchment areas) and in others it may be more ambiguous. On occasion the decision may be to take no action.

While the examples used above are linked with planned behaviour by producers, sometimes accidents occur, such as an unintended discharge of industrial waste into a river. Society has to be prepared to deal with such environmental disasters, and this often means spending on maintaining emergency facilities; international networks will need to be set up and maintained. Many negative externalities, especially water and air pollution, have to be tackled on a co-operative EU-wide basis as the causal chemicals are no respecters of national boundaries.

Other externalities are positive, in which case decisions made on the basis of private costs and benefits will result in levels of activity that are below the social optimum and more should be encouraged. An example is the benefit which a farmer who installs bees in his orchard to improve his own fruit yield has on the yields of neighbouring farms and gardens; they benefit without bearing any cost. Such benefits are 'non-excludable' and 'non-rival'. It is not practical to exclude any neighbouring grower's orchard from benefitting from the

Box 8.1 The concept of an 'optimum level of pollution'
(using nitrogen fertiliser pollution of water-courses as an example)

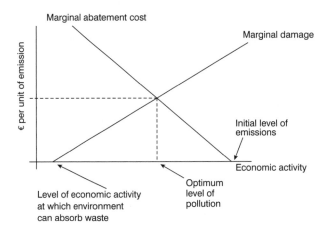

- The diagram shows that the marginal value of the damage to the environment of pollution emissions (e.g, nitrogen in water-courses) from an activity (such as applying nitrogen to growing crops) increases as the level of the activity rises. This is the additional damage caused by the last unit of nitrogen pollutant.
- At low levels of application the environment can absorb run-off without harm and the marginal damage is zero, though it rises beyond a certain level.
- The marginal cost of reducing pollution from its initial high level (that is, the cost of removing progressively each unit of pollution) is low at first but this abatement cost rises as nitrogen pollution is brought down.
- When pollution levels are high (the right hand end of the horizontal axis), the benefit from reducing emissions by a unit greatly exceed the costs of doing so, so there is a net gain to society. This net gain falls as pollution is reduced.
- At the 'optimum level of pollution' the 'marginal abatement cost' just balances the value of the marginal damage. To reduce pollution further would incur additional costs that exceeded the additional benefits.
- Alternatives exist for reaching the optimum, including the imposition of physical limits ('standards'), taxes and incentives.

bees, and the individual growers are not rivals, in the sense that the more bees there are for one person the more there is for everyone else. Where such positive externalities occur, the main way to correct for the market failure is to offer financial incentives out of public funds to encourage the activities that generate positive externalities. Positive externalities can also be social or economic. A village shop or pub can assist in bringing a sense of local community by encouraging people to meet together and have a social significance way beyond its importance as a supplier of consumer goods. And people who undergo training and education can often bring benefits not only to themselves (by building up their personal intellectual capital) but to the wider society by being more innovative, more productive and increasing the capacity of communities to adapt and change (building social capital).

Closely associated with externalities are 'public goods' which are, by definition, both non-excludable and non-rival (see Chapter 1). The prime example is a nation's security force, but a visually attractive countryside free from eyesore and an environment kept clean by collective action would also both qualify. Because of the differences between private and social costs, and benefits, the market mechanism alone cannot be relied on to deliver these, and some form of government intervention is likely to be necessary to reach the social optimum. The costs of keeping the environment clean will need a system to ensure that everyone contributes and the 'free rider' problem is tackled; free-riders will tend to be present where public goods are concerned because it will always be in the interest of beneficiaries to opt out of paying if they can, and government intervention is needed to avoid this possibility. Also there will be a tendency for natural resources such as stocks of marine fish to be exploited beyond the point of sustainability (sometimes termed the 'commons tragedy'), because it will not be in the interest of any individual fisherman to hold back activities to allow stocks to recover, requiring government (or international) intervention to deliver a socially preferable solution.

A sound rationale for public intervention, based on 'market failure', does not, of course, mean that public intervention should take place. This will depend on the costs to society of doing so balanced against the benefits gained. How these are distributed among different groups in society may also be influential. Many elements on both sides of the equation are difficult to quantify, so an element of subjectivity in the decision to act, and the extent of public intervention, is inevitable. Nevertheless, it seems clear that the greater awareness of environmental issues and the rising affluence of the population in general, will lead to an increasing role for policies which focus on sustainable development, including those that encourage farmers to use their land in ways which are consonant with the emerging ideas on how natural resources should be managed and used and what the countryside should look like.

8.3 Agriculture's role

National governments and the EU have come to recognise that agriculture and forestry production involves much more than just the supply of a range of food and non-food commodities that are sold on markets. Some of its production can be a means, directly or indirectly, of achieving environmental or human health ends in ways that the market mechanism does not recognise adequately, even perhaps when no commercial market exists, in which case public intervention to encourage these types of activities may be justified. Farming and forestry can also result in non-tangible outputs which are valued by the rest of society. Some of these, such as an attractive countryside appearance, may not be intentional. On the other hand, there are potential costs to society resulting from agricultural and forestry production that need to be identified and, where necessary, corrected by intervention.

Elements of EU policy to encourage agriculture to serve environmental aims can be traced back to at least 1975, when the Commission initiated support to farming in mountainous and other less favoured areas to compensate for the difficulties caused by natural conditions, principally for environmental and social reasons (Directive 75/268/EEC). Box 8.2 lists the more important pieces of subsequent legislation, both that which is part of the CAP and other Regulations and Directives that are important to agriculture. These represent a progressive 'mainstreaming' of environmental policy within the CAP; rather than treating it as an add-on.

Box 8.2 Key pieces of EU agri-environmental and related legislation

1975   Less Favoured Areas Directive (75/268/EEC) introduced aids to mountain and hill farming, and farming in Less Favoured Areas to compensate for the difficulties caused by natural conditions. About 40 per cent of the then EU-12 total Utilised Agricultural Area was classified as LFA. (55 per cent of EU-25 in 2006). At the outset the main forms of aid were 'compensatory allowances' (headage payments), investment aids and the abolition (in mountain and hill areas) or reduction (in Less Favoured Areas) of the co-responsibility levy on milk (thereby insulating LFA producers from this mechanism that reduced the amount of support provided by the CAP).

1979   Birds Directive (79/409/EEC) designated Special Protection Areas (SPAs), later incorporated into Natura 2000 sites (see below).

1985   New Agricultural Structure policy. Authorisation for Member States to introduce special aids in 'Environmentally Sensitive Areas' (ESAs) included in Reg 797/85. Farmers could receive finance where they agreed to follow production practices that protected the environment or landscape.

1988   Special 'crisis' meeting of heads of government (February European Council) Community 'set-aside' scheme introduced, at least 20 per cent of arable area to be set aside for at least five years and schemes to promote extensification.

1988   'The Future of Rural Society', the Commission's discussion document, identified the need to protect the environment and conserve the EU's natural assets.

1991   Nitrates Directive (91/676/EEC) aimed to reduce water pollution caused by nitrates from agricultural sources. Member States were required to (a) establish a code of good agricultural practice, to be implemented by farmers on a voluntary basis; (b) to designate 'vulnerable zones' in which to implement 'action programmes' under which certain measures become mandatory (such as conditions of applications and their timing, storage facilities). Implemented in the UK via Nitrate Sensitive Areas.

1992   Habitats Directive (92/43/EEC) established Special Areas of Conservation (SACs), designated by Member States. These, with SPAs (see above) form Natura 2000, a network of Europe's most valuable and threatened species and habitats. The establishment of this network of protected areas also fulfils a Community obligation under the UN Convention on Biological Diversity.

1992   'MacSharry' CAP Reforms included agreement by the Council that environmental protection requirements should be an integral part of the CAP, not an add-on. The 'accompanying measures' included provision for schemes which built on the Environmentally Sensitive Areas concept, such as long-term set-aside (20 years), encouragement of extensive livestock farming,

continued ...

Box 8.2 continued

addition of provisions to encourage organic farming, to encourage farmers to manage their land for public access and to help protect water quality. Annual allowances per hectare were payable for the above if the farmer made an undertaking for five years (20 for set-aside). Also provision was made for the education of farmers in environmental protection. Afforestation aid comprised payments for establishment (tree planting), for maintenance costs in the first five years, an annual allowance per hectare to cover losses of income (up to 600 ECU per ha), and for the improvement of woodland.

1999   Rural Development Regulation (Council Regulation (EC) No. 1257/1999), setting out what could be supported in Rural Development Programmes for the period 2000–06, brought together and continued much existing legislation on this topic, including agri-environment schemes and afforestation, and Less Favoured Area schemes.

2000   EU Water Framework Directive (Directive 2000/60/EC of the European Parliament and of the Council) establishing a framework for Community action in the field of water policy. It established an approach for water management based on river basins, the natural geographical and hydrological units and set specific deadlines for Member States to protect aquatic ecosystems. The Directive addressed inland surface waters, transitional waters, coastal waters and groundwater. It established several innovative principles for water management, including public participation in planning and the integration of economic approaches, including the recovery of the cost of water services.

2005   Rural Development Regulation (Council Regulation (EC) No. 1698/2005) set framework for rural development spending under the CAP for the period 2007–13. One of its three 'thematic axes' is 'improving the environment and the countryside'. Environmental measures were largely a continuation of what was available in the 2000–06 period.

2008   CAP Health Check removed set-aside but gave countries the option to use cross-compliance to help address the environmental effects of its ending.

Using agriculture as an instrument for achieving environmental aims has now moved into a core position in EU agricultural policy. Within the CAP's Pillar 2, the Rural Development Programmes in the current period (2007–13) are directed at four main areas of impact, as follows:

- **Reversing biodiversity decline.** This is a multifaceted concept and, in principle, each component within the diverse ecosystem might be measured separately (such as the numbers of each type of insect, animal, plant, fungus etc.). This makes changes over time difficult to assess, especially when some elements are improving according to their indicators while others are deteriorating. Where agriculture is concerned, the emphasis of policy falls primarily on constraining changes in agricultural practices that pose threats to species and their habitats, though there are examples where new actions are encouraged for the benefits they bring (such as planting crops which might not otherwise be grown to encourage bird populations). Currently in the EU the number of farmland birds is used as a proxy measure of biodiversity, as it is believed that this reflects changes in a wide range of other variables, such as the number of insects in an area.

- **Preservation and development of traditional agricultural landscapes and high nature value farming and forestry systems.** Though the terminology 'high nature value farming' is not familiar (and some Member States have had difficulty in defining what it means in their contexts), the general implication is clear. It implies relatively low-intensity farming in which 'traditional' systems are used, such as extensive beef and sheep farming in the hills and uplands of the UK. There is now an enhanced sensitivity among EU Member States to the importance that the public attaches to the appearance of the countryside, and a willingness to pay for the conservation of its special features. And a landscape shaped by 'traditional' farming systems may be attractive to tourists and firms looking for places in which to set up, bringing economic benefits to the local economy. This landscape/conservation character can be regarded as another output from the agricultural industry, since the land-using activities of farmers and others determine what the countryside looks like and influences the wildlife it contains. Agriculture is providing a service for the non-agriculturist, through recreation or just the well-being of knowing that the countryside is 'there' and being looked after, which is valued in the same way as its food-security role. Again, the emphasis in policy seems to be on discouraging changes in the practices of farmers and landowners that lead to deteriorations in landscape quality. It is rarer for new and attractive landscapes to be created afresh, though the re-establishment of farming on old industrial sites might be considered an example (such as the removal or remodelling of spoil heaps at coal mines and their grassing-over).
- **Contributing to combating climate change.** A relatively recent addition to the list of ways in which agriculture can be used as a tool to achieve environmental aims is in mitigating climate change. Agriculture (and forestry) is both a major source of greenhouse gasses (mainly from ruminants) and a means of combating their effect through capturing carbon. In particular, increasing the areas of land planted with trees is seen as contributing to combating climate change.
- **Improving water quality.** The quality of water is only in part influenced by agriculture and forestry, and in turn agriculture can only be expected to be instrumental in improving situations where pollution from these activities is a problem.

8.4 Instruments of agri-environmental policy within the CAP

Attention in this section focuses on CAP instruments that have environmental aims as their principal purpose. However, it should be borne in mind that the incidental impact of Pillar 1 support to agriculture, by far the larger of the two Pillars in terms of total public spending, has an environmental dimension. Mention was made in Chapter 6 of cross-compliance conditions that occupiers of agricultural land must respect in order to be eligible to receive Single Farm Payments. These link with the respect of standards of environment, food safety, human, animal and plant health and animal welfare, as well as the requirement to keep all farmland in good agricultural and environmental condition (GAEC). These conditions are seen as contributing to the environmental aims of the CAP. Farmers also have to observe statutory (that is, legal) requirements, which would mean fulfilling their conservation duties concerning the EU's network of Natura 2000 sites.

The CAP's Pillar 2 contains the more explicit ways in which agriculture and forestry is used to achieve environmental aims. The EU's Rural Development Regulation (No. 1698/2005) lists 'measures' for which EU funding can be used in this period (see Box 8.3); the measures grouped under Axis 2 in the Regulation are concerned with the environment and countryside. This Regulation, covering the period 2007–13, gives legal authority for the Commission to supply funds to national governments to assist them in implementing their Rural Development Programmes, which include schemes aimed at using agriculture and forestry to improve the natural environment. As with the other parts of rural development organised under the CAP, the EU only bears part of the public costs, the rest being paid from national budgets. In addition, some costs may fall on the pockets of users of the schemes (farmers and landowners).

As a case study, Box 8.4 illustrates how the environmental 'measures' of the Regulation are put into practice as schemes in the England Rural Development Programme for 2007–13. The Regulation for the previous programming period (2000–06) contained a very similar set of provisions and the RDP was constituted of similar schemes. Wales, Scotland and Northern Ireland have different schemes; as was noted earlier, each UK country has its own RDP.

In terms of planned expenditure from the EU budget on the environmental (Axis 2) aspects of rural development in the period 2007–13, the picture is dominated by agri-environment payments (51 per cent) followed by payments to farming in Less Favoured

---

Box 8.3 Environmental provisions of the Rural Development Regulation 1698/2005 and related programmes under Axis 2 – Improving the environment and the countryside

Measures
Support under this section shall concern:

(a) measures targeting the sustainable use of agricultural land through:
　(i)　natural handicap payments to farmers in mountain areas;
　(ii)　payments to farmers in areas with handicaps, other than mountain areas;
　(iii)　Natura 2000 payments and payments linked to Directive 2000/60/EC (the Water Directive);
　(iv)　agri-environment payments;
　(v)　animal welfare payments;
　(vi)　support for non-productive investments.

(b) measures targeting the sustainable use of forestry land through:
　(i)　first afforestation of agricultural land;
　(ii)　first establishment of agroforestry systems on agricultural land;
　(iii)　first afforestation of non-agricultural land;
　(iv)　Natura 2000 payments;
　(v)　forest environment payments
　(vi)　restoring forestry potential and introducing prevention actions
　(vii)　non-productive investments.

Box 8.4 Environmental schemes in the England Rural Development Programme for 2007–13

Measures of Rural Development Regulation 1698/2005 taken up in England to target the sustainable use of agricultural land under Axis 2 comprise: payments to farmers in areas with handicaps, other than mountain areas; agri-environment payments; support for non-productive investments. For forestry these are the first afforestation of agricultural land and first afforestation of non-agricultural land.

Measures *not* taken up in England comprise: natural handicaps; Natura 2000 payments etc; animal welfare payments; first establishment of agro-forestry systems; and restoring forestry potential and introducing prevention actions.

Measures and their implementation through national schemes

Measure: Payments to farmers in areas with handicaps, other than mountain areas
Support to farmers in the Less Favoured Areas, in particular in the Severely Disadvantaged Areas (SDAs), where farming is marginal yet necessary to deliver wider environmental and landscape benefits, is done through the Hill Farm Allowance (HFA). The HFA aims to preserve the farmed upland environment by ensuring that land in the LFAs is managed in a sustainable way. Area payments are made to (all) farmers using eligible land to keep extensively grazed sheep breeding flocks and suckler-cows for beef production. From 2010 it is proposed to incorporated HFAs into the Environmental Stewardship scheme (see below).

Measures: Agri-environment payments, and support for non-productive investments
The Environmental Stewardship (ES) scheme, launched in 2005 and incorporating several previous schemes, comprises three elements;

- Entry Level Stewardship (ELS): This whole-farm scheme is open to all conventional farmers and land managers in England and encourages simple yet effective environmental management which goes further than the Single Payment Scheme (SPS) to maintain land in good agricultural and environmental condition (GAEC). The scheme requires that land entered into it meets a 'points target'. This can be achieved through the adoption of management options which will be worth a certain amount of 'points'. Over fifty simple management options are available to suit most farm types. The agreements with Defra are legally binding and run for five years. A flat rate payment of £30 per hectare per year is made automatically every six months for land meeting the eligibility requirements. Land in the Less Favoured Area (LFA) receive £8 per hectare per year;
- Organic Entry Level Stewardship (OELS): a broadly based scheme aimed at organic farmers;
- Higher Level Stewardship (HLS:) a more targeted scheme aimed at the most valuable habitats and environmental features that require complex and locally adapted management. Examples of the management options and priority environmental features and situations include: hedgerows – e.g. maintenance to high environmental value; grassland – maintenance and restoration of species-

continued …

Box 8.4 continued

> rich semi-natural grassland or wet grassland; restoration and maintenance of lowland heath; wetlands – maintenance of ponds of high wildlife value and reed beds; resource protection – to prevent erosion and run-off. The Farm Environment Plan under HLS will identify whether capital investments in non-productive assets are likely to be needed. Support is offered for a wide range of non-productive investments that support the full range of objectives of the ES scheme. For similar assets on forested land, see the English Woodland Grant Scheme below.
>
> *Measures: First afforestation of agricultural land; first afforestation of non-agricultural land*
> The English Woodland Grant Scheme (EWGS) incorporates measures for the first afforestation of agricultural and non-agricultural land, forest environmental payments (called the Woodland Management Grant (WMG)), and support for (forestry) non-productive investments (three related schemes dealing with the environmental and social values of woodland, called the Woodland Planning Grants, Woodland Assessment Grants and the Woodland Improvement Grants.
>
> Source: Department for Environment, Food and Rural Affairs (Defra)

Areas (LFAs) facing natural handicaps, which sum to another 32 per cent (17 per cent to non-mountain areas and 15 per cent to mountain areas). Thus, more than four-fifths (83 per cent) goes on these categories. Far behind comes support for afforestation on agricultural land (6 per cent). Thus, schemes relating to all the remaining measures account for only some 10 per cent of spending under Axis 2. Of course, the balance can vary substantially between Member States, but agri-environment payments in non-mountain areas is the instrument with the highest financial allocation in most Member States. Its share is higher than 70 per cent in Belgium (82 per cent), Sweden (78 per cent), the Netherlands (75 per cent), Denmark (73 per cent) and in the United Kingdom (72 per cent). Some 14 of the EU-27 Member States have integrated this measure with payments to farmers in mountain areas, and this has the highest relative importance within Axis 2 in France (51 per cent).

Rather than review each of these categories of measures separately, it is helpful to group them according to how they operate.

8.4.1 Annual payments to compensate for income loss for delivering environmental services

Annual *agri-environmental payments* can be made to compensate land occupiers for agreeing voluntarily to use their land in a way that delivers environmental services that have been identified nationally as being desirable for biological or landscape reasons. Examples would be payments to manage meadows in ways that encouraged a diversity of native plant and animal species, and to leave arable field margins uncultivated. EU legislation stipulates that the payments are to reflect the extra costs incurred or income forgone by farming in this way rather than to be an incentive, though in reality there may be a small element of incentive built in (as without it the rational farmer would not bother, unless there were also non-financial benefits involved). These agreements are typically long-term (for 10 years, with an opportunity to reassess the situation after five years), a reflection of the period over which a change in land use is likely to bring an impact. As noted in Chapter 6, the length of such agreements means that there is an accumulated legacy from previous schemes. All these long-term residual commitments have to be funded, and they take a substantial portion of what is currently available, thereby restricting the possibilities for devising and applying new schemes.

Closely similar situations of making good income forgone and additional costs exist in relation to schemes for the *promotion of forestry on agricultural land, conversion to organic production, animal welfare payments* for commitments to keep livestock in ways that exceed statutory requirement, and the *implications of having Natura 2000 sites or similar features* on farm or forestry land. Taking organic conversion as an example, there will be a period when conventional agro-chemicals and fertilisers are phased out in preparation for registration as an organic producer. Yields are likely to be reduced but no premium for organically farmed produce can yet be gained, resulting in an income fall until registration is achieved. Several years of reduced incomes are likely to present a substantial barrier to anyone contemplating a switch to organic farming. Payments under a conversion scheme are ended to cover this period.

An important issue is how the level of income compensation payment is to be set. To minimise public expenditure in a system that involved every land occupier on a voluntary basis, negotiations would be needed between the national authority administering the scheme and each land occupier. After negotiations, the payments arrived at would be the minimum needed to achieve the desired management changes; there would be no deadweight (payments for what the occupiers would have done anyway). Higher rates could be paid to those farmers who found themselves with land that was particularly biologically interesting to the scheme managers, or who formed that last vital parcel of land needed to achieve a wildlife corridor which delivered benefits on a large scale. But negotiations with individuals are likely to be administratively too burdensome for schemes that involve large numbers of farm operators. Administrations may have neither the staff capacity nor the funds to pay for them.

A system simpler to administer is one that offers a flat rate of payment to all farmers who apply and meet eligibility conditions. Such systems may also be favoured by potential beneficiaries because the application process may be less time-consuming and involve them in less uncertainty. However, as Figure 8.2 indicates, some farmers will not be interested in taking up the scheme's flat rate incentive as their marginal cost of doing so (in terms of the net income foregone) is greater than the sum on offer. These are on the right-hand side of the diagram. It could well be that these are the farmers who are the most critical to achieving environmental aims, such as those currently using their land very intensively and earning high profits from doing so. Policy designers may be most keen to get them to change their way of farming, yet they will not be recruited by a flat rate system. Some might not be willing to farm in a way suggested by scheme managers whatever inducements were on offer. At the other extreme, on the left of Figure 8.3, there are some farmers for whom the flat rate is a more-than-adequate incentive to farm in the way the management agreement prescribes, so they are paid more than is necessary to secure their signature; they will be earning 'economic rent', the term applied to situations where factors of production receive more than they can earn in the best-paid alternative use (their transfer earnings). Perhaps these are already farming in a way that is close to what the scheme wants. At least some of the spending on such people will be 'deadweight'

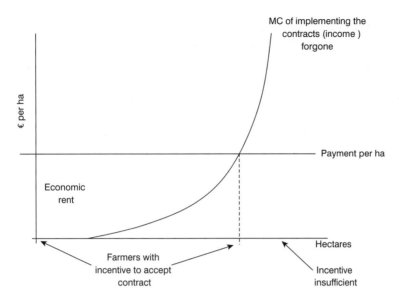

Figure 8.2 Using a flat rate payment for the supply of environmental services

as no change will result from it. Thus, a flat rate is likely to be inefficient in its allocation of support, in that more desirable outcomes could be achieved by redirecting resources from some beneficiaries (those over-compensated for change) to those that need more to participate. It also provides an example of 'adverse selection', in that those producers who the scheme administrators would like most to see become involved are less likely to join voluntarily, whereas those that would be most keen to sign up would be those that brought the smallest benefits in terms of environmental improvement.

Strategies for mitigating the problems associated with flat rates include, first, ensuring that the rate is appropriate as a group average by using case studies of individual negotiations covering a range of circumstances or by holding an initial tendering process whereby farmers bid to supply a range of environmental services. These could be the basis of a menu of actions for which farmers could seek financial support, knowing what payments were available for each. Higher rates could be offered in situations where the designers of policy were keenest to secure agreements. It may be useful to designate areas in which higher rates are on offer (such as in the hills and uplands). Extra payments could be available where farmers apply as a group and cover large areas capable of delivering environmental benefits that need scale to be effective. Second, where resources are inadequate to meet all likely claims from applicants, a points system based on the nature of the farm's environmental situation and its potential to contribute to improvement might operate, such as the number of features that are to be conserved or enhanced. Applicants can apply for payments that reflect the combination of what they are willing to supply, so that those offering greater levels of environmental services are offered the largest sums in exchange. However, when circumstances involve non-standard situations or where large amounts of money are involved, the balance between the better efficiency of using resources at the farm level and the transaction costs of administering the system is likely to favour individual negotiations.

8.4.2 Payments to farmers in Less Favoured Areas to compensate for natural handicaps

It will be seen from the list in Box 8.2 that support under CAP's Pillar 2 can be given to farming in mountain and hill areas and other special locations classed as Less Favoured Areas (LFAs) where the operators face natural handicaps, the purpose being to promote the sustainable use of agricultural land. Just over half (54 per cent) of the agricultural land area of the EU-27 in 2005 was classified as having LFA status, comprising 16 per cent mountain areas, 35 per cent other (mainly hill) areas, and 3 per cent in the remaining category that deals with specific restriction. There are wide differences in the relative importance of LFAs (taking all sorts together) between Member States; for example Denmark has almost none (1 per cent), but in contrast 95 per cent of Finland is LFA. In principle this means compensating farm operators in these LFAs for the additional costs and/or lower values of output obtained (smaller crop yields or rates of animal growth or lower prices). This is only a small step away from the logic of income compensation in the section above; the combination of lower revenues and/or higher costs will make incomes from farming in hill areas relatively unattractive and therefore farmers are more likely to quit. LFAs are typified by extensive cattle and sheep farming, traditional systems that conserve biodiversity and often generate landscape that is visually attractive. If a decline in the numbers of LFA farmers results in a deterioration in the environmental, social or economic conditions in hill areas (changes that are by no means certain), then LFA payments to encourage hill farmers to remain in the industry might be justified on these broader benefits to society.

Payments are currently made on a per hectare basis; a previous system of paying according to the number of animals kept was found to have the unintended negative environmental consequence of encouraging denser stocking rates (thus resulting in a deterioration in the environment), and attempts to control this by imposing physical limits proved complex. Per hectare payments are also more decoupled from production decisions, a feature sought in subsidies.

EU legislation (including the Rural Development Regulation 1698/2005) requires that over-compensation for the natural handicap faced by LFA farmers must be avoided, which has led some RDPs (including that of England) to err on the cautious side and only compensate partially.

There are practical issues to be confronted in calculating what the compensation should be. For example, a ready yardstick by which to assess the economic effects of the handicap of farming in a mountain or hill area may not be available. While milk production on a hill farm or a lowland farm is essentially the same activity, in reality there are very few dairy farms in the hills. The extensive beef production system found in LFAs is so different from that on lowland farms (breeds of animals, speed of growth, extent of housing, feeding system) that there is a danger of not comparing like with like. Comparisons are even less meaningful with a sheep system as practised in the UK, where lambs reared on upland farms may be transferred to lowland pastures for fattening, so that the two areas are integrated. Another issue relates to the degree of handicap. Areas where farmers qualify for LFA payments are designated primarily on geographical criteria (such as altitude). It follows that land just inside a designated area is likely to face only a small handicap compared with land just outside. Greater handicaps are faced by farmers further up mountains. If a single flat rate per hectare is paid, this will result in some farmers being over-compensated and others under-compensated. A way of coping with this is to designate two or more degrees of handicap (in the UK Disadvantaged Areas and Severely Disadvantaged Areas) but this only reduces 'border effects' rather than eliminates them. And there remains the general problem of inefficiency when a flat rate is applied to a range of circumstances.

Recently, doubt has been cast on the economic and social benefits of supporting farming in disadvantaged areas (at least for the UK). With farming accounting for such a small part of the jobs and incomes of rural residents, even in hill areas, the case for targeting this sector on economic and social grounds is weak. The main benefits are likely to come through the environment and landscape, as farming dominates land use. But if this is so, questions have to be raised about whether it would be preferable in terms of efficiency to replace LFA payments with agri-environment schemes that concentrate payments on delivering the biological benefits and countryside appearances that decision-makers have identified as their targets. In the UK, the administrations of both England and Wales have recently transformed their LFA payment schemes into agri-environment schemes, though at European level there seems to be a commitment to the support of farming there beyond the next reform of the CAP, to take effect in 2014.

8.4.3 Payment for supply of environmental services

In addition to the situations already described, it has been recognised that there are other circumstances where a continuing stream of support is needed if a flow of environmental services is to continue. A prime example relates to organic production and the environmental benefits that this is believed to bring. Experience suggests that assistance to farm operators to convert is not sufficient to establish a sustainable organic sector because actual returns after conversion have often been less than anticipated (with a smaller premium for organic produce than is needed to support this system of production). Consequently, a stream of regular payments will be necessary if organic production is to be kept going. Similarly, the management of woodlands to benefit the environment and society may be a continuing process that needs sustained support to achieve its aims.

8.4.4 Incentives to investment

One-off contributions toward the costs of capital investments are common. Partial public funding has justification in that the owner usually acquires an asset that is reflected in the market value of the land. Payments can be made for investments that bring environmental and landscape benefits, such as the restoration of stone field walls that are traditional in some rural landscapes. Financial assistance to tree planting is another form of investment that the RDR wishes to encourage, the costs being split between the EU, national budgets and the forest owner. Sometimes the assets constructed are non-productive (in the sense that they do not relate to agricultural or forestry output), which might include access paths for visitors and stiles that enable them to cross fenced boundaries more easily. It would be expected that public funds would bear all the costs (or nearly all) of such investments.

8.5 In conclusion

Chapters 6, 7 and 8 have concerned themselves with the implementation of policies that attempt to achieve the objectives set for the CAP in terms of the standard of living of the agricultural community, the economic situation of the broader rural community (particularly its ability to offer income and job opportunities to farmers and their families) and the environment. For each it is possible to demonstrate that problems exist for which a rational case for intervention using public funds can be built, though in the case of income support the evidence is far weaker than is often assumed. Each too has had to be set against the context of more general policies on economic growth, provision of jobs and sustainability, including not only policies emanating from EU institutions but also from national governments.

Next we turn to EU trade in agricultural commodities and encounter a rather different set of circumstances. Here there is a legacy of CAP policies and instruments that, while being aimed primarily at supporting EU farmers, have contributed in a major way to impeding the well-being of not only EU citizens but also of residents of other OECD and developing countries. The CAP has been a cause of current problems, though it would be unjust to lay all the blame at its door.

Further reading

Baldock, D., Dwyer, J., Lowe, P., Petersen, J-E. and Ward, N. (2001) *The Nature of Rural Development: Towards a Sustainable Integrated Rural Policy in Europe*. Report for the WWF, IEEP, London.

Brouwer, F. and Silvis, H. (2010) 'Rural areas and the environment.' Chapter 20 in Oskam, A., Meester, G. and Silvis, H. (eds) *EU Policy for Agriculture, Food and Rural Areas*. Wageningen Academic Publishers, Wageningen.

Defra (undated) *The England Rural Development Programme 2007–13: A summary*. Online at http://www.defra.gov.uk/rural/rdpe/pdf/rdpe-sum.pdf

Dupraz, P., van den Brink, A. and Latacz-Lohmann, U. (2010) 'Nature preservation and production'. Chapter 21 in Oskam, A., Meester, G. and Silvis, H. (eds) *EU Policy for Agriculture, Food and Rural Areas*. Wageningen Academic Publishers, Wageningen.

European Commission (2008) *Rural Development in the European Union: Statistical and Economic Information. Report 2008*. Directorate-General for Agriculture and Rural Development, Brussels.

Hill, B. (2006) *An Introduction to Economics: Concepts for Students of Agriculture and the Rural Sector*. 3rd edition. CABI, Wallingford. (See Chapter 7 'Market failure').

Moran, D., McVittie, A., Sayadi, S. and Parra-Lopez, C. (2010) 'The demand side of rural amenity: definition and valuation methods'. Chapter 19 in Oskam, A., Meester, G. and Silvis, H. (eds) *EU Policy for Agriculture, Food and Rural Areas*. Wageningen Academic Publishers, Wageningen.

OECD (1995) *Agriculture and the Environment: Issues and Policies*. Organisation for Economic Co-operation and Development, Paris.

OECD (2003) *Multifunctionality: The Policy Implications*. Organisation for Economic Co-operation and Development, Paris.

OECD (2005) *Multifunctionality in Agriculture: What Role for Private Initiatives?* Organisation for Economic Co-operation and Development, Paris.

Oskam, A., Meester, G. and Silvis, H. (eds)(2010) *EU Policy for Agriculture, Food and Rural Areas*. Wageningen Academic Publishers, Wageningen.

Polman, N., Slangen, L. and van Huylenbroeck, G. (2010) 'Collective approaches to agri-environmental management'. Chapter 21a in Oskam, A., Meester, G. and Silvis, H. (eds) *EU Policy for Agriculture, Food and Rural Areas*. Wageningen Academic Publishers, Wageningen.-

9

UNDERSTANDING THE CAP
AND INTERNATIONAL TRADE
AND DEVELOPMENT

Key topics

- Economic rationale for specialisation and exchange.
- The pattern of trade in agricultural commodities.
- International trade agreements to reduce restriction on trade.
- Trade and aid to developing countries.

9.1 Introduction

Economic theory can easily demonstrate that specialisation and exchange can result in higher levels of consumption possibility. In everyday life few, if any, individuals attempt to be completely self-sufficient in all aspects of existence. Typically households buy rather than make almost all their clothing, vehicles and energy sources, using money generated from selling their labour and other resources. As a result of specialisation and exchange, we are all better off than if we tried to do everything ourselves. This applies at all levels of analysis, from the individual up to the international scale.

Sometimes there is no alternative. Major surgery on oneself is not something to be contemplated except in extreme circumstances; the need for specialist knowledge is overwhelming. Growing grapes for wine making under arctic conditions is impossible but, shift the conditions a little, to the north of England and permit the use of heated glass houses, and it may be technically possible for ardent gardeners to grow tropical fruit there, though this obviously would be expensive, more so than the cost of importing them from countries where the climate is more suitable.

Less intuitive is the finding that specialisation and exchange is beneficial when the people and circumstances are basically similar. A commonly quoted example is that of a lawyer and a secretary working in the same office. The lawyer happens to be a more proficient typist than the secretary, in the sense that more pages per hour can be achieved. The secretary, though competent as a typist, does not have the skills or training to act as a lawyer. Should the lawyer type the letters? If this requires giving up highly paid legal work, the answer is no. It would be more profitable for the lawyer to specialise in law and to employ a typist at a lower hourly rate to type the letters. Both can be better-off as a result, and the standards of living of the community (of two) can increase. It is important to recognise that comparative advantage (differences in what has to be given up to do something – or put in another way, in opportunity costs) is at the root of why specialisation and exchange is beneficial. Absolute advantage (the fact that the lawyer is a faster typist than the person engaged as a typist) is irrelevant.

The same logic underpins why trade occurs between regions and countries, even when they are quite similar in terms of their natural resources and skills of their residents, as are EU Member States. Differences in opportunity costs (that is, comparative advantage) results in gains to be had by a degree of specialisation and exchange, which manifests itself as trade moving across regional or national boundaries. A major driver for setting up the EU was the economic benefits that unrestricted trade between member countries can bring. To some extent an agreement to lower or remove taxes and other restrictions between members can achieve benefits (a customs union), but more can flow from the formation of a single market covering all commodities (a 'free trade area'), and even more if this applies not only to goods and services but to the movement of factors of production as well (as in the EU).

In practice, in a market economy comparative advantage is reflected in differences in prices, which mean that there is an incentive to purchase from the cheapest source; if this is in another geographical area, movements of the goods or services will take place as a result.

Specialisation itself involves a shift in opportunity costs; these often tend to rise, which means that a degree of specialisation will take place and then proceed no further. But up to this point, competitive forces will mean that, while some activities are expanded, others have to contract because they become uncompetitive in terms of price. Moving the resources from declining industries to expanding ones represents a substantial challenge and takes time to achieve. Where countries have different currencies, shifts in exchange rates can cushion the impact of competitive forces, but where a single currency is used (as in regions of the same country) this cannot happen and governments will need to take a more active role.

There are several important implications of comparative advantage for agricultural commodities in market economies:

- Trade resulting from specialisation and exchange will occur through normal commercial entrepreneurial activities, as long as markets work (both in commodities and in currencies) and the costs of transportation and related trading expenses do not wipe out price differences. Thus, we should expect trade in agricultural commodities to be a normal activity.
- Self-sufficiency in food production is not something that would be expected at national or regional levels. Overall some regions and countries would be net importers (area with deficits, where consumption is greater than local production) and others would be net exporters (areas with surpluses). For individual commodities this will also be true, and it is quite possible for a country to be a net importer when all commodities are taken together, but for it also to be a net exporter of individual items.
- Trade will be associated with higher levels of consumption possibilities at aggregate level and higher national incomes than would happen in a no-trade situation.
- Because technology is constantly developing, comparative advantage will shift over time. A country that is an importer of a commodity at one time may find itself an exporter later if it happens to make large strides in the productivity of this type of production.

If specialisation and exchange has such positive connotations, what is the downside? This largely reflects the failure to follow the changes indicated by comparative advantage and international competition:

- Though the national economy gains with trade, not all sectors will benefit to the same extent, and some may be worse off in the short term. It would be possible, at least in theory, to compensate those that see their incomes fall and still leave a net gain to society, but this rarely happens. Instead, entrepreneurs in sectors that face stiff competition as market forces work towards their decline (in other words, they will be undercut by rival imports) start suffering reduced incomes and profits. They will wish to protect their interests and will seek ways of avoiding the effects of trade on them, at least in the short term. The costs of forming pressure groups to lobby on their behalf will have to be weighed against the likelihood and size of private gain.
- The gains from trade assume that resources no longer needed in sectors that are internationally uncompetitive can be used elsewhere in the economy. If they remain unused, the overall gain may be non-existent. Thus, importance has to be attached to facilitating the move of resources to other industries, and government interventions (such as providing retraining for labour and facilitating short-term credit) to achieve this end may be justified.
- Arguments that protection should be given to domestic industries often cite the need to give them time to adjust. However, once support is given against international competition, the pressure to adjust is reduced. It is likely that continued support will be asked for on account of the increased gap between what protected entrepreneurs receive and what it is assumed they would face if protection were removed.
- Sometimes protection can be justified for strategic defence and security reasons. For example, the government may see the need to ensure that the country can feed itself adequately if war or other events cut off supplies from abroad. A similar case could be made for retaining a basic capacity in the domestic energy industry. Retaining a degree of self-sufficiency in production is just one of the options for coping with the possible temporary interruption of supplies from abroad: others include retaining strategic reserves and working to maintain good international relations.

For agriculture, the process of specialisation and exchange brings pressure to adjust that can be particularly painful because of the location-specific nature of farming and the immobility of the resources it uses. For example, some types of fruit production (pears, some apples) became unviable in England once the sector was opened up to competition from France with its more appropriate climate. Orchards had to be removed and the land used for alternatives, a time-consuming and expensive process. Capital-demanding horticultural production under glass can become uncompetitive when exposed to trade with countries with more sunshine and higher temperatures; alternative uses may be hard to find. Farms already facing natural handicaps (such as beef producers in mountain and hill areas) can find themselves being further undercut but, with few other types of agriculture available to them because of climatic conditions, their responses may be limited to restructuring. Farm families might take off-farm jobs to supplement household income, enabling them to remain as independent operators on a part-time basis, or farms might amalgamate to form much larger extensively run units that can be competitive, though this will involve some people leaving the industry. As noted in Chapter 8, such structural adjustments may carry environmental and social implications that governments may wish to avoid. But payments to farm operators to maintain their numbers in hill and mountain areas will need to be on-going and are likely to become increasingly expensive as competition develops further.

9.2 Patterns of EU international trade in agricultural commodities

Caution has to be exercised over statistics on trade. As the EU has expanded, the pattern of its international trade has altered. Some of what was international trade between the EU and countries that were prospective members has become EU internal trade and thus has dropped out of the statistics. This does not alter the comparative advantage, but the statistics on trade between the EU and the rest of the world (RoW) will be affected. Trade statistics often make no distinction between what movements of goods and services are fully commercial in nature and those that take place with the aid of public subsidies, such as the export of surpluses generated by domestic agricultural policies.

That said, at the most general level, EU-27 is normally a net importer of agricultural products, but trade is not all one-way. In 2009, the EU-27 imported agricultural products to the value of €77.0 billion, but also exported €74.5 billion of them, giving a net negative balance of trade of €2.5 billion. As the balance is the difference between two relatively large numbers it is not surprising that this net balance can change quite markedly from year to year. Nevertheless, throughout the period 2000 to 2009 the balance was negative except for 2006, when the value of agricultural exports exceeded that of imports by €2.9 billion.

Figure 9.1 shows what agricultural products the EU-27 currently imports and exports. The largest import in 2009 was animal feed, but some was also exported (thus appearing twice on the graphic). Fruits formed the next category. Among the exports the largest in terms of value was wine (which also featured among the main imports), though this was closely followed by cereals (including for animals). Table 9.1 gives a more detailed breakdown by commodity of the net balance between imports and exports. This list covers a broader

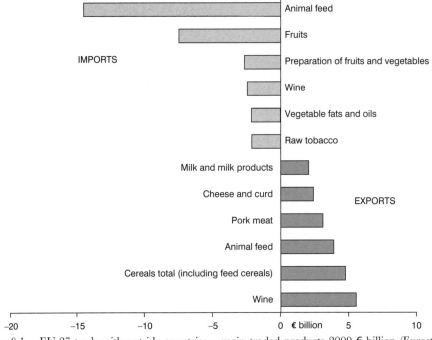

Figure 9.1 EU-27 trade with outside countries – main traded products 2009 € billion (Eurostat – COMEXT)

Table 9. 1 EU-27 trade balance with extra-EU-27 € million

	2000	2009	00/09
01 – Live animals	452	904	99.9
02 – Meat and edible meat offal	1,315	1,038	−21.1
04 – Dairy produce	4,400	4,579	4.1
05 – Products of animal origin	− 500	− 379	−24.2
06 – Live trees and other plants	13	104	681.7
07 – Edible vegetables, roots and tubers	−1,396	−1,333	−4.5
08 – Edible fruits and nuts	−7,014	−9,648	37.5
09 – Coffee, tea, maté and spices	−5,091	−5,284	3.8
10 – Cereals	1,262	1,096	−13.1
11 – Products of the milling industry	1,518	1,706	12.4
12 – Oil seeds and oleaginous fruits	−4,397	−5,480	24.6
13 – Lacs, gums, resins and other vegetable saps	66	50	−23.5
14 – Vegetable products not elsewhere specified	− 109	− 89	−18.4
15 – Animal or vegetable fats and oils	119	−2,829	−2,477.7
16 – Preparations of meat	112	− 813	−827.5
17 – Sugars and sugar confectionery	876	− 319	−136.4
18 – Cocoa and cocoa preparations	− 450	−1,954	334.3
19 – Preparations of cereals, flour, starch, etc.	2,459	3,978	61.8
20 – Preparations of vegetables, fruits, nuts and plants	−1,149	− 935	−18.6
21 – Miscellaneous edible preparations	1,478	2,695	82.4
22 – Beverages, spirits and vinegar	8,914	10,470	17.4
23 – Residues and waste from food industry	−3,868	−5,216	34.8
24 – Tobacco and tobacco products	− 462	1,635	−453.9
Other WTO products outside chapters 1–24	−1,892	3,518	−286
Total agricultural products	−3,344	−2,506	−25.1
– Commodities (e.g. bulk grain, wool)	−7,982	−7,838	−1.8
– Intermediate (e.g. wheat flour)	− 820	−3,944	380.9
– Final products (ready for consumers)	5,120	8,166	59.5
– Confidential trade	338	1,110	228.4
Total all products	−142,956	−104,120	−27.2

Source: Eurostat / COMEXT

range of food and drink products than Figure 9.1. These are classified in two ways. First they are broken down according to their type of origin as shown in the international standard classification. Secondly (and below the first in the table) they are grouped according to whether they are bulk commodities (such as wheat or soya-beans), intermediates inputs (such as prepared flour), or ready to be consumed (such as lamb meat). Beverages and spirits

Table 9.2   EU-27 agricultural trade by origin and destination (excluding all intra-trade)

	EU-27 imports by origin (%)		EU-27 exports by destination (%)	
Region	2000	2008	2000	2008
ACP	15.5	12.5	7.6	8.0
ASEAN	8.0	10.6	4.2	4.2
Australia and New Zealand	6.3	4.3	1.8	2.3
China	3.6	4.3	1.3	2.1
CIS	3.0	4.1	8.5	15
EFTA	3.2	4.0	9.2	10.9
Japan	0.3	0.2	7.6	5.3
LDC	3.1	2.2	4.1	4.2
MERCORSUR	18.6	25.5	1.9	1.4
Mediterranean Area	8.2	8.0	14.6	14.5
NAFTA	17.7	11.4	23.5	20.3
RoW	14.7	15.8	16.2	15.4

Notes:
1. ACP – 79 African, Caribbean and Pacific countries associated with EU Member States; ASEAN – Association of South East Asian Nations (10 countries); Austr. and N.Zealand – Australia and New Zealand; CIS – Commonwealth of Independent States (Russia and other former Soviet Republics); EFTA – European Free Trade Area (Iceland, Liechtenstein, Norway, Switzerland); LDC – 29 Least Developed Countries; Medit. Area – the 16 Mediterranean countries that are, with the EU Member States, in the Euro-Mediterranean Partnership (EUROMED); MERCORSUR – Brazil, Paraguay, Uruguay, Argentina;. NAFTA – North American Free Trade Area (US, Canada, Mexico): RoW – Rest of the World (not covered in the other groupings).
2. In 2000 total EU agricultural imports were €64.1 billion and its agricultural exports were €55.6 billion. In 2008 EU agricultural imports were €98.5 billion and its agricultural exports were €80.8 billion.

accounted for the largest net exports in both 2000 and 2009. In contrast, the largest net import category was 'edible fruits and nuts'.

Table 9.2 shows that, on the basis of trade for 2000 and 2008 broken down by region/ country, the EU-27 both buys agricultural products from and exports them to most of its trading partners; overall the balance was again negative in these years. The MERCOSUR group of countries (Brazil, Paraguay, Uruguay, Argentina) are unusual in that much agricultural material is imported from them but very little sold to them, while Japan buys from the EU-27 but very little is imported from it. The two largest purchasers of EU-27 agricultural products are this MERCOSUR group and the NAFTA group (US, Canada and Mexico). NAFTA is also the largest purchaser of EU-27 agricultural exports. The 49 Least Developed Countries are far less important as trading partners than the ACP group, the 79 African, Caribbean and Pacific area states that formerly had close links with EU Member States and have special trading concessions with the EU.

Overall, the EU-27 is the world's largest importer and also (in 2008) its largest exporter, though with NAFTA as a close rival (Table 9.3). A breakdown of trade by commodity is given in Box 9.1.

Table 9.3 EU-27 and other regions' shares in world agricultural trade (* excluding all intra-trade)

Region	% of world imports		% of world exports	
	2000	*2008*	*2000*	*2008*
ACP	3.3	3.8	4.7	3.1
ASEAN	5.7	6.0	8.9	11.9
Australia and New Zealand	1.3	1.6	9.0	6.2
China	3.0	8.6	6.0	6.0
CIS	3.0	6.1	1.0	2.3
EFTA	2.8	3.0	1.4	1.5
EU-27	23.1	23.9	22.2	19.8
Japan	15.6	10	0.9	0.6
LDC	1.0	1.0	1.2	0.8
Mediterranean Area	6.4	6.5	3.0	3.3
MERCORSUR	1.0	0.8	9.6	16.2
NAFTA	14.9	12.8	21.7	17.1
RoW	17.4	15.1	11	11.1

Notes: Percentages do not add to 100 in the original shown on the Europa website http://ec.europa.eu/agriculture/agrista/tradestats/2009/graphs/g1_p7.pdf. See also notes to Table 9.2 for details of the regional groupings.

Source: Eurostat COMTRADE

9.3 Agricultural policy and trade

The CAP's role in international trade has to be seen against the background of a general awareness that, in essence, specialisation and exchange is something to be encouraged as it increases the income and consumption possibilities of countries that engage in it. As noted above, there are circumstances in which there may be a rationale to restrict trade to achieve other policy goals, such as to prevent the import of goods carrying risks to human health or the export of arms to governments who use them to oppress their own peoples. In the short term, restrictions may be supported in order to give industries time to adjust where a sudden exposure to competition would cause economic waste and social disruption, though such restrictions carry a danger of becoming permanent if scaling them down over time is not built in from the outset. However, the economic benefits of trade are undeniable. Trade also encourages interdependence among countries, establishing links of an economic, social and cultural nature that build relationships and reduce the likelihood of conflict, motives that lay behind the creation of the EU.

The EU has for long appreciated the benefits that can flow from trade. In many places the 1957 Treaty of Rome committed Member States to the development of free and fair trade. For example, in Article 131, under the section on commercial policy, Member States stated that 'by establishing a customs union between themselves Member States aim to contribute, in the common interest, to the harmonious development of world trade, the progressive abolition of restrictions on international trade and the lowering of customs barriers'. This intention (with suitably modified wording) has carried forward to other Treaties, including the 2010 consolidated version of the Treaty on the Functioning of the European Union.

Box 9.1 EU-15 main markets for selected products – 2005

Cereals total: Out of a total import of €1,439m nearly 22 per cent was imported from the USA alone (€314m) making it the largest import origin for the EU-15 in 2005. The six main countries of origin for import, combined, added up to 82.5 per cent of all EU-15 imports. On the export side the partners were far more diverse. The six main exporting destinations reached a combined share of over 45.1 per cent. From a total of €2.495m that was exported out of the EU-15, Algeria remained, as in 2004, the most important destination, with €390m or a share of around 16 per cent.

Vegetables: The EU-15 imported €1,243m of vegetables in 2005. €370m (or 29.7 per cent) were imported from Morocco and €146.5m from Kenya. Exports stood at a total of €769m with Switzerland as the most important export destination (€183m or 23.9 per cent).

Fruits: In values, the EU-15 imported in 2005 over five times more fruit than it exported. Total EU-15 imports reached a level of €7,059m with the USA as the main importing partner (€1,241m or 17.6 per cent) and South Africa as second country of origin with €943m. EU-15 exports totalled €1,329m of which €327m was destined to Russia (or 24.6 per cent) and €296m to Switzerland.

Potatoes: The six main origins of EU-15 potatoes imports, out of which four were situated in the Mediterranean Area, accounted for nearly 100 per cent of all EU-15 imports (total €165m). Israel, with €85m, accounted for 51.7 per cent of all EU-15 imports, with Egypt being the second largest origin also with €63m. In contrast, the six main export destinations only reached 43.4 per cent of all EU-15 potatoes exports, which added up to a total of €204m. Main destination for potatoes was Algeria (€26m or 12.9 per cent).

Olive oil: In 2005 €512m of olive oil imports for EU-15 was recorded. The six main import origins – combined – reached 98.3 per cent of total olive oil imports with Tunisia being the main country of origin with €257m (or 50.2 per cent) for 2005. €1,175m worth of olive oil was exported of which €538m (or 45.8 per cent) went to the USA.

Vegetable oils and fats: €1,648m of imports of vegetable fats and oils were recorded, of which €337m (or 20.4 per cent) came from Indonesia as largest origin country. Argentina and the Philippines exported respectively for €299m and €225m to the EU. The EU-15 exports were more spread among destinations as the main export market, the USA, only accounted for €67m (or 12.7 per cent) out of a total exports of €530m.

Butter and butter fats: Historically the main origin of EU-15 butter and butter fats imports was New Zealand. This also was the case for the year 2005. Out of a total import of €135m, €124m or over 91 per cent originated from New Zealand. Exports for a total of €608m were mainly destined to Russia (€58m or 9.5 per cent) and to Mexico (€55m).

Milk and milk products: 95 per cent was the share of the six main origin countries for imports for milk and milk products – in *value terms* – which reached a total value of €32m. Main partner on the import side for the EU-15 was Switzerland, with €17m (or 52.8 per cent). In 2005 the EU-15 exports represented almost 60 times the value of EU-15 imports. A total value of

continued …

Box 9.1 continued

€1.869m was recorded as EU-15 exports. The main destination was Saudi Arabia with €178m (or 9.5 per cent) and, as second destination, Algeria (€151m) and also to Nigeria that showed an amount of €137m of milk and milk products being imported from the EU-15.

Skimmed milk powder: The EU-15 imported a total of €9.1m of SMP from third countries. Just 35.4 per cent, or €3.2 m, was imported from the USA and €3.1m from Switzerland. Exports of the same product reached over 30 times this amount and totalled €248m. The main export destinations were Algeria with €25m (or 10 per cent) and Indonesia with €24m.

Sugar: For the year 2005 the main import origin was Mauritius with €301m (or 26.6 per cent of a total of €1,131m). Main export destinations (total 2005 of €1.194m) were Syria with €122m (or 10.2 per cent) and Algeria with €115m.

Wine: In value terms, the EU-15 exported almost twice as much wine as it imported in 2005. Imports reached an amount of €2,380m against €4,628m of exports. Most important origin of import was Australia of which €844m (or 35.5 per cent) was imported. South Africa came as second origin with €427m. 42.7 per cent or €1,977m of all EU-15 wine exports were destined to the USA and €543m went to Switzerland.

Raw tobacco: For raw tobacco, imports reached a value of €1,577m against exports of €498m. The USA was the largest contributor to imports with €389m (or 24.7 per cent), followed by Brazil with €348m. The six main countries of origin accounted for – in value terms – a total of 68.7 per cent of total imports. Exports were mainly destined to Russia (€85m or 17.1 per cent) and to the USA €65m.

Beef meat (incl. live animals but excl. offal): 95.4 per cent of total imports value originated from the six main partners. Imports stood at €1,454m for 2005 and main contributors were Brazil with €784m (or 53.9 per cent) and Argentina with €388m. €151m (or 35.2 per cent) of beef meat exports were destined to Russia out of a total of beef meat exports of €429m. Second destination for export was Lebanon with €53m in 2005.

Pork (incl. live animals but excl. offal): Norway contributed for €12m (or 31.7 per cent) to all EU-15 imports (total €40m) of pork for 2005. All six main countries of origin combined added up to 95 per cent of all EU-15 imports, expressed in value terms. Exports stood at a much higher level and reached in total €2,431m of which €866m (or 35.6 per cent) were destined for Japan, €327m to Russia and €242m to the USA.

Poultry meat (incl. live animals but excl. offal and salted poultry meat): Poultry meat imports stood at €1,170m for 2005 with Brazil as the main contributor. €720m (or 61.5 per cent) of EU-15 poultry meat imports originated from Brazil. Thailand was the second country of origin with €305m and Chile came third with €44m. Combined, the six main countries of origin accounted for 97.6 per cent of total EU-15 poultry meat imports. Exports reached €823m of which €121m (or 14.7 per cent) went to Russia and €92m to Saudi Arabia.

Sheep and goat meat (incl. live animals but excl. offal): New Zealand, as the historically main country of origin for sheep and goat meat imports, obtained a share in EU-15 imports of 79.6 per cent or €895m out of a total of €1,124m for the year 2005. Exports with a total of only €25m went to Switzerland (€9.7m or 39.3 per cent) as main destination.

However, this general appreciation did not prevent the use within the CAP of instruments that impeded international trade (such as taxes on imports) and distorted international markets (such as subsidies on the export of surpluses generated by EU farming). Thus, from the outset there has been a tension between agricultural and trade policies. Once in place, the CAP's main instruments of support proved difficult to remove in the interest of more harmonious trade.

On the broadest scale, it has been found that freeing up international trade by lowering impediments can be best achieved if this is done in a multilateral way, that is by agreement negotiated between a group of countries covering as many commodities as they can agree on. Bilateral agreements (between pairs of countries) can usually achieve positive outcomes, as will those between subsets of countries such as among EU Member States (though there is a danger of diverting trade away from where international comparative advantage lies).

Under the auspices of the United Nations, the General Agreement on Tariffs and Trade (GATT) was set up in 1949. It worked through a series of 'Rounds' of negotiations by which barriers to trade were lowered and rules that its member countries agreed to observe in their trading behaviour, with the provision for judgements and sanctions if these were breached. Trade in agricultural commodities was largely left out of the negotiation for political reasons, though by the time of the 'Uruguay Round' of 1986–1994, which involved 123 countries, this was no longer acceptable, particularly to the 14 countries known as the 'Cairns Group'. This included many for which agricultural exports were highly important to their economies (such as Australia, Brazil, Canada, and New Zealand).

The Uruguay Round outcome, reached in December 1993, was not formally signed until 1994 (the Marrakesh Agreement). The agricultural component (the 'Agreement on Agriculture') remains both as key to trade in agricultural commodities and critical to the application of domestic agricultural policy by its signatories, including the CAP (the EU having negotiated as a single entity). In addition, in 1993, the GATT was updated (GATT 1994) and replaced from January 1995 by the World Trade Organisation (WTO). Whereas GATT was a set of trade rules agreed by nations, the WTO, now with 153 members, is an institutional body that settles disputes on whether actions by members are permissible under GATT rules. The original GATT text (GATT 1947) still in effect underpins the WTO framework, subject to the modifications of GATT 1994. Later attempts to hold a further 'Round' of talks to further free-up trade have so far proved unsuccessful; the Doha Round started in 2001 but an agreement is not in prospect.

The Agreement on Agriculture, details of which are shown in Box 9.2, facilitating trade by lowering taxes on trade (first requiring all border protection measures to be converted into tariffs and then reducing them by 36 per cent over six years), moving towards harmonisation of health standards on animals and crops (sanitary and phytosanitary measures) and gaining minimum access to markets (so that the possibilities for greater levels were in place if these proved profitable). But the Agreement went further by placing limits on two highly significant aspects of public intervention. One was on exports that received public subsidies and which tended to lower world prices; limits applied to both the value of subsidies and volumes of exports. The other was a limit on the value of subsidies that could be paid to producers that encouraged them to produce more (so called 'coupled' support). These became called 'Amber Box' measures. The rationale was that such subsidies had a significant impact on the markets for agricultural commodities and were therefore distorters of the pattern of trade that would have occurred if comparative advantage had been allowed to operate unconstrained. The value of these subsidies was reflected in an 'Aggregate Measure of Support' (AMS) for each

---

Box 9.2 The Uruguay Agreement on Agriculture (December 1993)

Conclusion of Uruguay Round of GATT, with an agreement to run from 1/7/95 until 30/6/01. The agreement is to be administered by the World Trade Organisation (WTO), a new organisation replacing GATT. Essence of the main agreement on agriculture:

Domestic support: Reduction of 20 per cent over six years, based on total Aggregate Measure of Support (AMS) with a base period 1986–88.

Market access: all import restrictions converted to tariffs *(tariffication)* in 1995; for OECD countries tariffs would be 'bound' at this level and reduced by an average of 36 per cent over six years, with a minimum cut of 15 per cent per product. Base period 1986–88. *(In retrospect choice of data and calculations by countries of tariff levels left room for creative accounting, such as estimating baseline tariffs as high as possible to minimise the need to cut in reality – 'dirty' tarrification).* Minimum access requirement of 3 per cent of domestic consumption (1986–88), rising to 5 per cent by end of agreement. Current access to be maintained.

Export subsidies: volume of subsidised exports to be reduced by 21 per cent over six years (base period 1986–90). Budgetary expenditure on export subsidies simultaneously to be reduced by 36 per cent over six years. The 'Peace clause' states that agricultural policy measures, as long as they do not directly contravene the agreement, are not subject to challenge through GATT panels or other dispute settlement channels, and this arrangement will last for three years beyond the six-year duration of the Round itself. There will be an overall review of the agreement on agriculture in 1999.

As a result, world prices of agricultural products were expected to rise by 10 per cent by year 2000. EU and USA were both required to cut back on agricultural export policies, but the full impact in both was reduced by the exemption from the normal schedule of cuts of the main channels of support to farmers (compensatory payments in the EU and deficiency payments in the USA). The 'Peace clause' in effect gave legitimacy to the CAP and meant that it could not be challenged internationally until 2003. Cairns Group of countries (including Australia and New Zealand) were expected to be net beneficiaries; these agricultural exporting countries would have higher prices for their produce and some guaranteed access.

---

country (taking the EU as one) and a commitment was made to limit the AMS to an agreed level and, if initially in excess of this, to scale subsidies back over a period. The value of these subsidies became 'bound' in that this upper limit set subsequently applied permanently.

Not all subsidies were subject to this commitment to reduction. No such limits were applied to subsidies judged not to significantly impact on production and trade, such as decoupled income payments, grants for training, and agri-environment payments. These were granted 'Green Box' status. Others put in a 'Blue Box' were exempt from commitments if such payments are made on fixed areas and yield or a fixed number of livestock, or if they were made on 85 per cent or less of production in a defined base period. Production was still required in order to receive the payments, but the actual payments did not relate directly to the current quantity of that production. In practice 'Blue Box' measures were often involved as transitional arrangements while agricultural policy was reformed, though this exemption ran out in December 2003. In addition, exemption applied to *de minimis* payments which, as the label infers, is where subsidies that are capable of distorting the market are of very small size (in developed countries where the value of product-specific support does not exceed 5 per cent of the value of production of the product in question.)

In retrospect it is not particularly useful to split responsibility for the changes made to the CAP between pressure to achieve a wider Uruguay GATT settlement, which would not have been possible without the Agreement on Agriculture, and other factors such as the rising budgetary cost of the CAP and criticisms of its inefficiency. But they all pointed in approximately the same direction and certainly reinforced each other. Reflecting that internal and external pressures were coming together, one of the objectives agreed for the reformed CAP as part of *Agenda 2000* was that policy should 'increase competitiveness internally and externally in order to ensure that Union producers take full advantage of positive world market developments'.

What is clear is that the main way of supporting agriculture that operated up to the MacSharry CAP reforms of 1992 and continued in diluted form up to the introduction of the Single Payment System by the 2003 CAP Health Check (see Chapter 12) has been firmly rejected. This involved the use of taxes on imports and, later as surpluses appeared, support buying and export subsidies as main ways of raising the prices of farm products and therefore the incomes of farmers, with the intention of providing them with a 'fair standard of living'

It is now realised that such an approach is counter-productive. It created a conflict between agricultural policy and other policies, such as economic growth. It was probably a poor way even to try to achieve the objectives of the CAP as stated in the Treaty of Rome (see Chapter 3). For example, as a way of ensuring living standards, trade restrictions are unsustainable and would prove increasingly costly. A better future lies in helping farming to adjust its structure (farm sizes, labour numbers etc.) to become internationally competitive. Even on the objective of assuring food supplies, shoring up inflated levels of output from EU agriculture is suspect, especially when that is dependent on imports of energy and other inputs. Prospects are better when international trade cements good international relations and when there is the opportunity to spread the impacts of natural disasters, which tend to be regional rather than global. Emergency precautions can deal with crises situations, such as outbreaks of communicable diseases and threats to human health, but these can be handled in an orderly way. Strategic reserves of essential commodities can also play a role.

9.4 The current situation

As was evident from Chapter 6, support to agriculture is now dominated by the largely decoupled Single Payment Scheme. What farmers produce is therefore in principle determined by market forces, in which what EU farmers receive reflects prices on international markets and the costs of transport. The CAP has turned from its former trade-distorting instruments. When trade is fully unrestricted, if there is a surplus in a particular commodity in the EU, it reflects a comparative advantage and can be exported without the need for subsidy. Imports represent situations in which the EU does not have comparative advantage, and buying them from abroad is economically rational.

In terms of the CAP as it stands, this situation is rather more muddied. Residues of instruments that impact on trade remain in some of the commodity regimes outlined in Chapter 6, and these go beyond residual powers to tackle emergencies. According to the European Parliament 8 per cent of 'tariff lines' still have a customs duty in excess of 50 per cent, and items covered include dairy products, beef, cereals and cereal-based products, sugar and sweeteners. The Doha Round was expected to focus on such items, but progress is stalled. However, the EU applies zero or minimum duty to 775 lines out of the total of 1763. Subsidies on exports are still used, but these summed to only €925 million in 2008 (2 per cent of Pillar 1 spending) for EU-27, much less than the €10,159 million for EU-12 in 1993 which accounted for 30 per cent of spending. Furthermore, the EU has agreed over the years a number of multilateral and bilateral agreements for preferential treatment of imports from, for example, the African, Caribbean and Pacific countries (ACP), MERCOSUR, the Euro-Mediterranean area, the European Economic Area, Mexico, Chile etc. There have also been unilateral waivers granted under the Generalised System of Preferences (GSP) (see section below). These preferential agreements must also be compatible with WTO rules and they explain the high quality of EU agricultural imports from developing countries.

Some 'Amber Box' support remains, but at a much reduced level; it was €81 billion at the start of the period covered by the Agreement but had fallen to €31 billion in 2003. The CAP reforms of 2003 and subsequent changes to the regimes that were then not altered have been largely converted into 'Green Box' measures that are not counted in the Aggregate Measure of Support.

Another example of the relevance to the Agreement on Agriculture are its rules on what can be regarded as 'Green Box' and how these can influence the design of CAP policy instruments. Concern has been expressed over the instability of incomes from agriculture and how this may increase now that EU commodity markets are far less regulated. *Agenda 2000* makes explicit reference to the policy aim of the CAP to contribute to the stability of farm incomes. Consideration has been given to the use of a 'safety net' mechanism, so that farmers receive support when their incomes are unexpectedly low but not when they are more normal. However, the Agreement (in its Annex 2, paragraph 7) lays down rather precise rules for any such scheme if it is to remain within the Green Box. Farmers are eligible only if their individual income from agriculture in a particular year falls to less than 70 per cent of the average of the previous three years (or of the previous five, leaving out the worst and best years), and the maximum payment they can be given must be less than 70 per cent of the difference between the particular year and the average. The farm-level data needed to operate such a system makes it impossible to operate in many EU Member States, and thus rules it out as a potential instrument for use by the CAP. A similar set of conditions (paragraph 8) governs when payments can be made to counter the effects of natural disasters.

To sum up, the shape of the CAP, both how it spends on domestic support and how it designs new instruments, is heavily influenced by what has been agreed in negotiations on international trade. They have achieved a substantial easing of trade restriction, with the potential of economic growth through specialisation and exchange. A turning back of the clock is highly unlikely. The former mechanisms that were employed to support agriculture by large-scale intervention in commodity markets using product-related subsidies, thereby distorting the pattern of trade, are unlikely even to be considered again.

9.5 Trade with Developing Countries

Trade in agricultural products is seen as highly important to the growth of incomes and jobs in developing countries and to national export earnings. But this is only one of the ways in which the EU relates to them. The Treaty of Rome (1957) created the European Development Fund (EDF) which was focused on giving technical and financial assistance to countries, mainly in Africa, with which the then seven Member States had historical links. The number of such countries was greatly expanded by expansion of the EU, particularly when the UK joined bringing with it the residues of its colonial past. These African, Caribbean and Pacific (ACP) states now number 79, to which may be added a further 21 overseas countries and territories (of which 12 are British, including the Falkland Islands and Pitcairn Islands).

The EDF is not formally within the EU budget (see Chapter 10) but is accounted for separately, using funds contributed by Member States. The EDF operates in a series of periods of about five years for planning purposes, each agreed at a Convention; the earlier periods were called Yaoundé conventions, followed by Lomé conventions and, since 2000, Cotonou agreements. The current Revised Cotonou Agreement, the tenth in the series, runs from 2008–13 and has been allocated some €22.7 billion, almost all of it going to ACP States. A Second Revision was agreed in 2010 and runs from November of that year. The instruments used include grants, risk capital, and loans to the private sector, with an increased emphasis on regional development. The European Investment Bank also contributes another €1.7 billion.

When the CAP was responsible for generating commodity surpluses, a way of disposing of some of them was to make gifts or sales on very advantageous terms to countries. While a role remains for giving food aid to countries facing humanitarian crises caused by natural or man-made disasters, it is generally accepted that streams of such food can be harmful. The production capacities of local agricultures can be undermined and dependency fostered, with both economic and political consequences.

Under the Fourth Lomé Convention, signed in 1989 for a period of 10 years, practically all products originating in the ACP States (99.5 per cent) had free access to the EU. Reciprocal arrangements (free access on ACP markets for EU goods) were not compulsory, though the ACP countries were required to give them the same good treatment as the best that was on offer to its other trading partners (i.e. giving the EU most-favoured-nation status). A system of stabilisation of export earnings from agricultural products (Stabex) applied, cushioning ACPs against market price movements and production. At the Convention's Mid-Term Review, provision was made to suspend countries from ACP concessions if they breached conditions on human rights, democracy and the rule of law.

The Cotonou Agreement (of 2000) and its revisions have extended the relationship between the EU and ACPs to become about much more than trade. The Agreement, which is expected to run for 20 years, emphasises the partnership between the EU and ACP States in the process of development, and in particular the Economic Partnership Agreements (EPSs) between the EU and regional groups of countries. It covers issues such as democracy, good governance, the involvement of civil society, and migration. A set of institutions (Council of Ministers, the Committee of Ambassadors and a Joint Parliamentary Assembly) is employed to operate the Agreement. Both the Council and the Parliamentary Assembly are expected to consult widely, not only with organisations involved with economic and social development but also with civil society. The purpose is to promote sustainable economic development in ACP States and their 'smooth and gradual integration into the global economy through a

Table 9.4   Trade volumes under Generalised System of Preferences and Value of Preferences, 2008

	GSP preferential imports (€ million)	Nominal duty loss (€ million)
Standard GSP	56,900	2,050
GSP+	5,800	577
EBA	5,800	657
Total	68,600	3,284

Source: European Commission (Europa website)

strategy combining of trade, investments, private-sector development, financial cooperation and regional integration. A policy priority is the reduction of poverty. As the largest importer from ACP States, the EU has considerable potential for providing aid through trade. It should be noted that the Stabex system, intended to bring stability of earning from ACP exports of agricultural commodities, which had been introduced in 1975 as part of the first Lomé Convention was abolished under Cotonou 2000 and replaced by a form of national-linked support that was expected to bring greater benefit to the poorest countries.

In addition, the EU operates a more general policy concerning trade with developing countries. Its Generalised System of Preferences (GSP) reduces tariffs on goods entering the EU from many of them without any condition that EU goods must be given similar benefits when entering their markets. It is brought into effect by a succession of Council Regulations covering three-year periods. The GSP covers three separate preference regimes:

- The standard GSP, which provides preferences to 176 developing countries and territories on over 6200 tariff lines;
- Special incentive arrangements in the form of additional tariff reductions (GSP+) to assist vulnerable developing countries in their ratification and implementation of international conventions in the areas of sustainable development and good governance. A country is considered 'vulnerable' in terms of its size relative to the EU's total imports under the GSP (it must be less than 1 per cent) or the limited diversification in its exports (using a formula). For the period 2009–2011, 16 beneficiary countries qualified to receive these additional preferences;
- The Everything But Arms (EBA) arrangement, which provides duty-free, quota-free access for all products for the world's 49 least developed countries (LDCs).

According to Commission figures, the overall volumes of EU imports under each of the three GSP regimes and the rough value of the preferences provided in terms of nominal duty loss if the same products had been imported and duties paid under the EU's standard MFN conditions of access were as shown in Table 9.4 for 2008.

Further reading

Anderson, K. and Martin, W. (2005) *Agricultural Trade Reform and the Doha Development Agenda*. CIES Discussion Paper 0517. World Bank, Washington, DC.

Hill, B. (2006) *Introduction to Economics: Concepts for Students of Agriculture and the Rural Sector*. 3rd edition. CABI, Wallingford.

Huige, R., Laperre, R., and Stanton, G. (2010) 'The WTO context'. Chapter 4 in Oskam, A., Meester, G. and Silvis, H. (eds) *EU Policy for Agriculture, Food and Rural Areas.* Wageningen Academic Publishers, Wageningen .

Irwin, D. A. (2005) *Free Trade Under Fire*, 2nd edition, Princeton University Press, Princeton, NJ.

Kuyvenhoven, A. and Stolwijk, H. (2010) 'Developing countries and EU agricultural and food policy: opportunities and threats'. Chapter 5 in Oskam, A., Meester, G. and Silvis, H. (eds) *EU Policy for Agriculture, Food and Rural Areas.* Wageningen Academic Publishers, Wageningen.

Mousis, N. (2009) *Access to European Union.* 18th edition (updated). European Study Service, Rixensart, Belgium.

Oskam, A., Meester, G. and Silvis, H. (eds) (2010) *EU Policy for Agriculture, Food and Rural Areas.* Wageningen Academic Publishers, Wageningen.

Swinbank, A. and Tanner, C. (1996) *Farm Policy and Trade Conflict: The Uruguay Round and CAP Reform.* University of Michigan Press, Ann Arbor, MI.

Useful websites

http://ec.europa.eu/agriculture/agrista/tradestats/2009/index_en.htm
http://www.wto.org/english
http://www.wto.org/english/docs_e/legal_e/legal_e.htm
http://www.OECD.org
http://www.worldbank.org

UNDERSTANDING THE COSTS OF THE CAP

Budget and finance

Key topics

- The EU's budget, the contributions by source and by Member State, and the way in which it is used.
- Decision-making on the budget.
- Agri-money matters – the present situation and a look at the past.

10.1 Introduction

The costs of the CAP can be viewed in a number of ways. Perhaps the most simple is to look at the amount that is spent by public bodies, both at EU and national levels, on putting the policy into operation. Such payments have to be financed, and this is done through the EU's budget with, for certain kinds of support, additional part-funding coming from national budgets. How contributions are made to the EU budget by Member State and by source, and how the resources it represents are used are matters of obvious interest to decision-makers and politicians. The Principle of Financial Solidarity (see Chapter 2), which lies behind EU policies in general, is that Member States contribute to a common fund according to agreed procedures that broadly reflect their abilities to pay, and this then finances the actions to tackle the problems faced wherever they occur. Despite this principle, there is a keen awareness in some countries (such as the Netherlands and the UK) of the balance between the amounts that individual Member States pay in and the amounts that they get out.

Here the particular concern is the budgetary costs of the CAP. As will become clear, until quite recently, spending on agricultural policy has dominated the EU budget and direct payments to farming and market price support even now absorbs almost a third of the total spent on all EU common policies. Of course, this is hugely larger than the share that agriculture represents as a generator of income or source of employment in the EU-27 (1.2 per cent in 2008) or any Member State (Poland was highest, with 6 per cent). It reflects the fact that, for many years, agricultural policy was the main common EU activity, forming the focus of economic and political cooperation between Member States. However, from the outset it was complemented by Communities to deal with problems in the coal and steel industry and the peaceful uses of atomic energy. Over time, the range of policy areas covered collectively at the EU level has grown considerably, some, like regional policy, absorbing large amounts of public funds. But none has been centralised to the extent that agricultural policy has, nor do they have the international trade features of the CAP that can lead to significant spending.

Another feature worth noting is the past tendency for the budgetary costs of the CAP to escalate. Various attempts have been made to limit this upward movement, at first not very successfully but, more recently, far more effectively (the 'Financial Perspective', discussed later). Shortage of available funds has also been a major driver of reform of the CAP.

As was evident from Chapters 5 and 6, in the past, much of the burden of the support given to agriculture fell on consumers in the form of higher food prices. According to OECD estimates, even in 2009 the annual economic transfer from consumers of agricultural producers in the EU was in the order of €21billion, though this was less than half the level of five years earlier. In comparison, payments from the EU budget on the CAP in 2009 was about €51billion (see later). The OECD publishes annual estimates of support to agriculture which, in its various forms, currently represent just over a fifth of the value of what EU farms produce (23 per cent of gross farm receipts in 2007–09). A broad view of costs would also take into account the economic consequences of distorting market prices, such as lost opportunities to use national resources in the most efficient way and consumer welfare effects (as reflected in consumer surplus). Over a period of time these distortions could harm the rate of growth of the economy, so a longer perspective on costs would be needed to reflect this dynamic aspect. And there may have been a whole range of environmental, social and other non-monetary costs associated with the CAP's use of intervention in markets. Fortunately, reforms to the way in which support is given, with the moves towards restoring the market as the incentive for farmers to produce, means that these broader costs not reflected in public expenditure have been much reduced. Consequently, when discussing the costs of the CAP, the outlay from the EU budget on agriculture and the smaller amounts of national spending now represent in a more satisfactory way the total economic costs of the CAP.

Other types of costs, however, should not be forgotten. In particular, the large amount spent on supporting agriculture has attracted criticism that the undue prominence given to the CAP may have hampered the growth of other common policies. The budget is an important factor that must be considered when looking at the way that EU policies have developed over time.

10.2 The general budget of the EU

The budget of the EU is important not only as an accounting device which brings together and summarises the resources for collective action and their distribution to various uses but also because the agreement of the budget is a significant element in the policy-making process of the EU. Moreover, the rule that budgets must balance and the difficulties in achieving this have caused recurrent crises that have acted as powerful catalysts in achieving change and reform in the EU's common policies.

As was pointed out in Chapter 3, the EU was founded on three separate Communities (the European Coal and Steel Community (ECSC), set up by the 1951 Treaty of Paris, the European Economic Community (EEC) and the European Atomic Energy Community (Euratom), both established in 1957 by the Treaty of Rome). Since 1970, the general budget has covered all the policies of the European Economic Community and Euratom (both research and investment); not included were the ECSC operating budget (this Community was abolished in 2002) and the European Development Fund (set up in 1959) which is accounted for separately (see Chapter 9). Here we are concerned with the general budget, referred to throughout this book as the 'EU budget'.

When examining the budget it is useful to bear in mind some of the terms used. First, there is a difference between commitments for a particular purpose in the financial year and the actual payments, the difference being that the latter also includes what is paid out arising from commitments in previous years.[1] Accounting systems will need to cater for both. Out-turns (actual spending) are often different from the budgeted sums, so figures published in the EU budget will not coincide exactly with those of EU's *Financial Report* for the same year. Sometimes out-turns are smaller than budgeted if, for example, Member States find that the uptake of a particular form of support is less than expected. Over-spends lead to consequences that depend on circumstances, which involve a second set of terms. Some expenditure in the budget is termed compulsory and some non-compulsory. The former is that which has to be spent in order to enable the EU to meet its obligations, both internally and externally, arising directly out of the Treaties, the remainder being non-compulsory. In practice, spending on the support of agricultural commodity regimes has historically been treated as compulsory, costs higher than expected leading to a squeeze on other spending such as on measures to assist changes in the structure of farming. And, third, some commitments and payments are non-differentiated, meaning that both commitments and payments should, in principle, be completed in a single budget year, whereas differentiated commitments refer to obligations spanning several financial years. The principles on which the budget is drawn up are contained in the Financial Regulation (Council Reg. 1605) of 2002.

10.3 The financial resources of the European Union

At the start of the European Economic Community the general budget was financed by contributions by the six founding Member States. This was only intended as a temporary measure. In accordance with the terms of the Treaty of Rome a move was made, starting with a decision in 1970, to give the Community its 'own resources', which may be defined as tax revenue allocated once and for all to the Community and accruing to it automatically without the need for any subsequent decision by the national authorities. These now consist of four forms:

- **Agricultural levies (and sugar and iso-glucose levies):** These are the taxes charged on the imports of agricultural commodities from countries outside the EU and on sugar and iso-glucose and inulin production in the EU. Though import levies were important as a source of revenue in the early years of the Community, since 1980 they have accounted for less than 10 per cent of total resources, in the early 1990s providing 3 to 4 per cent and down to less than 2 per cent in 2009 (Table 10.1).
- **Customs duties:** These derive from the application of the common customs tariff to the customs value of goods imported from non-EU countries. In the 1980s these were the second largest source of resources, in the 1990s accounted for about a fifth (18 to 22 per cent in the early years) and in 2009 were down to 15 per cent.
- **VAT resources:** This is the contribution which national exchequers make to the EU budget calculated from applying a Value Added Tax (0.5 per cent) to notional national VAT revenues (the VAT base), were a common VAT system to be in operation. It is important to note that the VAT resources paid to the EU are not a share of the actual VAT collected in each country, but the equivalent of what would have been collected if a 0.5 per cent VAT had been applied to the production of goods and services which are on the EU standard list. Thus, the fact that in practice some countries do not charge

Table 10.1   Sources of Contributions to the EU budget, 2009

	Million €	*Per cent of total*
Net agricultural duties	1,404	1.2
Net sugar and isoglucose levies	147	0.1
Net customs duties	17,656	15.4
VAT own resources	19,616	17.1
GNI own resources	75,914	66.2
Total	114,737	100.0

Source: European Commission EU Budget

VAT on certain items whereas others do (for example, children's clothes, books and newspapers and food are either exempt or zero rated in the UK) makes no difference to the amount which has to be paid by the UK Treasury to the EU budget. Soon after its introduction this resource became the budget's largest source of funds and from the early 1980s contributed more than half of the total. In the early 1990s, 54 to 59 per cent of revenue came in this form, but in 2009 it had shrunk to 17 per cent.

The VAT resource was intended to be the item which could be adjusted to balance the EU budget. Because of the principle of annuality on which the budget operates, which means that each year's budget must balance, the EU is not permitted to plan for a deficit (or a surplus) in any single year. Consequently, some adjustable item has to be used to bring the budget into balance. If expenditure to which the EU was committed was rising, then the VAT resource could be increased to accommodate it by raising the notional VAT rate. Member States will naturally wish to keep some control over EU spending and hence the costs to national exchequers, since this represents both a drain on the amount of tax revenue they can spend nationally without resorting to unpopular tax-raising and also a curb on the power of the EU institutions relative to national governments. This application of annuality is one way in which control is kept over the Commission's activities. Initially a ceiling of a notional 1 per cent VAT rate was imposed, which in the face of expanding CAP costs proved inadequate. In 1984, this ceiling was raised to 1.4 per cent from 1986 and intended to apply for another seven years. Again it proved inadequate; as soon as 1987, the Community's commitments implied a rate of 1.65 per cent. As interim measures, various forms of creative accounting were used (such as delaying the timing at which Member States were reimbursed for spending on Community policies). The rate was lowered to the present 0.5 per cent in 2000.

- **Gross national income:** In 1988 a *fourth resource* was created as the new topping-up mechanism, based on each Member State's gross national product (GNP), an indicator of the amount of economic activity in the country. With the revision of national accounting in 1995 this concept has been replaced by the similar gross national income (GNI). The present ceiling is 1.24 per cent. When this resource was introduced the proportion of total revenue coming in this form varied widely from less than 1 per cent (1990) to 22 per cent (1993); such wide variation between years was to be expected in a topping-up resource when the cost of running the CAP – a major item in the budget – was subject to unpredictable factors such as prices of agricultural commodities on world markets. However, with the reduction in the VAT resources this GNI source has jumped to be by far the largest contribution, in 2009 accounting for two-thirds of the total.

Table 10.2   Contribution by Member States to total own resources of the EU, 2009

Member State	%	€m	Member State	%	€m, 2009
Austria	2.27	2,414	Latvia	0.22	243
Belgium	3.02	4,879	Lithuania	0.30	337
Bulgaria	0.32	388	Luxembourg	0.27	282
Cyprus	0.15	193	Malta	0.05	58
Czech Republic	1.30	1,488	Netherlands	4.85	6,745
Denmark	2.09	2,364	Poland	3.28	3,611
Estonia	0.16	185	Portugal	1.44	1,537
Finland	1.67	1,761	Romania	1.21	1,400
France	17.45	18,125	Slovakia	0.55	645
Germany	19.95	22,639	Slovenia	0.33	421
Greece	2.20	2,374	Spain	9.60	10,617
Hungary	0.89	990	Sweden	2.78	3,152
Ireland	1.48	1,670	United Kingdom	8.70	11,421
Italy	13.48	14,796	TOTAL	100.00	114,736

Source: derived from European Commission Financial Report 2009

When the rules are applied, Member States contribute different amounts of 'own resources' to the EU general budget (see Table 10.2). Germany, France and Italy provide the largest sums. The 'fairness' of how much each country contributes is a long-running issue. As early as 1974 the UK was concerned with 'broad balance' in the burden of contributions, implying that an adjustment might be made if payments by a Member State exceeded what would have been paid had calculation been made on the basis of the country's share of the EU's total gross national product (GNP). The notion of 'budgetary compensation' was invoked to obtain a rebate for the UK in 1980 and 1982. In 1984, by an agreement at the Fontainebleau summit, this UK rebate was made automatic rather than determined by negotiation. The effect is to spread the rebate's cost between other Member States, Germany, Spain and Portugal have also invoked this 'compensation' principle.

Treasuries of Member States pay the sums due to the EU budget into special accounts set up by the European Commission in national banks or treasuries for the purpose. Sometimes the Commission requests sums to be credited in advance. These funds are then available for EU policy spending. In some cases, if the amounts paid into these accounts have been over-estimated, negative expenditures can be seen in the accounts, as some money is repaid to the Member State.

10.4 Uses of budgetary resources by the European Union

What is spent on agriculture and on the other areas of EU policy is the result of a complex political process, involving the institutions of the EU, national government and lobby groups. These were discussed in Chapter 3. What we see in the EU budget is the outcome of that process.

Agreements between the European Parliament, the Council and the Commission in the form of multi-year 'Financial Perspectives' (see Box 10.1) apply to EU spending, including

Box 10.1 The Financial Perspective

The first Inter-institutional Agreement (IIA) was concluded in 1988. It covered the 1988–1992 Financial Perspective, known as the Delors I package, to provide the resources needed for the budgetary implementation of the Single European Act. In view of the success of this approach, the institutions followed the same procedure in concluding a new IIA in 1993, with the Financial Perspective for the 1993–1999 period. The third IIA on the Financial Perspective for the period 2000–2006, relating to *Agenda 2000*, was signed in 1999, and was designed to reconcile the CAP and enlargement. In 2004 the Commission proposed a new agreement and a new Financial Perspective for the period 2007–2013 which led to the new IIA of 2006 providing for EU spending of up to €864.3 billion over the 2007–2013 period. The relevant figures are given below, including the agricultural guideline (figures adopted by the EP Temporary Committee on the Financial Perspective).

Million € at 2004 prices

Commitment appropriations	2007	2008	2009	2010	2011	2012	2013	Total
1. Sustainable growth	57,612	60,612	63,560	65,558	67,699	70,559	73,435	459,035
1a. Competitiveness for growth and employment	11,010	13,157	15,377	17,207	19,190	21,272	23,350	120,563
1b. Cohesion for growth and employment	46,602	47,455	48,183	48,351	48,509	49,287	50,085	338,472
2. Preservation and management of natural resources	56,744	56,866	56,980	56,747	56,524	56,299	56,088	396,248
of which: agriculture– market-related expenditure and direct payments (CAP Pillar 1)	43,120	42,697	42,279	41,864	41,453	41,047	40,645	293,105
3. Citizenship, freedom, security and justice	1,777	2,156	2,470	2,778	3,096	3,420	3,741	19,437
4. The EU as a global partner	8,235	8,795	9,343	10,050	10,782	11,434	12,060	70,697
5. Administration	3,675	3,815	3,950	4,090	4,225	4,365	4,500	28,620
Compensations	419	191	190					800
Total appropriations for commitments	128,462	132,434	136,493	139,223	142,326	146,077	149,824	974,837
Commitment appropriations over GNI	1.17%	1.18%	1.19%	1.18%	1.18%	1.19%	1.19%	1.18%
Total reduction compared to Commission's proposal								−47,518
Total appropriations for payments	116,403	120,003	123,680	126,154	128,966	132,365	135,760	883,329
Payments over GNI	1.06%	1.07%	1.08%	1.07%	1.07%	1.07%	1.08%	1.07%

Source: European Parliament 'Fact sheets'

Table 10.3 Spending on agriculture in the Financial Perspective for EU-27 2007–13. € billion at 2004 prices

	2007	*2008*	*2009*	*2010*	*2011*	*2012*	*2013*	*Total 2007–13*
CAP Pillar 1	43.1	42.7	42.3	41.9	41.4	41.0	40.6	293.1
CAP Pillar 2	10.0	9.9	10.2	9.9	10.0	10.0	10.0	69.2

Source: Balkhausen and Bause (2006) based on Agra Europe articles

the allocations to CAP's Pillars 1 and 2. These agreed figures are given separately for the period 2007–13 in Table 10.3. They are updated each year to reflect inflation as well as any negotiated changes within the (real terms) constraints of the Perspectives; notice that the figures quoted here are in real terms (at 2004 prices), though they also appear on official websites in current money values. It can be seen from Box 10.1 that, compared with the entire economic activity in the EU (as shown by gross national income), the combined cost of EU policies is small – barely above 1 per cent. Second, although the size of the EU budget is projected to rise slightly to 2013 in real terms, the amount used on 'the preservation and management of natural resources', which includes the CAP's two Pillars as the main components, is set to decline. Thirdly, Pillar 2 (rural development) spending (see Table 10.3) is only about one quarter the size of Pillar 1 (direct payments and market intervention). Spending on agriculture is considered in more detail later.

10.5 Budgetary balance by Member State

As noted on a number of previous occasions in this text, one of the guiding principles of the EU is financial solidarity; this means collective financing of EU programmes in which the funds of the EU, gathered according to agreed rules which presumably are judged to be fair by Member States, are used to tackle the problems which the EU faces wherever these are to be found, without taking overtly into account the balance between each country's contributions to the EU budget and spending within that country on EU policies. Nevertheless there is reason to keep an eye on this balance. For one thing, it may indicate that either the policies or the rules on national contributions may need adjustment; reflection might come up with a more equitable distribution of costs and policy benefits. For another, large national imbalances one way or the other might be expected to influence the direction of policy decision-making, in that countries which are net beneficiaries under EU policies will tend to try to retain the existing pattern, opposing change and maybe even pressing to expand the level of spending, whereas countries which are net payers will tend to wish to constrain programmes and constrain overall costs. These preferences could be expected to be reflected in voting patterns in the Council.

Table 10.4 gives the amounts of resources contributed by each Member State in 2009, together with the amount drawn from the budget to support spending on EU policies in each country. It is clear that the number of net payers is small (eight out of 27 in 2009). The main net contributors in that year (in terms of absolute figures) were Germany, France and Italy. The main net gainers were Poland, Greece, Hungary, Belgium and Portugal. In terms of the size of these payments as a proportion of the own resources contributed (which might be taken as an indication of the degree of burden or benefit) Germany, Denmark and Italy found themselves with receipts from the EU budget which formed only about two-thirds of their contributions.

Table 10.4 Resources contributed from and payments made to Member States, 2009 (€ million)

	National contribution to EU budget	Expenditure from EU budget on national support	Balance	Sustainable Growth (mainly regional policy)	CAP direct aids and market related	CAP rural development
				Use of spending		
EU-27	94378.7	102821.2	*	42425.5	41277.3	8739.5
Austria	2159.0	1816.6	−342.4	452.2	749.5	548.4
Belgium	3238.5	5629.3	2390.9	1184.8	210.2	61.0
Bulgaria	336.7	978.6	642.0	303.6	227.8	127.1
Cyprus	165.0	172.3	7.4	91.7	39.7	16.2
Czech Republic	1207.3	2948.6	1741.3	2040.6	499.3	366.7
Denmark	2208.1	1328.0	−880.1	203.4	955.3	53.9
Estonia	134.5	716.4.0	582.0	541.6	55.3	95.1
Finland	1699.0	1207.8	−491.3	399.5	561.9	191.4
France	18830.0	13631.9	−5,198.1	3312.4	8908.8	795.7
Germany	17564.0	11713.3	−5,850.8	4755.6	5702.3	930.7
Greece	2234.0	5434.0	3200.1	2483.6	2583.7	257.7
Hungary	816.0	3568.6	2752.6	2241.0	747.6	525.7
Ireland	1357.0	1378.0	21.0	240.6	740.7	329.9
Italy	13912.7	9372.3	−4,540.4	3174.7	4640.0	582.3
Latvia	197.2	710.3	513.1	485.9	80.0	104.5
Lithuania	282.0	1790.3	1508.4	1279.2	214.1	247.5
Luxembourg	276.0	1453.6	1177.6	115.3	38.9	13.7
Malta	54.6	71.5	16.9	41.9	2.7	3.4
Netherlands	1615.9	1849.5	233.6	688.5	945.9	45.0
Poland	2834.5	9252.9	6418.5	6210.7	1734.2	1043.8
Portugal	1519.1	3724.1	2205.1	2563.3	728.9	344.9
Romania	1218.0	2951.2	1733.2	965.2	600.4	565.9
Slovakia	628.0	1192.4	564.4	633.5	220.4	289.3
Slovenia	358.8	616.3	257.5	393.8	74.9	112.8
Spain	10168.1	11614.2	1446.1	4833.3	5950.7	621.3
Sweden	1485.3	1451.9	−33.4	469.0	744.4	106.8
UK	7879.6	6247.1	−1,632.5	2320.7	3319.9	359.0

*The difference between national contributions and expenditure is explained by factors such as resources that accrue to the EU budget from sources other than national contributions.
Source: derived from European Commission Financial Report 2009.

At the other extreme, Estonia, Lithuania and Luxembourg received back more than four times what they contributed; the net flows towards the first two are understandable in the light of their lower stages of economic development. Luxembourg is an important administrative centre for EU policies and, with Belgium, receives large sums from the budget for this purpose, far more than is spent in these countries on the policies themselves.

Also shown in Table 10.4 are the amounts spent on each of the two Pillars of the CAP – direct payments and market support that constitute Pillar 1 (see Chapter 6) and rural development Pillar 2 (see Chapters 7 and 8). The cost of 'sustainable growth' measures (in effect, regional policy) is also shown. In the case of Greece, the amount given in CAP Pillar 1 support alone was greater than that country's contributions to the budget. Further attention is given to these figures later.

10.6 Stages of the procedure for agreeing a European Union annual budget

The Financial Perspective forms a background against which the European Union sets its annual budget. By agreement between the Member States and parliaments the total available for the EU budget is 1.24 per cent of the EU's gross national income (GNI). Article 272 of the EEC Treaty stipulates the sequence of stages and the time limits which must be respected by the two arms of the budgetary authority, the Council and European Parliament, in setting the annual budget. The official timetable extends from 1 September to 31 December. In practice, however, a pragmatic timetable has been applied that starts far earlier.

The different stages of the procedure are as follows:

(i) **Establishment of the preliminary draft by the Commission and transmission to the budgetary authority (Council and European Parliament).** In April and May the Commission compiles the requests of all spending departments and arbitrates between conflicting claims on the basis of the priorities set for the year in question. It also receives the estimates of the other institutions and puts them all together in a preliminary draft budget, which is the overall forecast of revenue and expenditure for a given year. This preliminary draft is adopted by the Commission in May or June and sent to the budgetary authority (Council and European Parliament) in all the official languages. The preliminary draft can subsequently be amended by the Commission by means of a letter of amendment to allow for new information which was not available when the preliminary draft was established.

(ii) **Adoption of the draft budget by the Council of Ministers.** The Council conducts its first reading of the preliminary draft and on this basis adopts the draft budget by 31 July (by qualified majority), which it sends to Parliament.

(iii) **First reading by European Parliament.** When it has received the Commission's preliminary draft and the Council's draft, Parliament conducts its first reading in October; amendments to non-compulsory expenditure require the votes of an absolute majority of members. Proposed modifications to compulsory expenditure require an absolute majority of votes cast.

(iv) **Second reading by the Council of Ministers.** The Council conducts this second reading in the third week of November, after a conciliation meeting with a delegation from Parliament. The draft budget is amended in the light of Parliament's amendments (non-compulsory expenditure) or proposed modifications (compulsory expenditure). As a rule, the Council's decisions on second reading relating to compulsory expenditure determine the final amount: unless the entire budget is subsequently rejected by Parliament, the Council has the last word on this category of expenditure. The draft budget as amended is returned to Parliament towards the end of November.

(v) **Second reading by Parliament and adoption of the budget.** After the Council has had its last say on compulsory expenditure, Parliament devotes most of its December part-session to reviewing non-compulsory expenditure, for which it can accept or refuse the Council's proposals. Acting by a majority of its members and three-fifths of the votes cast, Parliament then adopts the budget. In accordance with the Treaty, the President of Parliament declares the budget adopted and it can then be implemented from 1 January.

Sometimes there are disagreements between the Parliament and Council that have led to rejection of the proposals by the Parliament and so the new financial year (starting in January) commences with no budget in place. This is a key power that the Parliament holds over the direction in which policy is progressing, though a rather blunt instrument where the objective is to influence agricultural policy. If this happens there are provisions to carry on using a system of 'provisional twelfths', which in essence rolls the previous budget forward in monthly steps. Meanwhile, an informal 'third reading' process takes place, where necessary using new budgetary proposals from the Commission, until the Parliament and Council come to an agreement.

In the event of unavoidable, exceptional or unforeseen circumstances, the Commission may propose during the year that the budget as adopted be amended; it does this by submitting preliminary draft supplementary and/or amending budgets. These are subject to the same procedural rules as the general budget, although, in practice, a supplementary or amending budget is sometimes adopted on first reading by the Council and Parliament, something which does not happen with the general budget.

10.7 The two agricultural funds

Drawing up a budget for EU activities should be distinguished from the arrangements set up to make the payments that put policies into operation – that is, financing them. In the context of the CAP two funds are of particular importance to its functioning. These are the European Agricultural Guarantee Fund (EAGF), from which Pillar I support is paid (direct payments such as the Single Farm Payment, and the cost of the remaining market intervention mechanisms) and the European Agricultural Fund for Rural Development (EAFRD) that pays for Pillar 2 (largely the cost of EU support to Rural Development Programmes in Member States). These two funds were created in 2005 by Council Regulation (EC) No 1290/2005 which established a single legal framework for financing CAP spending and superseded the single European Agricultural Guidance and Guarantee Fund (EAGGF) that had existed from the outset of the CAP. The 2005 Regulation sets out conditions under which the Funds operate; these include the accreditation of national agencies that actually make the payments to farmers and landowners and the systems needed to manage, monitor and control the payments. In England, the Rural Payments Agency makes payments to beneficiaries on behalf of the Department for Environment, Food and Rural Affairs (Defra), and the European Commission reimburses Defra.

Box 10.2 EAGF and EAFRD

European Agricultural Guarantee Fund (EAGF)

As regards expenditure managed jointly by the Member States and the Commission, the EAGF finances:

- refunds for exporting farm produce to non-EU countries;
- intervention measures to regulate agricultural markets;
- direct payments to farmers under the CAP;
- certain informational and promotional measures for farm produce implemented by Member States both on the internal EU market and outside it;
- expenditure on restructuring measures in the sugar industry under Regulation (EC) No 320/2006.

As regards expenditure managed centrally by the Commission, EAGF financing covers:

- the Community's financial contribution for specific veterinary measures, veterinary inspection and inspections of foodstuffs and animal feed, animal disease eradication and control programmes and plant-health measures;
- promotion of farm produce, either directly by the Commission or via international organisations;
- measures required by Community legislation to conserve, characterise, collect and use genetic resources in farming;
- setting up and running farm accounting information systems;
- farm survey systems;
- expenditure relating to fisheries markets.

European Agricultural Fund for Rural Development

The EAFRD finances rural development programmes implemented in accordance with the legislation proposed by the Commission [COM(2004) 490], solely where expenditure is managed jointly by the Member States and the Commission.

Source: Europa website

The Regulation lays down the conditions on which the Commission will reimburse the payments made to beneficiaries, obligations on Member States to prevent fraud, the reporting system to the Commission that has to be used, what happens if over-payments are made etc. Payments made to a Member State under the EAGF and EAFRD may be reduced or suspended where certain serious and persistent deficiencies are detected.

Although the EAGF and EAFRD operate similarly, each has certain specific features, such as the timing of reimbursement by the Commission. The areas which each finances are shown in Box 10.2. A spin-off of the separation of the Pillars is that it is now easier to carry out evaluations of policy. Evaluation is done in relation to particular funding lines in the budget. The fact that, in the past, rural development in some regions (those with Objective 1 status as the result of lagging behind economically – see Chapter 7) was financed by a mix of budget lines created practical difficulties (for example, in some parts of Wales diversification grants came from rural development spending whereas in others they came from regional policy programmes). Now all rural development is financed from the EAFRD wherever it is applied.

10.8 Spending on agriculture and rural development from the general budget

Support of agriculture is currently still the major use of the EU's budget. Spending on the management of natural resources (which includes both Pillars of the CAP, forestry, fishing and other categories) absorbs 41 per cent of the budgeted total in the current financial period, which runs from 2007–13. Of the €396 billion involved, some €293 billion is for Pillar I support, in the form of direct payments (mostly now Single Farm Payments and Single Area Payments), so this Pillar accounts for 30 per cent of spending by the EU on all its common policies. Nevertheless this represents a substantial decline in relative importance over the last four decades.

An extract from the budget for 2009 is shown in Table 10.5. The figures are similar to, but not identical with, those for 2009 that appear in the Financial Perspective; explanations for the differences include the updating of the latter. The key point is that the main form of spending is direct aids, which include Single Farm and Single Area Payments plus any remaining coupled direct payments. These account for 69 per cent of commitments and slightly more (73 per cent) of budgeted payments. Intervention in agricultural markets now costs only about one-tenth of the amount absorbed by direct payments. Rural development spending is the second largest category but this is far behind the cost of direct payments, at 25 per cent of commitments (and a rather smaller share of budgeted payments, at 20 per cent).

Analysis of actual spending for 2009 (in contrast with budgeted figures) reveals some interesting differences between Member States in terms of the relative size of spending on

Table 10.5 Budgeted spending on agriculture, 2009 (€m)

	Commitments	Payments	% of commitments
Administrative expenditure of agriculture and rural development policy area	133	133	0.2
Interventions in agricultural markets	3,410	3,410	6.2
Direct aids	37,779	37,779	69.1
Rural development	13,645	10,226	25.0
Pre-accession measures in the field of agriculture and rural development	122	341	0.2
International aspects of agriculture and rural development policy area	6	6	0.0
Audit of agricultural expenditure	−459	−459	−0.8
Policy strategy and coordination of agriculture and rural development policy area	44	40	0.1
Total	54,680	51,477	100.0

Source: European Commission, DG Budget

agriculture. Back in Table 10.4, sums used in the main policy areas for each Member State were given. Combining the expenditure on the CAP's two Pillars finds that overall 49 per cent of actual spending in EU-27 in 2009 was on agriculture and rural development (rather higher than the budgeted sums), though there were wide differences between countries (Table 10.6). More than 70 per cent went on agriculture and rural development in Austria, Denmark, France and Ireland, but less than a third in most of the EU-12 new Member States (a little more in Romania and Slovakia) and Portugal. In three countries (Belgium, Luxembourg and Malta) less than a tenth of what was received from the EU budget was used for agriculture; for the first two the explanation is the large amounts used for maintaining the EU institutions. A converse picture emerges when spending for 'sustainable growth' is considered. Typically more than 60 per cent of sums received from the EU budget by the new Member States (plus Portugal) went on these regional policies. The EU-27 average was 41 per cent. Further consideration of the sums budgeted for agriculture is given below.

10.9 Some characteristics of agricultural spending

A first characteristic is that spending on the CAP has shown a historic tendency to grow over time. This is not surprising when an industry is insulated from developments in world markets by a support system that gives incentives to production and protects against international competition. The history of the CAP up to 1988 was marked by relatively weak control over these rising costs and consequently a series of financial crises was precipitated. Though part of the growth in CAP spending was explained by enlargement, the cost of the Common Market Organisations (regimes) for the agricultural commodities was a main element, spending that was considered 'compulsory' under the Treaty of Rome. Various attempts were made to bring costs under control by reforming the regimes, intended to make producers more aware of the market reality, or introducing palliative measures (including milk quotas in 1984) to cope with the financial crises, but these involved only minor changes to the level at which support prices were set, changes that were insufficient to alter fundamentally the production incentives faced by farmers. Thus, production, surpluses and budget costs continued to rise. The levels of price cuts needed would have lowered incomes to an extent that was politically unacceptable.

Firmer resolve was tried in 1988. Discipline was increased by means of imposing an 'agricultural guideline' for expenditure on market support, a mechanism first tried in 1984, and laid down for the period 1988 to 1992 at €27.5 million for 1988 with a permitted annual growth 74 per cent of the rate of increase of the EU's GNP. An early warning system was put in place for each CMO to give adequate notice of emerging problems over spending, enabling actions to be taken, and a monetary reserve created (outside the 'guideline') to help cope with cost changes arising from movements in the exchange rate between the US dollar and the euro. This 'agricultural guideline' was not respected in this period, despite its inclusion within the 'financial perspective', because there were no effective constraints on the Agricultural Council (of Ministers) to ensure their price and policy decisions kept within the prescribed figures. Only in 1992, with changes to the support mechanisms (the 'MacSharry reforms') was CAP spending capable of respecting the Guideline. In 1992 the European Council extended the 'agricultural guideline' until 1999, then under *Agenda 2000* it was extended for Pillar 1 spending to 2006, and in 2002 it was further extended to 2013 (see Box 10.1). Though by definition the sums available under these 'guidelines' are allowed to expand, this is done in a predictable way. They have probably contributed to the shift in

Table 10.6 Relative size of actual spending of EU funds on agriculture and other policies, 2009 (percentages)

	Agriculture and rural development	Sustainable growth	Citizenship, freedom, security and justice	Other
EU-27	49	41	2	8
Austria	71	25	2	2
Belgium	5	21	2	72*
Bulgaria	36	31	2	31**
Cyprus	32	53	9	5
Czech Republic	29	69	1	1
Denmark	76	15	1	8
Estonia	21	76	2	2
Finland	62	33	2	3
France	71	24	2	3
Germany	57	41	1	2
Greece	52	46	1	1
Hungary	36	63	1	1
Ireland	78	17	1	4
Italy	56	34	7	3
Latvia	26	68	1	4
Lithuania	26	71	2	1
Luxembourg	4	8	1	88*
Malta	8	59	22***	11
Netherlands	54	37	3	6
Poland	30	67	1	2
Portugal	29	69	1	1
Romania	40	33	1	27**
Slovakia	43	53	1	3
Slovenia	30	64	2	4
Spain	57	42	1	1
Sweden	59	32	6	3
UK	59	37	1	3

*Mostly administration ** Mostly pre-accession aid *** Mostly related to solidarity and management of migration flows.
Source: Based on European Commission Financial Report for 2009.

balance of overall spending by the EU, whereby the share of the EU overall budget taken by agriculture has fallen from 67 per cent in 1988 to 42 per cent in 2009 (actual figures were rather higher in the latter year). Of course, this also reflects an expansion of other EU (non-agricultural) activities. Whether the previous relatively low levels of spending from the EU budget on these other areas was the result of the heavy commitments to agriculture or a lack of political will to develop these areas is a matter of debate.

Agriculture is an industry that, because it faces weather and other influences that are hard to control, is characterised by year-to-year fluctuations in outputs, prices and rewards. The budgetary cost of providing support to EU agriculture's revenues and incomes can also be expected to fluctuate. However, it is probably far more predictable now than at any previous period in the CAP's history. The last two decades have seen a gradual reduction of the elements of support that were unpredictable and whose costs could lead to budgetary crises. They have been replaced with mechanisms that, though not necessarily costing less (and sometimes more), are both more stable and inherently more predictable. For example, the direct payments under the MacSharry 1992 reforms that went hand-in-hand with the reduction in support prices for farm commodities were set in advance and linked to a maximum number of crop hectares or number of animals. These direct payments were increased under *Agenda 2000* when institutional support prices were lowered further, but this took place within the 'agricultural guidelines' provided by the 'financial perspective'. Likewise, the MTR and the introduction of the Single Farm Payment has carried this to a next (and even more predictable and stable) stage because entitlements are linked to a previous (historic) level of direct payments. Subsequent reforms to commodity regimes that were not covered by the original SFP have brought them inside it, with suitable adjustments to the levels and entitlements. Thus the degree of stability in the cost of supporting agriculture (and rural development) is much greater in 2009 than it was before 1992, and even more than in 2000.

As well as being more predictable, a case can be made that the revised system of support is more efficient. A characteristic of the previous system of instruments was its low transfer efficiency, a point the OECD made frequently. Estimates suggest that under the old instruments only one euro in four spent on agricultural support remained in the hands of farmers, while under the new direct aid-payment schemes now one euro in two reaches them. This leads to the claim that a much greater impact is being made, and that the transfer efficiency of the new EU systems is superior to that of the old one. However, a question remains over whether the benefits are in the right hands. As was pointed out in Chapter 6, the pattern of distribution is very skewed, with small numbers of recipients of large sums, many of whom are large companies rather than individual farmers, and large numbers of 'natural persons' (individual self-employed farmers and partners) who receive small payments. This raises the issue of whether the payments are being properly targeted.

10.10 State-level expenditure

The ability of national governments to spend outside the CAP in support of their agricultures is severely constrained by EU rules. The concept of a single market for agricultural commodities, at the centre of the CAP, implies that national aids that distort the competitive process are not permitted. State aids are only allowed under specific circumstances and with the permission of the European Commission, and, where approved, concern interventions that do not significantly affect competition.[2] In practice, securing this permission can be a complex and long process.

Within the CAP, while national support expenditure is not allowed for production activities that fall under Pillar 1, it forms a vital part of Pillar 2 spending. As was noted in Chapters 7 and 8, Pillar 2 covers rural development, which is organised at national (or sub-national) level into Rural Development Programmes. These cover schemes to encourage the restructuring of agriculture to make it more competitive (including potential assistance to entry and exit), agri-environmental schemes and payments to farmers operating in Less Favoured Areas, and other ways of improving the quality of life in rural areas. The principle of co-financing is used, in which EU funds provide a proportion of spending on schemes that are organised at national level. This proportion varies in a pre-determined manner, for example between holdings in or outside Less Favoured Areas and between the countries that joined in 2004/2007 and the EU-15 Member States. In addition, Member States are permitted to spend extra (to 'top up') on rural development schemes if they so wish, though not in an unlimited way; this also applies in the new Member States with their Single Area Payments. In Chapter 6, mention was made of 'modulation', an arrangement by which a minor proportion of funds allocated to Pillar 1 can be transferred to Pillar 2. Both compulsory and voluntary forms of modulation are found, the latter implying that Member States can choose to use it to boost spending on rural development.

Thus, the process of policy reform that has resulted in the establishment and expansion of Pillar 2 has involved Member States in a greater commitment to spending from national budgets. This has not always been welcomed. For example, poorer Member States will be less able to provide funds than richer ones. In addition, even in the more affluent countries national commitments will not fit well in a situation in which domestic economic policy is aiming to reduce the level of public spending. For such reasons the national enthusiasm for spending on Pillar 2 activities may be muted. In the UK's case, funds taken for rural development purposes may have an impact on the special rebate on the UK's contribution to the EU budget. Assessment of value-for-money of these schemes has to take into account the fact that, net, a far higher proportion of their costs falls on the national budget than is indicated in the nominal share of co-financing.

Of course, there are many other forms of support outside the coverage of the CAP that national governments can give to their agricultural sectors, directly or indirectly. These do not enter the EU agricultural budget nor, often, national agricultural budgets either. For example, the provision of post-school education and training is common, with university and colleges providing courses that are agriculturally focused but not limited to people working in the agricultural industry or intending to do so (a distinction that could be useful in separating it from vocational training, which is eligible for EU part-funding under the RDP but restricted to people working in agriculture, forestry etc.). There are also many tax concessions and special treatments for farm operators and owners of agricultural land found in EU agriculture (OECD 2005, Hill and Cahill 2007). These may carry implications for national tax revenues and national budgets (such concessions are often termed 'tax expenditures' since the tax forgone is often an alternative to schemes that would otherwise involve government spending) but they lie outside the conventional budgets and accounting systems of either the EU or Member States.

10.11 Living with multiple currencies

Though not strictly a budgetary issue, it is convenient to deal with the problems associated with operating a CAP across countries that use different currencies at this point.

In the development of the EU there is a strong subtext of political union (co-operation). The various stages in building the European Union are covered in Chapter 12. One aspect of political union closely allied to the economic aspects of the EU has been the objective of monetary union, implying the use of a single currency – the euro – and a single central bank – the European Central Bank – that sets basic interest rates. An advantage of a single currency is the elimination of costs associated with exchanging currencies. These include the differences between rates for buying and selling currencies charged by banks and exchange merchants, commission charges, and the costs that firms incur by protecting themselves against future adverse movements in the rates which could affect their profitability (various forms of insurance and hedging). The lower costs and greater price stability are expected to result in the benefit of a raised level of economic activity and hence higher national income and personal prosperity.

This is not the place to review European Monetary Union (EMU) and it must be conceded that not all politicians are in favour of moving to a single currency. At a more practical level, there are implications for the costs of the CAP and the level at which support is offered to agricultural producers. Texts written before the start of EMU and the formation of the Eurozone in 1999 would have contained detailed sections on agri-monetary matters that are now largely consigned to history. Fortunately, the task of explaining the relationship between currencies and the CAP is now far simpler.

The central issue is that decisions by the agricultural Council on support payments, incentives and commodity prices (where still used) are made in euro (€). This presents no problem for farmers in countries that have adopted the euro as their national currency, but outside the Eurozone recipients will normally wish to be paid in their national currency. For these countries (which include the UK) some mechanism has to be used to convert the results of policy decisions into equivalents in national currencies. Because of movements in the commercial exchange rates between currencies (including between national currencies and the euro), the choice of conversion coefficients is a politically sensitive issue, though less now than previously.

Great administrative problems would ensue if the commercial exchange rate for each day were applied to payments (so that the Single Farm Payment would vary in an unpredictable way, dependent on the day on which it was paid). Instead, a reference period is set, and that rate (known as the Green Rate) is applied for the whole season. This also means that farmers see support payments that are stable and predictable within the season, which should help their planning decisions. Clearly, the choice of day or period is critical, and disparities can develop over the course of a year between commercial exchange rates and the Green Rate.

For countries not part of the Eurozone, a fall in the relative value of the national currency will lead to an increase in the sums received in the national currency by their farmers when the Green Rate is next adjusted and realigned. Conversely, a rise in the relative value of the national currency to the euro will lead to a fall in receipts. These changes are outside the direct control of agricultural policy yet can make a substantial impact on the profitability and viability of farming in the countries concerned. Where farmers in non-Eurozone countries see falls in direct aids and market support measures (such as export refunds) because their national currency has risen in value against the euro), the agri-monetary system makes provision for compensation to be made available, but this is optional for the Member State.

Further reading

Ackrill, R. (2000) *The Common Agricultural Policy.* Sheffield Academic Press, Sheffield.

Bos, M. (2010) *The EU budget.* Chapter 3 in Oskam, A., Meester, G. and Silvis, H. (eds) *EU Policy for Agriculture, Food and Rural Areas.* Wageningen Academic Publishers, Wageningen.

European Commission (2009) *Financial Report 2009.* The Commission, Brussels.

Hill, B. and Cahill, C. (2007), 'Taxation of European Farmers', *EuroChoices*, 6 (1), 44–9.

OECD (2002) *The Incidence and Income Transfer Efficiency of Farm Support Measures.* Available online at www.OECD.org/AGR/CA/APM(2001)24/FINAL.

OECD (2005). *Taxation and Social Security in Agriculture.* Organisation for Economic Co-operation and Development, Paris.

OECD (2009) *Agricultural Policies in OECD Countries: Monitoring and Evaluation Report 2009.* Organisation for Economic Cooperation and Development, Paris.

OECD (2010) *Agricultural Policies in OECD Countries at a Glance 2010.* Organisation for Economic Cooperation and Development, Paris.

Useful websites

www.ec.europa.eu/budget/budget_glance/index_en.htm

www.europarl.europa.eu/parliament/

www.farmsubsidy.org

www.OECD.org/

11

UNDERSTANDING THE ASSESSMENT (EVALUATION) OF THE CAP AND RURAL POLICY

Key topics

- The evaluation process in relation to the policy process.
- General issues in evaluation – additionality, establishing the counterfactual.
- Efficiency, economy and effectiveness – the three Es.
- Cost-effectiveness and cost-benefit.
- Valuing the non-market costs and benefits.
- Assessment of programmes and policy as a whole.
- Evaluation within the EU and as applied to the CAP.
- Specific applications in relation to the CAP, including its contribution to the political development of the Union.
- Overview of the CAP in relation to EU agricultural and other objectives.

11.1 Introduction

When, in Chapter 1, the policy process was described, the point was made that the assessment (evaluation) of the performance of policy was part of that process. An understanding of the CAP therefore needs to be aware of how assessment is carried out in the EU. Reviewing effectiveness has always been a part of the European Commission's activities, and today there is a formal system, backed by legislation, to evaluate the performance both of the individual schemes and programmes within agricultural and rural policy and of the CAP as a whole. The rationale is that, on the basis of sound evidence, steps are then possible to improve the situation, in particular by not repeating past mistakes and by avoiding forms of implementation that have proved to be unsatisfactory. The CAP increasingly finds itself having to face competition from (and comparison with) environmental, regional, social and other policies as ways of using the funds that Member States contribute to the EU budget, and evaluations can contribute to decisions on resource allocation. Though as yet there seems to be no compulsion on decision-makers to prove that they have taken evaluations on board, the climate of opinion is towards a general application of assessment in all EU policies. Furthermore, there is now a legal requirement to assess the likely impacts of major changes in policy before they are put in place, including their effects on the environment.

In short, today much interest is shown in the relative success or failure of the CAP and rural policy, and the efficiency with which they use public resources. No longer can the Community budget be seen as a deep well from which to draw money without much thought as to the consequences. The CAP, which still absorbs nearly half of the total spending on all EU policies, has to be seen to be delivering value for money. Evaluation can also serve to increase the accountability of policy-makers and strengthen democratic principles. .

Here the main concepts which form part of assessment are first introduced. Assessment can be undertaken at various levels, and the concepts apply generally. It is most straightforward to apply to the individual schemes or instruments by which policy is implemented (such as national agri-environment schemes, or schemes to support farmers in hill areas for a mix of environmental and social reasons). Assessment can also be used for complete programmes that are made up of several schemes, such as Rural Development Programmes (RDPs) that apply to complete regions (covering farm modernisation, diversification, entry and exit assistance, hill farming support, agri-environment, afforestation etc. – see Chapters 7 and 8) . At this level account will need to be taken both of how well each scheme performs singly and how they work as a set; situations are possible in which each scheme is satisfactory but where the programme as a whole is not optimal, perhaps because too many resources go on some schemes and too few on others, or there are gaps, duplications, conflicts between schemes etc. And assessment can be applied at higher levels (such as Pillar 2 for the EU as a whole, which would need to consider how each RDP performed and contributed to the overall picture) right up to the complete CAP, where the contributions of both Pillars (and anything else that might be deemed to be part of agricultural policy) would need to be judged in relation to the aims of the CAP. At the higher levels the assessment tasks can be very challenging.

11.2 The concept of assessment and its definition

At the outset it is necessary to clarify terminology and basic concepts. Because of a lack of standardisation among authors and institutions, misunderstanding can result from the use of different words to mean the same thing, and the same word having different meanings according to context. For example, terms like assessment, appraisal and evaluation are interchangeable in general use but can have specific technical meanings, so confusion can arise. Whilst not dogmatically defending a single definition against all others, some preliminary explanation of how terms are used here will aid understanding.

The term assessment can be described as the formal process of applying procedures to formulate a set of programme objectives to meet aims, and to provide reliable data upon which judgements concerning the usefulness of the programmes designed to meet those objectives can be made and can be fed back into the policy-making cycle.

Thus, the assessment process is seen to be an integral part of the management of policy and the programmes by which policy is implemented. It is not a discrete, one-off and retrospective activity concerned with the evaluation of the performance of a policy after a number of years, but includes pre-implementation activity, continuous monitoring through the duration of the programmes and important feedbacks of the monitoring information and other evaluation exercises.

Just as policy can be envisaged as a set of inter-related stages, so too can the process of assessment. A useful acronym for recalling the steps in the assessment procedure is ROAME; this stands for **R**ationale, **O**bjectives, **A**ppraisal, **M**onitoring, **E**valuation. Sometimes **F** (for Feedback) is added (thereby forming ROAMEF), since without this, the lessons to be learned from the process are wasted. Each of these stages are dealt with below. Assessment results provide feedback to policy-makers to enable them to assess whether or not the policy effects coincide with the intended objectives and provide the basis of possible policy or programme adjustment.

It should be noted that the stages in the assessment process run parallel to those in the policy process, introduced in Chapter 1. The way the two processes relate are evident from Figure 11.1. The consequence of this close relationship is that the assessment process should be thought of as integrated with policy and not as a bolt-on.

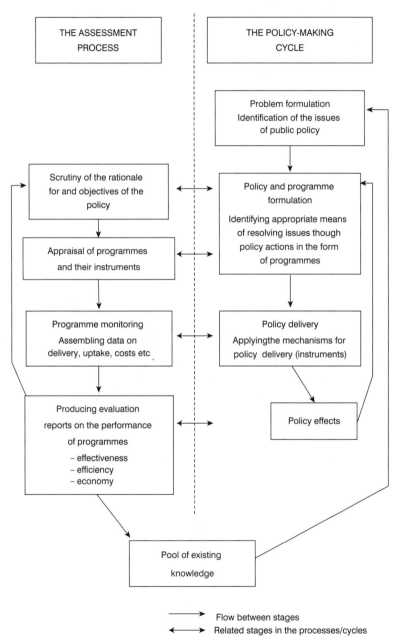

Figure 11.1 The assessment process in relation to the policy-making cycle

The wider implications of the assessment process should be recognised. The results of evaluation reports will contribute to the pool of existing knowledge of real-world conditions and their causes. Assessments can thereby contribute to problem formulation which forms the initial step of the policy-making process. For example, a study of the impact of CAP payments to encourage elderly farmers to retire may throw up important information on the goals and motive of farm operators and their plans to pass their farms to the next generation that helps explain why so many hang on to their businesses even though the incomes they produce are very low. Figure 11.1 shows this particular feedback loop.

Assessments may also point to the need for further, more strategic studies. For example, an evaluation study of farm modernisation schemes intended to make agriculture in a region more competitive might identify that modernised farms use less labour and hence exacerbate a problem of rural depopulation. Resolution of this issue would need research to understand why this occurs in order to fully complete the assessment work process by suggesting modification to existing legislation and policies.

11.3 Checking the rationale and objectives of policy

At the heart of all policy assessment is the questioning of the assumptions upon which the objectives and actions of policies, programmes or schemes are based. If they are false, it is highly likely that public resources devoted to them will be wasted. Consequently, the first step in any assessment is the questioning of the rationale and objectives of the CAP and its various parts. The evaluator will typically be concerned with issues such as the following:

- Why is the policy, programme or scheme being undertaken? What is the evidence that there are problems that need to be tackled?
- What is intervention using public resources intended to achieve (including who is intended to benefit)?
- What are assumptions underlying the actions being taken? Is there a pathway of logic between the interventions and the alleviation of the problems being addressed?
- Does the action conform with broader (non-agricultural) goals?

This stage of the assessment cycle is also involved with probing the indicators by which the success or failure of the policy, programme or scheme can be judged. For example, if there is a scheme (within a Rural Development Programme) to encourage farmers to set up new enterprises on their farms (such as holiday cottages, or small workshops to be let to local people) some way of measuring the amount of these activities will be needed (perhaps, the number of beds available in an area over a given time period, or the floor space to let) and some criterion of success established (such as raising the number of beds by 10 per cent).

11.3.1 Consistency of the hierarchy of objectives

Objectives exist at different levels. Clarity and consistency are important at all of them. If objectives are not clear and consistent with other parallel or higher aims, then the policy performance will be seriously constrained. Thus, all assessment work puts heavy emphasis on the quality of the objectives.

The CAP is one of a number of common policies that attempt to contribute to achieving the EU's broad goals through dealing with (in particular) food security and safety, the

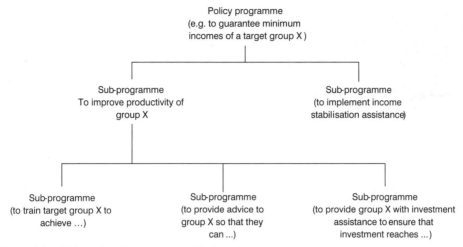

Figure 11.2 A hierarchy of programme objectives

environment, and the welfare of the agricultural community (see the objectives of the CAP described in Chapter 2). In turn, the CAP's various objectives are broken down and handled by programmes and sub-programmes, ultimately leading to the various schemes for operating direct payments, market support mechanisms, adjustment assistance and agri-environmental payments etc. that attempt to bring about the intended impact on the target groups in the agricultural and related industries.

As was described in Chapter 1, it should be possible to construct a hierarchy of objectives which relates to the various levels of policy operation; Figure 11.2 provides an example. An evaluator will wish to see evidence for a hierarchy being in place (though it may not be formally written out) and examine it for consistency between those at the lowest and higher levels. Lower levels in the hierarchy should provide the answers to how the higher objectives are to be achieved; the lower ones are intermediate to the final higher ones. Alternatively, the reason why objectives of lower levels, down to the implementation of schemes, have been set should be clear from the next higher level in the hierarchy. In a well-designed hierarchy, individual schemes should also be consistent with others, so there should be no examples of schemes that work in opposite directions (for example, some encouraging farms to amalgamate while others split them up) or that duplicate each other. Preferably there should be no gaps, and opportunities for synergy should be grasped (that is, where schemes work together to achieve an outcome better than they would in isolation).

Typically, objectives at the higher levels are couched only in general terms. This is true of the CAP (see Chapter 2). However, those of the lower levels will be more explicit and testable (i.e. when looking back it is easier to see whether they have been achieved, completely or partially). Usually lower level objectives will be quantifiable, using appropriate indicators and criteria by which the achievement of success can be measured (such as, numbers of jobs created by schemes in Rural Development Programmes and cost per job). Evaluation of individual schemes will often therefore be more straightforward than that of whole programmes or policies.

Success in achieving objectives in the higher levels of the hierarchy depends on cause and effect flowing from the lower to upper levels, an assumption that must not go unchallenged and un-investigated. For example, if the aim is to raise farmers' incomes by making their businesses more competitive and productive, does this actually happen, or is the net effect to drive down prices of agricultural commodities, leaving incomes unchanged but forcing many small farmers out of the industry?

Objective-setting for public policy interventions is a top-down procedure in which the objectives of individual schemes are derived from the higher objectives of programmes and policies. This does not preclude management responsible for operating the delivery process setting more detailed objectives and targets; for example, managing authorities in Member States may decide to set as a process objective that 80 per cent of applications for farm diversification grants must be handled within three months. Such process objectives can be useful tools though, if given too much prominence, managers may become primarily concerned with achieving performance targets (such as rapid turn-around of applications, minimising the costs of delivery and maintaining staff morale) and can lose sight of the underlying aims of policy. It is the responsibility of senior administrators to ensure that this does not happen.

Putting such a conceptual framework into practice encounters two main difficulties that, nevertheless, should not be allowed to disrupt the logic and force behind the hierarchy of objectives. First, it is much easier to apply a hierarchy when starting out on a new policy area than when taking over an existing set of policy measures which have not started from a unified set of objectives. An advantage felt by the CAP's Pillar 2 rural development policy is that, because Rural Development Programmes only run for seven years, each has to be designed afresh, which gives an opportunity to re-examine the hierarchy of objectives, though in practice much is carried over from one period to the next. In contrast, many of the CAP's commodity regimes ran for many decades without serious challenge of their objectives or the assumptions behind them. Second, there will be unforeseen outcomes in terms of side effects and interactions of unexpected magnitudes between individual programmes and schemes which may result in conflicts, needing modification in measures to minimise them. For example, there may be a genuine conflict of objectives between different government departments. This conflict may be on the basis of operations (e.g. the imposition of a measure has implications for another policy) or resources (e.g. limitations of financial allocations). Such conflicts should be acknowledged and an attempt made to quantify the desired balance. Thus, an environmental objective to reduce nitrogen pollution in groundwater may involve costs for farmers (in terms of reduced crop yields) and this may conflict with income support objectives of agricultural policy. The temptation will be to say that water quality policies should 'be in balance' with those covering the agricultural sector, although this is clearly not a satisfactorily quantified objective. A more desirable approach would be to seek a compromise, for example through introducing compensation of some kind, that is much more amenable to quantification.

In some cases, establishing testable objectives may be resisted as inappropriate for political reasons. Clearly where national interest is at stake this is an important constraint. For example, should the UK push for more precision in terms of income objectives for CAP policies, which may lead to a more efficient allocation of public funds but which may also involve additional net costs to the UK Exchequer (as could happen if CAP support were to be more targeted at low-income farm households which tend to be found predominantly in Italy, Greece and the new Member States). Keeping the aims of income support rather vague may enable payments to relatively high-income UK farm families to be continued and the UK government to achieve a politically acceptable balance between what it contributes to the EU budget and what it draws out. Clearly each country has to make a judgement between a more efficient CAP and budgetary self-interest.

11.3.2 Defining the target population

Who forms the target population for a programme should form part of the statement of objectives, since unless the target is clearly defined it will be difficult to determine the extent to which these people are reached. Once defined, assessing the participation of different groups will be crucial in determining the success of the policy, programme or scheme. Of particular interest will be coverage and bias; coverage refers to the extent to which a policy enjoys widespread target population participation and bias is the extent to which sub-groups of the target population participate. Clearly the two are related as a policy that achieves total coverage is obviously not biased in its coverage. However, few policies ever enjoy total coverage, hence bias is typically an issue.

It has already been demonstrated (Chapter 4) that, while the CAP is concerned with targeting the 'agricultural community', nowhere has this term been defined in EU legislation. The Single Farm Payment Scheme, which currently accounts for the overwhelming major share of the agricultural budget, bases its payments on a mix of past entitlements and farm area. There is no attempt to focus on those who might be mainly dependent on farming for their livelihood or whose incomes were particularly low. Whether this failure to specify the target population is deliberate, a political convenience, or results from a naive idea of the real nature of the agricultural community is open to debate. However, it is clear that a greater degree of targeting of income aid is likely to result in a more effective policy.

11.3.3 Identifying assumptions

At all levels, the design of policy involves assumptions that there is a chain of causality between planned actions and intended outcome – that there is a path of logic linking the achievement of intermediate goals with desired final changes. In the hierarchy of objectives in Figure 11.2 it is assumed that increased levels of investment (encouraged by the sub-programme to aid investment) would lead to higher productivity on farms, which would lead to higher incomes. Cause and effect assumptions link the lower levels of objectives to the higher ones in the hierarchy. Similarly, they also link intermediate outputs and final outcomes of individual schemes and may be particularly significant where a long time elapses between instigating a policy action and when its final outcome may become apparent. Consider, for example, the schemes that provide subsidised vocational training to people working in agriculture as a way of improving the industry's productivity and competitiveness (encountered in Chapter 7). While it is easy to measure the output of such schemes in terms of the number of people trained or hours of training delivered, the results of such training in terms of the benefits later accruing to the people who underwent training and the businesses on which they work is harder to quantify, and the outcome (or impact) that this training has on the performance of the agricultural industry as a whole is even harder to identify and measure. Yet the provision of training using public funds is repeatedly supported on the assumption (or belief) that such courses do lead to benefits.

While it would be impracticable to scrutinise every link in the chain, many assumptions are taken for granted and not thoroughly considered. Therefore any evaluation process should pay attention to the assumptions about causal links that are likely to be critical.

Another type of common assumption concerns what is happening in the external environment. The operation of a policy is seldom the only factor that determines whether its objectives are achieved or not. External factors are changing all the time and it is often difficult to disentangle the outcomes attributable to the policy inputs and those that would have happened anyway or came about for other reasons entirely. Again, by breaking objectives into a hierarchical order and focusing on the cause and effect linkages between them, should expose where there is a need to examine other variables that can influence the outcome of a policy.

11.4 Appraisal

Appraisal is an *ex ante* activity (looking forwards before the event) which helps to improve decision-taking by considering whether a proposed policy intervention is likely to be worthwhile and comparing in advance the different options for implementing it.

This exercise is akin to that of a farmer considering whether or not to buy additional land; he would attempt to rank, on one side, the known and likely costs of the purchase and on the other the additional income which the land might bring to his business, also taking into account the riskiness of falling short or exceeding expectations. Bearing in mind that income generated some time in the future is worth less now than income received today, discounting would be applied to estimate the aggregate present value of this extra income stretching into the distance (typically taking the cost of borrowing from banks as the rate at which to discount future income flows), which could then be viewed against the cost of the investment. The land purchase could also be compared with other forms of investment, for example in more modern machinery, or even in acquiring assets off the farm (starting up a local shop, or buying government securities).

A policy administrator will undertake a similar exercise, ranking probable costs against probable benefits for a range of possible instruments but, as noted in Chapter 5, factors other than cost–benefit analyses will need to be considered. For example, the capacity of the administrative system to deliver the selected instruments has to be reviewed, as have the attitudes of the individuals and firms affected and interactions with other areas of policy. An appraisal for a particular scheme, such as the use of financial incentives for farmers to convert surplus farm buildings to tourist accommodation, should include estimates of the number of potential recipients of grants, the likely rates of application and uptake among these farmers, the total cost to the farmers, the cost to public funds, the net income generated to farmer households, and so on. Sometimes a minimum rate of return on capital will be stipulated as a benchmark. The amount of 'red tape' involved will need scrutiny; schemes that make the application process too onerous to its intended beneficiaries, involving them with high private costs, are unlikely to be successful. Previous experience with similar programmes or schemes can be a valuable guide to risks of things going wrong. Clearly, the provision of on-farm tourist accommodation must not conflict with other policy aims on preventing encroachment of housing developments in protected landscapes.

Often the anticipated benefits are not easily quantified; for example, the aim might be to create better access to the countryside, in which case some value might be attachable to the enjoyment to be gained by the general public. The difficulties encountered with non-market goods in appraisal are the same as when these items enter into evaluation exercises, and they are dealt with more fully in that context below. Sometimes, as with pollution control aimed at preventing a catastrophic biological impact, appraisal might primarily concern itself with finding the least-cost way of achieving this; it assumes that the benefits exceed the costs, though the judgement of this is put off to later evaluation rather than avoided.

Appraisal is now formally required when drawing up Rural Development Programmes under the CAP's Pillar 2 (called '*ex ante* evaluation') and for other proposed major policy changes ('Impact Assessments') (see Section 11.8 below). Some proposals should be discarded at this appraisal stage because they are not likely to be successful in terms of impact or to meet other criteria of success. For example, the UK rejected CAP schemes of grants to assist young entrants set up as farmers that could have formed part of the Rural Development Programmes that started in 2000 and 2007 (see Chapter 7). Similarly the use of some instruments might be rejected, for example tax breaks if the target group are unlikely to be in a position to benefit because their incomes are too low for them to pay tax. However, it is clear that political factors sometimes weigh heavily in the decision to introduce measures. For example, in the light of past experience of the failure of the offer of pensions to farmers in the UK to encourage the elderly to leave this industry, it is surprising that such schemes are still considered periodically in the UK, but they are.

11.5 Monitoring

Monitoring refers to collecting information on progress towards achieving objectives as it happens. Often a large volume of data is generated through the administration of policy (for example, the details of subsidies paid to farmers under both Pillars of the CAP), though with some forms of policy instruments (such as legislation banning silage effluent pollution of water-courses) monitoring will have to be planned and carried out more purposefully. Questions to be posed include: is the policy reaching targeted groups or areas and how do these compare with expectations, are the necessary inputs (funding, administrative capacity etc.) being provided, are the original intentions being complied with, how effective is the management of the policy? Sometimes monitoring will enable an unsuccessful programme to be halted rapidly; if no-one applies for a particular financial incentive, then there is clearly something wrong with the policy's design or the performance of the delivery mechanism. Sometimes the administration procedures might be too complex and inhibiting; while the idea of means-testing assistance to farmers suffering from low incomes is attractive in principle, it could be that those in greatest need are also those who would not, or could not, fill in the various forms which would get them aid. Somewhat better-off and more capable farmers can cope with the paperwork and therefore secure the benefits. This is an example of adverse selection, where the system works towards benefiting those who are not the prime target.

Monitoring also provides much, though not all, of the data necessary for the later task of evaluation.

11.6 Evaluation

Though the term *evaluation* is often used in a general sense, it has a more specific meaning as a stage in the assessment process. Evaluation can be described as follows:

Evaluation consists of those *ex post* (after the event) activities and procedures which are carried out to measure the effectiveness, efficiency and economy with which policies are applied.

Effectiveness, efficiency and economy are known as the 'Three Es'. Effectiveness is concerned with whether the intervention (policy, programme, scheme or other action such as legislation) achieves an impact. If there is no effect, there is little point in taking the evaluation further. Efficiency looks at the value of the effect and compares it to the costs. To justify the use of public resources the benefits of a policy action must be at least as great as the costs. Sometimes a big effect can be achieved, but the cost of doing so may be so great as to make the action inefficient. Economy looks at whether a particular effect could be achieved is a less costly way, and is a useful concept when the benefits from policy action cannot easily be expressed in money terms. For example, if an environmental improvement can be achieved in more than one way, which was the least costly?

Evaluation enables the decisions taken as a result of appraisal to be reviewed rigorously in the light of evidence on what has actually happened and with the knowledge of any changes in the external environment which may have occurred in the meantime. Data collected during monitoring will be used in evaluation, though additional information will generally be needed that will have to be collected specially (thus involving further costs). The outcome of evaluation can normally be incorporated in a report that preferably should be published, since administrations are more likely to heed the results if aware that they are open to public scrutiny.[1] In order to protect the rigour of evaluation, it is desirable that the persons carrying out the evaluation are independent of the department administering the policy, or at least for the evaluation team to have some independent members. Regulations on rural development in the EU stipulate the independence of evaluators and set out a timetable for the various stages of the process.

The methodological challenge in undertaking an evaluation of policy can be formidable. Here are some of the major factors of which the evaluator of the CAP and its programmes and schemes has to be aware. Though here we consider them at the evaluation stage, many of these issues would also be confronted during appraisal.

11.6.1 Breadth of coverage – drawing the boundary round an evaluation

A policy intervention may invoke multiple consequences, and some of these will be side effects which can be important to an assessment of the performance of the overall policy process. For example, supporting the incomes of farmers in ways that encourage them to expand production and to use their land more intensively may have a negative impact on biodiversity and landscape appearance. There may also be effects on wages in the local economy and the viability of rural communities. An evaluator will need to decide which and how many of these side effects to bring into consideration – where to draw the boundary around the evaluation. Sometimes they will be trifling and best ignored but in other circumstances they may be of major importance. Evaluations that fail to encompass major impacts, where intended or not, will not be considered satisfactory. Capturing both side effects and the various multiplier effects (second- or third-round effects, such as when the higher incomes of farmers cause them to buy more from other sectors, which in turn raises income there and further increases the demand for goods and services provided by farmers) demands a great deal of the methodology and good judgement by the evaluator. These problems are magnified when a stream of benefits or costs is expected to flow over a long period of years.

11.6.2 Causality and measurement

The challenge is to design research to capture and measure the effects and to subject the data to analysis which will attribute causality – that is, the extent to which changes that have been identified through monitoring are the result of the policy instrument, or were caused by other factors. For example, if there is a rise in farm incomes, is this due to actions under the CAP or to rising prices on world commodity markets? There are often many linkages involved, and the influence of external factors can disrupt the best research design. In practice, the complexity is such that quantitative evaluation procedures are rarely if ever sufficiently comprehensive or accurate to allow conclusions to be drawn. A degree of subjective judgement is often needed, though by careful design of the evaluation process the areas where subjectivity is applied can be reduced.

11.6.3 Additionality

Critical considerations in relation to evaluation methodology are the issues of additionality and displacement. It is important to establish that impact is additional to what would have occurred anyway. For example, if a scheme is introduced to encourage elderly farmers to retire, account must be taken of how many would have retired anyway within the time period of the policy. Additionality aims to identify the additional (net) effect because of the policy. This involves establishing what would have happened in the absence of the policy – termed the counter-factual. Displacement (the extent to which impact occurs at the expense of 'stealing' from elsewhere) takes various forms:

- **Over time**: where a policy action (for example, an investment grant) may bring forward an investment, or delay it if the grant will be available only at some time in the future, but maybe leave investment in the longer term unchanged;
- **Over place**: for example, where higher grants to investments in upland areas can cause firms to switch their spending to these locations if they own farms in both;
- **Over sector**: for example, in rural areas the available labour force may be small, so a project that creates a significant number of new jobs may attract resources from existing firms, whose output may therefore decline.

Closely associated with additionality is the concept of deadweight. This is use of resources that fails to achieve a net effect because the change would have occurred anyway. For example, payments to farmers, at a standard rate per hectare, to convert to organic production would be regarded as deadweight if they would have done so for other reasons if no grant were available. (It should be noted that this term deadweight is also used for expenditure that goes to recipients other than those targeted. For example, in giving support to the poorest farmers, generally found on small farms, large payments may be made inadvertently to large, high-income producers.)

Establishing additionality is one of the evaluators' major challenges. Various techniques help. Baseline studies describe the situation before policies, programmes or schemes commence and provide an opportunity to compare situations prior to and after policy implementation. Rural Development Programmes now contain baseline information (key indicators) for the start of their seven-year periods by which progress at the end can be judged, though other influences may also cause change and must be considered when attempts are made to establish the counter-factual. Control groups of people, firms or areas not affected by the policy are useful for comparison, though often these are unlikely to be exact. For example, when looking at the effect of support to hill farms to enable them to overcome the extra costs they face because of natural handicaps, comparison with changes seen among livestock farms in lowland areas is undermined because their production systems are likely to be very different (their types of animal, intensity of stocking, climatic conditions etc.). Comparing what happens in alternating periods when the policy is applied and when it does not (policy-on/off) may be of some use, though if farmers are aware of this in advance they may adjust their behaviour appropriately, delaying or advancing actions to take advantage of incentives (an example of displacement over time). Each offers some indication as to whether the measured outcome of the policy inputs is due to the policy or some external factor and to identify the net effects of a policy beyond what would have happened anyway (the counter-factual).

11.6.4 Forms of evaluation

There is a spectrum of types of evaluation, ranging from detecting whether the policy has had any impact at all (if not, there is no point in going on to a more complex form of evaluation) to those which attempt to encompass all the costs and benefits associated with particular policy programmes.

Impact evaluation. The starting point for impact evaluation is the identification and clarification of the intended outcome of the policy, programme or scheme. In some cases it will not be possible to measure a goal precisely. For example, a policy intended to improve the living standard of farmers and their families will soon run up against the fact that 'living standard' is not a concept that is easily measured and, in practice, no data system exists for agriculture. If exact measures are not obtainable, suitable proxy indicators should be chosen. In this case, the disposable income of the farm household is often used, as this is what is available to spend on consumption or to save. The need to select indicators will have been encountered at an earlier stage in the assessment process, since clarification of objectives of policy inevitably draws attention to them.

Proxy indicators may be particularly necessary where objectives are set far forward into the future. In such circumstances, the objectives can be represented by indicators that relate to intermediate objectives, which form steps towards the ultimate objective. For instance, when vocational training is used as a means of improving the productivity and competitiveness of agriculture, the outcome is experienced some time after the training is given and stretches over many years. Even the results as seen in the earnings of individuals and the profits of the farms on which they work may take time to materialise, especially if the trained people choose to move between farms or even leave agriculture altogether. The most readily measured indicator is the output of the training (number of people trained, or number of training days delivered), but its use in evaluation depends heavily on the assumption that training leads to the desired outcomes.

Another point about the coverage of impact evaluation is the need to cover the policy *delivery system.* This is extremely important because the success or otherwise of a policy will depend on the way in which it is implemented. Thus, for example, it is possible for a grant scheme to be entirely appropriate in terms of concept to meet the objectives set for it but to fall down because of shortcomings in the delivery system. There are many possible reasons for this, including the breakdown of communications so that information on the scheme may not get to the target group (e.g. a newspaper notice intended to reach small farmers in hill areas will be ineffective unless it is carried by the papers or magazines they read) or the mechanism for administering the assistance may be inappropriate (e.g. the government office may be wrongly situated or have opening hours which are highly inconvenient for visits from farmers, or the details may be inappropriate, such as the demand that farmers provide proof of current income levels before aid is granted where farm incomes can only be calculated at the end of the financial year). These two aspects are termed access and specification. Improving access may include active campaigns to recruit participants, the provision of transport or visits by officials to the target population. In effect, the scrutiny of the delivery system amounts to an assessment of the efficiency with which managers in the public service deploy their resources (facilities, and financial and human resources). What is extremely important to untangle is whether it is the method of delivery which is at fault or the inherent nature of the policy intervention itself.

Closely related to impact analysis is the concept of *cost-effectiveness* or economy. This is used in contexts where there are clear policy choices involving alternative schemes which a government can potentially fund, or under fixed budgetary conditions. Thus, if the aim is to create employment in the countryside, this approach would be concerned with the cost per job of the various alternative ways of generating additional employment. For cost effectiveness measures both inputs and outputs need to be quantified, but only the inputs are expressed in monetary terms. Cost effectiveness measures allow the comparison and ranking of different programmes or schemes.

Because policy programmes are administered by bureaucracies, there is a danger of the objectives of the bureaucracy being substituted for those of the underlying policy. For example, one possible proxy for activity of a particular programme is the amount of money it uses; schemes that are taken up more strongly by farmers will need bigger budgets. However, spending money then becomes the aim of the administrators; among bureaucrats their performance as administrators may be judged by the size of the budgets they control, not by the effectiveness of the policy this spending supports. Consequently, the performance of the underlying policies may be left unquestioned.

Economic efficiency evaluation goes a step further than impact analysis and encompasses the values of both benefits and costs. In its most extreme form, termed cost-benefit analysis, all the various costs and benefits to society will be identified and expressed in money terms and compared with each other. There is a need to be sensitive to quality of output as well as its quantity.

Comprehensive cost-benefit analysis is difficult to apply. It faces two distinct problems: first, the identification of all costs and benefits; and, second, the expression of these costs and benefits in monetary terms. Agriculture is connected to the rest of the economy by a network of relationships, and farming change also has obvious repercussions for the environment, appearance of the landscape, composition of rural society and so on. Policy which affects agriculture is likely to ripple out to all these related parts, so in evaluating policy there will always be some dispute about how wide to cast the net. Where to put the cut-off line is inevitably a matter of judgement. A government department administering the CAP is likely to take a relatively narrow view as it will be primarily concerned with the agricultural sector; it is not likely to consider whether the expenditure could be better spent in another sector of the economy.

In practice, when evaluating the economic efficiency of particular programmes and schemes, a narrow approach is often taken, in which only the closest benefits and costs are covered, such as might happen when the impact on farm incomes of a particular scheme to provide management advice is evaluated. Even then, typically a number of the costs and benefits are intangible and difficult to measure and quantify. The various issues to be considered in relation to expressing these costs in financial terms are touched on below.

11.6.5 Valuing costs and benefits

When valuing costs and benefits, for many items a market price can be utilised to illustrate its cost or worth to society. However, circumstances may occur where such a price fails to reflect adequately social costs, or a policy output does not have a market price. To overcome these problems 'shadow prices' are normally estimated. One example is the cost of labour. Some authorities suggest that in developing countries the cost to society of labour used in rural projects should be valued not at the full wage rate but at zero, on the assumption that all new jobs created are taken up by previously unemployed people. Naturally this can make a great difference to whether a project's benefits exceed its costs.

Another issue concerns who bears the costs and who receives the benefits; that is, the distributional and equity aspects of a policy action. For example, if policy is aimed at supporting low-income farm families, the costs and benefits must be weighted accordingly. Income given to poor farm households should be valued more than that which goes to those who are not part of this target group.

Mention has already been made of discounting incomes (and costs) that lie in the future. But at what rate? Choice of rate can make a substantial difference to cost–benefit calculations. The appropriate rate will depend upon a variety of factors, but it generally reflects the rate of return which funds utilised in the policy could have achieved elsewhere. This is often referred to as the opportunity cost of capital (what an amount can be expected to gain if invested elsewhere in the private market). An alternative approach is to use a 'social discount rate', usually a lower figure which implies a relatively greater value to the benefits to future generations than do commercial rates. In order to overcome the problem of setting this rate empirically, in government-funded policies the choice of discount rate is often set administratively.

Particular problems surround the value of non-market goods and services, items that do not have a market-determined price. This occurs most notably in the area of evaluation of environmental factors (biodiversity, landscape etc.) that are of increasing importance to the aims of agricultural and rural development policies in the EU. As such, they constitute a major and increasingly significant component of evaluation exercises related to the CAP. Several methodologies are used to value such items and include the contingent valuation, contingent ranking, hedonic pricing and travel cost methods. These are outlined in Box 11.1.

The availability of data (or the cost involved in their collection) may be a crucial determinant of the choice of technique, as will the nature of the policy setting. In the context of rural policy issues, hedonic pricing and travel cost methods are the most appropriate for the valuation of rural amenities such as areas of outstanding natural beauty, environmentally sensitive areas and national parks. However, they only capture benefits accruing to direct users of an environmental good (people who buy houses or travel to sites). If there are significant benefits to members of society who do not participate directly in rural pursuits, these methods would understate the value of the countryside. In such circumstances the contingent valuation technique would be more appropriate as this could cover both users and non-users.

Box 11.1 Approaches to valuing non-market goods

Contingent valuation: Surveys are used to ascertain the 'willingness to pay' or 'willingness to give up' consumption of a public good. The intention is to simulate a market demand curve for the public good. The principal sources of bias are:

Strategic: the respondent believes that others may bear the cost of any actual change in environmental quality and so will overstate his willingness to pay for the change. Alternatively, if the respondent believes that he may be taxed by the amount of his stated willingness to pay, the incentive would be to understate his true preferences.

Information: When the survey is based on a hypothetical situation the response will typically not be based upon the same information as a real market activity and as such, may differ from the reaction to a similar situation based on actual past experience.

Hypothetical: This occurs when the interviewer only obtains hypothetical answers to hypothetical questions. To avoid this, the respondent must not only understand the proposed change and judge it to be feasible but must also believe that his answers will have some bearing on the magnitude of the change in the environment.

Instrumental: The respondent's valuation may depend upon the proposed means of payment and the degree of substitution possibilities that this offers.

The contingent ranking method: This is a variation of the contingent valuation method but preferences are ranked rather than any attempt being made to simulate a market demand curve.

Hedonic pricing method involves imputation of non-market good values from observed prices of closely associated market goods. The technique relies on the ability of the evaluator to identify a set of market goods and expenditure which may reasonably be assumed to represent values placed on the non-market good. For example, individuals choose the level of consumption of a non-market good such as freedom from noise pollution through their choice of residential location. Property prices on the edge of a busy road will be lower than for similar houses in quiet streets nearby. The difference represents the value people put on the absence of traffic noise. Unfortunately, house prices also reflect a number of other factors (number of rooms, age etc.). Distinguishing the effect of noise nuisance is therefore only likely to be approximate.

The travel cost method attempts to value a non-market good by using the amount of money that people are prepared to pay to visit/avoid a non-market good. For example, demand for a wildlife site can be estimated by assessing the amount of money that people are willing to spend to travel to the site to see wildlife. In order to undertake such an estimate data on the number of visits, the fixed price of a visit and income levels are required. Ideally, allowances should be made for the opportunity costs of travel time (such as any loss of earnings) as well as the direct monetary cost of travel. A complication with the technique is that the utility people derive from the visit may not depend merely on a site visit but also on the journey itself. Consequently, there may be difficulty in valuing travel time to the site, especially for very short trips. Also, by the nature of the technique it can only be of use in valuing non market goods that are site specific.

11.7 Assessing entire policy areas

In principle, the assessment process is applicable at various levels in policy for agriculture and rural areas, from overall policy at the top, through the programmes by which policy is implemented, down to individual grant schemes of management agreements on single farms. Although often associated with government and EU actions which involve public funds, in theory the process can be applied to all forms of intervention, including the use of tax concessions (or penalties) and planning controls. In order that meaningful evaluation can take place, objectives should be testable (which will often mean quantifiable) and should carefully define the target population.

In reality, the problems of evaluating whole policy areas (such as the CAP) are far greater than when individual programmes (or projects) are evaluated. There are several reasons for this. There may in practice be no consistent overall policy with a set of testable and coherent objectives at a high level. A seen in Chapter 2, the CAP's original objectives contained many imprecise terms (most notably the aims of 'reasonable' food prices for consumers and the 'fair standard of living' for the agricultural community). Often there are some inherent trade-offs between objectives, some of which are difficult or impossible to quantify. For example, increased food supply may mean environmental damage or loss of landscape features, but the precise relationship between the two and hence the optimum balance from the view of society is uncertain. We have also seen that policy objectives are not static. The CAP's objectives have evolved from those set out in the 1957 Treaty of Rome, with *Agenda 2000* adding some new objectives and omitting others. Broadening the CAP to include policy for rural areas (Pillar 2) has added further complications since aims are no longer restricted to the production of goods and services traditionally classed as agricultural, but now extend to other economic activities taking place in rural areas and the well-being of rural residents, whether or not they are involved in the use of farm resources. Where objectives relate to non-market goods and services (such as conserving biodiversity), though there are ways of attaching money values to them there may be a lack of agreement as to what these values should be. An evaluation of a broad policy area may have to be content with just noting these conflicts and difficulties.

Another complication is that not all policy objectives are set out explicitly. Though the European Commission may try to steer funds to those countries with the greatest apparent needs for policy intervention, in practice allocations will be heavily influenced by political factors. This means that there are likely to be hidden items on the agenda in decision-making, such as ensuring that Member States draw from the EU budget amounts commensurate with their contributions. Once funds have been allocated between Member States, the fact that public funds are being very effective at solving a problem in country X will be of only limited concern to the representatives of country Y. If the target is to reach some sort of commonality in result, the inefficient use of funds may be used as a lever to obtain *more* funds to achieve the desired ends. When dealing with such situations evaluators of policy have to face up to political reality and concede that their analysis only provides a partial coverage of objectives.

Practical issues are also important. Agricultural policy interventions typically build up in an *ad hoc* way in response to particular urgent problems ('firefighting') rather than as part of a coherent strategy. The introduction of milk quotas in 1984 as the response to a rapidly escalating crisis in the dairy sector that impacted on the overall EU budget balance was an example. There was little time to consider the implications for other sectors, or how quotas might be phased out. Periodically the various programmes will need rationalisation within an overall set of objectives, so that inconsistencies are removed and overlaps reduced. For the EU, *Agenda 2000* was an example of this with respect to the CAP.

Another practical issue is that policy is frequently *fragmented*. Typically, not only are policy decisions taken along sectoral lines, but they are also administered sectorally (such as by different Directorates General of the European Commission – see Chapter 3). Where policy responsibilities overlap (such as for rural areas where agricultural, regional and environmental administrations are involved, each with its distinct culture and sets of objectives and with relatively weak links between them), it may be hard for the evaluators to come to a picture of the EU overall policy performance. Even within agricultural policy, there is fragmentation and conflict of objectives. Success by the part of the Commission's Directorate-General for Agriculture and Rural Development responsible for providing direct payments for farmers can conflict with the aims of the sections concerned with making the industry more competitive, since when farming incomes are high the pressure for farms to enlarge and modernise and for the occupiers of small, low income holdings to exit from the industry is less. Good performance in one of the two areas does not necessarily imply good performance for agricultural policy as a whole.

Nevertheless, some general principles can be set out for a broad view of the performance of an entire policy area. It will be necessary to ensure that:

(a) there is broad agreement on a general set of objectives for the policy area among the individuals and organisations responsible for carrying out the policy;
(b) the objectives of individual programmes are set within the overall hierarchy of objectives for the policy area, so that overlap and conflicts are minimised;
(c) assessment of individual programmes is undertaken and adjustments made on the basis of the results, so that each programme performs as well as is possible;
(d) the performances of individual programmes are considered together, so that reallocation between them is possible.

11.8 Evaluation of EU policy for agriculture and rural development in practice

11.8.1 Evaluation at programme and scheme level

As described by the European Commission, 'evaluation is a judgement of interventions according to their results, impacts and needs they aim to satisfy'.

> Evaluation generates a wealth of relevant information that is essential to evidence-based decision-making for planning, designing and implementing EU policies as well as for managing the institution. Evaluation also enhances the legitimacy of decisions and the accountability of decision-makers. Moreover, where evaluation results are communicated properly, they enhance transparency and democratic accountability. Last but not least, evaluation also supports the Commission in better communicating the added value of the EU to the European citizen
>
> (Commission 2007).

In the EU, commitment to evaluation has gained weight over time and is now an integral part of the policy process. It started rather patchily in certain sectors, but from the mid-1990s was given a boost by the initiative to reform the management of EU spending, known as Sound and Efficient Management (SEM). In 2000, the Commission started a process of reforms that included encouraging evaluation generally. Now, legislation is in place that 'requires' impact assessments of major policy initiatives (introduced 2002 – see below) and the Financial Regulation of 2006 introduced general requirements for evaluations to be carried out. Today, Directorates-General concerned with spending EU funds each have their own Evaluation Units that are responsible for evaluations of their policy areas (a decentralised system that recognises the differences in approach that may be necessary) but with DG-Budget taking a lead role in setting guidelines and good practice, maintaining networks between staff undertaking this type of work and in providing training.

With agricultural and rural development policy, growth in the use of evaluation has been curiously lop-sided. It was introduced formally as part of the expansion of the Structural Funds in 1988. The legislation that enabled EU funds to be used to assist regions that were lagging behind (many of which were rural) and to help agriculture adjust to CAP reform (including rural development in regions that were otherwise performing adequately) also required evaluation of the expenditure to be undertaken. Following this lead, both the Rural Development Regulations covering programmes for 2000–06 (1257/1999) and 2007–13 (1698/2005) have required explicitly that evaluation takes place, set out the various stages in its process, state who is responsible for carrying it out and emphasise that evaluators should be independent. Thus, it was the CAP's structural policy programmes (comprising schemes to modernise and adjust the sizes of holdings, encourage older farmers to retire, improve marketing etc.) that were the earliest to be evaluated, though these together have accounted for only a minor part of total EU spending (even now barely a fifth of the EU agricultural budget). The much more expensive part of agricultural spending (the commodity regimes implemented from the early 1960s and transformed into the Single Farm Payment system from 2005) largely escaped evaluation until relatively recently. However, evaluations covering Pillar 1 are now conducted for the main schemes and programmes. Those published since 1998 are listed in the Annex of this chapter.

Evaluation is seen in its most systematic form when applied to programmes operated under these two Rural Development Regulations, which form the major part of the CAP's Pillar 2. For each seven-year cycle a well-defined series of studies has to be carried out. Each has to be published so that all stakeholders (including farmers and their representatives, other government departments and other Member States) can learn from these studies:

- First, there has to be an *ex ante* evaluation (which might also be called an appraisal of the RDP according to the terminology outlined above), which also establishes a baseline for key indicators, so that in retrospect it is possible to see how conditions have improved (or not). This *ex ante* study has to ensure that the RDP describes adequately the rural problems the region faces, conducts a SWOT analysis (listing the Strengths, Weaknesses, Opportunities and Threats faced there), specifies objectives, and describes the proposed schemes that are to be used to tackle them. Each scheme within the RDP has to be assigned quantified targets. The European Commission establishes Common Evaluation Questions (CEQs) corresponding to each Chapter in the Rural Development Regulation (such as afforestation, organic farming, investment in agricultural holdings etc.) and specifies indicators (numbers of jobs created by afforestation etc.) that are applied to evaluations across all Member States and that therefore are capable of being used to give an overall picture of rural development policy in the EU.

- The second is a *mid-term evaluation* which gives an interim judgement of the effectiveness, efficiency and economy of the schemes being undertaken and the RDP as a whole. Its timing partway through the period covered by the RDP allows adjustments to be made for the latter years if these are needed, for example in the delivery systems or the target groups of beneficiaries. If uptake of a scheme is disappointing, the cause may be because farmers find the application procedure complicated rather than because there is something seriously wrong in the rationale of the intervention. Interim answers to the CEQs are provided, and progress against targets of each scheme assessed.
- The third is an *ex post* evaluation (using the term as in the ROAME sense), undertaken a year or so after the RDP has come to its end, that takes a backward-looking view of the individual schemes and the RDP as a whole and forms a general view on the performance of the intervention in progress towards the objectives. Drawing comparisons between data at the end of the period covered by the RDP with the earlier baseline data can be a useful aid to assessing the extent to which conditions have changed, though evaluators need to be aware of the issues of additionality, displacement and changing external environment described earlier in this chapter.
- Running alongside the three stages, the European Commission has a responsibility to draw together the results of the individual evaluations and synthesise a view on how policy on rural development has performed for the EU as a whole. The common questions and their related indicators, for which all RDPs should provide information, are important in this exercise. The implication is that this synthesis is used in the design of rural development policy legislation in the next planning period. In practice, timing may be less than convenient, and sometimes new programmes have to be drawn up before the lessons from old ones have been fully learned.

The European Commission (both DG-Budget and DG-Agri) provides general methodological advice on how to carry out evaluations and suggests ways to tackle the problems listed earlier.

11.8.2 Broader approaches to evaluation

Two forms of evaluation undertaken in the EU that are of relevance to the CAP should be noted. Both take a rather broader approach than is usual with assessments of the performance of individual programmes and schemes against their own objectives. The first is Strategic Environmental Assessments (SEAs). The EC SEA Directive (2001/42/EC) of 2001 stipulates that *ex ante* assessments are to be undertaken by Member States alongside initiatives which are likely to have a significant impact on the environment, which would include agricultural and Rural Development Programmes. The aim is to ensure that programmes that use EU funding contribute positively to the high level of environmental protection now expected. Thus, the SEA broadens the scope of *ex ante* appraisal of national initiatives such as Rural Development Programmes to cover likely significant effects on the environment of proposed schemes and of reasonable alternatives. Such environmental effects have to be identified, described, evaluated and taken into account by Member States, with evidence presented to the European Commission, before planned action can be put forward as a proposal to the Commission for adoption.

The second is Impact Assessment (IA). As noted above, this is another form of *ex ante* study and is applied to substantial policy proposals or revisions to policy in the EU, including agricultural and rural development policy and the Regulations and Directives by which it is put into practice. Responsibility for carrying it out lies with the Directorate-General dealing with that area of policy. For example, an IA was carried out by DG-Agriculture and Rural Development as part of its proposals for the 2003 reform of the CAP and the introduction of the Single Farm Payment system. The Göteborg and Laeken European Council meetings, both held in 2001, introduced the requirement to consider the economic, social and environmental effects of policy proposals. This integrated, multi-dimensional approach, applied from 2002, was intended to provide an improved aid to political decision-making and replaced single-sector assessments.

IA identifies and assesses the problem in hand and the objectives pursued. It examines the main options for achieving the objective and analyses their likely impacts in the economic, environmental and social fields. It outlines the advantages and disadvantages of each option and examines possible synergies and trade-offs. As such, it is very similar to a conventional *ex ante* evaluation, and in some circumstances may replace it, though for individual Rural Development Programmes the legislation may require a separate exercise that concentrates only on the economic aspects. The Commission provides guidelines for impact assessment, available on its website.

11.9 The performance of the CAP as a whole

Assessing the performance of the CAP as a whole involves bringing together a multitude of evaluations undertaken at the level of individual schemes, programmes and regimes in relation to the CAP's objectives, being mindful of the multiplicity of aims, conflicts, trade-offs and synergies involved, and of the resources it absorbs. As was noted above, there are substantial impediments to making such an overall judgement. Commentators will tend to stress those aspects that are of most interest to them, and there are plenty of books that do this (see reading list at the end of this chapter).

Rather than attempting an overall judgement here, a subjective review is provided in tabular form of the extent to which each of the CAP objectives have been achieved, both those set out in the 1957 Treaty of Rome and the restatement contained in *Agenda 2000*. Table 11.1 shows that success is only partial or that only uncertain answers can be given. Much of this lack of clarity results from difficulty in establishing what would have been the situation had the CAP not been in place. For example, a case can be made that, if the CAP had not intervened in markets for agricultural commodities, competitive pressure and lower prices would have forced out inefficient producers, leaving only those able to compete internationally. The result would have been a smaller agricultural industry in terms of numbers of businesses (and hence numbers of independent farmers and farm families), but those that remained would have been larger on average, probably more appropriately equipped with capital, more modern in their production processes and more competently managed. Their incomes would have been likely to represent a satisfactory return on the resources they owned and to provide them with a standard of living at least comparable with what they could have earned in other occupations. Though the CAP purported to improve productivity and competitiveness, in practice the use of interventions in the markets for agricultural commodities that raised the prices received by farmers (as a way of supporting their incomes) provided some insulation from competitive pressures. Consequently some

Table 11.1 Subjective judgements on the attainment of CAP objectives

Treaty of Rome 1957	Agenda 2000	Comment	Assessment of attainment by CAP
To increase agricultural productivity by promoting technical progress and by ensuring the rational development of agricultural production and the optimum utilisation of the factors of production, in particular labour.	Increase competitiveness internally and externally in order to ensure that Union producers take full advantage of positive world market developments.	Concern has shifted from productivity and its impact on incomes of people in agriculture to the competitiveness of firms in this industry.	Uncertain. Arguments could be put that the CAP has improved the situation, or that it has hampered structural change and thus made it worse than would have been the case in the absence of the CAP.
Thus to ensure a fair standard of living for the agricultural community, in particular by increasing the individual earnings of persons engaged in agriculture.	Ensuring a fair standard of living for the agricultural community and contributing to the stability of farm incomes.	The 1957 Treaty linked living standards with improved productivity. *Agenda 2000* did not require this link, and gave an unqualified assurance.	Partial. Has only applied to some farm households. Many occupiers, especially of smaller farms, have quit because of inadequate incomes.
To stabilise markets.		Methods of support have often led to greater instability on foreign markets.	Achieved in part for domestic markets faced by EU producers.
To assure the availability of supplies.	Food safety and food quality, which are both fundamental obligations towards consumers.	Output of agriculture undoubtedly increased, but the concern with quantity has been replaced by issues of safety and quality. Dependence on imported inputs may affect production.	Uncertain. Greater food production might well have happened without the CAP. Possibly the CAP contributed to the causes of problems over safety and quality.
To ensure that supplies reach consumers at reasonable prices.		Dropped as an objective. Food prices almost certainly higher than without a CAP.	Uncertain. No longer seen of political importance.
	The integration of environmental goals into the CAP.	Realisation that the CAP was probably responsible for some damage to the environment came later.	Current CAP undoubtedly has adopted environmental goals, but whether they are fully integrated is open to question.
	Promotion of sustainable agriculture.	Reflects the increased concern with consumption of finite resources.	Success depends on the interpretation of 'sustainable'.
	The creation of alternative job and income opportunities for farmers and their families.	Recognises that the size of the domestic industry's workforce is in inevitable decline.	Partial success, but most of the non-farm opportunities arise outside the influence of the CAP.
	Simplification of Union legislation.		Partial, especially after the 2003 reforms.

of the poorer-performing farmers were able to survive, resulting in an industry that was less productive and competitive. In such circumstances, if the only aim was to improve the competitive performance of agriculture, it would have been preferable not to have intervened.

But in practice it is rather difficult to be precise about what shape the agricultural industry would have been in if the CAP had not existed, or what the environmental state of rural areas would have been, or the appearance of the landscape, or the level and mix of economic activities taking place in rural areas. So assessments of the overall impact of the CAP on the problems faced by society that are mirrored in the stated policy objectives are best treated with caution.

But perhaps this is too narrow a view, and account has to be taken of unstated objectives which may result in a far more favourable assessment. The key to this is the role the CAP has had in building the EU as a community of nations. For many years after its founding, the CAP was one of the very few policies that were 'common', in the sense that EU Member States agreed to operate on a collective basis to help solve shared problems. Consequently, the CAP can be seen as the essential mortar that held the bricks of the EU together. If the existence of this EU (and its predecessors including the European Economic Community) has maintained peace between the independent nations that are its Member States and has enabled them to cooperate in other ways (economically, environmentally, politically, socially etc.), then the incidental benefits have been huge. The political context of the CAP is considered as part of its historical development outlined in Chapter 12.

Further reading

Evaluation

Commission of the European Communities (1999) *The MEANS Collection– 'Evaluating Socio-economic Programmes'*. Six volumes. Directorate for the Co-ordination and Evaluation of Operations of DG XVI.

The following are available on the Europa website

Commission of the European Communities (1999) *Evaluation of Rural Development Programmes 2000–2006 supported from the European Agricultural Guidance and Guarantee Fund – Guidelines*, Directorate General for Agriculture. VI/8865/99- Rev.

Commission of the European Communities (2000) *The Communication on Evaluation* (SEC(2000) 1051).

Commission of the European Communities (2005) *Evaluation of EU Activities – An introduction*. DG Budget.

Commission of the European Communities (2006) *Rural Development 2007–2013: Handbook on Common Monitoring and Evaluation Framework*. Draft guidance document. Directorate General for Agriculture and Rural Development.

Commission of the European Communities (2007) *Responding to Strategic Needs: Reinforcing the Use of Evaluation*. Communication to the Commission from Ms Grybauskaite in agreement with the President. SEC(2007)213.

Others

Hill, M. (2006) *The Public Policy Process*. 4th edition. Pearson-Education, Harlow.

HM Treasury (2003) *The Green Book: Appraisal and Evaluation in Central Government – Treasury Guidance*. The Stationery Office, London.

OECD (2005) *Evaluating Agri-environmental Policies: Design, Practice and Results.* Organisation for Economic Co-operation and Development, Paris.

Tavistock Institute (2003) *The Evaluation of Socio-Economic Development: The Guide.* Tavistock Institute, London.

Timmer, P. C. (1988) 'The agricultural transformation'. Chapter 8 in *Handbook of Development Economics, Vol. I*, Chenery, H. and Srinivasan, T.N. (eds). Elsevier Science Publishers, Amsterdam.

Performance of the CAP

Ackrill, R. (2000) 'The Common Agricultural Policy', Chapter 6 in *An Assessment of the CAP: From Article 39 to Agenda 2000.* Sheffield Academic Press, Sheffield.

European Commission (2007) *The Common Agricultural Policy Explained.* Directorate General for Agriculture and Rural Development, Brussels.

Hill, B. (2000) *Farm Incomes, Wealth and Agricultural Policy.* 3rd Edition. Ashgate Publishing, Aldershot. (4th Edition, 2011, CABI, Wallingford).

OECD (annual) *Agricultural Policy Monitoring and Evaluation.* Organisation for Economic Co-operation and Development, Paris.

Annex: List of Evaluation reports commissioned by DG for Agriculture and Rural Development, 1999–2010.

Texts are in English except for those marked as being in French.

Market and income policies

2010

Evaluation of direct aids in the beef and veal sector (in French)
Evaluation of market effects of partial decoupling (in French)

2009

Evaluation of the Implementation of the Farm Advisory System
Evaluation of measures relating to the durum wheat sector within the context of the Common Agricultural Policy
Evaluation of the Common Agricultural Policy measures related to hops
Evaluation of measures carried out for the outermost regions (POSEI) and the smaller islands of the Aegean Sea within the context of the Common Agricultural Policy (in French)
Evaluation of measures applied under the Common Agricultural Policy to the rice sector (in French)
Evaluation of measures applied under CAP to the olive sector (in French)
Evaluation of measures applied under the Common Agricultural Policy to the protein crop sector
Mid-term evaluation of the implementation of the EU Forest Action Plan
Evaluation of measures applied under the CAP to the raw tobacco sector (in French)

2008

Evaluation of the Environmental Impacts of Milk Quotas
Evaluation of the CAP policy on protected designations of origin (PDO) and protected geographical indications (PGI)
Évaluation des mesures concernant les organisations de producteurs dans le secteur des fruits et légumes (in French)
Evaluation of the set-aside measure 2000 to 2006
Evaluation of the system of entry prices and export refunds in the fruit and vegetables sector
Evaluation de l'activation des paiements directs sur les cultures de fruits et légumes dans le modèle régional (in French)

2007

Evaluation of market measures in the beef and veal sector (in French)
Evaluation of the Environmental impacts of the CAP measures related to the beef and milk sector
Evaluation study of the Common Market measures for dried fodder (in French)
Evaluation of the extensification payment (in French)
Evaluation of the environmental impact of the CMO and direct support measures of the CAP for arable crops (in French)
Evaluation of the application of cross compliance as foreseen under Regulation 1782/2003
Evaluation of the environmental impacts of CAP measures related to cotton (in French)
Evaluation of withdrawals and crisis management in fruit and vegetable sector

2006

Study on the impact of export support measures and food aid on food security (in French)
Study on implementing the Energy Crops CAP Measures and Bio-Energy Market
Evaluation of the Information Policy on the Common Agricultural Policy

Evaluation of measures regarding fresh and processed peaches, nectarines and pears (in French)
Evaluation of measures regarding citrus fruits (in French)
Evaluation of measures regarding processed tomatoes (in French)
Evaluation of the Impact of Directive 2000/36/EC on the Economies of those Countries Producing Cocoa and Vegetable Fats other than Cocoa Butter

2005

Evaluation of the environmental impact of common market organisations in permanent crops (in French)
Evaluation of the Common Market Organisation (CMO) in the Cereal sector
Evaluation of the Common Market Organisations (CMOs) for Pigmeat, Poultry meat and Eggs
Evaluation of the Common Market Organisation (CMO) in Flax and Hemp (in French)
Evaluation of the market organisation for bananas (in French)

2004

Ex-post evaluation of the Common Market Organisation for wine

2003

Evaluation of the Common Market Organisation (CMO) for raw tobacco (in French)

2002

Evaluation of the impact of the main market-organisation measures in the olive oil sector (in French)
Evaluation of the Community policy for the promotion of agricultural products (in French)
Evaluation of the Common Market Organisation for milk and milk products and the regulation on milk quotas (in French)
Evaluation of the Community Policy for Starch and Starch Products
Evaluation of the impacts of the Community measures on Land set-aside (in French)

2001

Evaluation Community Policy on oilseeds (in French)

2000

Evaluation of the common organisation of the markets in the sugar sector
Evaluation of the common organisation of the markets in the sheep and goatmeat sector
Evaluation of the impact of measures implemented under the agricultural component of POSEIMA programme (for the EU's outermost regions, such as islands) (in French)
Evaluation of the impact of measures implemented under the agricultural component of POSEIDOM programme (in French)

1999

Evaluation Community Policy on durum wheat (in French)
Evaluation of the impact of actions implementing Regulation (EEC) No 2019/93 on the economic situation of the small islands in the Aegean Sea
Evaluation of the School Milk Measure
Evaluation of the impact of measures implemented under the agricultural component of POSEICAN programme (in French)

1998

Evaluation of the European Community's food programmes (in French)

Rural development

2008

Synthesis of Ex Ante Evaluations of Rural Development Programmes 2007–2013

2007

Evaluation on the impact of Nordic aid schemes in Northern Finland and Sweden

2006

An Evaluation of the Less Favoured Area Measure in the 25 Member States of the European Union
Synthesis of mid-term evaluations of LEADER+ programmes
Mid-term Evaluation of the Sapard Programme 2000–2003

2005

Synthesis of Rural Development mid-term evaluations
Evaluation of the agri-environment measures (in French)

2004

Impact assessment of Rural Development Programmes in view of post 2006 rural development policy
Methods for and Success of Mainstreaming Leader Innovations and Approach into Rural Development
    Programmes

2003

Ex post evaluation of the Community Initiative Leader II
Ex post evaluation of measures under Regulation (EC) No 950/97
Ex post evaluation of measures under Regulation (EC) No 951/97
Ex post evaluation of Objective 5b programmes 1994 –1999 (in French)

2001

Evaluation of the Community aid scheme for forestry measures in agriculture Regulation (EEC) No
    2080/92

1999

Ex post evaluation of the Leader I Community Initiative
Interim evaluation of Rural Development Programmes (Objectives 5a and 5b)

12

UNDERSTANDING THE HISTORY OF THE CAP AND EUROPEAN POLICY

Key topics

- An outline of the main strands of policy since the CAP was established, drawing attention to the political engine behind developments, periodic crises in agricultural policy, the broadening of policy to embrace rural development, and attempts to reform the CAP.
- A chronological list of events in the development of the CAP.

12.1 Major stands of development in the European Union

This book has been concerned mainly with explaining the CAP in its present form. While there is insufficient space to provide a full account of its history, some information on the steps by which the present has been arrived at is necessary to its understanding. Moreover, the forces that have shaped policies are still largely in existence, so anyone interested in explaining how changes are likely to be made in the future will need some knowledge of what has happened in the past, and why.

This chapter provides a guide to the main features and periods; a more detailed chronology of events in the life of the CAP is provided in list form at the end of this chapter. A number of themes running through the history are identified. Other commentators on the development of the EU may find other themes worth drawing out, but here we are concerned primarily with those that relate to agricultural policy. These are:

- the importance of political objectives to the development of agricultural and related policies;
- evolution in the way in which agricultural policy decisions are made;
- the saga of attempts to reform the CAP, including the long-running relationship with problems of financing the budget;
- changes in the aims of policies affecting agriculture directly or indirectly, including the rise of concerns with the environment, the desire to achieve freer international trade (specifically to reach a satisfactory outcome in international trade negotiations), and enlargement of the EU to embrace countries in Central and Eastern Europe.

12.2 The political engine of the European Union

The CAP has its origins in the political ambitions of a few men to build a European community from separate nations, in which an attempt to do something about the problems of agriculture was seen to play a part. Pressure to do so came from several quarters. In the immediate aftermath of the Second World War a new threat to peace in the West – the former ally Russia – had emerged. West Germany was at the geographical meeting point of East and West. America and Britain were of the view that West Germany must be reintegrated into the Western group of nations. Yet there was fear among some of the allies that a fully independent West Germany might pose a renewed threat to peace. The French Foreign Minister, Robert Schuman, was given the job of devising how this binding of West Germany into a larger European structure could be done. His plan involved building an economic community that included France and Germany but could embrace other countries that wished to take part. These nation-states had already engaged in two major wars during the twentieth century, with devastating consequences. If they could be brought together to work in an integrated way to tackle common problems, and if their economies were to become inter-dependent and linked by trade, to be encouraged by the dismantling of barriers, the likelihood of further war would be reduced and, perhaps, eliminated.

The notions of economic and political union (better understood as cooperation) were therefore central to the vision of men like Altiero Spinelli, Jean Monnet and Robert Schuman (see Box 12.1) for a post-Second World War Europe. The most effective way of building a community of nations was to concentrate on the collective solution of shared but manageable problems. At the time, a pressing economic problem was the need to restructure the coal and steel industries, which were central to the development of military hardware, to meet the new post-war conditions. Over-supply was already depressing prices. There was a danger of repeating the pattern seen between the two World Wars of forming cartels that exacerbated problems rather than providing solutions. To have these industries under shared control would limit countries' abilities to engage in war with each other. Later agriculture and the peaceful use of atomic energy were seen as industries where collective action was highly desirable and feasible.

There have been, and are, alternative views of the way in which this cooperation could be brought about, ranging from, on the one hand, a loose association of independent nation states agreeing to act collectively on matters where this is appropriate (a *confederalist* approach), to one in which the individual countries merge their sovereignties into a federation as close as a United States of Europe (the *federalist* approach), a notion of which even Winston Churchill was at one time an advocate (though he saw Britain as a promoter of such a federation rather than as a participant). There have also been differing opinions on the extent to which cooperation is best fostered by 'widening' to include more countries or by 'deepening' (that is, involving greater levels of cooperation between existing Member States).

Whatever the form of cooperation might take, the founding fathers realised that, in addition to doing things together, there had to be some institutional framework at Community[1] level to which nation states ceded some of their powers and which was thereafter recognised by the participating countries as having some authority over them. Simple voluntary cooperation between countries could not be relied on to build a Community; there had to be something more substantial. A set of independent institutions was envisaged whose authority rested on the powers that countries had willingly given to them. The setting up of the European Coal and Steel Community (ECSC) in 1951 by the Treaty of Paris brought

Box 12.1 Fathers of European political and economic integration

Altiero Spinelli (1907–1986) (Italian) was, from 1927, a political prisoner of the Italian government for his pro-Communist sympathies and opposition to the regime of the National Fascist Party. In 1941 he and Ernesto Rossi, a fellow prisoner, produced the Ventotene Manifesto Towards a Free and United Europe calling for a post-war federation of European democratic powers which would bind the nations together sufficiently strongly as to prevent them going to war. Spinelli was a founding member of the Movimento Federalista Europeo (MFE) that pressed for close international cooperation, and advocated a European constituent assembly to draft a European Constitution. Though a proposed European Defence Community did not materialise, the European Coal and Steel Community did, together with its institutions. Spinelli was nominated by Italy as to be a Commissioner from 1970 and in 1979 became a member of the European Parliament in the first round of direct elections. He pressed for increased integration and was influential in the process leading up to the Single European Act (1986) and the Treaty of European Union (Maastrich) 1992.

Jean Monnet (1888–1979) (French) was a successful businessman and financier who had gained a remarkable amount of political experience and responsibility during both World Wars. After the latter, Monnet was appointed head of France's General Planning Committee and was behind the plan to create the European Coal and Steel Community (1951). In 1955, in the face of the failure of the proposed European Defence Community, Monnet founded an Action Committee to drive forward European integration that led to the 1957 Treaty of Rome and the formation of the European Economic Community in 1958. Monnet was never an elected politician but had a pervasive and powerful influence on the development of the EU.

Robert Schuman (1886–1963) (born in Luxembourg of father with German nationality and became a French citizen in 1919) was a French MP and in the Second World War worked for the Vichy regime. After amnesty, he became Minister of Finance, then Prime Minister twice (1947–48), and later Foreign Minister and Minister of Justice. His first government advocated the creation of a European Assembly, which became the Council of Europe (1949). His vision was a community of nations built by working together in a supranational association rather than by conquest. In 1950 the Schumann Declaration appeared (a joint work with Monnet and others) which was adopted by the French Government, in which European countries were invited to manage their coal and steel industries jointly and democratically. This led to the 1951 Treaty of Paris that established the European Coal and Steel Community with its set of supranational institutions. He became the first President of the European Parliamentary Assembly (now the European Parliament).

Paul-Henri Spaak (1899–1972) (Belgian) was a socialist politician, holding ministerial positions from 1935 to 1966, being Foreign Minister from 1939 to 1949. After 1944 he advocated regional cooperation and collective security and promoted the creation of the customs union of the Benelux countries (Belgium, the Netherlands and Luxembourg). In addition he was the chairman of the first session of the General Assembly of the United Nations (1945) and President of the first session of the Consultative Assembly of the Council of Europe, and from 1952 to 1953 President of the Common Assembly of the European Coal and Steel Community. The 'Spaak Report', written on the instigation of European leaders, on the creation of a common European market was key to the Intergovernmental Conference on the Common Market and EURATOM (1956) that resulted in the Treaties of Rome (957) setting up the European Economic Community and the European Atomic Energy Community. Spaak was one of the Treaty signatories for Belgium.

Table 12.1   The Treaties that form the legal basis of the European Union

Date of signature	Treaty
18 April 1951	Signature in Paris of the Treaty establishing the European Coal and Steel Community (ECSC) which came into force on 23 July 1952 for 50 years. It was abolished in 2002.
25 March 1957	Signature in Rome of the Treaties establishing the European Economic Community (EEC) and the European Atomic Energy Community (EAEC or Euratom). They came into force on 1 January 1958.
17 and 28 February 1986	Signature in Luxembourg and The Hague of the Single European Act, which came into force on 1 July 1987.
7 February 1992	Signature in Maastricht of the Treaty on European Union which came into force on 1 November 1993.
2 October 1997	Signature of the Treaty of Amsterdam which came into force on 1 May 1999. Among other things, the texts of earlier Treaties were consolidated which *inter alia* affects the numbering of paragraphs.
26 February 2001	Signature of the Treaty of Nice which came into force on 1 February 2003.
13 December 2007	Signature of the Lisbon Treaty modifying the Treaty on European Union and the Treaty establishing European Economic Community, which came into force on 1 December 2009.

Source: The Lisbon Treaty Foundation Robert Schuman, December 2007 (updated in December 2009) www. robert-schuman.eu

into being such institutions; the ECSC High Authority (the forerunner of the Commission), its Assembly (which eventually became transformed into the European Parliament), its Council of Ministers and a Court of Justice. On this same model the European Economic Community (EEC) was founded a few years later by the Treaty of Rome (1957), together with the European Atomic Energy Community (Euratom) under a separate Treaty of Rome.

Despite divergences in views of the means by which the ends should be achieved, it is clear that the progress of the community of nations which now form the EU has been driven from its earliest days by the urge for closer cooperation in an increasingly wide range of aspects of life – economic, social, environmental, security, defence etc. The EU's history is peppered by declarations of intent for more integration, long-term collective goals of an economic and political nature, and official statements that various stages in the process of building the European Community/Union have been reached.

The main constitutional bases of the European Union as it now exists are the Treaties shown in Table 12.1. The principal features of these Treaties are described as part of their entries in the Annex. In addition there are the Accession Treaties that have taken the membership from the original six countries to the present 27.

When moving through the series of Treaties it is easy to spot a growth in the range of policies that are to be acted upon communally. This progression started with the restructuring of coal and steel production (1951), extended to agriculture and atomic energy (1957), the establishment of a customs union (1968) that gradually widened to a common (single) market for goods and services throughout the 12 Member States by 1993, and went on to embrace monetary union, a single currency and economic policy. Environmental, regional and social policy have also been areas in which collective action is now taken, with recent extensions into foreign affairs and security capabilities.

Almost inevitably, this broadening of community policy areas has involved transferring power from national to EU central institutions, and this has been accompanied by a reduction in the ability of Member State governments to act independently. However, to some extent the drift towards decision-making at the centre on issues of a strategic nature has been countered by a greater use of flexibility for Member States to take decisions over details at the local level. Rural development is a good example (see Chapters 7 and 8), where the strategic EU priorities and aims are set in Regulations adopted by the Council and European Parliament on proposals of the Commission, but where the design of programmes is drawn up at national or regional levels to allow for differences in problems and ways of tackling them. This is an application of the concept of 'subsidiarity',[2] which implies that decisions are taken at the lowest level or least centralised competent authority.

This gradual broadening of common policies has been the subject of a running debate and has not been without some dead-ends, such as the early rejection (by the French National Assembly in 1954) of the proposal for a European Defence Community (CDC). This CDC concept only returned to the agenda in the early 2000s with the drawing up of a draft Constitution for the EU (the 2004 text was not ratified by some countries in 2005 and therefore lapsed) and the 2007 Treaty of Lisbon that picked up some of the proposed Constitution's elements (eventually ratified after initial rejection by some countries). Some areas of policy cooperation for which a case could be made (such as rates of company taxation) have been firmly dismissed by Member States, primarily on political grounds.

The series of Treaties has changed the nature of the arrangements between Member States, with the transformation of the European Communities (one of which was the European Economic Community) into the European Union in 1993 (with the ratification of the Maastricht Treaty). The 2007 Treaty of Lisbon took this further, among other things giving the EU its own legal status and revising the role of the President of the Council.

Stretching over the period covered by the Treaties listed in Table 12.1 has been the desire, for largely political reasons, to bring further countries into Membership. For example, the accession of Spain and Portugal was agreed quite quickly even though they brought with them substantial numbers of small farmers and large volumes of production at a time when the CAP was struggling to deal with the problems of a Community of 10 countries. One important motive was the desire to underpin the newly established democracies of these countries by binding them into a Community in which the principle of democracy was fundamental. While the 1995 enlargement (Austria, Finland and Sweden) involved countries that were, in essence, very like the existing Members, the next rounds (2004 and 2007) included former Eastern bloc states. Bringing them clearly into the group of Western, democratic countries with market-based economies was likely to be of economic and social benefits to both parties, but it could also provide a buffer for the EU against unwelcome developments and instability further east.

12.2.1 Agricultural policy and the EU

The CAP has been a cornerstone for building the Union. From the outset, a Common Agricultural Policy (CAP) within the EEC was seen as important for the following reasons:

- agriculture was a major industry of the original six Member States (Belgium, West Germany, France, Italy, Luxembourg, Netherlands) which, as well as being of vital interest as a food supplier, faced income problems which required action;

- the high existing level of each government's intervention in their agricultural industries made the goal of a common market in these commodities particularly difficult to achieve without an explicit EEC policy;
- unless a common policy was achieved in agriculture, other common policies would be partly undermined, as different amounts of national support for agricultures would feed through to different food prices and hence distort competitive advantage in other industries and intra-EEC trade.

Common policies for agriculture, trade and transport were mentioned explicitly in the 1957 Treaty of Rome, with a provision for expanding into areas where this was subsequently found necessary, taken up after the Paris Summit of 1972 to establish environmental, regional, social and industrial policies. Despite progress being made in these areas, the CAP has carried great political valency because it has dominated the use of resources in the Union budget, in the early years accounting for the vast majority of spending on all EU activities (80 to 90 per cent) and even 50 years later still absorbing over 40 per cent of its funds (see Chapter 10).

After the mid-1980s there seems to have been a greater political willingness to develop other common policies that required substantial spending. A turning point was 1988, when the sum available to the Structural Funds then in existence was greatly expanded (the guidance part of the EAGGF, the European Regional Development Fund, and the European Social Fund). A major motive of this expansion was the wish to assist the poorer parts of the EU to participate in the additional prosperity that was coming to the EU as a whole. The rationale is part to do with equity; there is a tendency for the disparity between richer and poorer regions which have to compete in a single market to widen over time with the general rise in prosperity, and this may be seen as unfair. In part it is to do with self-interest; it is in the interest of richer regions for poorer regions to grow as this provides the former with an expanding market. The resolve that the richer parts of the EU should assist the poorer ones is known as 'cohesion' and the 1992 Maastricht Treaty provided extra resources via a Cohesion Fund to assist in achieving it; the beneficiaries were Spain, Portugal, Greece and Ireland.

There has been a further and larger-scale political dimension to helping the poorer parts of the Community. The conditions necessary for the next declared stages of EU development (economic and monetary union) first required a high degree of economic convergence among Member States (whereby their economic performances were required to move closer to one another, with a progressive levelling up towards the best performing country). The introduction of a single currency (the euro) and the setting of interest by the European Central Bank (1999) implied that Member States had to pursue domestic economic policies that prevented further misalignment. By participating in monetary union (MU) Member States were signalling their willingness to accept the conditions of MU membership and the constraints it imposed (including the 'Stability and Growth Pact') on its fiscal policy in exchange for the benefits that such a system was expected to bring (material and political, such as a stronger and more cohesive EU).

The lesson from the above is that there has been a clear political impetus towards greater integration and cooperation between Member States. The dominant tendency so far has been towards greater collective policy action and a strengthening of EU institutions relative to those in Member States. However, this has created a tension with those parts of society that are keen to not let the central EU institutions become too powerful, to rein back what is seen as a drift to centralisation and a reluctance to develop additional common policies. The pressure has been relieved to some extent by the 2007 Lisbon Treaty's clarification of the areas in which the EU has 'exclusive competence' (such as the Customs Union and competition rules), where there is 'shared competence' between the EU and Member States (such as in agricultural and environmental policy), and where Member States hold sole competency (such as industry, culture and tourism). Furthermore, national parliaments were given a specific role by the Lisbon Treaty to check that agreed divisions of competence were being observed and to notify the Commission, using an 'early warning mechanism', where the subsidiarity principle is in danger of being violated by EU institutions, requiring the Commission to review the proposals.

12.3 Evolution in the ways in which agricultural policy decisions are made

In the development of the CAP, changes have occurred in four main aspects of decision-making.

12.3.1 Role of the European Parliament

Viewed at EU level, over the series of Treaties there has been a gradual strengthening of the role of the European Parliament. This is sometimes referred to as making good the 'democratic deficit', a term used to describe the situation whereby progress in the quantity of resources administered collectively resulting from the widening and deepening of the sphere of influence of EU policies had not been matched by greater accountability to its citizens. In particular the 1986 Single European Act (SEA), the 1992 Maastricht Treaty and the 2007 Lisbon Treaty have increased the powers and responsibilities of the European Parliament.

Up to the coming into force of the Lisbon Treaty in December 2009, and in contrast with the general picture, for most agricultural policy legislation there had been very little change. For most actions covered by the CAP the processes set out in the Treaty of Rome still applied. Under these, the European Parliament had the right to scrutinise and pass an opinion on the proposed legislation coming from the Commission (as has also the Economic and Social Committee), and this opinion may (or may not) have led to the Commission modifying its proposal. Once the opinion was received, decisions on agricultural matters were taken by the Council of Ministers, or by the committees of the Council and the Commission to which powers had been devolved by the Council, becoming EU law without the opportunity for the Parliament to confirm or change. This was unlike the process for most other legislation which, following the SEA and the Maastricht Treaty, had to go back to the Parliament for one or more readings before passing into law. The 2007 Lisbon Treaty has given significantly greater powers to the European Parliament on agricultural matters, bringing decision-making in this policy area into line with the 'ordinary legislative procedure' (see Chapter 3 for details).

Two reasons have been offered for retaining for so long the old procedure for agricultural legislation. First, up to the introduction of the Single Farm Payment system of support that was part of the 2003 package of reforms, many CAP decisions were very detailed and complex and had immediate commercial implications. Especially with price decisions, the outcome was a package covering many different commodities, a compromise reached behind closed doors. The European Parliament could pass an opinion on the proposals, but it was felt that a second, post-Council scrutiny stage would have tended to unravel the political compromise. In addition, farmers could not be expected to wait to make production decisions in a state of uncertainty while the Parliament deliberated on a set of provisional prices for various agricultural commodities, with the possibility of change. Meanwhile, traders of agricultural commodities might make large speculative transactions. Now that the former regimes to support the prices of farm products have largely been dismantled, this argument is far less relevant. Second, a view has been expressed that the other institutions (including national governments) were agreeable to an extension of power of the European Parliament only in EU activities 'which did not matter much' while retaining for themselves powers in areas such as agricultural policy where the bulk of Union budgetary spending was concentrated. The gradual shrinking of the CAP's dominance of the budget has eroded this incentive to resist change.

12.3.2 Use of qualified majority voting

Within the Council of Ministers there has been a shift towards the use of qualified majority voting. Though the Treaty of Rome provided for qualified majority voting in agriculture, in practice, in the early years, unanimity seems to have been striven for. The Luxembourg Compromise of 1966 – a 'gentlemen's agreement' designed to put aside qualified majority voting on issues that any single Member State could declare was of 'vital national interest' – that provided, in effect, a veto on politically sensitive issues – had fallen into disuse by the early 1990s. Though similar arrangements have been attempted (see Chapter 3 for details of the Ioannina Compromise and a new version tried in 2007 as a ploy to gather support for the Lisbon Treaty), with progressive enlargement from six to 27 Member States (in 2007), qualified majorities have become normal. Nevertheless, it must be recalled that, if the Council wishes to amend a Commission proposal, then unanimity is required. This was common in the past at Council meetings; when setting annually agricultural support prices, a political compromise frequently had to be worked out, covering many commodities, but the shift in support away from market intervention towards direct payments has lessened the need for such complex packages.

12.3.3 Subsidiarity

Another general development in CAP decision-making has been the greater application of subsidiarity. Allowing decision-making at a local level has long been a feature of the application of EU regional policy to give assistance to regions lagging behind; while the EU set general guidelines and the Commission had to approve proposals, local bodies (typically regional government) in collaboration with national governments identified local priorities for spending and were responsible for the first stages of assessing the effectiveness of these policies (see Chapter 7). Up to the mid-1990s, when the CAP was implemented primarily through the support of commodity markets, most of the major decisions were made centrally. The ability of Member States to exercise national independence within the CAP was quite limited and was confined to relatively unimportant (in terms of expenditure) parts of policy, such as a degree of local flexibility in the application of some structural instruments, in setting local rural development objectives to tackle local problems, and in their choice not to introduce national legislation to implement EU policy if they felt it to be inappropriate to their conditions.[3]

The role of national (or even more local) decision-taking was expanded under the guidelines for future development put forward by the Commission in 1995 in its *Agricultural Strategy Paper* and was taken up in *Agenda 2000,* which further reduced the amount of intervention in the markets for agricultural commodities, gave a heightened attention to the broader problems of rural development (in the form of its Pillar 2, in which environmental and social considerations were important) and gave greater weight to further 'simplification', code for greater influence over policy actions by Member States. The growth in the part played by national and regional administrations has been taken forward in the Rural Development Programmes for the planning periods 2000–06 and 2007–13. National (or regional) governments are able to identify their strategic priorities within the framework established for the EU as a whole, including setting their own sets of objectives for the environments, economic performance of farming and forestry, and living conditions in rural areas. These, and the balance between them, vary widely across the EU. Member States can then choose from the menu of possible measures under the Rural Development Regulations to formulate a Rural Development Programme to assist their rural areas appropriate to their particular set of circumstances (see Chapters 7 and 8). However, it must be recalled that Pillar 2 of the CAP remains far less substantial than Pillar 1.

Within Pillar 1, though there is some flexibility in the implementing arrangements for the Single Farm Payments (such as the way in which such payments are calculated and in how much modulation can be employed to transfer a small share of funds from Pillar 1 to Pillar 2), in essence the degree of subsidiarity is quite limited. This was not always the case. When Monetary Compensation Amounts (MCAs) existed (before January 1993) there was an opportunity for Member States to apply different MCAs to different agricultural products, thereby engineering a set of prices which favoured those products of which it was a major producer. This form of national action has now largely disappeared with the introduction of Monetary Union and the euro. For the countries that are not members of MU (including the UK), support payments received by farmers (in national currencies) are affected by exchange rates with the euro, though in reality the exchange rate is determined by external factors (such as the anticipated performance of the whole economy) and cannot be manipulated solely to achieve aims related to agriculture.

Whether this devolution of powers has gone far enough is open to question. At least in rural development, a case exists for breaking down the design of policy to units smaller than regions, so that individual localities can identify problems and propose solutions. The LEADER initiative has attempted to do this through local action groups (a bottom-up approach that performs well in identifying local problems and devising solutions) (see Chapter 7). Introduced in 1990, LEADER has been progressively expanded and has been mainstreamed in the latest programming period of rural development (2007–13), implying that this approach is seen to have a role in formulating and delivering both the economic, environmental and quality-of-life aspects of the CAP's contribution to rural development, though in practice it seems to be applied particularly in the last of these three.

12.3.4 CAP and national agricultural policies

There is only room here to touch on one further aspect of CAP decision-making – the relationship between the EU policy for agriculture and national agricultural policies. An element of national policies towards agriculture and rural areas has always existed alongside the CAP. The Community has allowed national support measures that provided benefits where there was little or no direct connection with the prices in the markets for farm commodities (such as research and genetic improvement, and agricultural education). Also certain forms of support (such as taxation concessions to farmers) are considered politically sensitive and thus have to be left in the hands of the governments of individual Member States. Some forms of national aid might be judged as affecting prices; free advisory services for farmers in one country could be expected to affect their competitiveness and output. However, the EU test for whether a national aid is to be objected to as unfair depends not only on whether it distorts competition, trade and exchange but also that it does so 'to an extent contrary to the common interest'.

No clear picture emerges over how the balance between common EU policies for agriculture and national policies has evolved. In part this is because there is a close link between giving national policy a greater role and greater subsidiarity. The former is usually cast in a less favourable light than the latter. However, there could well be circumstances where local action, based on a knowledge of local problems and targeted at them using national resources, makes more sense from a EU perspective than a uniform policy that is inappropriate for the vast majority of situations in which it is applied. For example, as long as a Member State respects overall rules on state aids (see Chapter 10), it might be preferable for a country in which small farms are considered to be socially important (but whose combined output contributes very little to the market) to be allowed to adopt support mechanisms targeted at them, whereas other countries that did not value such farms so highly need not take such actions.

12.4 The saga of attempts to reform the CAP

At the outset of the CAP the problems faced by the original six Member States were seen, primarily, as ones linked to improving the productivity of agriculture, that is, the efficiency with which it used resources, in particular, labour (see Chapter 2). If this could be raised, then it was believed that food production from domestic agriculture would be increased, important when the degree of self-sufficiency was relatively low and the memory of food shortages still vivid in the minds of politicians (the distinction between productivity and production should be noted). Also, incomes in farming would be improved, and resources (most significantly, labour) could be transferred to industries where its marginal product was greater, thereby improving the prosperity of the whole economy. The main instrument chosen to achieve this was higher prices for the commodities produced by domestic farmers, brought about by taxing imports of these commodities from abroad.

With the passage of time, this situation, and in particular the use of product price support, ran up against a number of difficulties, many of which can be linked to the success story of improving productivity in agriculture. These difficulties included the following;

12.4.1 Increased self-sufficiency and surpluses

In contrast with the lower degree of self-sufficiency at the outset, the EU became more than self-sufficient in most of the agricultural commodities that its farmers could produce. This change came about as the result of a number of factors; the higher prices offered to farmers, the improvements in productivity in agriculture, and the enlargement of the Community to include some Member States that were major agricultural producers. However, this change meant that import taxes could no longer be used as the principal way of raising the prices for domestic producers, as there were no imports to tax. Instead, support buying had to be used. Difficulties were aggravated by the restrictions placed on the EU as part of international trade agreements (under GATT); these restricted its ability to impose taxes on some agricultural commodities from abroad that competed with domestic products (for example, on cereal substitutes in animal feed, such as manioc).

12.4.2 Inadequate agricultural restructuring

In the longer term many observers agree that, in the face of improving productivity and rising production, a restructuring of agriculture was (and still is) required, with fewer but larger farms. This meant fewer people in agriculture, and probably less land being used for farming. Changes in this direction were already taking place, but progress was too slow (linked with the immobility of labour in agriculture – see Chapter 2) and structural adjustment was impeded by product price support, higher prices cushioning farmers from the need to change. The CAP has from the start envisaged aid for structural adjustment to run in parallel with product price support, though the two are essentially conflicting. However, in practice the sums spent on agriculture's structural policy (such as early retirement schemes, retraining schemes, farm enlargement, and farm modernisation) were small compared with product price support. Only in 1988 was a reasonably bold step taken, with a doubling of the amounts available to the EU's Structural Funds and the closer integration of support to agriculture with support to rural areas more generally. Schemes for farm restructuring and modernisation have continued in all subsequent packages of support and the sums allocated to them have expanded, but the conflict has also continued between, on the one hand, achieving a farming industry of appropriate size and structure and, on the other, giving support to farmers that insulates them at least in part from the economic forces that are necessary to bring about such changes.

12.4.3 Costs of market support

The budgetary cost of the CAP has tended to rise rapidly. Whereas the original main instrument for raising market prices (the import levy) raised funds for the EU budget, support buying and the costs of surplus disposal, were drains on the budget. The more farmers produced, the greater the costs and there was a tendency for this cost to increase rapidly, faster than the increase in the overall EU budget.[4] Consequently, the history of the CAP is marked by various budgetary crises, with attempts to contain costs, by devices such as (in approximate historical order of introduction) Co-responsibility Levies, quotas at regional or farm level, Maximum Guaranteed Quantities attached to production (beyond which levels of support prices are lowered), set-aside etc. Several attempts have been made to restrict the overall costs of the CAP, most notably at the Fontainebleau Summit of 1984 and in 1988 as part of 'budgetary discipline' (see below).

12.4.4 Opposition to fundamental reform of the CAP

Reform of the CAP to reflect new conditions has been difficult to bring about. Fundamental reform implied reducing the role played by product price support (which meant lowering prices received by farmers to nearer the world level), tackling the underlying structural problems and grasping the nettle of how to move to a system which better respected the underlying market and technical situations. Up to the early 1990s agricultural ministers from Member States, acting as the Council, were unwilling to lower the prices for agricultural commodities because of the political backlash that was feared in some countries because of the assumed impact on incomes of farmers. Under the system of decision-making, it was difficult for countries advocating lower prices to win the day. The tendency was to tinker with individual CMOs, without changing their main characteristics and without taking a view across all of them towards the basic reasons why support was being given. Even when decisions were taken that support prices (in the EU currency) were to be held at a given level, it was often possible for Member States with relatively weak currencies to engineer a price rise (in national currency terms) for their farmers by making adjustments in Green exchange rates (see Chapter 10).[5] Added to this, the structure of the Commission, which kept agricultural policy matters in the hands of one Directorate-General and further split responsibilities for commodity regimes and structural measures, meant that radical agricultural reform was not welcomed; too many people had an interest in keeping the system in its existing form.

Support for radical change only came in the early 1990s when a combination of external influences (the need to conclude trade agreements, enlargement of EU membership, and budgetary costs) threatened a political and financial crisis and when a system of compensation for farmers had been devised that would make them as a group no worse off than they would have been under the old system of CAP support. Furthermore, a rising awareness that the unreformed CAP was aggravating environmental and food safety problems heightened the public perception of the need for change. The realisation that a revised system of support could give farming and forestry a role in alleviating such problems suited both the agricultural interests and legitimised the continued use of public funds for spending via the CAP. Once the tide of reform had turned, marked by the MacSharry reforms of 1992, further change in the same broad direction met less resistance.

12.5 Phases in the reform process

Several distinct phases in the history of the CAP can be detected. The shift from one to the next is usually marked by a particular piece of legislation that changes, or reforms, the CAP.

12.5.1 Reform of the CAP up to 1988

Soon after the CAP had started operating in the early 1960s, centred on the support of the prices received by farmers for commodities, there was a realisation that it was going in the wrong direction, with the prospect of overproduction, surpluses and high budgetary cost. In 1968, Sicco Mansholt (the Dutch Minister of Agriculture who had become the first Commissioner for agriculture) proposed a plan for accelerated structural change combined with a more realistic price policy. Among his suggestions were that farms should be restructured to provide 80–120 hectares of cropland and 40–60 cows, that some 5 million people should leave agriculture in the 1970s, assisted by early retirement schemes or retraining, and that the agricultural area should be reduced by 5 million hectares (out of 70 million hectares), with 3 million fewer dairy cows. Not surprisingly this plan engendered violent opposition from farmers and their professional (trade) organisations. Only a very diluted set of Directives was eventually passed by the Council in 1972, providing EU support for national schemes aimed at the modernisation of agricultural holdings, early retirement of older farmers, and the provision of vocational training.

The first serious incident in the reform process history was the EU budgetary crisis of 1982. This led to a 1983 internal discussion document from the Commission (*Common Agricultural Policy* (COM(93) 500)) dealing with the issue of imbalance in the markets for agricultural products. The problems of CAP costs led to the 1984 Fontainebleau Summit of heads of government which agreed a need to apply budgetary constraints to agricultural spending. But, at the same time, the Summit sanctioned an increase in the sum available as a way out of the crisis.[6] It is perhaps not surprising that the growth of agricultural spending continued. After a new set of Commissioners had taken office in January 1985, the Commission issued its 1985 Green paper *Perspectives for the Common Agricultural Policy*. This described the nature of the problems facing agriculture and how these had changed since the CAP started in 1962. In the first 15 years of the CAP, a fairly rapid exodus of labour from farming had first been absorbed by the buoyant non-agricultural part of the Community's economy, but the less favourable conditions (including relatively high unemployment) now presented a problem. For social and environmental reasons it was necessary politically to retain a substantial number of people in agriculture.

Yet the problems of mounting surpluses made it important that farmers be dissuaded from producing with the intention of selling to the CAP's intervention agencies; basic market forces should be given a greater role in guiding supply and demand. Doing so, whether by cutting support prices or applying quantitative restrictions, would have implications for incomes in agriculture. Various forms of income aids were considered to assist with adaptation to the new market conditions and to the restructuring of agriculture, including the 'social approach' (which was a form of direct income support that brought the total income of farmers – from agriculture and other sources – up to an acceptable level) and the 'buying out approach', which was a payment to farmers who gave up the right to produce.

Following public debate, a second document later in 1985, *A Future for Community Agriculture: Commission Guidelines,* contained a more sober catalogue of measures that the CAP intended to follow. The message of a more realistic price policy was continued, together with measures to assist farmers with obtaining advice and information, for improving product quality and developing better marketing and new outlets, for schemes to assist farmers to leave the industry and for new entrants, for the support of farming in Less Favoured Areas and provision for schemes that encouraged environmentally friendly farming. Environmental objectives were put on a firm legal footing by being explicitly added to the aims of the EU in the Single European Act of 1986 (which came into effect in 1987). In short, the general direction was confirmed, with the more imaginative elements of the 'Perspectives' document omitted, shelved for the time being.

Actions in the prescribed directions had already commenced. Up to 1983/84 the Council of Ministers, when reaching decisions on commodity prices, had in the forefront of its collective mind the income situation in agriculture. However, from the 1984/85 year (fixed early in 1984) market and price policy became heavily influenced by budgetary constraints. Agricultural prices were frozen or reduced in ECU, and even in national terms they rose at less than the rate of inflation. In 1984 there was a substantial reduction and even dismantling of certain guarantee schemes. In 1984 quotas were applied to milk deliveries as the most appropriate way of dealing with a rapidly expanding supply which would have required very substantial price cuts to contain, cuts of a size that was politically unacceptable. Subsequent cuts in dairy quotas saw spending on that sector fall, even in nominal terms, but this was replaced with increased spending on other surplus-generating sectors, most notably cereals and beef.

Despite the actions taken in the market support arrangements and in socio-structural policy, the overall situation of rising supply and accumulating surpluses did not improve substantially. Consequently, the Commission submitted further proposals to strengthen budget stabilising measures (COM(87) 410 and 512) which were adopted at the European Council of February 1988.

12.5.2 Phase 2 of reform, 1988–1991

The changes agreed at the February 1988 European Council, together with subsequent agreements made by foreign ministers, resulted in the following major reform steps:

- The extension to all important CMOs, of Maximum Guaranteed Quantities (MGQs). Production in excess of the MGQ, would lead to reductions in institutional support prices and other steps designed to restrict the budgetary costs of the CMO. These stabilisers, which varied for each commodity, were set largely without taking detailed account of agricultural or social criteria, such as the level of farm incomes. Initially the proposals had been for a stabilisation of budgetary spending, but this was a step too far for the Council, which agreed production stabilisers in the form of MGQs.
- The application of a more severe budgetary discipline than that stemming from the 1984 Fontainebleau Summit. Annual increases in EAGGF Guarantee spending was not to exceed 74 per cent of growth in Community GNP. With a base amount, this led to the calculation of a strict ceiling on spending, termed the 'financial guideline' (In addition, by agreement between the Council, the European Parliament and the Commission, a 'financial perspective' was later developed; this sets out a multi-annual programme of separate ceilings for each major sector of Community expenditure, including the three Structural Funds (the European Regional Development Fund, the European Social Fund, and the Guidance part of the European Agricultural Guidance and Guaranteed Fund – see Chapter 10).
- At the same time the 'own resources' of the Community were increased, changing the rules determining how the contributions of Member States were to be comprised and introducing a 'Fourth Resource', related to each country's GDP. The intention was that this expansion in available funds should not be swallowed up by agricultural commodity support because of the Guideline, permitting greater sums to be directed to other Community policies. In reality, the mechanisms intended to constrain agricultural spending were inadequate to ensure that it respected what was set in the 'financial perspective'.
- The doubling of the sums allocated to the Community structural funds between 1988 and 1993, which included measures to support agricultural restructuring to cope with reform of the CAP and rural development (see Chapter 7 for details). All three structural funds were to operate in Objective 1 areas (regions lagging behind, many of which were rural) and their activities were to be integrated. Rural development was also to be promoted in parts of other regions, designated as 5b areas.
- The introduction of socio-structural measures of a complementary nature (a) to reduce the area under cultivation (set-aside and to encourage cessation of farming or early retirement); (b) to compensate farmers for the adverse effects of stabilisers on their incomes (a scheme for direct aid to incomes and for extensification or conversion to products not in surplus).

274

Set-aside, extensification and conversion schemes were compulsory for Member States (that is, such schemes had to be introduced, though they were optional for farmers) whereas the income aids and early retirement schemes were optional at Member State level. Other facets of policy also underlined were, *inter alia*, the encouragement of the non-food uses of agricultural commodities and the use of Community cereals in animal feeding stuffs.

These steps were insufficient to bring a balance back into the agricultural markets and to eliminate the increase in intervention stocks, though the pressure on the budget was eased because high world prices reduced the size of export subsidies per unit and offered greater export opportunities. The socio-structural measures were not very effective; set-aside and extensification were taken up less than had been anticipated, income aids were only applied in three Member States and pre-pensions in only one. The problems associated with the subsidised exports continued to attract attention as the Uruguay round of the GATT talks, that started in 1986, failed to find a solution. A more fundamental reform was called for. Late in 1990 the new Commission (which had been appointed in 1989) announced that such a reform was to be proposed.

Within this period the Commission published its document on the *Future of Rural Society* (1988). Primarily concerned with the broader problems of rural areas rather than more narrow ones of farming, the place of agriculture was given prominence both in its role as the cause of some problems and as the means by which solutions could be found. The social and job-creating aspects of agriculture in rural areas continued a theme found in the 1985 'Perspectives' Green paper. However, it was clear that the Commission did not see the support of agricultural production and incomes as a central element in its strategy for many accessible rural areas, though farming could contribute to environmental protection. Only in the most remote parts was agriculture seen as the central core of the local economy. This signalled a broadening view of agricultural policy, so that it became part of a wider strategy to tackle the problems of rural areas. However, agriculture absorbed the overwhelming majority of resources directed at rural areas. The steps taken in 1988 to reform the Structural Funds went some way to correcting the imbalance, though it would be expected that further re-allocation would be necessary in the future.

12.5.3 Phase 3 of reform, 1991–1997

A root-and-branch approach to CAP reform started with a Commission paper in 1991 *The Development and Future of the Common Agricultural Policy: Reflections Paper of the Commission* (COM(91) 100) which was followed up later in the year by *The Development and Future of the Common Agricultural Policy: Proposals of the Commission* (published as Green Europe 2/91), dubbed the 'MacSharry proposals' after the then Commissioner for Agriculture and Rural Development under whose period of office they appeared. These reforms mark the watershed in the development of the CAP, and therefore deserve attention in some detail.

The background was the familiar story of a continued build-up of surpluses in beef, skimmed milk powder, tobacco and wine. Cereal stocks were rising and utilisation falling. Only in oilseeds was there much success in achieving market balance. There was also increasing concern with the fact that, though the costs of support had been rising (from ECU 4.6 billion in 1975 to ECU 31.5 billion in 1991) agricultural incomes were growing only very slowly. Most of the support from the EAGGF went to the relatively few large farms (MacSharry stated that 80 per cent of the spending went to 20 per cent of the farms, presumably the largest ones). There were large disparities of income between farmers in different Member

States, linked with the patterns of farm size. There was continuing concern of the impact of agriculture on the environment.

The 1991 reforms proposed were indeed radical. However, they were not complete; they proposed starting with the CMOs for cereals, oilseeds and protein plants (to form a COP or 'arable' CMO), with the intention of spreading later to other commodities. Some of the initial proposals were rejected by Member States. These included a limit on the size of dairy herd on which some forms of support were paid and, significantly, an attempt to 'modulate' support to the benefit of smaller farmers; though an element of this remained in the version accepted by the Council of Ministers in 1992 it had been considerably watered-down by the political compromises necessary to get the passage through the Council.[7] The notion of providing dairy farmers with an income bond (yielding an income flow over 10 years, though the bond could be sold for immediate cash) in exchange for reducing their milk quota was also dropped.

The main features of the agreed reform were:

- Over a three-year period, (1993–94 to the 1995/96 marketing years) a substantial cut in the support prices of cereals (–29 per cent) would be made, to levels close to those anticipated for the world market when this had adjusted to the reduced amount of subsidised exports coming from the EU. The use of stabilisers and MGQs was discontinued.
- The lower market prices would be offset by 'compensatory aid' per hectare, calculated according to regional yields and historic prices (i.e. in a past reference period). They were receivable at the predetermined level whatever happened to market prices. These aids were thus 'decoupled' from the factors on which farmers made their current decisions on production, at least partially. Market prices of outputs (which were now lower) and inputs were envisaged as the main determinants of such decisions.
- Compensatory aids would be conditional on farmers with cereal area equivalent to 92 tonnes or more of production (regionally determined) setting aside a certain proportion of their arable area (base area of cereals, oilseeds and protein plants). For set-aside that rotated around the farm this share was to be 15 per cent (higher for non-rotational set-aside), but this figure could be varied in light of market developments. Additional aid would be payable on set-aside land (not modulated by farm size, as was in the original proposals).
- For oilseeds and protein plants, the former system of guaranteed prices was disbanded. Compensatory aid would be paid per hectare at a rate calculated on the assumed relationship between cereal price and oilseed prices.

There were knock-on effects for other sectors, particularly those livestock enterprises that used cereals as feeding stuffs. For the beef sector prices were reduced, in line with the lower costs of cereal feed, offset by the payment of premiums per head, subject to conditions on stocking levels, an arrangement intended to benefit producers who reared using extensive grazing systems and hence who would not benefit from lower cereal prices. The support arrangements for pigmeat and eggs and poultry already included an element that took into account the changing costs of cereals.

The changes made in 1992 for the other sectors represented only minor adaptations, designed mainly to constrain output (see the details given in the chronological list). The outcome was that virtually all the major agricultural commodities found themselves limited by forms of quantitative restraint at the farm or regional level, with disincentives of various degrees of severity for exceeding them (quotas for milk, sugar and tobacco, entitlements for premiums for beef and sheep, oilseeds and protein crops). There was also the (by now usual) range of socio-structural and environmental provisions ('accompanying measures') for environmental programmes, for the afforestation of agricultural land and an extension of the programme of early retirement for farmers, that had been established in 1988.

Some features of the 1992 reforms and their expected impacts are worth noting:

- The budgetary guidelines established in 1988 (negotiated as part of the package for the European Community Budget overall) were continued on an updated basis. However, the ceiling on agricultural expenditure now applied to spending on market policies (including set-aside), supplementary measures (including items previously covered under heading 5a of the Structural Funds), the cost of income support and expenditure on the Guarantee Fund for fisheries.[8] Nevertheless it was anticipated that the reformed CAP would cost more in terms of budgetary expenditure than the unreformed version as the burden shifted from the consumer and more towards the taxpayer.
- For farmers, the degree of compensation for lower market prices was expected to vary substantially from individual to individual, depending on what was grown and the farm's size and location.
- For consumers, food prices were expected to fall, the extent varying between food types and depending on factors such as the proportion of the final price represented by the unprocessed material, the economic behaviour of the food processing and distribution industry etc.
- For industries supplying goods and services to agriculture, the demand for inputs into farming was seen as likely to decline. This could also be reflected in falling land prices where there were no production entitlements attached.
- For administrators, the use of direct payments to farmers required a detailed and sophisticated system of administration and control, including reliable knowledge of cropping and stocking patterns at the individual farm level. These forms of payment are susceptible to fraud, so policing would be required. This bureaucratic burden was expected to be costly and thought possibly beyond the capabilities of some Member States.
- For critics of the CAP, the greater transparency of the payments made to farmers was welcomed as it opened them up to scrutiny. Where the recipients of large sums were large-scale farmers in no obvious need from a welfare viewpoint, these payments were expected to be vulnerable to adverse comment. Though the compensatory aids were not thought to be limited to a time period (though there were contradictions in statements to this effect), some commentators thought that in practice political pressure might build up for them to be terminated or the amounts given to any one individual farmer or holding capped.

In practice, before the 1992 reforms had chance to fully run their course, other factors impinged on EU agriculture. These included in 1992 the withdrawal of the UK from the Exchange Rate Mechanism (ERM) and the subsequent large increase (in sterling) in the level of support payments (which were designated in ECU), the GATT agreement of 1993 (see below) and short-term movements of commodity prices on the world market, notably an increase in cereals prices. In terms of the impact on farm incomes, among cereal producers it was found that the direct payments (based on a historic period and thus 'decoupled') more than compensated them for any falls in price support, so that they saw their profits rise. The rise in world market prices also reduced the costs of export subsidies and hence held the costs of the CAP to below budgeted levels. From 1996 onwards there was, in addition, the widespread impact of the BSE health scare (disrupting the process of reform by the need to deal with the policy actions to control the disease, to pay for control measures, to counter the impacts on the market for beef and the income of farmers etc.).

Though not strictly part of the CAP reform process, the GATT agreement of 1993, the belated conclusion of the Uruguay round of the GATT talks, carried implications for the way in which the CAP had to change. Indeed, significant reform of the CAP, and specifically the need to move away from price support that distorts production and trade on world markets, was a prerequisite for the Uruguay agreement. On oilseeds there was an agreement which reduced the area on which area payments were made, with no additional market support expenditure. More generally, there was a commitment to reduce the amount of market-distorting domestic support, based on the concept of the Aggregate Measure of Support (AMS)(see Chapter 9), to give a minimum market access, to reduce both the budgetary expenditure on subsidised exports and to reduce the volume, all by specified percentages (for details see the Chronological list and Chapter 9). As part of this, the EU was committed to change its various systems of protection of domestic producers into one based on fixed tariffs (rather than variable tariffs – or levies – that changed with the level of world price, and other mechanisms). This process of tariffication exposed the degree of support, and thereby facilitated its scaling down over time.

Forms of support were classified. Amber Box measures (where support affected prices and there was a clear impact on trade) were subject to the commitments to reduce support. Green Box measures (not being price support and having only minimal impact on trade) were exempt from the commitments. A third type formed the Blue Box (support that would otherwise be classed as Amber but where there were restrictions on how much farmers could produce), and these were also exempt from the reduction conditions.

There was dispute over the extent to which the conditions of the GATT agreement were compatible with the reformed CAP. The new compensatory aids introduced as part of the MacSharry reforms qualified for inclusion in the Blue Box so the CAP had little difficulty in meeting the requirement of less coupled domestic support. The main problem area appeared to be in lowering the volume of subsidised exports.

The changes of 1992 and those associated with GATT left several CMOs still to be revised. The prospect of some of the countries in Eastern and Central Europe joining the EU early in the twenty-first century prompted the consideration of a number of options for further reform, as it appeared unlikely that the accession of these could be carried out before change among the existing Members had at least been set in motion.

In late 1995, the Agricultural Commission issued an *Agricultural Strategy Paper* that identified and discussed options; for the most likely of these (which continued the pattern of the 1992 reforms) three streams were set out:

(a) improving the competitiveness of EU agriculture, which meant continuing to dismantle market support, extending this to commodities for which moves towards lower 'world' prices had not yet been made, and accompanying these where necessary with more 'compensatory' direct payments to farmers;

(b) shifting the emphasis from the support of agriculture to one of rural development in which farming and farmers play a part, which implied encouraging on and off-farm diversification, and the support of other activities and facilities in rural areas that were more effective at maintaining incomes, employment and the environment;

(c) simplification which, as has been previously mentioned, means less central control of policies and greater responsibility given to Member States to implement policy. This greater use of subsidiarity went together with the idea of rural development operating within general principles agreed at EU level, but with Member States having freedom to decide on the priorities of local objectives, and how they should be achieved.

12.5.4 Phase 4 – 1997 to the present – Agenda 2000, its 2003 Mid-Term Review, the 2008 Health Check and prospects for policy from 2014 onwards

In 1997, the Commission issued a major discussion document, *Agenda 2000*, that dealt with four main areas of importance to the future development of the EU:

(a) the enlargement of membership to include candidate countries mainly in Central and Eastern Europe;

(b) the future financing of the EU (the 'financial framework'), which included, *inter alia*, the need to review the reduced contribution made by the UK (the UK 'rebate');

(c) reform of the CAP; and

(d) reform of regional policies.

The agricultural section of the *Agenda 2000* paper continued the approach put forward in 1995 in a climate of increasing certainty that the EU would allow the accession of some applicant countries in the first decade of the next century. (The Commission had initially recommended that negotiations for accession should start with Hungary, Poland, Estonia, the Czech Republic, Slovenia and Cyprus). It was concerned with agricultural policy up to 2006. Cereals and beef changes included the further lowering of price support, but with enhanced direct income payments. In the dairy sector, though quotas were to be retained up to 2006 (but relaxed a little), support prices were to be lowered, compensated by the introduction of direct payments. There was to be an attempt to place a ceiling on the amount that individuals could receive in the form of direct income payments, though the poor performance record of such ceilings in the US suggested that perhaps this was an item destined to be abandoned in the move from proposals to actual reform of policy. An enhanced role was proposed for agri-environmental payments, reflecting the multifunctional nature of farming in providing not only agricultural products but also environmental services, for which an increasing demand seemed to come from the public. These payments formed a convenient and politically acceptable way of continuing income support, particularly to farmers in mountainous and other Less Favoured Areas, now that the market intervention was being scaled down.

Of particular note, rural development was promoted to the status of a 'second pillar' of the CAP; it was to be implemented using a reorganised system of support for sustainable rural development incorporating a simplified typology of areas at which support was to be directed. This Pillar 2 represented a clear Commission acceptance of the inevitability of the changes that agriculture was having to face in market developments, market policy and trade rules. These changes would impinge not only on farmers and their households, for whom other forms of economic activity would need to be found – often locally in rural areas – but also, in many regions, on the other sections of society. Thus, the problems of agriculture had to be put in the wider context of rural development policy.

Perhaps most interesting among the *Agenda 2000* proposals was a restatement of the objectives of the CAP. Though these clearly do not carry the weight of the objectives contained in the 1957 Treaty of Rome, they at least revealed how the Commission reinterpreted the earlier set in the conditions of the 1990s. The Commission's objectives for the CAP were (and remain):

- increase competitiveness internally and externally in order to ensure that Union producers take full advantage of positive world market developments;
- food safety and food quality, which are both fundamental obligations towards consumers;
- ensuring a fair standard of living for the agricultural community and contributing to the stability of farm incomes;
- the integration of environmental goals into the CAP;
- promotion of sustainable agriculture;
- the creation of alternative job and income opportunities for farmers and their families;
- simplification of Union legislation.

These formalised the main lines put forward in 1995 (competitiveness, rural development, environment, simplification). The continuing commitment to the vague but potent notion of a 'fair standard of living for the agricultural community' which has been used to justify so much misdirected spending, should be noted.

Agenda 2000 was adopted in principle by the Council in 1998. There followed a series of specific proposals for each of the major commodity regimes that put the outlines into practice, agreed as a package by agriculture ministers in March 1999. The outcome was along the lines of the proposals, though with some modifications needed to secure acceptance. It was expected to be more costly than the support system it replaced because the reform elements involved extra spending; the cost comfortably exceeded the amount that heads of government had set for agriculture (€314 billion in contrast with €307 billion). The price cuts for major agricultural commodities were to be staged and the start of cuts delayed (to 2000 for arable crops and beef, and 2003 for dairy products). Cross-compliance (with environmental considerations) was included as an element that it was foreseen Member States would wish to see implemented, though without specific details. Attempts to cap the amount received per farmer were dropped and any modulation tailing off support to the larger producers left as a national decision. The difficult issue of 'degressivity' – scaling down direct aids over time – was left out of the agreement by the Council of agricultural ministers, though it was thought that it might be later introduced (by a session of the European Council) as a way of limiting CAP costs and of achieving an agreement on the way of financing the EU.

The attention of the Berlin European Council of 24/25 March 1999 was largely diverted to the consequences flowing from the resignation of the entire Commission (following an independent report on corruption, fraud and lack of accountability, in the face of a probable vote to dismiss it by the Parliament) and conflict in the Balkans. The compromise which was necessary to secure unanimity of support for the complete *Agriculture 2000* package further watered down the agricultural reforms, principally by lessening the price cuts for cereals and also the accompanying compensation payments, and by delaying reform in the dairy sector (which included the introduction of compensation payments) to 2005. (Though these were not the only factors involved, France saw it necessary to protect its agricultural interests by blunting the reforms, while the UK had put great political weight on retaining the rebate on its net contribution to the EU budget). This achieved the reduction in CAP budgetary expenditure that enabled it to fit into the new Financial Framework without resort to politically difficult matters such as degressivity of compensatory payments; under the final *Agenda 2000* agreement, limits on agricultural spending were set to 2006.

To implement Pillar 2, and reflecting the broadening of concern in the CAP beyond agricultural activity, in 1999 a special Rural Development Regulation (No 1257/1999) set out the framework for future support to rural areas by consolidating previous legislation that stretched back in some forms to 1972 (which was thus repealed). In particular, it brought together the 'accompanying measures' that had formed part of the 1992 MacSharry reforms (early retirement, agri-environment and afforestation), the Less Favoured Areas schemes, and measures to modernise and diversify agricultural holdings (farm investment, setting up of young farmers, training, investment aid for processing and marketing facilities, additional assistance for forestry, promotion and conversion of agriculture) (see Chapters 7 and 8) and applied them in national or sub-national Rural Development Programmes for the seven-year period 2000–6. Some €4.3 billion per year was allocated from EU funds for rural development, though this only represented some 10–13 per cent of total planned CAP spending in the then 15 Member States. Even though Member States were required to part-finance RDPs, as a second pillar of the CAP, rural development remained quite spindly.

The European Councils of December 2000 (Nice) and June 2001 (Göteborg) moved towards the accession of 10 countries by the time of the next round of European elections in 2004. The accessions of Bulgaria, Romania and Turkey were treated as possible, but only at some later date. This timetable added pressure to ensuring that the agricultural reforms incorporated in *Agenda 2000* were operating effectively.

In June 2002, the Commission published its Mid-Term Review of *Agenda 2000* containing a further set of proposals for change. To some countries the provisions appeared to go far beyond a review and constituted a substantial reform of the CAP; some countries (particularly France) were opposed to making reforms in this way. The Commission's aim was to 'enable the EU to ensure a transparent and more equitable distribution of income support for farmers, and to better respond to what our consumers and taxpayers want', which implies a concern with a better justification of spending rather than lower spending. The continuing significance of the income strand of policy should be noted. A package of changes was adopted by the Council in January 2003. The key elements of this 2003 reform were:

- The introduction of a single payment that bundled together and replaced other forms of direct payments associated with commodity-linked support. Various options were offered to Member States on how the payments at farm level (the Single Farm Payment or Single Area Payment – SFP/SAP) could be calculated (see Chapter 6). An important characteristic was that these payments at farm level were made independent from current production (that is, they were 'decoupled'). Though this was not total, in that to be eligible, recipients had to be occupiers of agricultural land, they were more decoupled than were the direct payments introduced as part of the MacSharry reforms of 1992.

- The use of Single Area Payments would enable the system of support payments to be applied to the 10 new Member States that were to join the EU in 2004.
- Linking these payments to standards in environmental, food safety, animal welfare, health, occupational safety standards and the maintenance of land in good condition ('cross-compliance').
- A stronger rural development policy, with more funds and new measures.
- A reduction in direct payments ('modulation') for larger farms to generate additional funds for rural development and to finance further reforms.
- Revision to the market policy of the CAP, including (a) a final 5 per cent cut in intervention price for cereals and higher direct payments; (b) wider ranging and accelerated reform in the milk sector, with differentiated price cuts for butter and skim milk powder and the maintaining of the milk quota system until 2014/2015; (c) reform in the rice, durum wheat, nuts, starch potatoes and dried fodder sectors.

The introduction of the Single Farm (or Area) Payment (SFP or SAP) represented a very substantial change in the basis of payment and the incentives to production given to farmers. By decoupling support payments, farmers' decisions on how much to produce of what commodities became dependent on market signals, not on supported prices. How farmers were expected to react to a mixture of lower product prices and very-low-risk SFP/ SAPs was a matter of debate; though a case was made that economically rational producers would lower outputs, they might be encouraged to launch into more risky enterprises and investments that they otherwise might have avoided. But the impact of structural change on industrial production is also difficult to predict. While the SFP/SAP may encourage some farmers to remain who might otherwise have left, the land of those who quit agriculture is likely to be taken over by more productive operators, so it is conceivable that output could rise (though this would be still at market prices).

In 2008, the Commission published its *CAP Health Check*, which now applied to a policy for an EU of 27 Member States. This was a scheduled (planned) review and adjustment of the mechanisms of the CAP, the result of which was a set of steps in the directions already underway. Agreement was reached in the November 2008 Agriculture Council on the following main reforms that were to be implemented early in 2009:

- further decoupling of direct farm payments from production in sectors such as arable crops where Member States still had some options for maintaining some coupled direct payments;
- further limits on market controls, including the abolition of compulsory set-aside and the introduction of a tendering system for wheat intervention;
- agreement on the process for phasing out milk quotas by 2015, including a basic 1 per cent per year increase in quotas over the next five years, though with some differential increases for some countries;
- reducing red tape for farmers through some simplification of direct farm payments and the requirements of cross-compliance;
- increasing the rate of `compulsory modulation' across the EU from 5 per cent to 10 per cent by 2012, and therefore increasing the share of CAP funding that goes towards environment and rural development schemes;
- the option for countries to use cross-compliance to help address the environmental effects of ending set-aside;

- Extending SAPS: EU members applying the simplified Single Area Payment Scheme are to be allowed to continue to do so until 2013 instead of being forced into the Single Payment Scheme by 2010;
- Additional funding for EU-12 using SAPS (€90 million) to make it easier for them to make use of 'Article 68' (which enables Member States to retain 10 per cent of their national budget ceilings for direct payments for use for environmental measures or improving the quality and marketing of products);
- Investment aid for young farmers under Rural Development is increased from €55,000 to €70,000.

The ratification of the Lisbon Treaty meant that, from December 2009, the European Parliament's role in decisions about agricultural policy was much enhanced. Subsequently, proposed reforms to the CAP are subject to the 'ordinary legislative procedure', involving co-decision between the Council and European Parliament (see Chapter 3). The implications for the speed and direction of CAP reform, compared with when the Council alone held responsibility for most decisions, is yet to emerge. Scenarios could be imagined in which the Parliament was more reformist than the Council, or vice versa. What is clear is that proposals drafted by the Commission have now to treat the Parliament as seriously as it does the Council.

In November 2010, the Commission published a consultation document on the shape the CAP should take in the period 2014 to 2020, though it had been widely leaked some months earlier. In *The CAP Towards 2020: Meeting the Food, Natural Resources and Territorial Challenges of the Future*, the Commission described why further CAP reform is seen to be necessary. It saw a set of 'new challenges', notably:

- to address rising concerns regarding both EU and global food security;
- to enhance the sustainable management of natural resources such as water, air, biodiversity and soil;
- to deal with both the increasing pressure on agricultural production conditions caused by on-going climatic changes, as well as the need for farmers to reduce their contribution to GHG emissions, play an active role in mitigation and provide renewable energy;
- to retain and enhance competitiveness in a world characterised by increasing globalisation and rising price volatility, while maintaining agricultural production across the whole European Union;
- to make best use of the diversity of EU farm structures and production systems, which has increased following EU enlargement, while maintaining its social, territorial and structuring role;
- to strengthen territorial and social cohesion in the rural areas of the EU, notably through the promotion of employment and diversification;
- to make CAP support equitable and balanced between Member States and farmers, by reducing disparities between Member States taking into account that a flat rate is not a feasible solution, and better targeted to active farmers;
- to pursue the simplification of the CAP implementation procedures and enhance control requirements, and reduce the administrative burden for recipients of funds.

(COM(2010) 672 final)

Contrary to the Commission's claim, few of these challenges are new; most represent issues of long concern to the CAP, though they may have become more pressing. Environmental issues are given prominence. However, it is of interest to note that food security is listed once again, something that had taken a low profile since the CAP's earliest days because of the rise in agriculture's production levels. The Commission view is that the EU should be able to contribute to the worldwide demand for food, that is anticipated to continue to rise. There is a commitment to maintain agricultural production (which may not always be rationale economically).

The overall architecture of CAP support is not to be changed (Pillars 1 and 2). Perhaps the most radical aspect is the mention, on grounds of equity and balance, of targeting support to 'active farmers', a term that is capable of a multitude of interpretations. The payments themselves are envisaged as providing basic income support (with capping on what is received by the largest farmers). A component of them is to be 'greened' in a way that goes beyond mere cross-compliance. Farmers facing natural handicaps (presumably as in LFAs) are to receive additional area-based payments, the rationale of which is not spelled out. A simple and specific support scheme for small farmers is envisaged. Among the market measures, the emphasis is on streamlining and simplifying, with the retention of facilities to intervene in crisis conditions. There is renewed commitment to the ending of dairy quotas in 2015 and to the expiry of the sugar/isoglucose regime in 2014/15, but what arrangements are needed subsequently are unclear. There are no major reform proposals for rural development policy within the CAP, though improvements in the performance of delivery mechanisms are envisaged.

Three broad policy options are outlined (for more details see Table 12.2):

- Option 1 represents maintaining the status quo, with further gradual changes, an approach that 'would ensure continuity and stability with the current CAP, thus facilitating long-term planning for operators along the food chain'.
- Option 2 is to make major overhauls of the policy in order to ensure that it becomes more sustainable, and that the balance between different policy objectives, farmers and Member States is better met. This would be done through more targeted measures, implying greater spending efficiency. 'Such an orientation would allow to address EU economic, environmental and social challenges and strengthen the contribution of agriculture and rural areas to the objectives of Europe 2020 of smart, sustainable and inclusive growth'.
- Option 3 would be a 'more far reaching reform of the CAP with a strong focus on environmental and climate change objectives, while moving away gradually from income support and most market measures'.

As a package, the proposed reforms look modest. In particular, the system of direct payments to farms (SFP/SAPs) and the link with land occupancy are retained. Clearly the argument that complete decoupling of SFPs should take place (the link with farm occupation should be broken, so that entitlement no longer depends on occupying land) has not won the day within the Commission. Furthermore, the long-term sustainability of such payments has not been called into question. As the SFPs are based on entitlements to previous (coupled) direct payments linked to commodities, and these were themselves compensations for cuts in support prices, it is reasonable to ask about the length of time such payments should last and how they should be phased out. Criticisms on equity grounds have also been made more

Table 12.2   The Commission's proposals for the CAP after 2013

	Direct payments	*Market measures*	*Rural development*
Option 1	Introduce more equity in the distribution of direct payments between Member States (while leaving unchanged the current direct payment system).	Strengthen risk management tools. Streamline and simplify existing market instruments where appropriate.	Maintain the Health Check orientation of increasing funding for meeting the challenges related to climate change, water, biodiversity and renewable energy, and innovation.
Option 2	Introduce more equity in the distribution of direct payments between Member States and a substantial change in their design. Direct payments would be composed of: • a basic rate serving as income support; • a compulsory additional aid for specific 'greening' public goods through simple, generalised, annual and non-contractual agri-environmental actions based on the supplementary costs for carrying out these actions; • an additional payment to compensate for specific natural constraints; • and a voluntary coupled support component for specific sectors and regions*. Introduce a new scheme for small farms. Introduce a capping of the basic rate, while also considering the contribution of large farms to rural employment.	Improve and simplify existing market instruments where appropriate.	Adjust and complement existing instruments to be better aligned with EU priorities, with support focused on environment, climate change and/ or restructuring and innovation, and to enhance regional/local initiatives. Strengthen existing risk management tools and introduce an optional WTO Green Box compatible income stabilisation tool to compensate for substantial income losses. Some redistribution of funds between Member States based on objective criteria could be envisaged.
Option 3	Phase-out direct payments in their current form. Provide instead limited payments for environmental public goods and additional specific natural constraints payments.	Abolish all market measures, with the potential exception of disturbance clauses that could be activated in times of severe crisis.	The measures would be mainly focused on climate change and environment aspects.

*This would be equivalent to coupled support paid through Article 68 of *Agenda 2000*
Source: Annex of Commission (2010) *The CAP Towards 2020: Meeting the Food, Natural Resources and Territorial Challenges of the Future.* (COM(2010) 672 final)

potent because of the greater transparency of SFPs, and there is now open information on who receives what in SFPs and other grants and subsidies from the CAP (see Chapter 6). While there is validity in paying larger sums to occupiers of large farms for agri-environmental reasons for the provision of larger volumes of services, it is far harder to justify continuing large direct payments as compensation for a change in policy that happened in the early 1990s. A more rigorous reform might make the SFP relate to the farmer rather than the farm and start phasing it out, or at least transform it into something for which environmental, social or cultural benefits are received in exchange from the farming community.

The shape of the CAP for the period from 2014 onwards is thus likely to be rather similar to the present. Radical change will be avoided as there does not appear to be a driver or event that demands it. The Commission's proposals seem to be compatible with budgetary guidelines, the Doha round of WTO talks does not seem to demand major restructuring of agricultural policy, and further potential enlargements of the EU only involve rather small countries as long as Turkey's accession is stalled. Though unanticipated events might trigger change, known pressures do not make it imperative.

It is convenient at this point to reflect on the process of reform to the CAP and to draw general lessons that might be useful in understanding future events.

12.6 General observations of the reform process

Despite the forces impeding reform, it is clear that significant change in the CAP has taken place, particularly since the mid-1990s. Characteristics of how this has been brought about that are worth noting are:

12.6.1 Windows of opportunity to reform under crisis conditions

Chapter 3, when discussing the bureaucratic and political nature of the CAP's decision-making process, pointed out that there is a tendency for institutions to prefer the status quo and for decision-takers to respond to pressure by only making marginal changes. Fundamental reform has only been considered seriously and implemented when a crisis was imminent that threatened the existence of the entire CAP, even perhaps of the entire apparatus of the EU. Usually this has taken the form of a budgetary crisis or, in the later decades, elements of both budget and trade issues. Examples we have already met in this chapter include the following:

- In 1983 the problems of CAP costs led to the 1984 Fontainebleau Summit of heads of government which agreed a need to apply budgetary constraints to agricultural spending. In 1987, a new financial crisis led to the introduction in 1988 of what attempted to be a more binding form of budgetary discipline (though effective control was not achieved until later) and other changes, including the enlargement and a new role for the Structural Funds.
- The significant MacSharry reforms, put into effect in 1992, arose from a mixture of budgetary problems and political pressure to achieve a settlement in GATT, failure to do so threatening a disruption to international trade and trade 'wars', especially with the USA, that would have had consequences beyond the confines of agriculture.
- The reforms proposed in 1997 as part of *Agenda 2000* were in the face of an urgent need to prepare the CAP for the entry to the EU of the first wave of candidate countries in Central and Eastern Europe, since lack of reform might prove to be costly both in a

short-term budgetary sense and, on a longer perspective, in sending wrong signals to their agricultures about the way that they should develop and the sorts of support that might be on offer beyond the millennium.
• Changes made to the CAP in the 2003 Mid-Term Review were also stimulated by the impending accession of 10 new Member States and the need to have in place a support system capable of operating for an EU of 25 (later 27) countries.

These crisis periods provide windows of opportunity during which Member States could be persuaded to accept proposals for change that, under more normal circumstances, would be resisted.

12.6.2 Ratchets in the change process

The inability to make reform as radical or as complete as perhaps would be desirable always delivers only partial success, and this seems to be reflected in the strategy of the Commission, the institution responsible for making propositions for reform. A pattern can be discerned in the way that it introduces changes. Typically, the Commission publishes a discussion document (after issuing initial internal papers for consideration by the Council); examples include the *1985 Perspectives on the Common Agricultural Policy* (following the internal document with COM(83) 500), the 1988 *Future of Rural Society* document, and the 1991 'MacSharry' proposals, aired in two forms, first as a communication from the Commission to the Council (COM(91)100 final) and, second, as a more generally available Green Europe 2/91 *The Development and Future of the Common Agricultural Policy: Proposals of the Commission*. The *Agenda 2000* proposals document of 1997 is another example, as is the 2010 *The CAP Towards 2020: Meeting the Food, Natural Resources and Territorial Challenges of the Future* which considers changes in the CAP for the period from 2014. These early documents usually take quite a radical approach, perhaps more so than the Commission thinks necessary to meet the immediate policy problems. However, the Commission knows that much at this stage will be rejected by decisions made in the Council; while ministers from some Member States are likely to want to go further in making changes than the Commission, decisions on policy have to be reached by the procedures in place and they may not be able to persuade their colleagues. However, ideas can be sown; when the time is ripe, the Commission may re-propose some of them, with greater likelihood of successful acceptance.

One example of seeding ideas concerned direct income payments to farmers; these were mooted in the 1985 Perspectives paper but only for debate, not implementation. However, in 1992, a form of direct payment became a central plank in the reformed system of support. By the late 1990s direct income payments (the term is used overtly in *Agenda 2000*) were seen as the main way forward for support, coupled with environmental payments and stimulants to the rural economy, as interventions in commodity markets were to be reduced to one of stabilisation, not support. The 2003 Mid-Term Review of *Agenda 2000* transformed most direct payments into a Single Farm Payment (operational from 2005) that was largely decoupled from production decisions, thereby completing a process that was first mooted some 20 years earlier. Though this method of making progress is to be found in many large organisations, it may sometimes be overlooked that the Commission is capable of taking a strategic attitude to changes in the interest of the Union as a whole. Its position gives it an overall view of what the problems are and the policy responses needed. Perhaps this is best seen working when the Commission acts on behalf of the EU in trade negotiations.

12.6.3 Broadening of the perspective of agricultural policy over time

It is apparent that the policy towards agriculture is increasingly seen within the context of other policies – regional policy, environmental policy, trade policy etc. The compartmentalism which resulted in the CAP being conceived and operated more-or-less in sectoral isolation, with very weak links to other policies, is breaking down. For reasons of institutional structure and history, before 1988 the problems of rural areas were predominantly considered as separate from those of agriculture, despite the obvious link between farming and the rural economy. However, from 1988, with the reform of the Structural Funds and the publication of *The Future of Rural Society*, the two have come together, so that now it is hardly possible to consider agricultural policy measures without at the same time taking into consideration their impact on rural society and, in turn, recognising that agriculture can be affected by changes in the rural economy (for example, by providing job opportunities for farm families). Indeed, the maintenance of rural society is often a major element justifying agricultural support.

Now rural development priorities, set at EU level, give particular weight (in terms of expenditure) to the environmental role of agriculture. Though schemes are supported that aim to improve the competitiveness of agriculture, the broader context in which farming takes place is predominant. Much the same broadening could be said to have taken place in the connection between agricultural policy and trade and foreign policy. In particular, the 1993 GATT agreement had a very strong impact on the CAP, and CAP decisions now have to consider their trade environment. While the Doha Round (under the auspices of the WTO) has not yet reached a successful conclusion, it is clear that it has had influence on the way that support is given under the CAP, in particular the switch to the Single Farm Payment system which is far more decoupled and thus less trade-distorting than previous methods of supporting EU agriculture.

12.7 A model of the reform process

The final section in this chapter presents a simple model of the reform process that may be useful in understanding future CAP changes. Looking back at past reforms gives some indication of forces at work on shaping policy from which some generalisations are possible. Figure 12.1 (based on work by Moyer and Josling) shows that decision-making operates under a number of pressures and influences. It follows that changes in these can lead to change (reform) in the policy.

As noted previously, policy is a continuous process and so the decisions in previous periods are a major factor explaining the shape of the present policy, and today's decisions will largely determine the CAP of tomorrow (indicated in Figure 12.1 by the decisions in t–1 and t+1).

Decisions are taken within a political environment (in the case of the CAP that provided by the EU) and reflect the existing 'agricultural policy paradigm', the predominant view of agriculture and what policy is trying to achieve. For many years the 'paradigm' was that of supporting agricultural production and thus the incomes of producers. However, neither are unchanging. Political developments (such as the notion that the EU should be enlarged) and political shocks (such as unrest in the Balkans which might make it suddenly in the EU's broader interests to allow the more stable states there rapid entry to EU membership) will change the environment in which decisions take place. They will also change the dominant view of agriculture; with increasing interests by voters in the environmental and social aspects of policy, decision-makers may see the role of agriculture as less concerned with food production and more to do with the provision of environmental and social services (keeping rural communities going etc.) Economic trends, such as productivity growth and the continual decline in the numbers of people working in agriculture, will also help shape the political environment and policy paradigm. But it is the shorter-term economic shocks (sudden financial crises brought about by, for example, oil price rises, or animal disease outbreaks) that often trigger action. Of course, politics and economics are closely linked (hence the joining arrow in Figure 12.1); perhaps the BSE crisis that started in 1996 is the best example, with both a sudden political pressure for action and a major shock to the economic situation of beef producers combining to change the circumstances in which decisions take place and hence the nature of the decisions.

Another factor determining the surroundings of decisions is the international pressure that can come from other governments and international institutions. The prime example of this is objections to the CAP's support of agriculture in ways that distorted markets and trade patterns and thereby harmed the interests of other agricultural exporting countries (see Chapter 9).

Figure 12.1 shows that these pressures and shocks are transmitted via people, firms and organisations that have interests in the outcome of policy decisions. The most direct

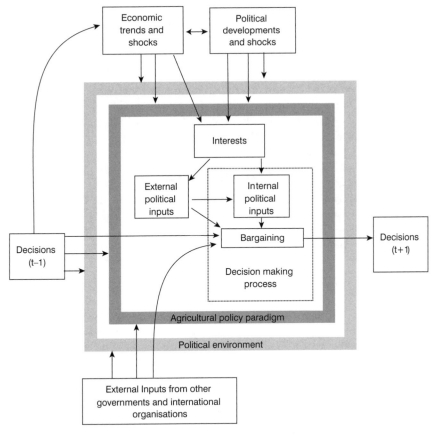

Figure 12.1   The dynamic agricultural policy-making process (after Moyer and Josling, 1990)

route is by influencing people who take part in the decision-making process, such as the Commissioners and their staff and (now) MEPs (the 'internal political inputs'). More likely, this influence is transmitted by lobbying by pressure groups (European-level organisations such as unions representing farmers or trade groups representing the haulage industry); these are outside the decision-making circle ('external political inputs') but try to influence those who actually take the decisions, including the politicians whose job it is to bargain among themselves and reach a decision. Other governments may bypass the administrator level of the decision-making process and go straight to the ministers making the decisions.

From this model it should be clear that policy will always be subject to change as the political and economic environment alters; many of the technical and economic forces behind these changes are well established. However, this change is not a process that happens rapidly and smoothly. Often it needs the momentum of an economic or political shock to overcome the inertia of the decision-making process. Thus, when looking forward to the way in which the CAP may change in the future, though the direction in which change is anticipated may be reasonably clear, the details and the speed are not so predictable. Shocks are, by their nature, unpredictable in their timing.

12.8 Postscript – a chronology of events

This chapter contains as an annex a list of the more significant events in the history of the CAP and the EU of which it is a major part. This is provided in the hope that the complicated series of happenings, drawn on in this chapter and referred to in many of the preceding ones, may be somewhat more comprehensible. Sometimes it is helpful to have development in a summary form to jog the memory. Though more weight is given to the most recent decade or so, explaining the CAP of the second decade of the twenty-first century (and beyond) should not underplay the importance of what happened in the earlier formative years; though the passing of time may have diluted the significance of some of their details, they helped set the foundations of what we see today. Path dependency is an important feature of the CAP.

Further reading

Ackrill, R. (2000) 'Understanding the process of CAP reform'. Chapter 5 in *The Common Agricultural Policy*. Sheffield Academic Press, Sheffield.

Blandford, D. and Hill, B. (eds) (2006) *Policy Reform and Adjustment in the Agricultural Sectors of Developed Countries*, CAB International, Wallingford.

European Commission (2006) *Scenar 2020 – Scenario Study on Agriculture and the Rural World*. Commission, Brussels.

European Commission (2009) *Preparing for Change: Update of Analysis of Prospects in the Scenar 2020 Study*. Final report.

European Commission (2010) *The CAP Towards 2020: Meeting the Food, Natural Resources and Territorial Challenges of The Future*. Communication from the Commission to the European Parliament, the Council, the European Economic and Social Committee and the Committee of the Regions. Brussels, 18 November 2010, COM(2010) 672 final.

Fennell, R. (1997) *The Common Agricultural Policy – Continuity and Change*. Clarendon Press, Oxford.

Gardner, B. (1996) *European Agriculture: Policies, Production and Trade*. Routledge, London

Garzon, I. (2007) *Reforming the Common Agricultural Policy: History of Paradigm Change*. Palgrave Macmillan, London

Meester, G. (2010) 'Future developments and policies'. Chapter 24 in Oskam, A., Meester, G. and Huib, H. (eds) *EU Policy for Agriculture, Food and Rural Areas*. Wageningen Academic Publishers, Wageningen.

Moyer, H. W. and Josling, T. E. (1990) *Agricultural Policy Reform: Politics and Process in the EC and USA*. Iowa State University Press, Ames, IA.

Moyer, W. and Josling, T. (2002) *Agricultural Policy Reform: Politics and Process in the EU and in the US in the 1990s*. Ashgate Publishing, Aldershot.

Ockenden, J. and Franklin, M. (1995) *European Agriculture: Making the CAP Fit the Future*. Royal Institution of International Affairs, London.

OECD (2002) *Agricultural Policies in OECD Countries: A Positive Reform Agenda*. Organisation for Economic Co-operation and Development, Paris.

OECD (2010) *Agricultural policies in OECD Countries at a Glance – 2010*. Organisation for Economic Co-operation and Development, Paris.

OECD (2011) *Disaggregated Impacts of CAP Reforms: Proceedings of an OECD Workshop*, OECD Publishing, Paris.

Oskam, A., Meester, G. and Huib, H. (eds) (2010) *EU Policy for Agriculture, Food and Rural Areas*. Wageningen Academic Publishers, Wageningen.

Ritson, C. and Harvey, D. R. (1997) *The Common Agricultural Policy*. 2nd edition. CAB International, Wallingford. (Especially parts 1 and 5)

Swinbank, A. and Tranter, R. (eds) (2004) *A Bond Scheme for Common Agricultural Policy Reform*. CAB International, Wallingford.

Thurston, J. (2002) *How to Reform the Common Agricultural Policy*. European Rural Communities Paper 1. Foreign Policy Centre, London. Available online at http://www.cepii.fr/anglaisgraph/communications/pdf/2002/141102/thurston.pdf

Tracy, M. (1989) *Government and Agriculture in Western Europe 1880–1988*. 3rd edition. Harvester Wheatsheaf, Hemel Hempsted.

Tracy, M. (1993) *Food and Agriculture in a Market Economy: An Introduction to Theory, Practice and Policy*. APS, La Hutte, Belgium.

Veerman, C. (2010) 'Agriculture: a binding factor for Europe?' Chapter 23 in Oskam, A., Meester, G. and Huib, H. (eds) *EU Policy for Agriculture, Food and Rural Areas*. Wageningen Academic Publishers, Wageningen.

ANNEX: A CHRONOLOGY
OF THE EU AND CAP

1946

Winston Churchill (in a speech in Zurich) proposes a United States of Europe, with Franco-German co-operation as an essential element. Britain was seen as a promoter rather than as an active participant.

1948

The Organisation for European Economic Co-operation (OEEC) came into being on 16 April 1948. It emerged from the Marshall Plan to provide American aid for a post-War recovery programme for Europe and the Conference of Sixteen (Conference for European Economic Co-operation), which sought to establish a permanent organisation to continue work and in particular to supervise the distribution of aid.

Belgium, France, Luxembourg, Netherlands and UK form the Western European Union for the purpose of mutual assistance and political consultation on military matters.

Congress organised by the European Movement in the Hague called for unity, with various subsequent failed attempts at integration.

1949

Council of Europe set up as an intergovernmental organisation by Belgium, Netherlands, Luxembourg, France and the UK (others joined later), but its Consultative Assembly could only discuss issues and its resolutions could be vetoed by the Committee of Ministers.

1950

Chairman of the OEEC Council, (Stikker) put forward an action plan for the economic integration of Europe through specialisation of activities, division of labour and the creation of a single European market. Countries with heavy state trade were asked to issue long-term purchase contracts at reasonable prices, and a joint list of objects for freeing was proposed.

Robert Schuman (French Foreign Minister, born in Luxembourg) announced his Plan, developed from a proposal by Jean Monnet (of the French National Plan Commission). Political reasoning lay behind it: in the face of the threat from Russia, there was a need to bring West Germany into the Western group of nations. The elements were: (i) to eliminate the old rivalry between France and (West) Germany, but other countries could be involved too if they wished; (ii) to build solidarity by uniting action on a limited but decisive target (the need to restructure the coal and steel industry which was over-capacity and pushing prices down); (iii) the idea that merging economic interests would help raise standards of living and pave the way for the establishment of an economic community; (iv) that an independent authority (HIgh Authority) would be created whose decisions would be binding on participating countries, and enforceable. France and West Germany were supportive of the Plan.

Idea of a European Defence Community (with a single army) put forward by the French (brainchild of Jean Monnet) as part of a broader supra-national Community (Pléven Plan).

1951

Treaty of Paris setting up European Coal and Steel Community (ECSC) by the Six (Belgium, West Germany, France, Italy, Luxembourg, Netherlands) to run for 50 years. Components: High Authority (fore-runner of the European Commission), Parliamentary Assembly (forerunner of the European Parliament), Council of Ministers, Court of Justice.

1952

Two new communities proposed European Defence Community (EDC) and European Political Community. EDC Treaty signed in Paris.

1954

European Defence Community opposed by French National Assembly, in effect killed off. In the light of this, Germany and Italy join Western European Union (WEU).

1955

Jean Monnet creates the Action Committee for a United States of Europe.

1956

Spaak (Paul-Henri – Belgian statesman) Report proposes European Economic Community (EEC) and European Atomic Energy Community, approved by foreign ministers. The UK was not interested in EEC membership, disliking the supra-national nature of some elements such as the Commission, preferring a free trade area.

1957

Treaties of Rome (European Economic Community with six members) and European Atomic Energy Community (Euratom) to come into force on 1 January 1958
(Note the subsequent formation in 1960 of the European Free Trade Association (EFTA) by seven countries: Austria, Denmark, Norway, Portugal, Sweden, Switzerland, UK)

1958

1 January the two Treaties of Rome come into force and new Communities come into being, so that there are now three separate Communities (EEC, ECSC, Euratom) with three Commissions, three Councils, shared Parliamentary Assembly and Court of Justice. Robert Schuman president of EEC (also known as the 'Common Market').

Main objectives of all three Communities – economic expansion and higher standards of living, accompanied by political union of the peoples of Europe. EEC immediate objectives are a customs union, with free movement of goods, dismantling of quotas and barriers to trade, free movement of persons, services and capital.

Common EEC policies provided for on agriculture, transport, competition, social policy, trade policy and harmonised legislation – also provision for other common policies if need arose e.g. regional, environment, consumer protection. Rome Treaty silent on general economic policy and monetary policy – in hands of individual members.

Specific recognition of responsibilities for former colonies.

Stresa Conference worked out broad lines of CAP, vital in the EEC context. Aimed at easier movement of goods (i.e. a free market) faced by economic, social and political problems.

Basic principles of CAP:
  (a) establishment of a single market and consequently common prices for most agricultural products;
  (b) assurance that those working in agriculture will enjoy a standard of living comparable to that enjoyed by workers in other sectors;
  (c) community preference (meaning that support mechanisms should not provide an incentive to import into the EEC rather than use commodities produced within the EEC);
  (d) financial solidarity (implies Member States pay into to a central fund which is used to fund policies wherever problems arise, with no automatic balance between what a country puts in and what they receive).

European Investment Bank set up (under Rome Treaty) to provide loans and guarantees for industry, energy, infrastructure and mechanisation.

European Parliamentary Assembly (later renamed the European Parliament) meets for the first time.

1959

Cuts in customs duties started (not for agricultural commodities). Common external tariff.

Greece and Turkey apply to become associated states of the EEC.

1960

European Social Fund instituted (as part of EEC) to help create jobs and promote vocational and geographical mobility in industries not covered by the ECSC. EFTA set up (Stockholm Convention) by non-EEC countries.

1961

Moves towards political union:
(a) Regular summits (of heads of government) start to be held;
(b) Christian Fouchet (France) puts forward two plans for political union – not well received.

Greece strikes association agreement (ultimately Greece accession)

UK, Ireland, and Denmark apply for membership.

First easing of controls on labour movement in the EEC comes into force.

Brussels conference held with dependent developing countries.

1962

Council decrees that EEC has reached the second stage of integration prescribed in the EEC Treaty. Temporary financing arranged (to last to 1965) giving the Community its 'own resources'.

Spain and Portugal make approaches for association.

Common Agricultural Policy effectively introduced, with financial solidarity operated through the European Agricultural Guidance and Guarantee Fund (EAGGF or FEOGA, its French acronym). Norway applies for membership.

1963

UK and other country negotiations break down – de Gaulle doubts political will of UK. Contact with UK to be maintained via Western European Union.

Yaoundé Convention agreement (valid five years) signed between the Community and 18 less developed countries: aimed to promote commercial, technical and financial co-operation.

Turkey – associations agreement signed. Trade agreement made with Iran.

1964

Kennedy Round of GATT reduces external tariff by 35–40 per cent (agricultural products excepted)

EAGGF/FEOGA starts operating. Market organisations set up – uniform prices agreed, to be used from 1967.

Necessity for new financing arrangements (especially to finance CAP) W. Hallstein (President of the Commission) proposals for 'own resources' from levies and subject to review by European Parliament.

1965

No agreement on new financing (Council meeting in Brussels) 30 June. As part of this, France withdraws from Council and COREPER over negotiations to finance the CAP and increase European Parliament powers over the EC budget, thereby operating an 'empty chair' policy that prevents decisions from being taken.

Treaty signed in Brussels to merge the executives of the three Communities (actual merger in 1967).

1966

'Luxembourg Compromise' reached which encourages France to return to meetings: this enables a country to state that a 'vital national interest' is at stake on an issue, when the others agree to proceed only by reaching decisions unanimously within 'a reasonable time'. Majority voting (scheduled for 1966) is thus foiled on big issues, where in effect a veto by any Member State operates.

1967

New Kennedy GATT round aims for further tariff reductions.

Greece association put on ice (because of colonel's revolution). UK, Ireland, Denmark and Norway reapply for EEC membership, but this is not progressed because of reluctance on the part of the French President (de Gaulle).

1967

Single Council and Commission formed by merger. Term 'European Community' (EC) used, from now on (replacing EEC or reference to Communities in plural).

1968

Customs Union completed by abolition of remaining internal customs duties, and common external tariff (CET) is introduced.

Sicco Mansholt Plan (former Dutch Minister of Agriculture, now the Commissioner for Agriculture) proposed, involving:
- accelerated structural change combined with a more realistic price policy;
- farms should be 80–120 hectare of cropland and 40–60 cows;
- 5 million people should leave agriculture in the 1970s by early retirement or retraining;
- agricultural area to be reduced by 5 million hectare (out of 70 million hectare) and dairy cow numbers by 3 million;

The plan engendered violent opposition from farmers and organisations.

1969

Heads of government in Hague Summit declare that Treaty of Rome is now in its definitive stage, with: calls for economic and monetary union; expression of favourable views on enlargement; sees need for strengthening community institutions and thereby provides an impetus to political co-operation. Summit agrees that the Community should be given its 'own resources' and to an increase in Parliament's budgetary powers.

Adoption of definitive arrangements for the CAP.

1970

Davignon Report (on political co-operation) agrees to periodic meetings of foreign ministers and staff, to promote mutual understanding of world issues and to act collectively where possible, so that the EC has a single voice on all major international problems.

New negotiations for UK, Ireland, Denmark and Norway accession.

Pierre Werner Plan (a Luxembourger) for greater economic and monetary integration adopted by Council. Its aim was full economic and monetary union by 1980.

Treaty of Luxembourg (came into effect 1971) providing for the gradual introduction of an 'own resources' system for the Community and extends the budgetary powers of the European Parliament. It also introduces the distinction between compulsory and non-compulsory expenditure.

1971

Non-associated developing countries offered preferential tariff treatment.

1972

Signing of Treaties of Accession for UK, Ireland, Denmark and Norway (Norway does not join following a referendum); Britain, Ireland and Denmark actually join in 1973.

March, resolution by the Council on the steps to achieve economic and monetary union, with UK, Ireland and Denmark as members. The EU-6 introduce a currency 'snake', with agreement to limit the margin of fluctuation of currencies to 2.25 per cent. In June UK and Ireland withdraw (as does France in 1973).

Three Directives agreed, forming a weak response to the Mansholt Plan, aimed at improving agricultural structures. These were horizontal measures, that is applicable in all Member States, though national legislation was required to turn them into practical schemes. Directive 72/159/EEC related to the modernisation of holdings (primarily investment incentives for new buildings etc. which in the UK took the form of the Farm and Horticulture Development Scheme); Dir. 72/160/EEC to encourage early retirement; Directive 72/161/EEC for vocational training.

1973

Tokyo round of GATT begins.

Yaoundé Convention II – enlarges to embrace UK's less-developed country associates and others (ACP countries: Africa, Caribbean and Pacific – some Commonwealth members).

Agreement between Community and EFTA countries which have not joined the Community come into force. The common external tariff is not applied to them; as a consequence they are in the Community's free trade area, but are not covered by the Common Policies.

Energy crisis – Yom Kippur war (OPEC raised oil price four-fold) Failure to reach agreement on the need for a Common Energy Policy.

1974

Paris Heads of Government meeting decided (i) to set up the European Council with regular meetings (from 1975); (ii) direct election to European Parliament (from 1979). Also decided to drop the voting rule that unanimity was needed on every issue (not effective in practice but marked a softening).

1975

UK referendum to stay in the EC (following 1974 election of Labour government).

Lomé I Convention agreement between EC and 46 ACP states:
1   tariff-free access to EC for most ACP products;
2   guarantees home countries stable export earnings from 36 commodities;
3   provides for industrial and financial cooperation;
4   operates through joint institutions.

Treaty giving the European Parliament wider budgetary powers and establishing the Court of Auditors is signed, entering into force in 1977. European Council decides on the election of the European Parliament by universal suffrage by 1978, on passport union and single Community representation for the North-South dialogue.

European Council creates the European Regional Development Fund (ERDF) and a Regional Policy Committee.

1975 Greece application for EC membership.

Tindemans (Leo, Belgium PM) Report on European Union proposes a common external policy, economic and monetary union, social and regional policies etc.

Directive 75/268/EEC introduces aids to mountain and hill farming, and farming in Less Favoured Areas to compensate for the difficulties caused by natural conditions. Eventually these areas were to be extended to 52 per cent of the EC's total Utilised Agricultural Area. The main forms of aid are 'compensatory allowances' (headage payments) and investment aids.

Trade Agreement with Israel.

1976

Trade Agreement with Magreb countries (Tunisia, Algeria, Morocco).

1977

Agreement with Mashreq countries (Egypt, Syria, Jordan, Lebanon).

(The three above agreements represent a global Mediterranean policy by the EC).

Co-responsibility levies introduced to CAP commodity regimes which should convert into price reductions for 'excess' production.

Regulation (EEC) No 355/77 adopted, a horizontal structural measure intended to strengthen processing and marketing structures for agricultural products.

Court of Auditors set up (inaugural meeting).

Spain and Portugal applications for EC membership.

1978

First new Community Instrument set up which allows the raising of loans to help finance energy, industry, infrastructure.

European Councils are largely devoted to sorting out economic difficulties and paving way to replace the 'currency snake'.

1979

European Monetary System (EMS) instituted, with four components:
(1) the European Currency Unit (ECU); (2) an exchange and information mechanism; (3) credit facilities; (4) transfer arrangements.

EMS implies greater convergence of economic policies. Measures are also planned to boost economic potential of less prosperous EC countries, but five realignments had to take place 1979–1982 by agreement. The UK does not take a full part.

UK requests special measures to reduce size of UK contribution to the EC budget (1500–2000 million ECU.) Agreed ad hoc measures for 1980, and subsequently up to 1983. Only UK and Germany are net contributors to the Community budget at this time.

Treaty of Accession of Greece – became a member in January 1981.

First direct elections to European Parliament with 410 MEPs from nine Member States. President is Simone Veil (formerly French Minister of Health and Family Affairs).

Three Wise Men Report (Dell was the UK representative) on ways of progress towards European Union (There was no substantial follow up).

Lomé II agreement – reaffirms and improves Lomé I and was valid for five years.

GATT Tokyo round concludes, with further reductions in customs tariffs. It provides limited coverage of agricultural products (for the first time).

Birds Directive designated Special Protection Areas (later incorporated into Natura 2000 sites).

1980

Regime for sheepmeat introduced to the CAP. Common Fisheries Policy (CFP) established.

EC budget crisis: with a pledge to radically reform budget contributions by the UK.

Crisis in steel industry: package of measures (inclusive of social provisions for workforce) include planned and co-ordinated scaling down of production across the Community, planned by European Commission with Council of Ministers' support.

1981

Greece joins as a Member State (EU-10). Number of MEPs increases by 24 to 434.

ECU replaces EUA (European Unit of Account) as the unit in Community general budget.

International summit at Cancun on North–South dialogue.

Document from the Commission 'Guidelines for European Agriculture' (COM(81) 608), contains outline of ways in which Community must adapt its agricultural production so that supply is brought more in line with demand.

1982

Common Fisheries Policy (CFP) introduced. Referendum in Greenland (which had joined EC with Denmark) voted for leaving (CFP being a major issue) but retains its 'Overseas Countries and Territories' status, with an association agreement and certain EC rights for its citizens.

Agricultural Council: price settlement – agreement to make (trivial) adjustments in price of cereals, and milk if output exceeded 'Guarantee Threshold' levels.

1983

European Council: Solemn Declaration of European Union (reaffirming general principles and direction of progress).

Document from the Commission *Common Agricultural Policy* (COM(93) 500) dealing once more with the issue of imbalance in the markets for agricultural products.

1984

Production quotas brought in for milk to counter crisis of rising production and expenditure.

European Parliament adopts the Draft Treaty establishing the European Union, the aims of which are to increase the Community's powers and to strengthen its democratic legitimacy.

Lomé III Convention (ACP + EEC and Angola and Mozambique) to run 1985–90. Provides for 8,500 million ECU of aid (7,400 million from ECU European Development Fund, 1,100 million ECU from European Investment Bank).

Fontainebleau Summit (EC). As part of a package own resources raised to a 1.4 per cent standardised VAT ceiling. UK budget contribution argument dealt with, giving a rebate in 1985 of 1,000 million ECU relating to 1984. New regime starts on 1 January 1985.

1985

Re-launch of progress towards political integration, involving a dispute over whether the Treaty of Rome should be revised or not (UK position on the latter was defeated).

New Agricultural Structures policy. Authorisation for Member States to introduce special aids in 'Environmentally Sensitive Areas' (ESAs) included in Regulation 797/85. Farmers can receive finance where they agree to follow production practices that protect the environment or landscape.

Integrated Mediterranean Programmes (IMPs) initiated (Regulation (EEC). No 2088/85) to improve the socio-economic structures in Greece, southern France and Italy to enable them to cope with the latest enlargement of the Community. These areas suffer from structural weakness (underdeveloped agriculture, difficult natural conditions, difficulties in marketing their products, unemployment, low-technology small and medium enterprises (SMEs), industries in crisis, tourist industries which are large but which create socio-economic imbalances, and poorly organised administrations). IMPs are multiannual (maximum length seven years), cover all sectors and must be consistent with other Community policies (including the CAP). Each IMP involves co-ordinated assistance from the various structural funds and includes aid from both the Community budget and the Member State budget.

Commission's Document 'Perspectives for the Common Agricultural Policy' (Green Paper) Main features:
1 mounting over-production requires drastic action; the surplus problem is only solvable by giving the market a greater role in determining supply and demand, i.e. a more restrictionist price policy;
2 as a counterbalance, more resources should be given to options in each of the following fields: agriculture as a protector of the environment; agriculture in regional development (an important recognition of agricultural policy as part of rural policy); restructuring of agriculture with the help of direct income aids.

Options were outlined:
- for agricultural markets, price policy or quantitative restrictions (quotas etc.);
- for income aids, to cope with the consequences of either market option and to promote the restructuring of farming, various forms of income aid were proposed: pre-pension for farmers aged 55+; temporary flat rate payment (per hectare and per head) for 'professional' farmers to give them breathing space to get out; income supplements to comparable income level (perhaps linked to environmental practices); buying out (abandoning rights to produce);
- for environmental protection, various ways of regulating and controlling practices harmful to the environment; of promoting practices friendly to the environment.

Document *A Future for Community Agriculture: Commission Guidelines*. Follow-up to the Green Paper after public debate of its proposals. Confirmed the aim of a more restrictive price policy which provides farmers with an effective indicator of market dynamics. Intervention should revert to a safety net role. Adjuncts to this will be structural measures that: emphasise product quality and facilitate disposal (e.g. better marketing); contain the harm done by intensive agriculture (protection of sites and aid to friendly production methods); promote structural change by encouraging early retirement and aid new entrants; reduce production potential (set-aside, afforestation); provide information and advice to farmers to adjust; support for social reasons to farmers in LFAs etc.

1986

Accession of Spain and Portugal to the EC. Raises number of MEPs to 518 (EU-12)

Uruguay round of GATT starts.

New level of Community resources (Fontainebleau) proved inadequate to stop escalating costs of the CAP. Concerning agricultural support prices: co-responsibility levy on cereals introduced; additional levy on sugar producers; additional guarantee threshold of fruit and vegetables; change in threshold system for oilseeds (agreed in principle 1982/3 but ineffective till now)

December, Heads of State agree to package of measures to cut costs of milk and beef regimes.
- 9.5 per cent reduction in milk quotas, spread over two years;
- further restrictions on availability of intervention for milk powder, butter and beef;

Commission makes proposals for:
- early retirement pre-pensions linked to set-aside;
- aid to young farmers provided land is used for non-surplus products;
- extension of aids in LFAs.

Single European Act (SEA) signed in Luxembourg by governments of Member States, but also requires ratification by national parliaments.

1987

Single European Act comes into force.
Four main parts
- political co-operation (foreign policy);
- completion of internal market by 1992;
- changes in law relating to common institutions;
- changes in the way that common institutions operate.

European Parliament (EP) is now officially called that (formerly European Assembly). EP is given the responsibility of ratifying (assent procedure) treaties of accession, association agreements and financial protocols concluded by the Community.

Main changes to policy-making:
- increased use of conditions under which a qualified majority can be used;
- introduction of new 'co-operation procedure' with EP.

Formerly the Council took note of EP opinion on proposals from Commission (could be ignored). Now after a Council qualified majority, legislation goes back to EP which may:

- approve;
- fail to take a position (Council would simply adopt proposal);
- reject by absolute majority (in which case Council can only adopt if Council is unanimous);
- amend Council's position by absolute majority.

In practice this was likely to mean only a reversion to the previous EP opinion. Failure to get an absolute majority would cause the proposal to go back to the Commission for possible redrafting. Council can then approve without going back to EP.

Under the title 'Economic and Social Cohesion' the SEA defines the Treaty of Rome's commitment to 'harmonious development', making the completion of the single market dependent on the achievement of economic and social cohesion, thus giving a firmer legal foundation to structural policy (and its social dimensions).

Also under the SEA, environmental policy was given a firm legal base by a statement of aims, enabling the Commission to propose actions where these are better taken at European level rather than at Member State level.

Commission proposals for agricultural policy:
- direct income aids (transitional) to allow 'main' income farms to adjust;
- Community 'pre-pension' scheme;
- framework for national aids.

CAP price review:
- price freeze and a few additional restrictions on intervention but green money conversions meant rises in national currency terms;
- oils and fats tax proposed.

Increasing financial problems – Commission package of proposals under the name 'budgetary stabilisers' covered, in some form, most products.

WEU adopts a joint defence policy platform in the Hague.

1988

Special 'crisis' February meeting of heads of government (European Council) agrees 'budgetary discipline' to ensure that Community expenditure does not outstrip resources. Legally binding ceiling on CAP price policy spending (EAGGF guarantee) of 27.56 billion ECU) and the annual rate of increase in spending must not exceed 74 per cent of growth in Community GNP.

Stabilisers agreed in principle;
- cereals: Maximum Guaranteed Quantity (MGQ) 160 megatonnes for the four marketing years to 1992 and provision for an additional co-responsibility levy of 3 per cent (in addition to the 1986 price cut). If production exceeds MGQ, price cut of 3 per cent;
- exemption of small farmers from co-responsibility levy;
- oilseeds and protein products: reduction in production aid when MGQ exceeded.

Later, foreign ministers endorse stabilisers for;
- milk: extension of period of quota;
- wine: reduction in payments, restricted replanting;
- sugar: additional controls;

- tobacco: MGQ;
- sheepmeat: regime to be reviewed.

Community 'set-aside' scheme introduced; at least 20 per cent of arable area to be set-aside for at least five years.

Schemes for extensification, conversion to crops not in surplus, and pre-pension aids for not using land on retirement.

Increased spending on Structural Funds (to be doubled by 1993).

Inclusion in budget of a 'monetary reserve' of ECU 1000 million to cover shifts in ECU/$ market rates.

An early warning scheme on trends in agricultural expenditure.

Introduction of Multiannual Financial Perspective for the EC budget, and a new 'Fourth Resource'.

Under the Reform of the Structural Funds, three Funds (ESF, ERDF, FEOGA (guidance section) are to be linked and their activities co-ordinated. Areas are designated by 'objective.' Funds allocated to rise from 7 billion ECU in 1989 to 14 billion ECU in 1993 (by then expected to represent a quarter of total Community budget spending on agriculture).

Objective 1 – promoting the development and adjustment of regions whose development is lagging behind (in terms of GDP/head) e.g. the whole of the island of Ireland. This is to be the main absorber of funding (over half).

Objective 2 – converting regions etc. seriously affected by industrial decline.

Objective 3 – combating long-term employment.

Objective 4 – facilitating the occupational integration of young people.

Objective 5 – with a view to reforming the agricultural policy.
- 5a 'horizontal' measures: adapting production, processing and marketing structures in agriculture and forestry (e.g. schemes for farm diversification/agri-environmental/set-aside/establishment of young farms/early retirement / LFA.
- 5b 'vertical' measures; promoting rural development (in England this applies to Cornwall and parts of Devon).

In UK, introduction of EC set-aside scheme, Farm Woodland Scheme, Farm Diversification Grant Scheme. These reflect the greater concern with the environment and with ways of supporting agriculture which do not encourage production of commodities in surplus. Agricultural Improvement Scheme ended.

'Future of Rural Society' (FRS) document
- linked to the doubling of structural funds;
- recognises the desire to broaden community assistance to rural areas from agricultural commodity support to rural development in which agriculture plays a part.

FRS reflects
- (a) the commitment under the Treaty of Rome and Single European Act to be active in the promotion of economic and social cohesion; this meant that the EC could not

tolerate the impoverishment of rural areas outside the mainstream of national and Community life;

(b)   that the CAP was committed to returning to the market as the means by which agricultural decisions were made (influenced by budgetary expedience, economic efficiency, trade problems, surpluses etc.);

(c)   the need to protect the environment and conserve the Community's natural assets.

FRS identified three types of rural area with associated sets of problems:

- those under urban pressure (e.g. most of England), that is they were faced by the pressures of modern life on rural society (such as land demand for development, environmental pressure, recreation, changes in rural society e.g. encapsulation of rural poor). Aims of policy for this type of area are less of stepping up the pace of economic development and more of environmental protection and of allowing these areas to take full advantage of the growing demand by urban dwellers for green spaces;

- where there are problems of population loss, ageing of those left, depletion of rural services, economic isolation of non-agricultural businesses and limited credit opportunities. Solutions proposed are to encourage farm diversification and new economic activities in the rural economy generally, improved marketing, training facilities and better infrastructures (for example, parts of Wales).

- the extremely disadvantaged areas which are relatively inaccessible, sparsely populated and suffer natural and structural disadvantages (e.g. some mountain and hill areas, islands). Agriculture will remain the only significant activity, and the support of farming and other businesses will be needed on a permanent basis. The environment and cultural values of the population should be protected and opportunities for new business ventures (e.g. integrated forestry and timber products) supported. Support of agriculture is necessary permanently.

Joint declaration on the establishment of relations and future cooperation between the Community and Comecon signed in Luxembourg.

1989

New Commission takes office, with Ray MacSharry as Commissioner for Agriculture.

Consolidation of CAP and its preparation for re-launched GATT round.

CAP price review includes:

- price freeze;
- aids to small producers;
- increased aid on durum wheat;
- olive oil (change in definition of small producer);
- milk (abolition of co-responsibility levy for farms in LFAs and small producers);
- reductions in intervention periods for cereals, rice and oilseeds;
- revised sheep regime to be introduced.

Stocks situation forming a context:

- decline in stocks of cereals, beef, butter, skimmed milk powder (almost totally gone);
- increase in stocks of alcohol and tobacco.

Rise in ECU led to reduced cost of support.

Revolutions in Eastern Europe, leading to overthrow of Communist governments and introduction of market economies.

Austria applies to join the Community.

Fourth Lomé Treaty between the Community and 69 ACP countries.

Social Chapter introduced.

UK, start of food quality scares (salmonella in eggs).

1990

UK Nitrate Scheme (Nitrate Sensitive Areas).

Intergovernmental conferences in Rome on Economic and Monetary Union (EMU) and on Political Union.

Schengen Agreement on the elimination of border checks adopted (by Belgium, Germany, Spain, France, Italy, Luxembourg, Portugal).

GATT Uruguay Round restarts.

Agreement establishing the European Bank for Reconstruction and Development signed in Paris.

Germany reunified.

Cyprus, Malta apply to join the Community.

Two Intergovernmental Conferences open in Rome, on Economic and Monetary Union, and on Political Union.

Community initiative LEADER (one of several, including YOUTHSTART, INTERREG) designed as a model programme for the support and development of local rural development initiatives.

Setting up of the European Environment Agency (EEA) by EEC Regulation 1210/1990 (later amended by EEC Regulation 933/1999 and EC Regulation 401/2009), becoming operational in 1994. Its purpose is to establish a network for monitoring the European environment. Its management board contains representatives of the governments of EU Member States and of other member countries.

1991

July – start of first phase of Economic and Monetary Union, involving action to improve cooperation between Member States in the economic and monetary fields, to strengthen the European Monetary System (EMS) and the role of the ECU and to extend the work of the Committee of Central Bank Governors.

Another potential CAP budgetary crisis.

Agreement on creating a European Economic Area signed between Community and EFTA countries, but not including Switzerland.

Nitrates Directive (91/676) aimed to reduce water pollution caused by nitrates from agricultural sources. Member States are required to (a) establish a code of good agricultural practice, to be implemented by farmers on a voluntary basis; (b) to designate 'vulnerable zones' in which to implement 'action programmes' under which certain measured become mandatory (such as conditions of applications and their timing, storage facilities). Implemented in the UK via Nitrate Sensitive Areas.

(February) MacSharry reform proposals 'Development and Future of the CAP' published.

Spurs for reform mentioned include: rapid deterioration of the agricultural budgetary situation, growth of unsold stocks of cereals, beef and dairy produce, difficulties in keeping agricultural markets in balance, problems faced in the context of international trade and GATT.

Main features of the proposals: starting with the CMOs for cereals, oilseeds and protein crops (COPs), price cuts compensated by direct payments per hectare. Existing stabiliser arrangements would be withdrawn once the new system came into effect. The basic co-responsibility levy was to be phased out. For livestock, reduction in the support prices would be made commensurate with the lower costs of cereals (as feeding costs would be less). Price of beef and milk products cut proposed, with direct payments to compensate producers who farm in an extensive way, since they would gain less than intensive producers from the lower prices of concentrated animal feed. Arrangements are made for long-term set-aside, for forestry and other environmental purposes

1992

(May) Adoption of a modified package of CAP reforms. These are a blunted form of the proposals above, especially with regards to 'modulation' in favour of small farms. Three main guidelines laid down by the Commission are followed by the Council:
- a substantial reduction in the prices of agricultural products to make them more competitive both within the Community and elsewhere;
- full and on-going compensation for this reduction through compensatory amounts or premiums not related to the quantities produced;
- implementation of measures to limit the use of the factors of production (set-aside, headage limits, stocking levels) alongside the retention of more drastic rules, such as quotas.

At the same time, the package strengthens measures to protect the environment, farmer retirement and use of land for non-agricultural purposes, such as forestry.

Main features:
- Cereals: support prices reduced by 29 per cent over three years; 15 per cent rotational set-aside (small producers exempt); optional non-rotational but at a higher per cent figure (not stated, to be determined later); all set-aside land will be compensated (not up to a maximum as in the proposals); set-aside to be run on a regional basis (not on an individual farm basis).
- Beef: price reduction of 15 per cent over three years from 1993; headage limits on suckler cow numbers at farm level not imposed. There are now four types of premiums; 'special' (ordinary), suckler cow, processing premium and extensive breeding premium.

Both 'special' and suckler cow premiums limited to maximum numbers (of 'claims') on a regional basis, with proportionate reduction in premiums if these are exceeded. Suckler cow premiums are transferable. Additional premium for Member States where a high proportion of cattle are autumn-slaughtered cattle (including Northern Ireland).

- Sheep: new premium to be paid on quotas of animals at the individual farm level. Quotas are transferable (by sale) without land necessarily changing hands, though when no land is involved, some will be siphoned off to form a national reserve for new entrants and other priority producers. The proposed headage limits on payment of premiums are not adopted.
- Milk: cut in butter price. Proposals for dairy cow premium and cut in quota in first year are not adopted.
- Tobacco: global quota of 350,000 tonnes by 1994 with a further review in 1996.
- Environment: Council agrees that environmental protection requirements should be an integral part of the CAP, not an add-on. Provision of scope for schemes which build on ESA, such as long-term set-aside (20 years), encouragement of extensive livestock farming, addition of provisions to encourage organic farming, encourage farmers to manage their land for public access and to help protect water quality. Annual allowances per hectare payable for the above if farmer makes undertaking for five years (20 for set-aside). Also provision for education of farmers in environmental protection.
- Afforestation aid: payments for establishment, maintenance costs in first five years, annual allowance per hectare to cover losses of income (up to 600 ECU per hectare), and for the improvement of woodland.
- Early retirement: for farmers and farm workers aged at least 55. Retirement grant, or annual payment not dependent on area released, annual allowance per hectare (to a maximum of 10,000 ECU per holding), retirement pension supplement.

Reform of the Structural Funds. Modest revisions, but Objectives 1 and 5 that affect rural areas and their development hardly changed. Restructuring of fisheries sector now under Objective 5b (financed by the new Financial Instrument for Fisheries Guidance (FIFG) structural fund).

September 16, Wednesday: UK leaves the Exchange Rate Mechanism. The commercial exchange rate between ECU and sterling changed; between August and October the pound depreciated by 11 per cent. As support prices and other CAP payments are set in ECU, this led to a substantial rise in the prices received by UK farmers (in pounds, though calculated using 'green' rates of exchange) and a surge in their incomes. Italy also withdraws from the ERM.

(November) 'Blair House' agreement between EC and US on agricultural trade and protection which was necessary before a GATT agreement could be achieved. The EC Commission concludes that the conditions of reduced support to home producers and improved access should be compatible with the changes already agreed as part of the CAP reform of 1992. Main features:

- Internal support: to be measured in an agreed formula as 'Aggregate Measure of Support'(AMS). Total AMS to be reduced by 20 per cent (over six years) when compared with the base of 1986–8, with credit for reductions already made since 1986. Direct aids (per hectare or per head) are not subject to this reduction of support as long as they are part of a production-limiting programme (in effect, on a fixed quantity base and yield base).

- Access: border protection measures to be changed into customs tariffs (tariffication); at the beginning these tariffs will be equal to the difference between the world price of the product and its intervention price on the Community market, increased by 10 per cent. Tariffs to be reduced by 36 per cent over six years; each tariff must be reduced by a minimum of 15 per cent over six years. Provisions for 'special safeguard clause' (temporary variable tariff) when import price falls by more than 10 per cent below the average 1986–8 import price into the EC. Clause covering minimum access (3 per cent of internal EC consumption, rising to 5 per cent). Bananas are exempt.
- External commitments: reduction, product by product, of direct export subsidies by 36 per cent over six years, from the average outlay 1986–90. Volume reduction, product by product, of subsidised exports by 21 per cent over six years from the average 1986–90. Food aid not included.

Oilseeds: agreement to reduce the area on which crop-specific oilseeds payments are made, to be reduced by the annual set-aside rate for arable crops fixed by Council (not less than 10 per cent). No additional market support expenditure. Other details agreed, (e.g. special treatment of some imports into Portugal).

Treaty of European Union (TEU) (Maastricht Agreement), December 11 between EU prime ministers and heads of state, requiring ratification by national parliaments in Member States. It extends Community action to areas not previously covered by the EC Treaties, especially Economic and Monetary Union and defence. Agreement changes articles of the Treaty of Rome and adds new ones; also agrees new protocols to go with the Treaty for new policy areas within the European Union. A social chapter agreed with 11 Member States will not form part of the Treaty but will be implemented via the EC institutions. The text says:

> This Treaty marks a new stage in the process of creating an ever closer Union among the peoples of Europe, where decisions are taken as closely as possible to the citizens.

The Maastricht Treaty organised the European Union around three main pillars:
- First (community) Pillar which corresponds to three communities (the European Community (EC); the European Community for Atomic Energy (EURATOM); and the European Coal and Steel Community (ECSC) (due to be abolished on 22 July, 2002);
- Second Pillar: dedicated to the common foreign and security policy;
- Third Pillar, dedicated to police and judicial cooperation in criminal matters.

Main contents of the Treaty:
- Subsidiarity: 'In areas which do not fall within its exclusive competence, the Community shall take action, in accordance with the principle of subsidiarity, only if and in so far as the objective of the proposed action cannot be sufficiently achieved by the Member States and can therefore, by reason of the scale or effects of the proposed action, be better achieved by the Community';
- Citizenship of the Union: rights to stand for election, vote etc. throughout EC;
- Powers of the European Parliament – Commission and its President subject to approval of Parliament at the start of their five-year term (extended from four from 1995 to coincide with Parliamentary term). Increased powers of co-decision with Council. Can now request Commission to submit proposals where Parliament decides by overall majority that new EC legislation is required.

Other detailed changes:
- Proposals for Common Foreign and Security Policy;
- Justice and home affairs and immigration: provisions for common policy on a wide range of issues, including combating fraud, immigration policy, exchange of police information;
- Social agreement: provision for common policies on issues such as health and safety, working conditions, social security, redundancy protection. Some are by qualified. majority, some by unanimity;
- New policy initiatives: Cohesion Fund (to finance projects in fields of environment and transport infrastructure); Committee of the Regions (to be consulted where specific regional interests are involved); trans-European networks (transport, communications etc.); consumer policy; culture, education, vocational training, youth; environment; health; industry; insurance, access to information; implementation of Community law; ombudsman for EC maladministration by institutions; own resources (provision for system of contribution of poorer Member States); other policy areas are allowed for (energy, civil protection, tourism);
- Timetable for progress towards Economic and Monetary Union: including single currency by 1999 – a logical extension to the creation of a single market for goods, services, capital and people.

Finland and Switzerland apply to join the Community.

Habitats Directive established Special Areas of Conservation (SAC), designated by Member States. These, with SPAs (see above) form Natura 2000, a network of Europe's most valuable and threatened species and habitats. The establishment of this network of protected areas also fulfils a Community obligation under the UN Convention on Biological Diversity.

1993

Completion of the Single Market (effective 1 January).

February: Edinburgh European Council decides the locations of the new institutions of the European Community: European Environment Agency (Copenhagen); European Training Foundation (Turin); European Monitoring Centre for Drugs and Drug Addiction (Lisbon); European Agency for the Evaluation of Medical Products (London); Agency for Health and Safety at Work (Bilbao); European Monetary Institute (Frankfurt); Office for Harmonisation in the Internal Market (Alicante); Europol (The Hague); European Centre for the Development of Vocational Training (CEDEFOP) (Thessaloniki); Foundation for the Improvement of Living and Working Conditions (Dublin).

June: European Council (Copenhagen) agrees in principle that countries in Central and Eastern Europe could join the EU. 'Accession will take place as soon as an associated country is able to assume the obligations of membership by satisfying the economic and political conditions required'.

June: Commission issues the White Paper 'Growth, Competitiveness, Employment': The challenges and ways forward into the twenty-first century to tackle the EU's problems of a shrinking rate of economic growth, rising unemployment, falling investment rate, worsening international competitiveness. Action is proposed on (i) making the most of the internal market, by removing or harmonising regulations on companies; (ii) supporting the development and adaptation of small and medium-sized enterprises; (iii) pursuing cooperation and joint decision-making by the two sides of industry; (iv) creating the major European infrastructure networks (trans-European Networks (TENs) (for transport on rail, roads etc, gas and electricity, telecommunications); (v) laying the foundations for the information society (research and technological development, information communications technologies, biotechnology, audio-visual industries).

1 November: Treaty on European Union (TEU) comes into force. The European Community becomes the European Union.

December: formal conclusion of Uruguay Round of GATT, with an agreement to run from 1 July 1995 until 30 June 2001. The agreement is to be administered by the World Trade Organisation (WTO), a new and more powerful body replacing GATT Secretariat. Essence of the main agreement on agriculture: domestic support: reduction of 20 per cent in trade-distorting measures over six years, based on total Aggregate Measure of Support (AMS) with a base period 1986–88. Market access: all import restrictions converted to tariffs (tariffication) in 1995; for OECD countries tariffs would be 'bound' at this level and reduced by an average of 36 per cent over six years, with a minimum cut of 15 per cent per product. Base period 1986–88. (In retrospect choice of data and calculations by countries of tariff levels left room for creative accounting, such as estimating baseline tariffs as high as possible to minimise the need to cut in reality – 'dirty' tariffication). Minimum access requirement of 3 per cent of domestic consumption (1986–88), rising to 5 per cent by end of agreement. Current access to be maintained. Export subsidies: volume of subsidised exports to be reduced by 21 per cent over six years (base period 1986–90). Budgetary expenditure on export subsidies simultaneously to be reduced by 36 per cent over six years. The Peace clause states that agricultural policy measures, as long as they do not directly contravene the agreement, are not subject to challenge through GATT panels or other dispute settlement channels, and this arrangement will last for three years beyond the six-year duration of the Round itself. There will be an overall review of the agreement on agriculture in 1999.

As a result, world prices of agricultural products were expected to rise by 10 per cent by year 2000. EU and USA were both required to cut back on agricultural export policies, but the full impact in both was reduced by the exemption from the normal schedule of cuts of the main channels of support to farmers (compensatory payments in the EU and deficiency payments in the USA). The Peace clause in effect gave legitimacy to the CAP and meant that it could not be challenged internationally until 2003. Cairns Group of countries (including Australia and New Zealand) were expected to be net beneficiaries; these agricultural exporting countries would have higher prices for their produce and some guaranteed access.

Agreement on further enlargement of the Structural Funds for the period 1994–99, including expansion of areas given Objective 1 status (in UK now included Highlands and Islands, and Merseyside), 72 per cent increase in areas given Objective 5b status at EC level, and amounts given to the Community Initiatives (including LEADER for rural development).

1994

Formal signing of the GATT Uruguay Round agreement in Marrakesh, Morocco.

1 January: European Economic Area comes into being. Austria, Sweden, Norway and Iceland now share the four freedoms of the Treaty of Rome, although the agreement does

not extend to agriculture or remove border controls. Switzerland, which rejected membership in a referendum, and Liechtenstein are not in the EEA.

Second stage of European Monetary Union starts. European Monetary Institute inaugurated, based in Frankfurt; forerunner of European Central Bank.

Agreement on new voting system for the enlarged Union following accession of the applicant countries (Austria, Finland, Norway, Sweden). Total votes 90 (raised from 76); blocking minority raised to 27 (from 23) with provision for 'reasonable delay' on legislation where a minority of 23 to 26 votes oppose legislation to allow the Council to do 'all in its power' to reach a satisfactory conclusion. This provision seems to be a face-saving device for the UK and, to a lesser extent, Spain who opposed the changes. Provision is known as the Ioannina Compromise.

1995

Enlargement of the European Union to 15 Member States by the accession of Austria, Finland and Sweden after referendums in each country in 1993. Norway's government agreed to join the EU, but the referendum in November 1993 rejected membership. This required a revision of the previously agreed voting arrangements in the Council, in the new Commission (from January 1995), in the new Commissioner designated to look after fisheries (who would have been from Norway) and in membership of the European Parliament. Norway stays in the European Economic Area.

Objective 6 added to the Policy under the Structural Funds to cater for sparsely populated area (Nordic regions).

Ten reports on the agricultural and food situation in countries of Central and Eastern Europe presented (CEECs) as a step on the way to accession – Bulgaria, Czech Republic, Estonia, Hungary, Latvia, Lithuania, Poland, Slovakia, Slovenia, Romania).

New Agrimonetary Regulation due to come into force, with the elimination of existing monetary gaps by raising support prices (in ECU) but lowering the value of the Green ECU to its market level (implying no change in prices in national currencies), the elimination of the switchover mechanism, and the introduction of procedures designed to prevent the further continuation of monetary gaps where they arise through currency revaluations and devaluations.

December: Agricultural Strategy Paper from Agricultural Commissioner Fischler ('Study on alternative strategies for the development of relations in the field of agriculture between the EU and the associated countries with a view to future accession of these countries') plots ways forward for the CAP. The most realistic scenario (Option 3: Developing the 1992 approach) points toward three main lines of CAP development: (i) towards higher competitiveness, continuing and extending the dismantling of product price support, accompanied where necessary by compensatory direct payments, which may have environmental and social connotations; (b) towards an integrated rural policy, which would strike a more sustainable balance between agriculture and other activities, and in which farmers would be called on to be rural entrepreneurs, to diversify and develop the other roles they increasingly play, as suppliers of non-food items, stewards of the countryside, managers of natural resources etc.; (c) simplification, in which more latitude is given to Member States within a generally agreed framework set at EU level, possibly set at five-yearly intervals. The move away from market support to other forms (such as rural development) would help in this longer-term planning.

1996

Dislocation in the beef sector, with a collapse in demand, resulting from health fears linking CJ disease in humans with BSE ('mad cow' disease) in cattle fed with material taken from others with the disease. Export of UK beef to any other country (EU and outside) banned. UK temporarily pursued a policy of non-cooperation in all decision-making requiring unanimity. BSE crisis reputedly slows progress on reform of CAP.

Inter-governmental conferences (IGC) on monetary and political union starts.

Cork Declaration on rural development, following a conference, that refers to making a new start in rural development policy. Declaration contains 10 points: 'preference' of sustainable rural development as the basis of rural policy; integrated approach (multisectoral and multidiscipline, territorially targeted); diversification (of rural economy), giving support to initiatives to become self-sustaining; sustainability (policies should sustain landscape, biodiversity cultural environment etc.); subsidiarity (decentralisation and bottom-up approach where possible); simplification of legislation; programming (approach to rural development); finance (co-financing and involvement of private sector and banking); management (technical assistance to local administration); evaluation and research (must take place and involve stakeholders).

1997

Treaty of Amsterdam – at the end of an IGC – provides for cooperation and for incentives to help boost employment. Regulations that form part of the stability pact in preparation for the third stage of economic and monetary union (EMU). New sections on freedom (of labour movement), security and justice; UK and Ireland are allowed to keep border controls. Strengthened environmental measures. Revised sections on foreign and security policy, with provision for common strategies. Modest increase in qualified majority voting in the Council. Little progress on institutional reform (such as number of Commissioners, votes etc.)

This Treaty also consolidates the text of earlier Treaties establishing the European Community. In particular, the objectives of the CAP, originally set out in the 1957 Treaty of Rome (Article 39) becomes Article 33 of the Consolidated Treaty, though with no change to the wording.

Agenda 2000 – publication containing the Commission's broad outlook for the development of the EU and its policies beyond the turn of the century, the impact of the enlargement of the Union, and the future financial framework. It recommends that negotiations for accession be started with Hungary, Poland, Estonia, the Czech Republic, Slovenia and Cyprus. It proposes revisions to the Structural Funds and the Cohesion Fund, with a reduction of the number of objectives from seven to three (two regional objectives and one for human resources). The CAP was to continue its progress in lowering market price support for cereals (with set-aside reduced) and beef, but with more direct income payments. With milk, quotas were retained but there was a commitment to lowering price support with the introduction of direct yearly payments per cow.

New objectives for the CAP were put forward:
- increase competitiveness internally and externally in order to ensure that EU producers take full advantage of positive world market developments;
- food safety and food quality, which are both fundamental obligations towards consumers;
- ensuring a fair standard of living for the agricultural community and contributing to the stability of farm incomes;
- the integration of environmental goals into the CAP;
- promotion of sustainable agriculture;
- the creation of alternative job and income opportunities for farmers and their families;
- simplification of Union legislation.

1998

Preparation for monetary union dominates EU political thinking. European Central Bank established.

1999

1 January: introduction of Monetary Union and a single currency – the euro (€) replacing the ECU though not yet as a currency in circulation – for 11 Member States (not including Denmark, Greece, Sweden and UK) who form the Eurozone.

March 11, deal reached on proposals contained in *Agenda 2000* by the Agricultural Council. This represents a stage in CAP reform, and was estimated to cost €314 billion over the seven-year reference period (to 2006), in contrast to the financial guide from the European Council of €307 billion.
Main provisions:
- Arable crops – intervention price cut by 20 per cent in two equal stages between 2000 and 2002; cereals direct aid increased; oilseeds and linseed aid progressively reduced (three years) to bring in line with cereals aid by 2002; set-aside basic rate 10 per cent in 2000 and 2001, falling to zero from 2002.
- Beef – intervention price lowered by 20 per cent in three equal stages, starting in 2000; direct headage payments increased; new slaughter premium; system of private storage aid plus safety net intervention to operate from 2002; extensification aid increased, with greater national flexibility; 'national envelope' package of aid.
- Dairy – support prices cut by 15 per cent over three years starting 2003; compensation phased in from 2003 as dairy cow premium; small increases in quota (some countries in 2000, others from 2003); quota system to be reviewed, aiming to run them out by 2006.
- Table wine – abandonment of 'preventative distillation', compulsory distillation and 'support distillation' and replaced by 'crisis' distillation, the resulting alcohol becoming the property of the Union (not of Member States). Organisation of grubbing up measures partly now the responsibility of Member States. Ban on the general planting of vineyards but with a flexible system of planting rights with a priority to new entrants.
- Rural development – investment in holdings will need to cross-comply with environmental and animal welfare requirements; revised early retirement package, now extended to 75th birthday; higher rate of support to investment by young farmers; payment to cover losses from afforestation.

Note:
- There was no mention in the final *Agenda 2000* agreement of capping direct aid payments per holder or holdings, or of 'degressivity' of these payments (scaling down over time);
- The package was 'declared' by the chair (Germany) to have qualified majority support, but no vote was taken. This called into question how fixed its details were;
- The agreement was subject to ratification by the Berlin European Council (March 24/25), at which further changes were made (see below).

15 March: entire Commission resigned, following an independent report on corruption, fraud and lack of accountability, in the face of a probable vote to dismiss it by the Parliament. The report had been initiated in January 1999 as a compromise to former accusations and Parliament's calls for resignation by two individual Commissioners. Caretaker Commission proposed; the Commission was due to be replaced at the end of 1999 anyway at the end of its five-year term.

24–25 March – *Agenda 2000* – European Council reaches agreement on a modified set of proposals for the CAP that further waters-down the extent of the reforms agreed by the earlier Agricultural Council in the following ways:
- Cereals; prices to be cut by only 15 per cent (c.f. 20 per cent) phased in over two years (2000 and 2001) and with compensation payments reduced from €66 to €63. Cut of oilseed aid to €63 after two years. Basic rate of set-aside at 10 per cent, continuing to 2006 (rather than a phased reduction). Escape clauses on oilseed aid cut that could further dilute the impact of reform. Portugal given increased Maximum Guaranteed Area for durum wheat.
- Dairy; countries promised extra quota would still receive this in 2000 and 2001, but other changes were delayed until 2005 (including the 15 per cent price cut, compensation, and the 1.5 per cent quota increase). Each year of dairy reform was to save approximately €2 billion in budgetary expenditure (and there were other savings from cutting cereals compensation).
- Beef; basic elements of March agreement were retained, but the system giving the Commission discretion on intervention buying in was retained (rather than being automatic).
- Limits on agricultural spending agreed to 2006 (averaging €40.5 billion) as part of the Financial Framework that also secured the 'rebate' on the UK's contribution to the EU budget.
- Reform of the Structural Funds agreed (with reduction in Objective areas to three), though with less funds than originally proposed. Objective 1 (less developed regions, with GDP per head less than 75 per cent of the Community average, and including former Objective 6 regions), Objective 2 (areas confronted with restructuring problems and including all territorially based objectives, including rural development not covered in Objective 1 regions), Objective 3, education and training systems in other areas. Total was limited to €195 billion over seven years (2000 to 2006 inclusive) plus €18 billion Cohesion Funds. Funds for accession allocated from 2002, of which a small part was for agriculture (a third in the first years, falling to about a quarter in 2006).

Rural Development Regulation (No 1257/1999) brought together much existing legislation on this topic, falling into two groups (a) the 'accompanying measures' of the 1992 reforms (early retirement, agri-environment schemes and afforestation, and Less Favoured Area schemes; (b) measures to modernise and diversify agricultural holdings (farm investment to improve efficiency and quality, setting-up of young farmers, training, investment aid for processing and marketing facilities for farm products, additional assistance for forestry, promotion and conversion of agriculture and other schemes).

Proposed start of World Trade Organisation 'Millennium Round' of talks in Seattle to further free trade ends in disarray.

2000

'Lisbon Agenda (or Strategy)' launched under the Portuguese Presidency to deal with the low productivity and stagnation of economic growth in the EU, through the formulation of various policy initiatives to be taken by all Member States. The broader objectives set out by the Lisbon strategy were to be attained by 2010. (It was re-launched in 2005 and 2006 and influenced the reform of agricultural and rural development policy, with an emphasis on innovation, building human capital, and social and environmental renewal).

New Commission starts five-year term.

Treaty of Nice agreed at December Inter-Governmental Conference (IGC) under French presidency to prepare EU for enlargement. This involves rebalancing of votes in Council between Member States and allocation to candidates when they become Members. Extension of qualified majority (QM) voting to many new areas of policy (but not to taxation, social security, most immigration policies and trade in audio-visual products); QM set at 258 votes out of 342 (89 being the blocking minority) but also requires a 62 per cent minimum representation of the EU population. European Parliament is expanded (to 738 MEPs when all 12 candidates join). Plans to restrict size of Commission, large countries giving up their second Commissioner in 2005 and total kept to below 27 Commissioners, possibly by smaller countries appointing in rotation. European Council confirms that applicant countries that are ready would be received into the EU from the end of 2002, enabling them to participate in the 2004 European elections (confirmed by Göteborg European Council of 2001). Enlargement required ratification of the Nice Treaty by all Member States (initially not ratified by Ireland, but later passed).

EU Water Framework Directive (Directive 2000/60/EC of the European Parliament and of the Council) establishing a framework for the Community action in the field of water policy. It establishes an approach for water management based on river basins, the natural geographical and hydrological units and sets specific deadlines for Member States to protect aquatic ecosystems. The Directive addresses inland surface waters, transitional waters, coastal waters and groundwater. It establishes several innovative principles for water management, including public participation in planning and the integration of economic approaches, including the recovery of the cost of water services.

Cotonou Agreement for the EDF covering the period 2000–2007. The Stabex instrument designed to help stabilise the agricultural export earnings of ACP States was abolished, but a system of rolling programming was introduced, making for greater flexibility and giving these countries greater responsibility.

2001

The EU sustainable development strategy (SDS) is agreed by the European Council in Göteborg in June 2001(the Göteborg Declaration). This proposes measures to deal with threats to quality of life. This strategy is composed of two main parts. The first proposes objectives and policy measures to tackle a number of key unsustainable trends in the EU and globally. The priorities are to:

- combat climate change;
- ensure sustainable transport;
- address threats to public health, such as chemicals pollution, unsafe food and infectious
- diseases;
- manage natural resources more responsibly and stop biodiversity decline;
- combat poverty and social exclusion; and
- meet the challenge of an ageing population.

The second part of the strategy revises the way that policies are made. It calls for a new approach to policy-making that ensures the EU's economic, social and environmental policies mutually reinforce each other. It also stresses the global dimension of sustainable development and the contribution that the EU can make to helping all nations reach a sustainable development path.

The SDS is intended to complement the Lisbon strategy (2000) of economic and social renewal. Its effectiveness is reviewed on a periodic basis.

2001 'Strategic Environmental Assessment' – SEA Directive (2001/42/EC) ensures that plans, programmes and projects likely to have significant effects on the environment are made subject to an environmental assessment, prior to their approval or authorisation. Consultation with the public is a key feature of environmental assessment procedures. As an example, Rural Development Programmes are required to undergo SEA at their *ex ante* stage.

Outbreak of foot and mouth disease in UK disrupts livestock industry and trade in animals and red meat.

 UK government reorganisation created the Department for Environment, Food and Rural Affairs (Defra). The main elements were the former Ministry of Agriculture, Fisheries and Food (MAFF) and part of the (then) Department for the Environment, Transport and the Regions (DETR). The latter was reformed as Department for Transport, Local Government and the Regions (DTLR) which was further rearranged in 2002, one element of which became a separate Department for Transport (DfT).

(Jan) Euro replaces national currencies in circulation for Eurozone countries. Greece joins the EMU.

Agreement that Cyprus, Czech Republic, Estonia, Hungary, Latvia, Lithuania, Malta, Poland, Slovakia and Slovenia should join EU, with a target date of 2004.

2002

France and Germany lead an agreement to maintain CAP spending in real terms through to 2013. However, no increase is to be made to spending on agriculture when 10 new Member

States join in 2004 (though this does not apply to rural development). This implies a cut for EU-15 of about 5 per cent.

First meeting of the Convention on the Future of Europe with a wide remit to draw up draft constitution suitable for an EU of 25 (or so) Member States. In part a 'tidying up' activity to make the EU workable, but in part an opportunity to make advances in common policies.

European Coal and Steel Community abolished.

Mid-Term Review of *Agenda 2000* phase of the CAP, leads to package adopted in 2003.

2003

January; Commission adopts package of proposed reforms, based on the Mid-Term Review (MTR) of *Agenda 2000*. With some changes (such as dropping proposals for a final cut in cereals support prices) the package is agreed by the Council in June. The key elements of the reform are:

- The introduction of a Single Farm Payment Scheme for EU farmers, the single payment being independent from production, decoupling support and simplifying the CAP. It consolidates direct payments of all main commodities. This payment, which could be made from 2005 or delayed to 2007, is to be based on payments received in a three-year reference past period (2000/2002). There is no requirement to maintain stocking levels or intensity of land use, or crop patterns, but farmers would have to keep land in good agricultural and environmental condition. Set-aside is to be maintained as in the reference period, but with flexibility to better meet environmental objectives (e.g. strips on field margins). The payments would be transferable by sale separate from the land, though they are to be based on land occupancy. Limited coupled elements can be maintained in specific circumstances to avoid land abandonment;
- Linking these payments to complying with standards in environmental, food safety, animal welfare, health, occupational safety and the maintenance of land in good condition (cross-compliance);
- A stronger rural development policy, with more funds and new measures to promote environment, food quality and animal welfare and to help farmers to meet EU production standards starting in 2005;
- A compulsory EU-wide reduction in direct payments rising from 3 per cent in 2005 to 5 per cent from 2007 onwards (dynamic modulation, with €5,000 being returned to each farmer) to generate additional funds for national environmental programmes and rural development (these actions are part-funded by national budgets);
- Revision to the market policy of the CAP, including (a) halving monthly increments in intervention prices for cereals (b) differentiated price cuts for butter and skim milk powder, compensated by a Dairy Premium (direct payment) based on the amount of quota held by a farm in a reference period, which may be combined with the Single Farm Payment; the milk quota system is to be maintained until 2014/2015 (c) reform in the rice, durum wheat, nuts, starch potatoes and dried fodder sectors.

Second draft of Constitution for the EU (Valéry Giscard d'Estaing) with proposals for extension of collective activity (common foreign and security-defence policy), more EU economic policy decisions taken by the single-currency Member States, an EU 'foreign minister', an elected European Council Chair ('President'), Presidency of Council by a team of three Member States (to give greater continuity), revised rules of qualified majority voting, a European public prosecutor, and legally enforceable. Incorporates Charter of Fundamental Rights (covering social and labour policy).

2004

Enlargement of EU to 25 Member States on 1 May by the accession of 10 countries (Cyprus, Czech Republic, Estonia, Hungary, Latvia, Lithuania, Malta, Poland, Slovakia, Slovenia). Population grows 25 per cent to 500 million, but total GDP increases by only 5 per cent.

Number of Commissioners now 25. Qualified majority voting rules for Council voting: if a majority of Member States (or in some cases a two-thirds majority) approve *and* if a minimum of 232 votes (72.3 per cent of 321 total) are cast in favour *and* a Member State may ask for confirmation that the votes cast in favour represent at least 62 per cent of the total population of the EU.

Treaty establishing a Constitution for Europe signed by Member State leaders on 29 October. To come into effect it requires ratification by Member States. In 10 Member States this involved a referendum (Czech Republic, Denmark, France, Ireland, Luxembourg, Netherlands, Poland, Portugal, Spain, UK), but in Luxembourg, the Netherlands and UK these were only consultative (not binding on the government).

2005

In February 2005, the Commission publishes an initial stocktaking of progress on sustainability, following the 2001 Gothenborg Declaration, and has to admit that several unsustainable trends still continue. The European Council of June 2005 therefore adopts stronger Guiding Principles for Sustainable Development. The Commission presents a review of the SDS on 13 December 2005.

In March 2005 European Council endorses a new streamlined approach to the (Lisbon) Growth and Jobs Strategy and in June adopts the single set of guidelines on which each National Reform Programme is to be based. They are: first, making a decisive leap in investment for higher education, research and innovation; second, cutting red tape and creating a business climate that encourages businesses to start and to grow; third, helping people of all ages to find jobs and removing barriers (such as lack of childcare) that prevent them from doing so; fourth, guaranteeing a secure and sustainable energy supply. These are reflected in subsequent agricultural and rural development policy.

Referendums fail to ratify the EU Constitution in France and Netherlands. As an interim, procedures set out in the Treaty of Nice (2000) continue to apply.

Rural Development Regulation (Council Regulation (EC) No. 1698/2005) sets framework for rural development spending under the CAP for the period 2007–13. It is focused on three objectives implemented through four 'thematic axes':
- improving the competitiveness of the agricultural and forestry sector;
- improving the environment and the countryside;

- improving the quality of life in rural areas and encouraging diversification of the rural economy.

Some funding must be reserved for applying the **LEADER** approach.

Proposed ending of milk quota system under *Agenda 2000* (delayed to 2014/15 under 2003 reform agreement).

2006

End of programming first period for regional policy under the Structural Funds (Objectives 1 and 2) and of the Rural Development Programmes under the Rural Development Regulation 1257/99.

2007

Second Round of Rural Development Programmes starts to operate (period to 2013).

January: Accession of Bulgaria and Romania, making an EU of 27 Member States.

Lisbon Treaty agreed by Member States but needing ratification by some countries before it can apply. Some proposals are taken over from the EU Constitution. With regard to the institutional clauses, (part 1 of the 'Constitution'), the Lisbon Treaty contains the following clauses:
- the Union becomes a legal entity;
- the three pillars are merged together;
- a new rule of double majority is introduced for decisions in the Council;
- affirmation of the co-decision rule between the European Parliament (EP) and the Council of Ministers as the ordinary legislative procedure. This would extend the role of the EP in agricultural policy-making;
- a stable presidency of the European Council (for a duration of two and a half years), renewable once;
- creation of the position of: 'High Representative of the Union for Foreign Affairs and Security Policy';
- right of citizens' initiative;
- enhancement of democratic participation, etc.

The Lisbon Treaty distinguishes three main categories of competences:

The EU's exclusive competences in areas where it legislates alone:
- Customs Union;
- establishment of competition rules necessary for the functioning of the internal market;
- monetary policy for Member States which use the euro as legal tender;
- conservation of the biological resources of the sea as part of the common fisheries policy;
- common trading policy;
- the conclusion of an international agreement when this is within the framework of one of the Union's legislative acts or when it is necessary to help it exercise an internal competence or if there is a possibility of the common rules being affected or of their range being changed.

Shared competences between the EU and Member States, with the States exercising their competence if the EU is not exercising its own:

- internal market;
- social policy with regard to specific aspects defined in the Treaty;
- economic, social and territorial cohesion;
- agriculture and fisheries except for the conservation of the biological resources of the sea;
- environment;
- consumer protection;
- transport;
- trans-European networks;
- energy;
- area of freedom, security and justice;
- joint security issues with regard to aspects of public health as defined in the Lisbon Treaty;
- research, technological development and space;
- development cooperation and humanitarian aid.

Areas where the Member States have exclusive competence but in which the EU can provide support or coordination on European aspects of these areas:

- protection and improvement of human healthcare;
- industry;
- culture;
- tourism;
- education, professional training, youth and sport;
- civil protection;
- administrative co-operation.

Member States coordinate their economic and employment policies within the Union and that the common foreign and security policy is governed by a special system.

2008

Referendum in Ireland fails to ratify the Lisbon Treaty, followed by suspension of the ratification process in the Czech Republic and Poland. However, ratification is later completed, and the Lisbon Treaty comes into force on 1 December 2009.

CAP Health Check. Scheduled review and adjustment of the mechanisms of the CAP. Agreement is reached in the November Agriculture Council on reforms that are to be implemented early in 2009:

- further decoupling of direct farm payments from production in sectors such as arable crops;
- phasing out the remaining processing aid schemes for dried fodder, starch, flax and hemp;
- further limits on market controls, including the abolition of compulsory set-aside and the introduction of a tendering system for wheat intervention;

- agreement on the process for phasing out milk quotas by 2015, including a basic 1 per cent per year increase in quotas over the next five years, though with some differential increases for some countries;
- reducing red tape for farmers through some simplification of direct farm payments and the requirements of cross-compliance;
- increasing the rate of 'compulsory modulation' across the EU from 5 per cent to 10 per cent by 2012, and therefore increasing the share of CAP funding that goes towards environment and rural development schemes;
- the option for countries to use cross-compliance to help address the environmental effects of ending set-aside;
- extending Single Area Payment Scheme: EU members applying the simplified SAPS will be allowed to continue to do so until 2013 instead of being forced into the Single Payment Scheme by 2010;
- additional funding for EU-12 using SAPS (€90 million) to make it easier for them to make use of 'Article 68' (which enables Member States to retain 10 per cent of their national budget ceilings for direct payments for use for environmental measures or improving the quality and marketing of products);
- investment aid for young farmers under Rural Development will be increased from €55,000 to €70,000.

Revised Cotonou Agreement for the EDF covering the period 2008–13.

2009

Treaty of Lisbon comes into force (1 December). The 'ordinary legislative procedure' becomes operative for agricultural policy decisions, in which the European Parliament and the Council have powers of co-decision.

2010

Consolidated versions of the Treaty on European Union and the Treaty on the Functioning of the European Union (formerly the Treaty of Rome) agreed and published in the Official Journal. In the latter the objectives of the CAP are given, unchanged from the 1957 original, with the same Article numbering (39).

Commission issues the discussion paper outlining options for the CAP after 2013. *The CAP Towards 2020: Meeting the Food, Natural Resources and Territorial Challenges of the Future.* Three broad options are outlined, which might be interpreted as respectively maintaining the status quo, greater targeting in the interest of efficient policy, and radical reform. The third is unlikely to be chosen for operation, the most likely outcome being a mixture of the first and second.
- Option 1: Direct payments – the system is unchanged but with some reallocation on grounds of 'equity'. Market measures – streamlined and simplified where appropriate, and risk management tools are strengthened. Rural development – the increased funding related to climate change, water, biodiversity and renewable energy, and innovation, agreed in the 2008 Health Check, is maintained.
- Option 2: Direct payments – some reallocation and substantial change in design, to comprise (a) a basic rate serving as income support; (b) a compulsory additional aid

for specific 'greening' public goods through simple, generalised, annual and non-contractual agri-environmental actions based on the supplementary costs for carrying out these actions; (c) an additional payment to compensate for specific natural constraints; (d) a voluntary coupled support component for specific sectors and regions. Also the introduction of a new scheme for small farms and capping of the basic rate for large farms, while also considering their contribution to rural employment. Market measures – improve and simplify existing market instruments where appropriate. Rural development – support focused on environment, climate change and/or restructuring and innovation, and enhancing regional/local initiatives. Strengthening of existing risk management tools and introduction of an optional WTO Green Box compatible income stabilisation tool to compensate for substantial income losses. Some redistribution of funds between Member States based on objective criteria could be envisaged.

- Option 3: Direct payments – phase-out of direct payments in their current form, providing instead limited payments for environmental public goods and additional specific natural constraints payments. Market measures – abolish all market measures, with the potential exception of disturbance clauses that could be activated in times of severe crises. Rural development – the measures would be mainly focused on climate change and environment aspects.

NOTES

2   Understanding the agricultural policy problems and objectives of the European Union

1   This can be shown in a number of ways. Figures in Table 2.1 refer to people who say that their main occupation group is in agriculture, forestry and fisheries. Consequently there will be some in other occupation groups who will have agriculture as a secondary activity. Other measures could be the number of people who work on agricultural holdings (full or part time), or the volume of labour used by agriculture in full-time worker equivalents (Annual Work Units). In 1987, when the numbers in the agriculture, forestry and fisheries occupation group was 9.9m at EUR 12 level, the number of people working on farms was 17.7m (of which 0.23m were regularly employed non-family members). Between 1977 and 1987 the total AWU in EUR 10 agriculture fell by 19% from 8.5m to 6.5m.

3   Understanding the policy decision-making process in the European Union

1   These include the following, with the year in which the Council approved their establishment shown:

*   European Environment Agency (Copenhagen) (1990).
*   European Training Foundation (Turin) (1990), mainly concerned with training in designated Central and Eastern European Countries.
*   European Monitoring Centre for Drugs and Drug Addiction (Lisbon) (1994).
*   European Agency for the Evaluation of Medical Products (London) (1995).
*   Agency for Health and Safety at Work (Bilbao) (1989).
*   Office for Harmonisation in the Internal Market (Alicante) (1994), concerned with trade marks, design and models.
*   European Police Office (Europol) for police co-operation in certain activities such as prevention of terrorism (the Hague).
*   European Centre for the Development of Vocational Training (CEDEFOP)(Thessaloniki), originally established in 1975 but relocated by decision in 1992.
*   Foundation for the Improvement of Living and Working Conditions (Dublin) (1975).
*   European Monitoring Centre on Racism and Xenophobia.
*   Translation Centre for Bodies in the European Union (Luxembourg) (1994).
*   Community Plants Rights Office (1995).
*   The European Central Bank (ECB) (1998) grew out of the European Monetary Institute (Frankfurt, 1994) that was concerned with the co-ordination of monetary policies, the development of the European Currency Unit (ECU) and preparation for the European System of Central Banks, which were necessary for the transition to Stage 3 of Economic and Monetary Union. The ECB has an Executive Board made up of nominations by participating Member States. Monetary Union was achieved in 1999 for 11 Member States (not Denmark, Greece, Sweden, or the UK) when the euro currency was established. The ECB is responsible

for the conduct of a single monetary policy; this policy is formulated by the ECB together with the national central banks of the participating Member States.

2 A distinction should be made between the European Council and the altogether different *Council of Europe*, a non-EU body which contains country members who are not EU Member States. The potential for confusion is exacerbated by the fact that the EU's European Parliament when it meets in Strasbourg uses the headquarters building of the Council of Europe.

3 A distinction should be made between this body and the European Court of Human Rights (ECHR), which is not an EU organisation but belongs to the Council of Europe (the intergovernmental European organisation, now with 47 country members, for political, cultural, social and legal cooperation, established in 1949 and whose Parliamentary Assembly elects the members of the ECHR). The European Convention on Human Rights is a product of the Council of Europe and came into force in 1953.

4 The European Bank for Reconstruction and Development (EBRD), set up much later (in 1990), provides finance to enable the countries of Central and Eastern Europe in their transition to open market economies. Though 27 of the 61 countries that own the EBRD are EU Member States and, in addition, the European Investment Bank and the European Commission are on its board of directors, it is not exclusively an EU institution. It is the largest single investor in Central and Eastern Europe.

5 See Consolidated Version of the Treaty on the Functioning of the European Union, para 42(3).

6 Detailed rules of procedure are available on the European Parliament's website.

7 See, for example, the writings of Michael Tracy, a former Director in the Secretariat of the Council of Ministers, especially his *Food and Agriculture in a Market Economy*, APS. 1993

8 Occasionally changes can be made between the 'political' agreement in the Council and the publication of the legal texts. This happened with sugar. The February 2006 legislation included a compulsory quota cut that was not part of the original agreement, but which was needed in order to help deliver the required schedule of quota cuts established in November 2005.

4 Evidence-based policy: information and statistics for policy decisions

1 These statistics, initiated by Eurostat in the late 1980s to meet a CAP need, were suspended in 2002 for a mix of reasons that included problems with quality, lack of basic data, and low priority ascribed by Eurostat and some Member States. A feasibility study was undertaken in 2007 for re-launching the series using a uniform methodology based on microeconomic data sources, but no decision to go ahead has been made.

2 The word 'farm' is avoided in EU agricultural statistics. Instead 'agricultural holding' is used, which has a technical definition. However, for the purpose of this chapter, the terms are taken as interchangeable.

3 Dates in quotation marks indicate a three-year average centred on the date mentioned.

5 Understanding the instruments used to implement the CAP

1 'Community Aid for Investment in Agricultural Holdings', which in the UK became the 'Farm and Conservation Grant Scheme'

2 This might be described as the administrators facing low transaction costs. Farmers, the recipients of support, also faced low transaction costs as their involvement was largely passive; prices of farm commodities increased without the farmer being involved in making out applications etc.

3 In his Preface of the European Commission's CAP reform proposals of 1991, Ray MacSharry, the Agriculture Commissioner, stated that under the existing arrangements 80 per cent of the support went to only 20 per cent of the farmers. By implication these were the larger producers.

6 Understanding the support of agriculture in the EU: Pillar 1 of the CAP (direct payments and market support)

1 74 per cent of the 2011 Draft Budget.
2 Council Regulation (EC) No 1782/2003
3 Specific support schemes were introduced or initially maintained for the following products: durum wheat, protein crops, rice, nuts, energy crops, starch potatoes, milk and milk products, seeds, cotton, tobacco, olive groves and grain legumes and there was a separate payment for sugar (only for those new Member States applying the Single Area Payment Scheme (SAPS)).
4 These apply to durum wheat, protein crops, rice, nuts, energy crops, starch potatoes, milk and milk products, seeds, cotton, tobacco, olive groves and grain legumes, and there is a separate payment for sugar (only for those new Member States applying the Single Area Payment Scheme).
5 The legislation is set out in Regulation (EC) No 1782/2003.
6 A ruling of the European Court of Justice in November 2010 relating to privacy of individuals has caused the withdrawal of details of payments from the websites of Member States. In 2011 the Commission was intending to pursue the publication of payments to recipients who were not 'natural persons'. If this is accepted, while amounts paid to individual farmers operating as sole proprietors or partners will remain confidential, details of payments to companies, charities, trusts etc. will be published. Farms arranged as companies are therefore likely to have their payments made public, important for countries such as the UK where many larger farms take this business form. The UK government was in favour of restoring full transparency (that is, publication of all payments).

7 Understanding the support of agriculture and rural development in the EU: Pillar 2 of the CAP

1 For example, in the 5(b) area in Devon and Cornwall in the UK the funds were concentrated on support to the city of Plymouth and nothing was drawn from EAGGF, the agricultural Structural Fund

10 Understanding the costs of the CAP: Budget and finance

1 According to the Financial Regulation (Council Reg. 1605/2002) 'Commitment appropriations shall cover the total cost of the legal commitments entered into during the current financial year, subject to Articles 77(2) and 166(2). Payment appropriations shall cover payments made to honour the legal commitments entered into in the current financial year and/or earlier financial years'.
2 In the UK one such state aid is the Agricultural Development Scheme, applied in England. This has been used to assist with the improvement of marketing, collaboration and competitiveness but in a flexible way that allows Defra to respond to particular crisis situations rapidly. As a scheme that is 'permanently on the shelf' it can be deployed without the need to re-apply for State Aid exemption.

11 Understanding the assessment (evaluation) of the CAP and rural policy

1 Where poor policy performance is the result of poor design, an issue arises as to who is responsible. If it is not clear who is accountable for a particular project or scheme, administrators will be sheltered from the consequences of their decisions. This is an example of *moral hazard* in management.
2 The term *deadweight* is also applied to payments made to beneficiaries who are outside the target group. For example, a system of support that is intended to benefit low income farmers on small farms but does so by raising the prices they receive for their output will, inevitably, benefit larger,

higher income farmers. The cost of the support this latter group receives is often considered as a form of deadweight.

12 Understanding the history of the CAP and European policy

1 Unlike in the rest of this book, this chapter uses the term European Community, mostly to apply to situations before the European Union formally came into being on 1 November 1993. Similarly, ECU and euro (€) are both used.

2 The principle of appropriate responsibility at appropriate levels. This states that anything which can be done by those at lower levels of responsibility must not be done by those at higher levels. Gondrand, F. (1991) *Eurospeak: A User's Guide.*

3 For example, the UK chose not to implement the system of 'transitional income aids' that were provided in the mid–1980s.

4 Once the Community achieved self-sufficiency in a particular commodity, a relatively small increase in overall production would increase the amount taken into intervention disproportionately. For example, if self-sufficiency is achieved at output 100, if output rises from 101 to 102 as a result of improved productivity, the amount by which production exceeds consumption has risen by 100% (from 1 to 2). If the cost of support is solely determined by the amount bought into intervention storage, then the cost will have risen also by 100% as the result of this very modest overall increase in production.

5 Some idea of the divergence between prices in ECU and in national currencies for the EU are given in the accompanying table:

Period	Increase in price in ECU	Increase in price in national currency	Annual rate of inflation in the economy in general
1983/84 EUR9	4.2	6.9	7.8
1984/85 EUR9	−0.5	3.3	5.8
1985.86 EUR9	0.1	1.8	5.3
1986/87 EUR10	−0.3	2.2	3.8
1987/88 EUR10	−0.2	3.3	3.4
1988/89 EUR10	−0.1	1.6	3.7
1989/90 EUR12	−0.1	1.3	4.5
1990/91 EUR12	−1.1	0.3	5.0
1991/92 EUR12	0.0	0.5	4.5

Source: quoted in European Parliament PE 162.500

6 By raising the ceiling of the VAT-base part of the Community's own-resources from 1 per cent to 1.4 per cent.

7 The UK was particularly hostile to the preferential treatment of small farms, since the UK would be unlikely to benefit from these provisions because of its predominantly large farm size structure. The UK government also held substantially different views on the social aspects of the CAP from the dominant view in the EU-12.

8 Items excluded from the Guideline included the monetary reserve, guidance spending of the EAGGF on Objective 5b (rural development) items, such as aid for modernisation, compensatory allowances (headage payments) for livestock in LFAs, and aid to help young farmers establish themselves.

INDEX